TAXATION AND RESENTMENT

PRINCETON STUDIES IN
AMERICAN POLITICS

Historical, International, and Comparative Perspectives

Paul Frymer, Suzanne Mettler, and Eric Schickler, Series Editors

Ira Katznelson, Martin Shefter, and Theda Skocpol,
Founding Series Editors

A list of titles in this series appears in the back of the book.

Taxation and Resentment

RACE, PARTY, AND CLASS IN AMERICAN TAX ATTITUDES

ANDREA LOUISE CAMPBELL

PRINCETON UNIVERSITY PRESS
PRINCETON & OXFORD

Published by Princeton University Press
41 William Street, Princeton, New Jersey 08540
99 Banbury Road, Oxford OX2 6JX

press.princeton.edu

GPSR Authorized Representative: Easy Access System Europe - Mustamäe tee 50, 10621 Tallinn, Estonia, gpsr.requests@easproject.com

ISBN 9780691137858
ISBN (pbk.) 9780691137865
ISBN (e-book) 9780691266237

British Library Cataloging-in-Publication Data is available

Editorial: Bridget Flannery-McCoy and Alena Chekanov
Production Editorial: Jaden Young
Jacket and Cover Design: Chris Ferrante
Production: Lauren Reese
Publicity: William Pagdatoon
Copyeditor: Cindy Milstein

This book has been composed in Arno

10 9 8 7 6 5 4 3 2 1

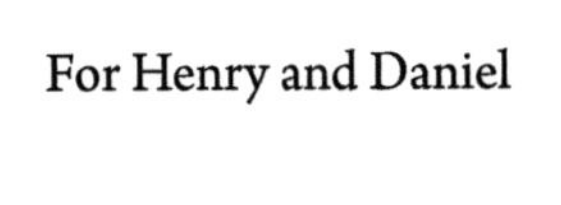

For Henry and Daniel

CONTENTS

ILLUSTRATIONS

Tables

PREFACE

I HAVE SPENT my career studying big domestic spending programs, and writing books and articles about Social Security, Medicare, and Medicaid, among other projects. My first book, *How Policies Make Citizens*, examined how the development of Social Security enabled the transformation of senior citizens from the least participatory to most participatory age group in US politics. *The Delegated Welfare State*, with Kimberly Morgan, explored the causes and consequences of the increasing privatization of social policies, focusing on the case of Medicare. A catastrophic car accident left my sister-in-law paralyzed, and I wrote a third book, *Trapped in America's Safety Net*, about her difficulties navigating Medicaid and other means-tested programs. Many of these projects look at how the designs of public programs shape the attitudes and behaviors of members of the public, and vice versa. Throughout, I have worked to develop policy feedbacks theory, the notion that public policies are not just the outcomes of political processes but also crucial inputs, shaping the very possibilities for subsequent policymaking. A fourth, short book with Daniel Béland and Kent Weaver provides an overview of extant work in the policy feedback realm. Projects in other areas—the Affordable Care Act, COVID-19 pandemic, and state preemption of local governing authority—dot my résumé too.

One can't study these large programs for long, however, before starting to wonder how we pay for them. I have always been fascinated by taxes (I know), and I do think that if I hadn't become a political scientist, I might have become a personal financial adviser. But the larger policy piece has always held my imagination: Why do we get tax policies that seem to go against the self-interests, and as I show here, abstract preferences, of nonrich taxpayers? And going back to my roots as a political behavior scholar, What are the tax attitudes people hold, and how can we explain them? I hope the findings here will pique readers' interests, and spur more sorely needed research on tax attitudes and policy among political scientists.

I have been working on this project, in fits and starts, for a long time. I have many people to thank and apologize to anyone I have inadvertently left off the list. This was supposed to be book number two for me; now it's book number five.

For my tenure file, I wrote an initial version that was more historical and based on existing public opinion polls. Although I had already joined the MIT faculty, Dan Carpenter was kind enough to sponsor a book conference at Harvard back in 2007 together with then MIT department head Charles Stewart. I thank Larry Bartels, Jennifer Hochschild, Gabe Lenz, Robert Shapiro, Joe Thorndike, and Julian Zelizer for their comments, and Phil Jones and Ellie Powell, then Harvard grad students, for taking notes. Others in attendance provided helpful comments as well: Lucy Barnes; the late, wonderful Anya Bernstein; Hahrie Han; Dan Hopkins; Sunshine Hillygus; Meg Jacobs; Alex Keyssar; Marjorie Kornhauser; and Eileen McDonagh. Some of the material from that earlier version can be found in my chapter "What Americans Think of Taxes" in *The New Fiscal Sociology: Taxation in Comparative and Historical Perspective*, edited by Isaac William Martin, Ajay K. Mehrotra, and Monica Prasad (Cambridge University Press, 2009). Later I shifted gears considerably because I was dissatisfied with that version, and concluded that the historical polling record was too thin in terms of both outcomes and explanatory variables (although legal scholar Steven Sheffrin's insightful 2013 book *Tax Fairness and Folk Justice* demonstrated that much could be done with existing survey data). The present volume is based largely, although not exclusively, on modules I placed on the 2012, 2016, and 2019 Cooperative Congressional Election Study (now Cooperative Election Study) surveys. Many thanks to CES principal investigators, the team at YouGov, and especially Samantha Luks for her guidance.

Between the first and second versions of this book, many things ensued—three other books, a term as department head, and the pandemic. When I finally completed the new draft, my colleague Devin Caughey's Pioneer Valley reading group kindly agreed to read it. I held another book conference and benefited from the brilliant advice of Antoine Banks, Larry Bartels (again!), Devin Caughey, Spencer Piston, Eric Schickler, Laura Stoker, Joe Thorndike (again!), and Nick Valentino. I thank MIT grad students Ayelet Carmeli and Helen Webley-Brown for taking notes, and my assistant Morgan Gillespie for handling logistics. I cannot say how grateful I am to have had *two* all-star groups of scholars enrich the book with their insightful comments. Laura Stoker later spent even more time with me patiently puzzling over many title ideas. I am eternally appreciative of my political science colleagues' generosity and care.

Over the years I have presented various permutations of the work at Brown, Duke Sanford School, Harvard Government Department, Harvard Kennedy School, Johns Hopkins Center for Advanced Governmental Studies, Michigan, Minnesota, Missouri, MIT, Notre Dame, NYU Law School, Oxford, Princeton, University College London, University of California at Berkeley, University of California at Los Angeles Law School, University of California at Santa Barbara, Virginia, Wisconsin, and Yale. I am thankful for helpful conversations with Lucy Barnes, Adam Berinsky, Henry Brady, Devin Caughey, Jack Citrin, Jasmine English, Archon Fung, Isaac Martin, Susan Moffitt, Paul Pierson, Monica Prasad, Ken Scheve, Theda Skocpol, Charles Stewart, Patty Strach, Paul Testa, Margaret Weir, Rebecca Weitz-Shapiro, Rick Valelly, and Vanessa Williamson. A sabbatical stint as the Kluge Chair in American Law and Governance at the John W. Kluge Center at the Library of Congress was instrumental in advancing the new version of the book manuscript. I am thankful to the wonderful Kluge and Library of Congress staff, and will always cherish the opportunity to go to work every day in the most beautiful building in the United States.

I could not have written the book without the help of numerous research assistants: Ayelet Carmeli, Sara Chatfield, Daniel Feinstein, Francisco Flores-Macias, Jacob Jameson, Zeyu (Chris) Peng, Mike Sances, Kyle Shohfi, and Tess Wise. Back when he was a grad student, Dan Hopkins cleaned and concatenated the Advisory Commission on Intergovernmental Relations survey data for me (yes, *that* Dan Hopkins. You know you have been working on a project too long when your research assistant is a full professor). I am especially grateful to my most recent MIT research assistant, Benjamin Muñoz, for doing a tremendous amount of careful analytic work to get me over the finish line, and research support associate Morgan Gillespie for helping me in an immense number of ways from analytic to editorial. Both are true gems who despite being in the beginning of their careers, are already immensely talented social scientists—smart, detail oriented, organized, and thoughtful. I cannot begin to thank them enough.

I thank the Princeton University Press editors who have championed this book over the years: Chuck Myers, Eric Crahan, and Bridget Flannery-McCoy. Chuck was instrumental to my career, publishing my first book and believing in this one, despite my failure to finish it on his watch, which I regret to this day. Eric too was a champion, first as politics editor, and later as editorial director for the humanities and social sciences. Bridget lent her unflinching support despite my testing her patience repeatedly (you also know you have been working on a project too long when you've gone through three editors, and your third editor has completed two maternity leaves). Politics assistant editor Alena Chekanov was a great help throughout. Cindy Milstein copyedited with tremendous care and attention to detail. Beth Nauman-Montana created the wonderfully detailed index. Jaden Young capably and cheerfully ushered the book through the production process.

There are numerous people to whom I could dedicate this book. One is Larry Jacobs, who was asked many times to review my dossier for one promotion or another, and saw the manuscript in multiple forms. After the last review, he urged me to just finish it already because he "never wanted to read that damn thing again." At least he had a smile on his face. I think. I could also dedicate the book to my husband, Allen Feinstein, who has supported "Andrea's big book o' taxes" (his title) for years. But in the end, I dedicate the book to my two sons, Henry and Daniel, who have been hearing about this project their entire sentient lives and are now taxpayers in their own right. Thank you for your patience. It's finally done.

ABBREVIATIONS

ACIR	Advisory Commission on Intergovernmental Relations
ANES	American National Election Study
BTU	British Thermal Units (referring to a broad-based energy tax)
CCES	Cooperative Congressional Election Surveys
CTC	Child Tax Credit
EITC	Earned Income Tax Credit
FDR	Franklin Delano Roosevelt
GDP	Gross domestic product
GOP	Grand Old Party (Republican Party)
GSS	General Social Survey
IRA	Individual retirement account
IRS	Internal Revenue Service
ITEP	Institute on Taxation and Economic Policy
NORC	National Opinion Research Center
NPR	National Public Radio
NYT	*New York Times*
OECD	Organisation for Economic Cooperation and Development
TANF	Temporary Assistance for Needy Families
TARP	Troubled Asset Relief Program
TCJA	Tax Cuts and Jobs Act (of 2017)
VAT	Value-added tax

TAXATION AND RESENTMENT

1

Introduction

THE UNITED STATES is a low-tax country. Revenues collected by federal, state, and local governments combined amount to a smaller share of the economy than any of the nation's economic peers (Canada, Germany, France, and so on). Some say low taxes make economic dynamism possible. Others point to a lack of investment in physical infrastructure and human capital as a threat to that very economic dynamism and a reason to raise revenues. But doing so is difficult: the total size of the government as a share of the economy has been the same for sixty years.

Why is it so hard to raise taxes in the United States? Why is it so difficult to fund government? This book examines one factor: the nature of American public opinion on taxes. It explores how Americans react to the tax system in place and how in turn their attitudes shape the possibilities for further policymaking. It argues that the progressive system of taxes in the United States, especially at the federal level, is self-undermining. Ordinary Americans support the abstract notion of progressive taxation, the idea that higher-income groups should pay not just more but instead progressively more, with tax rates that climb with income, in order to help fund government on an "ability-to-pay" principle. This is the philosophy behind the federal income tax, the main source of federal revenues, and as we'll see, the most salient and high-profile tax in the United States around which much of the politics of taxation revolves. The difficulty is that progressive taxes take the most from the most well-resourced, organized, and vocal elements in society. The privileged have spent the century since the enactment of the federal income tax in 1913 trying to lower their effective rates of taxation—what they actually pay as a share of income. They have been spectacularly successful, achieving reductions not just in the federal income tax but also in other progressive taxes: the capital gains tax, estate tax, and corporate tax. Ironically, the rest of the public, the nonrich, have often been unwitting allies in the quest of the well-heeled to minimize their taxes, in contradiction to both their material self-interest and abstract commitment to progressive taxation. The puzzle is why the public has served this role contra its own interests. The answer lies in a toxic brew of tax structures, race, racism, and party.

Because taxes are an economic issue, attitudes should be based on self-interest: the objective costs and benefits associated with this form of public policy. Tax attitudes, however, typically do not differ systematically with such material stakes. Instead, they vary sometimes with partisanship, and among whites, vary strongly with levels of racial animus. Many whites resent taxes because they believe they fund benefits for undeserving nonwhites. In the meantime, Black and Hispanic taxpayers are penalized by tax policies that overburden them relative to similar whites, for both intentional and inadvertent reasons. The result is that everyone has a reason to dislike taxes. The factors underlying tax opinion ultimately have consequences for who pays and how large government is. Public opinion is far from the only influence on tax policymaking, but it is a facilitating force; it is easier to get policies enacted if the public is on board. The rich tend to prevail in their efforts to minimize their taxes due to the failure of the rest of the public to serve as an effective counterweight, with the result that funding the government is incredibly difficult.

Taxes in the United States

Governments need revenues to conduct all of their other functions, from building roads to providing for citizen well-being to ensuring national defense. Raising money from taxes on individuals and corporations is the main way governments do so. In the United States, all levels of government levy taxes. The federal government imposes individual and corporate income taxes along with payroll taxes that support Social Security retirement and disability benefits and Medicare health benefits for older Americans. Estate taxes, customs duties, and excise taxes on gasoline, alcohol, and cigarettes generate smaller amounts of revenue. Most state governments also tax individual and corporate incomes and impose a retail sales tax. Many have an estate or inheritance tax as well. Local governments typically employ property taxes and sometimes sales taxes to fund their operations. Altogether, taxes total just under 28 percent of gross domestic product (GDP). Relative to the size of the economy, taxes in the United States are lower than in most other high-income democracies. Tax revenues as a share of the economy have also been virtually unchanged since the 1960s.

Moreover, taxes are complicated in the United States. One reason is that every level of government can impose taxes (as opposed to, say, the federal government collecting all taxes, and then redistributing them to states and local governments). Taxes are levied on different resources: earned income, unearned income from capital gains and dividends, wealth in the form of estate or property taxes, and consumption in the form of sales or gas taxes. They are also imposed in different ways. Some are effortless, like the sales taxes that are taken with each purchase or payroll taxes that are withheld from paychecks. Some are difficult to pay, either because the bills arrive in lump sums, like property taxes, or because filing them and reconciling one's payments with one's tax liability is arduous, as with the federal income tax.

Another reason that taxes, especially the federal income tax, are complicated is because of the machinations of the rich to reduce their burden. In their long campaign to get their effective taxes minimized, the privileged have sought both reductions in the tax rates they pay and tax breaks—credits, deductions, and preferential rates that reduce income taxes owed. These tax breaks, collectively called the tax expenditure system, benefit lower- and middle-income taxpayers too: the Earned Income Tax Credit (EITC) refunds the federal taxes paid by low-wage workers, essentially acting as a wage supplement; the tax exclusions for employer-provided health insurance and retirement plans frees from taxation the premiums workers (and their employers) pay along with the contributions they make to their retirement savings. Tax breaks, or "indirect" spending, have become a default way to enact social policy in the United States because partisan gridlock makes passing direct spending programs difficult. Tax expenditures are easier politically because they solve some social problem, which Democrats desire, but do so by reducing tax revenues, to the satisfaction of Republicans. There are scores of such tax breaks in the federal tax code. But while the nonrich do benefit from some important tax breaks, the vast majority of the tax savings go to the affluent. And tax breaks create a plethora of other problems that affect tax attitudes. They are outstanding examples, although not the only ones, of tax policies and structures that affect public opinion.

Tax Policy and Tax Attitudes

Surveys show that large majorities of Americans support the notion of progressive taxation—that those with more should pay more to support the government, not just proportionately more, but progressively more (higher rates on higher incomes). Indeed, progressive taxation and the ability-to-pay principle that it encapsulates was the basis for the modern federal tax system as adopted in the early twentieth century. And yet the American system has become far less progressive over time, with effective tax rates—taxes as a portion of income—falling, especially for the rich.[1] The federal system, centered around income taxes, remains progressive, but less than in the past. State and local taxes are regressive on balance, and have become more so over time, taking a greater share of the incomes of low earners than of higher earners. The result is an overall system that is nearly flat: each income quintile pays about the same share of all taxes as it earns of all income. Meanwhile, large majorities of survey respondents say the rich and corporations do not pay enough.

Why have taxes for the privileged fallen so much, counter to the abstract preferences of the majority of ordinary taxpayers? This book argues that the progressive tax system fails to generate sufficient political support among those who should favor it. It examines how individuals react to the tax system, shaped so much by the privileged in their own interest, in ways that undermine the interests of the nonrich.

Standard political economy models assume that people will think about taxes according to their material stakes, with the nonrich desirous of high taxes on the rich. In the abstract, people's preferences do comport with this self-interest-driven view. And tax policy has long been upheld by public opinion researchers as one of the few issue areas where attitudes vary with material stakes. But exploring a broader array of tax attitudes, I find that self-interest shapes tax attitudes only sometimes.

Nor do tax attitudes vary reliably with partisanship or ideology. Given that taxes define the scope of government activity, we might imagine sharp divisions between partisans and ideologues, as the size of government is supposed to be a central divide between Republicans and Democrats, conservatives and liberals. Instead, Republicans are especially more likely than Democrats to express antitax attitudes when they are cued and reminded to think in this way. And one reason that partisan differences are relatively muted is that while the majority of Republicans think many taxes are unfair, so do large minorities of Democrats. And independents are particularly likely to find a variety of taxes unfair and want them decreased. It turns out attitudes do not vary as much as we anticipate by partisanship and ideology, because partisans of all stripes tend to like and dislike the same taxes to relatively similar degrees.

I do find one factor that is consistently related to tax attitudes among white Americans: racial resentment. Indeed, racial sentiment is the single-largest influence on whites' tax attitudes. Moreover, the racially resentful particularly oppose progressive taxes, yet another boon to the rich in their efforts to reduce them.

Why is the role of self-interest—costs and benefits—so minimal when it comes to tax attitudes? Why don't partisans differ more in their preferences, and why does racial sentiment play such a strong role in whites' tax attitudes? One element of American tax policy that feeds all of these phenomena is the tax break system. Tax expenditures introduce a plethora of problems into the economics and politics of tax policy that undermine support for progressive taxation even as they reduce its bite. As tax expenditures have proliferated, often at the behest of the rich seeking to reduce their own tax burdens, taxes have become more complicated, undermining the ability of people to see their costs and benefits clearly. Tax breaks help reduce partisan differences in tax attitudes by making Democrats and independents, not just Republicans, angry about taxes. And they exacerbate the racial politics of taxing and spending to a profound degree.

To the extent to which nonrich taxpayers benefit from tax expenditures, they tend not to recognize the concomitant tax reductions as government benefits, as political scientist Suzanne Mettler (2011) has written. But tax breaks have an even more harmful effect on public opinion, creating confusion about who benefits from government spending, thereby heightening the racial politics of taxation. Taxes and direct spending on social welfare policies are highly visible to white Americans, and racialized, with whites who harbor more animus toward Black Americans less supportive of social spending, which they believe goes to the undeserving (Rosenthal 2021). At the same time, social policy benefits that people derive from the tax break system are not visible because they come in the form of taxes not collected, hiding the government subsidy. Large shares of white Americans thus think they pay taxes that fund visible benefits for others who they find unworthy while failing to realize that they too benefit from government benefits. This makes for a pernicious tax politics, dating back to the post–Civil War era, of white Americans perceiving themselves as taxpayers and nonwhites as tax eaters (Walsh 2018). In contemporary public opinion data, these age-old perceptions manifest as a strong relationship between racial resentment and tax attitudes.

While white Americans, especially the racially resentful, grouse about confiscatory taxation, the bigger victims of US tax policy are Black and Hispanic households.[2] Tax expenditures play a role here too. As scholars of critical tax theory in law and sociology have argued, tax policy has been written by whites, for whites.[3] Sometimes taxes have been used as a deliberate tool of racial repression. The fiscal regime adopted in many southern states in the 1930s is one example, with high sales taxes and low property taxes enacted to shift the tax burden onto low-income Black residents, and away from white property owners (Newman and O'Brien 2011). The excessive assessment of Black-owned homes for property tax purposes is a historical practice that continues to this day.[4] In other instances, the racial penalty has been more inadvertent, at least initially. Tax expenditure policies written to benefit white taxpayers overtax nonwhites who have less access to employer-provided benefits. Numerous such "race-neutral" provisions have differential effects across race, resulting in the greater taxation of Black and Hispanic households compared to similar white ones.[5] Some discriminatory tax policies are well-known, such as the overassessment of Black-owned homes mentioned above. Others, like differential Black access to the tax expenditure system, are more subtle and less publicized. Either way, taxation is one of the most coercive functions of government for any taxpayer. And communities that have suffered government coercion in other arenas such as the criminal justice and social welfare systems have every reason to be concerned about government coercion in the tax sphere as well. Indeed, even though Black and Hispanic Americans are more supportive of a wider role for government and government spending, they have more negative attitudes toward taxes than do white Americans.

In the end, many Americans have reasons to dislike taxes. And many of these reasons derive from the efforts of the rich to get their taxes reduced. These attempts have greatly complicated the tax code, making it difficult for the nonrich to recognize their stakes in tax policy. They have resulted in the overtaxation of nonwhites because of lesser access to the tax expenditure system at the same time that whites do not recognize their own benefits from that "indirect spending" system and think their tax dollars only go to direct spending programs, which they resent. These patterns in public opinion have profound implications for the politics of tax policy. At an abstract level, nonrich Americans prefer progressive tax systems, and think the rich and corporations should pay more. As a conceptual matter, many Americans support the ability-to-pay principle on which most federal taxation (and some state taxation) is based. These are class-based, self-interested stances. Many Americans, however, also have great difficulty connecting these abstract preferences to attitudes on specific taxes, where their preferences often stray from an embrace of the ability to pay and their own material stake. Middle-income Americans should like federal income taxes, which fall lightly on them, and estate taxes, which they do not pay at all (almost no one does). They should dislike sales taxes, which are costlier as a share of their incomes (and perhaps payroll taxes for Social Security, although the associated benefits are visible, offsetting tax regressivity). Instead, their attitudes are the opposite, resembling those of high-income people: acceptance of regressive sales and payroll taxes, and pronounced dislike of progressive income and estate taxes. Enmity among ordinary people toward income and estate taxes is a great boon to the rich, easing the reductions in these taxes that the rich seek. Even though ordinary taxpayers say those at the top pay too little, they support policies that result in exactly that situation.

Progressive taxation is not the only way to raise government revenues. The tax systems of peer nations in Europe rely on regressive taxation to a greater extent than does the United States (especially via a value-added tax (VAT), a consumption tax that the United States does not have). But progressivity is the foundation on which federal taxation in particular was built, and it is the form of taxation that nonrich Americans prefer in theory. In a country with pronounced and growing income inequality, where incomes among high earners have soared in recent decades, progressive taxation may also be just, depending on one's political views. But progressive taxation has waned in the United States due to the concerted efforts of the privileged to get their effective rates of taxation reduced. This book shows how the nature of public opinion among the nonrich has inadvertently aided and abetted these efforts.

Why This Examination of Tax Attitudes Is Needed

Taxation and Resentment seeks to fill a number of holes in our understanding of Americans' attitudes about taxes. In exploring variation in tax opinion and the factors behind these preferences, I try to address political scientist James Stimson's (2004, 49) concern that "most of what is said about attitudes toward taxes in American politics is based on assumptions, not facts."

First, although there are many studies of public opinion toward government spending, there are far fewer about tax attitudes. We know some basics from compendiums of survey questions by public opinion analyst Karlyn Bowman and associates as well as other researchers (Bowman, Sims, and O'Neil 2017). Consistent time series of tax questions are rare, as pollsters tend to ask questions about a topic when it is in the news, perhaps returning to the issue periodically, but often dropping it altogether. Ongoing issues such as taxes tend to get less coverage (Bowman 2019). But one can distill some generalizations about American tax attitudes from the available historical data.

Many express skepticism about the magnitude of taxes and use of tax revenues. When asked to make predictions for the coming year, most say taxes will go up. Majorities say the rich and corporations do not pay enough, and that they themselves pay too much—as do middle-class households (where most Americans place themselves). Majorities think the government wastes a lot of the money that "we pay in taxes." Extant surveys also reveal many contradictions, such as large shares of survey respondents saying the rich should pay more and professing support for progressive taxation, but many more opposing the government use of taxation to achieve redistribution. As valuable as these compendiums are, they do not offer explanations for these attitudes nor explore their consequences. Nor do they show how these attitudes might vary across different taxes and types of individuals.

For their part, political scientists have tended to examine Americans' tax attitudes only at certain moments and for certain taxes, such as the property tax during the tax revolt of the late 1970s, and the estate and income taxes when the George W. Bush tax cuts were enacted in the early 2000s.[6] And yet collecting taxes is a key government function, without which all other functions would be impossible. We might think that taxes, and attitudes toward them, would be a central focus for political scientists.[7] Thus another goal of this book is simply descriptive: What do Americans of different demographic and political subgroups think about various types of taxes? Do high- and low-income people have different opinions of income, estate, and property taxes? What about taxes beyond the three most typically studied? Who thinks state sales taxes are unfair? What about the capital gains tax, which is lower than the income tax? Or the gas tax, which is rarely examined, or the payroll tax? One important function of the book is to establish the opinions held among a broad range of societal groups on a broader array of taxes than previously examined.

A second goal is to explore the factors behind tax attitudes. Can we explain variation in tax attitudes with self-interest? With partisanship and political ideology? One would think "yes" in both cases. A durable finding in public opinion research is that attitudes are rarely congruent with basic measures of self-interest. Individuals who seemingly would have distinctive attitudes about a given issue based on their material stakes often do not have preferences that differ from those whose interests are less implicated. But taxes have long been thought an exception to the usual irrelevance of self-interest. Perhaps the most well-known example comes from the tax revolt: homeowners were more likely than renters to support Prop 13, the 1978 California ballot initiative that limited property taxes (Sears and Citrin 1985). A few other examples have cropped up over the years as well.[8] We might also expect tax attitudes to vary with partisanship and ideology, since taxes get to the heart of partisan and ideological battles about the size and scope of government. Especially in an era of political polarization, we might imagine that tax attitudes differ systematically between Democrats and Republicans, liberals and conservatives.

What we'll see, as noted above, is that tax attitudes are only sometimes correlated with self-interest, party identification, and ideology. Perhaps this is not a surprise with regard to self-interest, which is somewhat of a straw man in public opinion research (although it is not supposed to be a straw man with regard to tax attitudes). But the fact that party identification and ideology are not consistent predictors of tax opinion is startling.

What does predict tax attitudes? In chapter 6, we will see that among whites, racial resentment is a powerful influence. It drives attitudes toward every tax, with the exception (barely) of the sales tax. The strong influence of racial resentment helps solve some conundrums in existing tax opinion research. Previous scholars examining the estate tax have been perplexed over the seeming irrationality of people who will never, ever possibly pay the estate tax supporting its repeal (Graetz and Shapiro 2005). Analysts have also puzzled over the lack of a relationship between inequality concerns and estate tax attitudes (Bartels 2016). But we'll see that neither a class- nor inequality-based lens is useful in understanding estate tax attitudes. Instead, these attitudes are about race and racial resentment. Almost all wealth in the United States is owned by whites (Wolff 2017). The groups that the estate tax supposedly harms—farmers and small business owners—are white coded. The analyses here show that the racially resentful are less supportive of progressive taxation as a general concept, more supportive of regressive taxation, and concomitantly more likely to say that specific progressive taxes are unfair and should be decreased, from the estate tax on down. Racial resentment is also an important correlate of attitudes toward tax expenditures. Scholars may characterize the tax expenditure system as "the hidden welfare state" (Howard 1997), but it's not entirely hidden: people have impressions about which groups benefit from which tax breaks. These impressions shape their attitudes. Just as with taxes, the racially resentful prefer tax expenditure policies that help the economic elite and diminish progressivity, like the low capital gains rate, and disapprove of tax breaks that help lower-income groups, such as the EITC. At the same time, racial resentment bears no relationship to policies that are white coded, whether that's federal spending on Social Security, the payroll tax itself, or tax breaks that these respondents believe go primarily to the middle class, such as the tax exclusions for employer-provided health and retirement benefits. Among whites, attitudes toward federal spending, taxes, and tax expenditures all have the same structure: the most important correlate is racial resentment. This is yet another attitudinal characteristic that helps the rich (who are mostly white) in their enduring efforts to get their own taxes reduced. They have allies among the public who are on board not for self-interested reasons but rather racialized ones.

As potent a factor as racial resentment is on white tax opinion, a third goal of the book is to turn the lens from whites to Black and Hispanic taxpayers. Not only have political scientists focused less on taxes than have economists, fiscal sociologists, historians, and legal scholars. When they have examined tax attitudes, they have tended to concentrate on whites' attitudes.[9] As historian Andrew Kahrl (2019, 191) puts it, tax scholarship has centered on white opinion, with Black and Hispanic people appearing only as the object of white displeasure, not as "taxpayers in their own right." Black and Hispanic Americans have long been on the receiving end of many forms of government coercion, from historical instances of the dispossession of assets to the modern, highly punitive criminal justice and welfare systems, which disproportionately affect Black and Hispanic individuals, families, and communities. Since extracting revenues from individuals to fund its operations is one of the most coercive functions of government, it is easy to imagine that those facing coercion in other arenas might be skeptical of this one as well. It turns out that there is structural racism woven into American tax provisions at all levels of government that lead to Black and Hispanic Americans paying more than comparable whites. As mentioned, at the local level, Black homeowners are often overassessed for property tax purposes. At the state level, sales taxes are high, with fewer exemptions for necessities, in states where Black citizens are concentrated. At the federal level, Black taxpayers are less likely to benefit from the tax expenditure system that reduces the tax liability for whites (such as the tax breaks on employer-provided benefits along with the low capital gains and dividends rate). Although some of these inequalities are well-known, others are less visible. I do not think that they affect Black and Hispanic Americans' tax opinions directly through a material stake mechanism, which seems unlikely as Black and Hispanic Americans also have lower levels of formal tax knowledge than whites. Instead, the mechanism is more likely to be concern over a coercive state as it carries out a particularly coercive set of policies. The upshot is this. Hispanic and especially Black survey respondents are generally more positive toward government than whites, with one exception: they have more negative attitudes toward nearly every tax. The irony is that many whites see themselves as the victims of tax policy, but Black and Hispanic taxpayers are the actual victims. And this harm at the hands of government is all the more problematic because much tax policy seems race neutral but in fact is not.

As this review of the book's goals hopefully makes apparent, I bring the sensibility of the policy feedbacks school of thought to this project.[10] Much of my scholarly work examines how public policies are not merely the outcomes of political processes but also key inputs. The designs of public policies can shape public attitudes. This plays out in the following way in tax politics. Progressivity is redistributive, which the nonrich are supposed to prefer (Meltzer and Richard 1981). And they do, in their theoretical support of progressivity, but not in their preferences on particular taxes, which resemble those of the rich (a dislike of income and estate taxes, for example). Complex designs obscure the costs and benefits, confusing taxpayers and rendering them unable to think about taxes in clear, self-interested ways (the "fog of tax," to use legal scholar Edward McCaffery's [2008] term). Even partisans do not consistently differ in their tax attitudes, in part because of the obscuring designs. As tax complexity sends the usual factors that structure policy attitudes off the rails, nonrich whites are left vulnerable to racialized entreaties. What is supposed to be a class politics of tax, as political economy models assume, is actually a racial politics of tax. At the same time, tax structures disproportionately penalize Black and Hispanic taxpayers.

This pattern of tax attitudes, arising in part from the designs of existing tax policies, greatly complicates support for specific progressive taxes and the prospects for reforming the tax system in the progressive direction that nonrich taxpayers say they want in the abstract. Some political scientists have shown that public policy, despite many challenges, is roughly responsive to public opinion.[11] Others have argued that policy is much more responsive to the preferences of the economically privileged.[12] The issue in tax policy is that the preferences of the nonrich resemble those of the rich. The mass public's preferences are upside down. As a result, it is difficult to enlist the public as an ally in tax reforms that would make people better off. And electoral politics cannot solve the problem because the GOP wins both Republican and Democratic votes with an antitax stance. Meanwhile, the rich are pretty happy with this situation, as they have capitalized on the public's confusion to chip away at virtually every progressive tax since the Reagan revolution of the 1980s.

Data

This book explores what we can learn about public opinion on taxes from both extant and new survey data. I will examine attitudes across time, taxes, and different types of people. Note that because these are survey data, I have information on the attitudes of the affluent—say, the top 20 percent of the income spectrum—but not the attitudes of the truly rich. Hence the attitudes I report are for the "nonrich," as I term them.

Almost all the data are observational and descriptive. Except for a couple of survey experiments that I conducted, I will be reporting relationships among variables, testing hypotheses against each other, and assessing the generalizability of findings from existing interview-based work, but for the most part, not reporting causal relationships. Some scholars have begun to perform survey experiments on tax attitudes, mostly around tax expenditures, and I will reference that work.[13] My chief purpose, however, is to look at the basics of what people think of taxes and the correlates of those attitudes in order to set up experimentally minded researchers with a series of hypotheses to explore going forward.

In part I rely on historical surveys. The longest-running survey question on taxes is a Gallup item asking respondents whether the federal income tax they will have to pay that year is too high, too low, or about right. Gallup has asked this item regularly, although not quite annually, since 1947; the General Social Survey (GSS) began asking this item in 1976. Several scholars have examined the national marginals of this "too high" question, as I'll refer to it, in their studies of aggregate public opinion.[14] I have concatenated the entire series in order to perform individual-level analysis. Another historical source is the polling conducted by the Advisory Commission on Intergovernmental Relations (ACIR), a federal commission established by Congress to collect data and perform analyses on federal, state, and local governments, and abolished after Republicans took control of Congress in the mid-1990s. Between 1972 and 1994, the ACIR conducted nearly annual surveys asking Americans a variety of questions, including what they thought "the worst tax is—that is, the least fair." I employ individual-level data from 1983 through 1994 (the individual-level data from the earlier survey years seem to have been lost to history). In 2003, Kaiser, National Public Radio (NPR), and the Harvard Kennedy School conducted a particularly rich survey of tax attitudes (hereafter referred to as the 2003 NPR Taxes Study or simply NPR), although it lacks key explanatory variables such as racial animus. One measure of political scientists' relative neglect of tax policy is that there are few questions on taxes in the flagship American National Election Study (ANES), and it too excluded racial resentment measures on several of the rare occasions when tax items were included. In chapter 6, I look at a few ANES cross-sectional datasets that included individual tax items and relevant explanatory variables.

Because of the limitations of existing datasets, most of the analyses in the book come from modules I placed on the 2012, 2016, and 2019 Cooperative Congressional Election Surveys (now known as the Cooperative Election Study, although I will continue to refer to this source as the CCES). I replicated earlier questions from the ACIR and NPR studies to see what had changed in the intervening decades. I also expanded the list of taxes included and broadened the array of explanatory variables. We will learn not just about attitudes toward the federal income, estate, and local property taxes that political scientists have previously examined but about attitudes toward many others as well: state income, state sales, payroll, gas, and capital gains and dividend taxes (which I often term "investment" taxes in the text). We will learn about attitudes not just on direct federal spending, as has been included in the ANES and GSS—and analyzed—for years, but also on "indirect" spending in the form of tax expenditures (tax breaks for employer-provided health and retirement benefits, excess medical expenses, home mortgage interest, and charitable contributions; the preferential rate on unearned income [that is, the lower rate on capital gains and dividends; I analyze investment taxes both as taxes and as tax breaks]; and the Child Tax Credit [CTC] and EITC). Moreover, the timing of these surveys allows me to delve into attitudes at moments when taxes were not explicitly on the agenda, as was the case with earlier examinations of tax attitudes that focused on the late 1970s' tax revolt or Bush tax cuts. These CCES surveys were conducted when elite discourse was quieter. And I have data in hand from both the Barack Obama and Donald Trump presidencies as well as the Gallup and GSS items on the federal income tax back to 1947. Variation in party control of the presidency is important because it affects some relationships (Republicans only say their federal income taxes are too high when the president is a Democrat), but not others (Black Americans are always more likely to say their income taxes are too high, regardless of who is president).

The book's appendix discusses the analytic approach and modeling choices, and contains question wording for all survey items utilized as well as some supplementary figures. An online appendix contains the variable coding and descriptive statistics, regression tables underlying the figures in the text, and some additional figures.

The Plan of the Book

Chapter 2 provides a thumbnail sketch of the American tax system to inform later analyses and findings. It describes why each revenue source was chosen, how it is designed (what is taxed, who is taxed, and where the money goes), and how each tax has changed over time. It describes the ways in which tax policy, especially at the federal level, has become more complex, and how the privileged have benefited from reduced rates and tax breaks that make the system less progressive. It also discusses the American tax system in cross-national context, how tax revenues are lower than in peer nations, and how both reliance on progressive taxes and tax complexity is greater in the United States.

Chapter 3 is the first of five empirical chapters that explore the nature of American public opinion about taxes, assessing various factors in tax attitudes and the toll taken by system complexity. It asks what attitudes toward different taxes would look like if people thought about them in terms of their material stakes. Chapter 3 explores two barriers to the operation of self-interest: the obscuring effects of tax designs and effect of low information levels. The rich know a great deal about taxes and have little difficulty performing self-interested cost-benefit analyses. For everyone else, the story is quite different. With a few exceptions, attitudes do not vary across taxes in expected ways with regard to objective costs and benefits. Chapter 4 continues the investigation of self-interest by examining variation across individuals, with similar results: those individuals who pay more do not necessarily have more negative tax attitudes. Figures 1.1 and 1.2 offer a preview of these findings. For both the progressive federal income tax and regressive state sales tax, income, a leading indicator of stake in tax policy, is not correlated with the perceived fairness of the taxes or a desire to see them reduced.

Chapter 5 turns to the main alternatives to self-interest as an explanatory factor in attitudes: partisanship and ideology. These symbolic political attachments are usually highly correlated with individuals' policy preferences. Given that taxes are a principal factor in the size and role of government, we might imagine that tax attitudes vary significantly by party and ideology too. As with self-interest, however, the results are unexpected. Sometimes tax attitudes differ between Republicans and Democrats, conservatives and liberals, but often they do not. We see these inconsistencies in figures 1.1 and 1.2. Among all respondents, independents and Republicans are more likely than Democrats to say that the federal income tax is unfair and should be decreased, all things

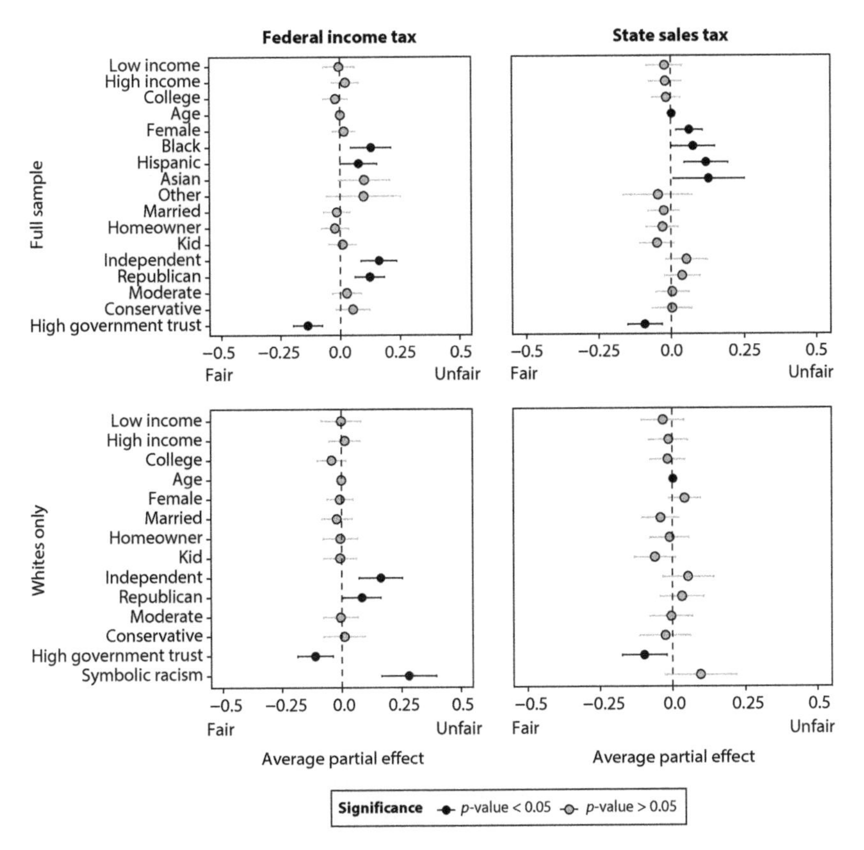

FIGURE 1.1 Correlates of Tax Unfairness
Note: Outcome coded so that tax very unfair is high. Average partial effects from ordinary least squares models. High income is the top quintile. Reference group for party identification is Democrat; for ideology, it is liberal.
Source: 2016 CCES.

being equal. But moderates and conservatives only differ from liberals in their desire to see the tax decreased, not in their fairness evaluation. And consider the sales tax. Partisanship and ideology bear no relationship to sales tax attitudes. We will see that pattern repeatedly: when partisans differ in their opinions, it's over progressive taxes; on regressive taxes, not so much. The other common pattern in descriptive data is that many political independents harbor strong antitax feelings, as do large shares of Democrats. These similarities help undercut partisanship as a correlate of tax attitudes. Politically they mean that the Republican Party has much to gain from an antitax stance, garnering support from its own partisans, a fair share of Democrats, and a

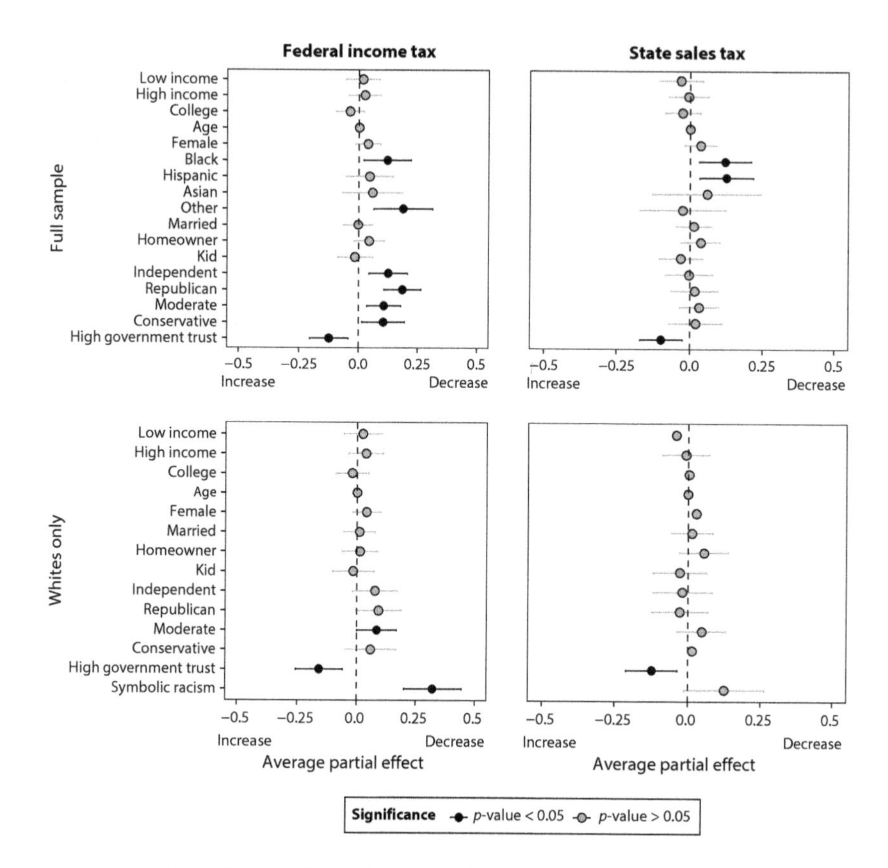

FIGURE 1.2 Correlates of Tax Change Preferences
Note: Outcome coded so that decrease tax is high. Average partial effects from ordinary least squares models. High income is the top quintile. Reference group for party identification is Democrat; for ideology, it is liberal.
Source: 2016 CCES.

large share of independents, who are even more antitax than Republicans on average.

If self-interest and symbolic attachments had inconsistent relationships to tax attitudes in chapters 3, 4, and 5, chapters 6 and 7 demonstrate the powerful associations between race and tax attitudes. Among white Americans, the symbolic attachment of racial resentment is strongly and consistently associated with tax attitudes. From previous work we knew that federal spending attitudes are strongly correlated with racial resentment. This chapter reveals that attitudes toward both taxes and tax expenditures are strongly associated with racial resentment as well. Figures 1.1 and 1.2 show that among whites, those who are more racially resentful are much more likely than others to deem the federal income tax unfair and in need of a decrease, even above and beyond other demographic and political factors as well as government trust. Symbolic racism is not a statistically significant correlate of sales tax opinion—the only tax for which that is the case. Over and over again, we will see a strong relationship between racial resentment and views on federal spending, taxes, and tax expenditures. They all have a similar attitudinal structure. The issue for tax politics is that racial resentment is chronically available in the United States, not only due to the nation's sorry racial history, but also to the active efforts of political elites, especially on the Right, to connect race, social spending, and taxes together in white Americans' minds.[15] These sinister—and cynical—stratagems take advantage of the nature of attitudes among the non-rich and help lawmakers achieve tax reduction for the economic elites who support them.

Chapter 7 examines the tax attitudes of Black and Hispanic Americans. Normally Black Americans hold more progovernment attitudes than whites. But Black Americans are more likely to say nearly every tax is unfair. In figures 1.1 and 1.2, we see that Black Americans are more likely than whites to say the federal income and sales taxes are unfair, and need to be decreased. The distinctiveness of Black (and often Hispanic) opinion will be found on both progressive and regressive taxes. Some of the few groups that otherwise support a strong role for government are punished at the hands of government in tax policy as in other policy areas.

Chapter 8 summarizes the book's findings and contemplates the lessons of the book's analyses for future tax reforms. Many of the pathologies of American politics are reflected in and exacerbated by tax policy. In combating progressive taxation, economic elites get a two-for-one deal with tax expenditures. These provisions lower their taxes yet simultaneously confuse and anger the public, undercutting the public's ability to see their true stakes and creating antitax sentiment that elites can harness for their own further tax-cutting purposes. The role of race also complicates reform of the nation's revenue system. To consider one example, peer nations use regressive VATs to fund expansive human capital and infrastructure investments (VAT is a consumption tax imposed on the value added in each stage of the production of a good or service).[16] On the one hand, regressive taxes are more popular than progressive taxes among the American public (one of the departures from self-interest that the book reveals). Perhaps the United States too could raise more revenues with a national consumption tax. On the other hand, the long history of elite-fanned linkages between taxes, spending, and race makes such a regressive tax–progressive spending bargain unlikely in the United States: the role of race undercuts the possibilities for increased redistributive spending. In these and many other ways, the design of tax policies shapes public opinion, which in turn constrains the possibilities for policy reform.

Finally, a brief word about government trust. The empirical chapters focus on self-interest, partisanship and ideology, and race and racism. As is clear from figures 1.1 and 1.2, trust in government is a strong correlate of tax attitudes as well: those who trust government more are less likely to deem taxes as unfair or in need of a decrease (the relationship exists for other taxes besides the two shown here).[17] This makes sense: if one trusts government, one is more sanguine about handing over one's hard-earned dollars to fund its operations. Scholars have long argued that government trust is a facilitating factor in policymaking as it shapes the openness of citizens to government activity. Individuals are more supportive of government policy—more willing to give government action a chance—when they are more trusting.[18] One consequence of the enormous decline in the United States in government trust since the 1960s is that low trust makes taxation more difficult.[19] Because government trust is so proximate to tax attitudes, I do not feature a separate chapter on it. But I do include it in all the empirical models in which it is available. Thus the effects that I show for partisanship, race, or racial resentment are above and beyond government trust. That is, when independents, Black Americans, or racially resentful whites say a tax is unfair compared to their Democratic, white, or racially sympathetic counterparts, it's not merely because they are less trusting of government.

2

History and Nature of the American Tax System

UNDERSTANDING THE NATURE of Americans' attitudes toward taxes begins with an exploration of the tax system's evolution. The basic design of today's system, including the list of taxes Americans pay, has largely been in place since World War II. Earlier in the nation's history federal revenues were often based on regressive sources that placed a relatively heavier burden on lower-income groups. But starting with the Populist movement of the late nineteenth century, the emphasis has been on progressive taxation, with a heavier burden on higher-income and higher-wealth groups because of their greater ability to pay. In response, those privileged groups have sought to reduce their effective rates of taxation—what they pay as a share of their income. Given the great permeability of the American political system to the influence of the organized and highly resourced, they have succeeded in blunting the system's progressivity. Federal taxes are far less progressive now than in the past; state and local taxation has always been regressive, and has become more so over time. Why has progressive taxation failed to generate more support? Why has it proven so difficult to sustain? This chapter provides a brief overview of the development of the tax system and points to features that might shape public attitudes, which are then examined in subsequent chapters.

In some respects, the contemporary structure and politics of taxation represents continuity with history. Because taxation is one of the most coercive functions of the state, raising revenue has always been difficult in a country deeply skeptical of government power. The chronic presence of race too has shaped tax policy and politics, with the fear of white tax dollars extracted to assist Black people a continuous thread. Ironically, as we will explore more in chapter 7, Black Americans have long paid more in taxes than similar whites for both visible reasons (overassessments of Black homes for property tax purposes) and less visible ones (greater income taxation of Black households that are less likely to qualify for various tax breaks, among many other examples) (Brown 2021). It seems that everyone has a reason to dislike taxes. The difficulty of funding the American state has deep roots.

In other respects, the contemporary era stands apart, chiefly in the commitment of the Republican Party to a relentless antitax stance. The various factions that constitute today's GOP—fiscal conservatives, social conservatives, libertarians, and the populist Right—may not agree on everything, but they have coalesced around an antitax philosophy. Public opinion is implicated as Republican politicians have come to see an antitax stance as a decisive electoral advantage given widespread antigovernment sentiment, and among some white voters, racial resentment as well. The asymmetry of taxes—people would rather not pay them, and the benefits are hard to see—leaves the Democratic Party hamstrung because it is so difficult to defend the state.

This chapter offers a thumbnail sketch of the structure of the American tax system in preparation for subsequent chapters that examine the attitudes that arise from this structure.[1] It shows how taxes transformed from being a quiet, technocratic arena to a noisier political one in which the public became a player. Of course, there have always been complaints about taxation as well as partisan contestation over the details of tax policy. But public opinion really began to matter in the 1970s. During the 1950s and 1960s, taxes rose precipitously as the nation waged the Cold War, increased the scope of social policies, and educated the large baby boom generation. Strong economic growth blunted the impact, though. Then came the 1970s' economic downturn, which exposed the size of the tax burden that had accumulated. A new GOP coalition centered around antitax sentiment found a receptive audience among a tax-burdened public, including among whites whose racial animosity was triggered by the racialization of poverty, fanned by slanted media coverage (Gilens 1996).

In the meantime, taxes had become complicated because the privileged worked vociferously to get their effective tax rates reduced, both through lower rates and a plethora of tax breaks that ate away at progressivity. In contrast, the public has long supported the principle of progressive taxation, believing the rich should pay more, as chapter 3 will show. Their anger at the tax system was inflamed by periodic media reports, beginning in the late 1960s, revealing that some of the rich paid little or no taxes. At the same time, the growing complexity of taxes—and elite obfuscation when talking about taxes—made it difficult for ordinary people to understand the stakes and channel their anger in ways that tied their abstract principles to specific tax attitudes. As we will also see in chapter 3, although nonrich taxpayers uphold progressive taxation as a desirable principle, they most dislike progressive taxes, in contradiction to both those principles and their own material stakes.

The overall American tax system remains progressive, imposing a greater burden on those at the top of the economic spectrum, but it is less progressive than it used to be. There are many reasons for the decline, including the great permeability of the policymaking system to organized interests, private financing of election campaigns that heighten the influence of economic elites, and so on. Yet in the perennial efforts of the privileged to get their taxes reduced, an important ally has been the public itself. Although many Americans believe otherwise, the public sector is quite small in the United States, with taxes accounting for a smaller share of the economy than nearly any other rich nation. This chapter begins to show why the nation's predominant form of public finance, progressive taxation, has failed to generate more public support, constricting the entire fiscal state.

A Brief History of American Tax Policy

Each level of government in the American federal system—national, state, and local—can impose taxes. Taxes vary in their object: income, consumption, and wealth. Taxes also differ in their redistributive effects. Some, like the federal individual income tax, are progressive, meaning that the rate increases as the amount taxed increases, posing a greater burden on higher-income people. Others, like the sales tax collected in most states, are regressive. Lower-income people spend a larger share of their income than do higher-income people, and so sales taxes constitute a greater share of income for the poor than for the rich, even though the rate may appear flat, the same for everyone. Taxes vary in their design elements too. Some are highly visible—such as a lump-sum property bill that arrives in the mail each quarter—while others are less visible either because they are withheld by an employer (payroll and income taxes) or taken a bit at a time (sales taxes). Some taxes deliver highly visible benefits—such as the Social Security retirement pensions funded by the payroll tax—whereas others, such as income or most sales taxes, simply go into federal or state governments' general revenue pots, where linking taxes paid to benefits received is far more difficult. This chapter explores how this complex system came into existence and starts to look at the implications for public attitudes.

Funding the Early American State

Many of the taxes Americans pay today are relatively recent developments, in part because government used to be small in scope. Moreover, the federal government, the focus of so much antigovernment ire in contemporary politics, was actually smaller than state and local governments in revenues as well as expenditures until the New Deal and especially World War II forever expanded its purview. For most of the country's first 140 years, just a few regressive taxes (tariffs on imported goods and excise taxes), along with the occasional sales of public lands, provided sufficient funds for the relatively limited list of federal government activities. These included paying off the states' Revolutionary War debts; paying pensions to Revolutionary War veterans; engaging in conflicts such as the War of 1812, Mexican War of 1846–48, and wars against Native American tribes; maintaining a customs union; constructing roads, canals, and public buildings; and distributing public land (Brownlee 2016, chap. 2). State and local governments were primarily funded by property taxes, a practice predating the Revolutionary War (Fisher 1996).

Federal revenues centered on the tariff for legal, practical, and political reasons. The US Constitution permitted only "indirect" taxes on commerce that individuals would pay through intermediaries, not "direct" taxes on individuals themselves (Brownlee 2016, 31).[2] Tariffs were also easy to collect and protected domestic industries, while other sources of revenue, such as property taxes, were already being utilized by local and state governments (Einhorn 2006). In addition, historian Robin Einhorn has argued that the tariff was chosen because taxing either income or property would have necessitated a national debate about taxing slavery—because slaves were property and produced income. Congress ducked the issue, realizing it "could design a tax on imports without talking about slavery," putting off for seven decades the fundamental conflict at the heart of American democracy (Einhorn 2006, 117). The tariff remained the chief source of federal revenue until the Civil War, and the only federal tax from 1817 to 1861.

Financing the Civil War

The great fiscal demands of the Civil War ushered in the first income tax. Much of the Union's war effort was funded through government bonds, but as spending soared, congressional Republicans sought new revenues. At first Republicans enacted higher tariffs and excise taxes—regressive taxes that they preferred because they fell more heavily on lower-income groups, the start of a "class-conscious politics" of taxation that has characterized American tax regimes ever since, according to historian W. Elliot Brownlee (2016). Nonetheless, Republicans worried that regressive taxes would be unpopular, and sure enough, after a military draft commenced, riots broke out in New York City in summer 1864. Civil War finance remained regressive overall, but to counter shouts of "rich man's war and poor man's fight," Congress first adopted an income tax focused on the privileged in 1861 and then raised the rates in 1864.[3] It would not be the last time that war reshaped American taxation.[4]

The Civil War income tax was short-lived, but had many features that characterized federal income taxation later. It was progressive, aiming at higher earners by exempting the first $800 in income (about the average income at the time). Initially it featured one flat tax rate, but later, graduated rates (Witte 1985). It also included the first tax break: a lower tax rate on the interest from the huge number of bonds the government issued.[5] The first estate tax, another progressive element, was established as well (formally, it was an inheritance or "legacy" tax applied to the transfer of property after death). The Lincoln administration also introduced two other aspects of modern tax collection: the precursor to the Internal Revenue Service (IRS), the Commissioner of Internal Revenue, and for employees of the government and some large corporations, withholding at the source, with employers deducting taxes from pay and sending them directly to the government.[6]

The Creation of the Modern Federal Income Tax

After the war, the estate and income taxes were repealed, with support for income tax repeal coming mainly from members of Congress from the Northeast and California—regions that faced the brunt of the tax—while those from the South and West voted overwhelmingly to retain it (Hill 1894, 442–43). With the repeal of the progressive wartime taxes, federal revenues once again centered on tariffs and excise taxes. Both were regressive, but benefits, mostly the Civil War pensions that consumed 45 percent of all federal receipts by the 1890s, were progressive (at least in the Union states) (Skocpol 1992).

The high tariffs proved controversial. Supporters included manufacturers and workers who benefited from tariffs' protection from foreign competition. Opponents included southerners who had to pay them, but who failed to benefit (they were shut out of the Civil War pension system, for example). Trouble was also brewing among farmers, who felt they bore the brunt of state and local taxation, which was more significant than federal taxation and centered on the property tax, harming rural interests whose landholdings were more extensive. Matters worsened after the financial panic of 1893 caused agriculture prices to fall while interest and freight rates soared (Ratner [1942] 1967, 160–61). Wealthy interests seemed to be profiting on the backs of farmers. With the elimination of the Civil War income tax in 1872, they seemed to be "escaping taxation almost entirely" as well (Seligman 1911, 495). The Populist movement in the South and West was born.

One desire was to make the rich pay more. A new, bipartisan rural-urban coalition of farmers and middle-class property owners ultimately triumphed in the creation of the modern federal income taxes on individuals and corporations. Congress first attempted to create an individual income tax in 1894, but the Supreme Court declared it an unconstitutional "direct" tax (even though the court had ruled the Civil War income tax constitutional). Ratification of the Sixteenth Amendment in 1913 overcame that barrier, giving Congress the "power to lay and collect taxes on incomes, from whatever source derived, without apportionment among the several States, and without regard to any census or enumeration." Republicans from the Northeast opposed income taxation, as they had in 1894, as did many wealthy individuals, even as some of the rich saw an income tax as a way to fend off more radical calls for industrial democracy—that is, employee participation in management decisions.[7]

With the Sixteenth Amendment in place, newly elected Democratic president Woodrow Wilson immediately proposed an individual income tax applying to a small percentage at the top of the income spectrum.[8] A new corporate income tax had been enacted a few years earlier, in 1909 (it was considered an excise tax and therefore avoided the constitutional barrier that the individual income tax had faced).[9] And the modern estate tax was created in 1916, in part to shore up federal finances when tariff revenues fell during World War I.

With the adoption of these three taxes, the basis of federal revenues shifted from regressive to progressive sources.[10] The animating philosophy during this Populist period was the ability to pay, with new taxes focused on high-income and high-wealth individuals who were deemed most able to afford it. This philosophy was embraced by much of the public, and is echoed in assertions from contemporary nonrich survey respondents that the rich and corporations do not pay enough (see chapter 3). Justifications for taxing wealth also had a long intellectual history, with arguments about redirecting concentrated wealth to benefit society arising from nineteenth-century intellectuals and political actors. Jeremy Bentham (1843) and John Stuart Mill (1848) advocated restraint in wealth accumulation, while President Theodore Roosevelt argued for "a constantly increasing burden on the inheritance of those swollen fortunes which it is certainly of no benefit to this country to perpetuate" (quoted in Herzig 2018, 1178). Even industrialist Andrew Carnegie (2006, 7–8) deemed the estate tax the "wisest" of all forms, inducing "the rich man to attend to the administration of wealth during his life" and benefiting the "community from which it chiefly came."[11]

Financing World War I with Progressive Taxes—and Cutting Them Afterward

The outbreak of World War I reproduced a familiar pattern. First, Congress cranked up progressive taxes to help fund the war effort—in this case, raising the top income tax rate to 77 percent and imposing an excess profits tax on corporations along with the estate tax previously mentioned. Indeed, until the Iraq and Afghanistan conflicts under President George W. Bush, major wars were always accompanied by tax increases.[12] This was especially true of progressive taxes, a way for the affluent to "sacrifice" money as the working class sacrificed its children (Scheve and Stasavage 2016). The second pattern we see repeated is that the rich seek tax cuts as soon as hostilities cease. This happened after the Civil War, and would happen again after World War II. After World War I, the rich pressured the newly Republican governments of the 1920s to lower income tax rates, reduce the estate tax, and abolish the excess profits tax. Nonetheless, there was a rachet effect: Congress reduced the top income tax to 25 percent, down from the 77 percent wartime rate, but still more than the prewar 7 percent rate (Mehrotra 2013, chap. 7).

The Great Depression and Advent of Payroll, Sales, and Gas Taxes

The Great Depression and later World War II forever changed the scope of government in the United States. The vast new obligations that the federal government in particular took on required unprecedented levels of revenue. The question became how to finance these new efforts. Soak the rich? Create new broad-based taxes? American governments at the national and state levels did some of each between 1932 and 1945. By the end of this period, the modern fiscal state was in place, and most of the taxes that Americans pay today were established.

In the face of the Great Depression, federal government revenues dropped precipitously. The Revenue Acts of 1932 and 1935 shored up federal receipts by greatly raising income taxes, with top marginal rates climbing to 62 percent in 1936 and 69 percent in 1940, erasing the declines of the 1920s. But the income tax remained a narrow tax only paid by a small share of households. Could it provide enough revenue? Congress debated but ultimately did not pass a national sales tax, which was favored by some business interests and opposed by southerners, farmers, and other important groups. Instead, the income tax increases of 1932 and 1935 were accompanied by consumption taxes on specific goods—some, like furs and jewelry, because they were luxuries, and others, like cars, chosen because they promised to raise a great deal of badly needed revenue. Those who championed the consumption taxes argued that the regressivity was tempered by the inclusion of luxury goods in the long list of taxed items and because the singling out of particular goods for taxation enabled more consumer choice than a broad national sales tax would (Thorndike 2013, chap. 2).

Although a national sales tax was not adopted, the 1930s were especially notable for the creation of other new taxes. Most of these were regressive, and applied to income groups far beyond the rich and affluent who paid the income and estate taxes. For example, the federal gas tax was enacted in 1932, providing for the federal funding of highway and bridge construction, with a smaller share for mass transit. Many, including Franklin Delano Roosevelt, thought it a "perfect tax" because it was essentially a user fee: only those who drove would pay the tax (Thorndike 2013).

More significantly, a broad-based payroll tax was adopted with the creation of Social Security. The Social Security Act of 1935, part of FDR's New Deal programs aimed at the social needs laid bare by the Great Depression, created two programs for older Americans. Old Age Assistance, meant to address the immediate problem of senior poverty, was a means-tested program funded by general revenues (replaced by Supplemental Security Income in 1975). Old Age Insurance, the retirement pension we know today as "Social Security," was at first smaller than Old Age Assistance, but soon eclipsed it. A payroll tax was chosen for funding Old Age Insurance because it was not clear that the progressive income tax—imposed on only 10 percent of households at the time—would produce enough revenue to cover the new pension program (Leff 1983). The payroll tax was only imposed up to a wage cap and therefore was regressive. But this was counterbalanced with a progressive scheme of benefits, which replaced a greater share of lower-income workers' earnings in retirement. Moreover,

FDR felt that a payroll tax would create a sense of earned entitlement—a "legal, moral and political right to collect their pensions," he quipped in 1941—and differentiate the new pension program from the dole, preserving participant dignity (quoted in Derthick 1979, 230). "With those taxes in there, no damn politician can ever scrap my social security program," he added (quoted in National Archives, n.d.). Senior citizens' defense of Social Security over time has proven him right (Campbell 2003). The payroll tax began in 1937, with employers and employees each paying 1 percent of the first $3,000 in earnings. Just over half of the workforce—generally workers in commerce and industry, from whom it was easier to collect payroll taxes—were included in the system (US House Ways and Means Committee 1998, 59).[13]

New Deal programs also instigated changes in state and local taxation. Through the early twentieth century, property taxes had been the main source of revenue for states. During the Great Depression, states handed over these revenues to local governments, leaving states in need of new revenue sources, especially for New Deal programs that required joint federal-state funding. Before the Depression, about half the states had been aiding the needy blind and elderly, and nearly all aided dependent children, but the benefits were modest (Patterson 1969, 8). The 1935 Social Security Act both created more generous benefits for these populations and required states to pay a share (Brownlee 2016). In response, the majority of states implemented individual and corporate income taxes during the 1930s (ACIR 1980, 95).[14]

Competition with the federal government and each other, however, limited states' abilities to raise revenue using income taxes. The federal income tax increases in the Revenue Acts of 1932 and 1935 constrained state action; interstate competition also dissuaded states from raising too much revenue with new income taxes.[15] For additional funds, states turned to regressive taxes, especially sales taxes. Mississippi passed the first retail sales tax in 1933, with twenty-two more states following during the Depression. Many states instituted gas and cigarette excise taxes as well (Hansen 1983, 144). These new levies allowed states to almost double their revenues between 1930 and 1940, despite the poor economic conditions (Patterson 1969, 98). Over time, the main sources of state revenues shifted dramatically, from property taxes, excise taxes, and license fees in 1900, to sales and other consumption taxes, income, and corporate taxes by the postwar era.[16] It's worth noting that southern states especially oriented their revenue systems around low property taxes and high sales taxes in order to shift revenue burdens from white property owners to Black residents (Newman and O'Brien 2011).

World War II and the Vast Extension of the Income Tax

World War II changed the American tax regime still further, with the federal government extending the income tax from the affluent to most households. As of the late 1930s, only about 10 percent of households paid the income tax, while regressive excise taxes still produced one-third of federal revenues (Leff 1984, 12). The enormous revenue needs of the war—World War II cost twice as much as a percentage of GDP as World War I—prompted a massive expansion of the income tax, forever changing the complexion of American taxation.

To fund the war effort, Congress first expanded the corporate tax dramatically and increased the top marginal income tax rate to 94 percent in 1944 and 1945, the highest in American history.[17] But the most consequential change was the extension of the income tax to the majority of households in revenue bills in 1941 and 1942, drawing ordinary Americans into the politics of the income tax. The number of taxpayers increased by a factor of ten, from 3.9 million in 1939 to 42.6 million in 1945, with 90 percent of the labor force submitting income tax forms and 60 percent paying federal income taxes by the war's end (Brownlee 2016, 146).[18] Despite the fact that most Americans were paying the federal income tax for the first time, surveys showed that it was quite popular. In March 1945, as they were readying their income tax returns (the deadline moved to April in 1955), 85 percent of Americans told Gallup (2024b) they thought the income tax they would have to pay was fair.

The 1950s and 1960s: Rapidly Expanding but (Temporarily) Popular Government

The nature of American government fundamentally changed with the New Deal and World War II. The federal government overtook state and local governments in total revenue. The vast fiscal expansions needed to fund New Deal programs and the war effort put in place most of the taxes Americans pay today: the majority of households paid federal and state income taxes; workers paid payroll taxes; consumers paid state sales taxes as well as federal and state gas taxes; homeowners paid local property taxes; and the wealthy paid estate taxes.

This tax regime was remarkably popular for a time. Yes, the rich engaged in the same behaviors they had after World War I, seeking reductions in their top marginal income tax rates as well as reductions in the corporate income tax and repeal of the excess profits tax, all granted by the Republican-led Congress elected in 1946. And yes, both the rich and other taxpayers grumbled when

Congress raised income tax rates for every tax bracket when the Korean conflict broke out in 1950, with the percentage of adults telling Gallup that the taxes they had to pay that year were "too high" rising from 43 percent in 1949 to 52 percent in 1951 and 71 percent in 1952.[19]

But the 1950s and 1960s were mostly marked by a quiet politics of tax. Taxes did rise, but a booming economy hid the toll (and the Cold War provided a compelling justification). A bipartisan sense of fiscal responsibility reigned, particularly among the conservative coalition of Republicans and southern Democrats who dominated congressional policymaking—and the tax-writing committees—in this period. During the 1950s, Republican president Dwight D. Eisenhower too refused several opportunities to cut taxes, citing a need to maintain a balanced budget. The share of Americans saying their federal income taxes were too high fell, to just 46 percent by 1961 (Bowman, Sims, and O'Neil 2017, 2).

The seeds of discontent were planted during these decades, however, as overall taxes rose substantially. Not so much the federal income tax, which only increased 34 percent for the "average" family between 1953 and 1974. Other taxes rose rapidly, however, especially the local property tax (77 percent), payroll tax (436 percent), and state income tax (533 percent; the rapid increase in these taxes during this period can be seen in figure 2.5). Payroll taxes increased with expansions of Social Security eligibility and benefits as the program became nearly universal along with the addition of Medicare in 1965, the public health insurance program for senior citizens, whose hospital insurance portion was funded by an additional payroll tax on employers and employees. State and local government taxes grew sharply as well, with the majority of the new spending dedicated to educating the baby boom generation, and after 1965, covering states' share of Medicaid, the public health insurance for low-income people enacted alongside Medicare (Penner 1998, 2–3).[20] Combined federal, state, and local taxes for the average family increased by a staggering 98.3 percent over this two-decade period (from 11.8 percent of an average income of $11,000 to 23.4 percent of an average income of $13,000) (ACIR 1975, 3–6).

The Tax Revolt and the Forging of the Republican Antitax Strategy

Twin oil crises in 1973 and 1978 brought the postwar economic boom to an end, rendering the tax burden highly visible.[21] Unemployment surged, as did inflation, causing real wages to fall most years between 1973 and 1982. Inflation had always pushed households into higher federal income tax brackets because the brackets at the time were fixed. This "bracket creep" was modest in the 1960s, when inflation hovered around 2 percent, and easily offset by periodic tax cuts. But with inflation ranging up to 13 percent per year, the personal exemption fell in value and households were pushed into steeply progressive higher tax rates at a rapid clip (there were twenty-five brackets for married couples in the 1970s, compared to seven in 2024).[22]

In the meantime, the high levels of trust in government that had bolstered the revenue system in the postwar era slid, with growing opposition to the Vietnam War after 1967 and the Watergate scandal of 1973–74.[23] New objections to government spending emerged, especially to antipoverty programs that were increasingly portrayed in the media—and increasingly associated in white taxpayers' minds—with Black urban poverty.[24] The share of Americans saying their federal income taxes are too high rose (Bowman, Sims, and O'Neil 2016, 2–3).

In California, a property tax revolt broke out. Dissatisfaction with high property taxes had been brewing for some time. In 1972, the media picked up a report from the ACIR that showed that while property taxes on average came to just 2 percent of homeowner income, they were 8 percent for the elderly, and in the Northeast, 30 percent for low-income elderly.[25] When the ACIR inaugurated its survey that year asking respondents "What is the worst tax?" the property tax was number one. Then homeowners began losing favorable systems of "fractional assessment" in which they only paid property taxes on a portion of their home's value. When new systems were adopted that centralized and standardized assessments—ending homeowners' arbitrary but cherished undertaxation—people rebelled, passing property tax limits first in California in 1978 (Proposition 13) and then around the country (Martin 2008). Taxes had arrived on the agenda.

Conservative politicians took notice. None more so than Ronald Reagan, who deftly reshaped this vehement but amorphous antitax sentiment into a new Republican coalition of fiscal conservatives and libertarians, always eager to limit the role of government, together with social conservatives newly energized over government tax rulings that didn't go their way.[26] Tax cutting became a central strategy for Republican Party building and the all-purpose GOP solution to whatever ailed (Blessing 2014). Privileged interests seized the opportunity to press for reductions, securing lower income tax rates (under Reagan, Bush, and Trump); lower tax rates on unearned capital gains and dividend income (Bush); estate tax reductions

(Bush and Trump); corporate tax reductions (Trump); and more tax breaks (throughout).[27]

Reagan oversaw two major tax bills: the 1981 tax cuts and 1986 Tax Reform Act (tax increases in 1982 and 1984, meant to address budget deficits arising from the 1981 cuts, drew less attention).[28] The tax changes reduced income tax revenues sharply, from 9.1 percent of GDP in 1981 to 7.4 percent a decade later. Most consequentially, these laws cut the number of tax brackets to just two, reduced the tax rates to 15 and 28 percent (down from 70 percent when Reagan took office), and indexed the brackets to inflation.

Together, these changes constituted a one-two punch to the economics—and politics—of the income tax. The number of brackets has increased modestly since the Reagan era, up to seven. But the notion that there should be only a few brackets capping out at a relatively low income level persists, limiting the ability of the federal income tax system to extract progressively more from the highest earners, even as rampant economic inequality has sent those earnings into the stratosphere (causing wags to quip that CEOs earning in the tens of millions pay the same marginal tax rate as their dentists earning a few hundred thousands). The other change, indexation, ended the bracket creep that pushed middle-income taxpayers into higher brackets. Indexation, though, also means that what accrues automatically are not budget surpluses but instead budget deficits. Before, when Congress had to take action, it was to pass periodic tax cuts as surpluses accrued, popular among the public. With the indexation of brackets, revenues rose more slowly, and it was budget deficits that automatically materialized; the action confronting Congress became whether to raise taxes, and on whom, or whether to resort to more debt financing. Thus the Reagan era both made tax cutting the centerpiece of the Republican agenda and guaranteed that Congress would repeatedly confront fiscal challenges—defining tax politics to this day.

An analysis of presidential nomination acceptance speeches and general election TV ads over time that I have reported elsewhere illustrates the increased focus on taxes among politicians and the public. During the late 1950s and 1960s, there were few mentions of taxes in electioneering, and then a rapid increase during the late 1970s and especially during the 1980s. Over the same period, tax mentions rose as a share of all likes and dislikes of the political parties that respondents mentioned in ANES data, indicating that taxes were rising in salience for voters too (Campbell 2009, 60–64).

George H. W. Bush was the rare vice president to follow his predecessor into office, but in some ways Reagan's tax cuts doomed his presidency. In 1986,

Grover Norquist launched his Taxpayer Protection Pledge in which the signatories (mostly Republican politicians) promised to oppose all increases in income tax rates for individuals and businesses, and oppose any reductions of deductions and credits unless matched by further rate reductions. In keeping with the zeitgeist, Bush pledged in his 1988 nomination speech, "Read my lips: no new taxes." Indeed, he hoped to out-do Reagan in lowering the capital gains tax rate from the 28 percent income tax rate to just 15 percent.

Once in office, however, Bush felt pressured to address the budget deficits lingering from the Reagan years. While Republicans clashed—Bush representing the old-school fiscal responsibility arm of the party, and Republican whip Newt Gingrich representing the new conservatives eager for more tax cuts—congressional Democrats crafted the 1990 Omnibus Budget Reconciliation Act, which left the capital gains tax untouched and raised the top income tax rate to 31 percent (Brownlee 2016). In signing the law, Bush reneged on his tax pledge. Also facing a recession, he lost his 1992 reelection bid.

Budget deficits undercut his successor's plans too. Bill Clinton promised a middle-class tax cut during the 1992 campaign, but his economic advisers urged him to tackle the budget deficit to satisfy the financial community. "You mean to tell me that the success of the [economic] program and my reelection hinges on the Federal Reserve and a bunch of [expletive] bond traders?" he raged (quoted in Woodward 1994, 84). The first round of proposals included a new BTU tax on all forms of energy. Although such a tax would simultaneously aid deficit reduction and encourage energy conservation, it was both regressive and opposed by gas-and-oil-state senators, who defeated it in the Senate Finance Committee, demonstrating the difficulties of passing a new type of tax in the American context. Ultimately, Clinton signed the 1993 Omnibus Budget Reconciliation Act, which passed the Senate only with Vice President Al Gore's tiebreaking vote (Brownlee 2016). It did not include a middle-class tax cut, but did increase the top marginal rate again, to 39.6 percent, expanded the EITC (which refunds some of the federal taxes paid by low-wage workers), and raised the federal gas tax by 4.3 cents—the last time that tax has been raised. This legislation was followed in 1997 by the Taxpayer Relief Act, which provided the promised middle-class relief with tuition tax credits and CTCs. It also established Roth IRAs and lowered the capital gains rate from 28 to 20 percent, with both provisions benefiting the affluent more, while increasing Medicare taxes for the affluent by eliminating the wage cap and subjecting all wages to the Medicare payroll tax. On balance, Clinton era tax changes were progressive, with average federal tax rates falling for the bottom 60 percent of earners, and rising for top earners between 1990 and 2000 (Steuerle 2004, 189–96).

That both Bush and Clinton raised taxes, and then suffered electoral losses (Bush his reelection bid, and Clinton his Democratic congressional majority in the 1994 midterm), seemed to indicate that raising taxes was a political loser (and all of this on the heels of Walter Mondale's whopping forty-nine-state loss to Reagan in 1984 after quipping in his nomination speech, "Mr. Reagan will raise taxes, and so will I. He won't tell you. I just did."). Never mind that Bush lost during a deep recession, or that the early Clinton years were marked by missteps such as the failed health reform effort and the "Don't Ask, Don't Tell" controversy over the military service of nonheterosexual people. Tax increases seemed to be the reason. Or as Norquist put it, raising taxes "ruined" Bush's presidency and "cut it in half" (quoted in Good 2012).

The second president Bush made sure not to suffer his father's fate. Individual income tax receipts peaked at nearly 10 percent of GDP in 2000—the highest ever, due to the Clinton rate increases and a booming 1990s' economy. At previous moments when individual income tax revenues surged, tax cuts tended to ensue. But the Bush tax cuts of 2001 and 2003 went further, reshaping the politics and economics of federal taxation yet again. Federal taxes fell for most taxpayers, and the middle class benefited from a higher CTC and "marriage penalty relief" that reduced taxes for some married couples. But overall the cuts were substantially skewed toward high earners: income tax rates fell to 35 percent at the top, capital gains tax rates fell to 15 percent, and the estate tax was hollowed out.

The Bush tax cuts were a triumph for the wealthy, with the successful assault on the estate tax perhaps their most emblematic feature. For many years the estate tax was a "little-noticed" part of the tax code (Slemrod and Bakija 2017, 68). It began to attract attention during the 1970s because the exemption amount had been left unchanged since 1942, and the share of estates subject to the tax rose from 1 percent in 1940 to nearly 8 percent in the 1970s (Joint Committee on Taxation 2015, 25). A 1976 adjustment doubled the exemption amount, reducing the share of estates subject to the tax to its historic norm, just below 2 percent. Nonetheless, after Republicans seized unified control of the federal government in the 2000 election, the estate tax became a target of the same coalition of ad hoc antitax groups, business organizations, think tanks, and conservative advocacy groups that lobbied hard for income tax cuts.[29] These groups fanned misperceptions among the public that family businesses would have to be liquidated or farms broken up to pay the estate tax (even though advocates could not produce any business owners or farmers to whom such fates had befallen) (Graetz and Shapiro 2005). The 2001 Bush tax cuts wound down the estate tax by increasing the exemption amount and reducing the tax rate annually through 2010, when the estate tax disappeared altogether, leaving the estate of New York Yankees owner George Steinbrenner, among others, untaxed. These political forces did not succeed in eliminating the estate tax entirely; it returned later, but with huge exemptions that today exclude most estates from taxation.

The Bush tax cuts were enormous, costing 2 percent of GDP and reducing federal revenues to a level not seen since shortly after World War II (see figure 2.5). They also broke with precedent in two ways. Bush became the first president to fight wars (in Afghanistan and Iraq) with no accompanying tax increases, undermining the power of conflict to be one of the few occasions during which American taxes can be raised. Second, the GOP shed its long-standing concern with fiscal responsibility, with the tax cuts, wars, and a new Medicare prescription drug benefit forcing the federal government to borrow twenty-five cents of every dollar it spent. Reflecting the party's new stance (at least when it occupied the White House), Vice President Dick Cheney declared, "Deficits don't matter" ("O'Neill Says Cheney Told Him" 2004).[30]

Obama campaigned for the presidency by pledging to attack economic inequality. He did succeed in increasing the top marginal income tax rate from 35 to 39.6 percent (from the Bush level to the Clinton one) and in increasing the capital gains rate for high earners from 15 to 20 percent (although still lower than the rates on earned income). His health care reform, the Affordable Care Act of 2010, was financed in part through progressive means, with an increased Medicare tax and capital gains tax for high earners.[31] The estate tax was also restored, at a high tax rate, which Democrats desired, but with a high exemption, which Republicans desired (the estate tax would only be imposed above $5 million per person—$10 million per couple—with these exemptions indexed to inflation).[32] On balance, the Obama era tax changes made the federal system modestly more progressive than it had been. But they kept in place the Bush tax cuts for the large majority of taxpayers—an affirmation of what historian Elliot Brownlee (2016, 245) terms the "retro-liberal" tax agenda of low federal taxes for most.

The third round of tax cuts for those at the top, the Trump era Tax Cuts and Jobs Act (TCJA) of 2017, reversed the trend toward increased progressivity under Obama. Income tax rates for top earners fell again. The TCJA doubled the estate tax exemption and continued the inflation indexing, so that the exemption reached $13.61 million for individuals and $27.22 million for couples by 2024.[33] Between the high exemption and extensive tax planning by the wealthy, the estate tax barely exists: fewer than 0.1 percent of decedents leave taxable estates, generating less than 0.7 percent of federal revenues.[34] "Only morons pay the estate tax," former Trump chief economic adviser and Goldman Sachs CEO Gary Cohn supposedly remarked (quoted in Davis and Kelly 2017, 18).[35]

Most significantly, the TCJA achieved what the Reagan and Bush tax cuts did not: enormous reductions in corporate taxes. It reduced the top corporate tax rate from 35 to 21 percent and eliminated the graduated system of brackets that dated back to the 1930s. In addition to these cuts for C corporations taxed through the corporate system, the TCJA lowered taxes on S corporations, the "pass-through" companies that are taxed in the individual tax system, and that constitute 95 percent of all businesses and 60 percent of all business income in the United States (Slemrod and Bakija 2017, 38). By allowing most S corporation owners to deduct 20 percent of their qualified business income, the TCJA reduced such business owners' effective rate of taxation.[36] These tax cuts for small businesses and large corporations both benefited the affluent most of all (ITEP 2019). And unlike many of the TCJA's changes to the personal income tax, which expire at the end of 2025, most of the corporate tax changes are permanent.[37]

The Contemporary American Fiscal State: Falling Progressivity, Low Revenues, Great Complexity, and the Enduring Influence of Race

Four phenomena arising from this brief history of American tax policy are worth underscoring. First, progressivity has fallen tremendously, with the effective rates of taxation of the affluent and rich falling more than for any other economic group. Second, American tax revenues are low in cross-national comparison. In no rich democracy is government as small as in the United States, and total revenues as a share of GDP have essentially been flat since the 1960s, despite a plethora of needs including an aging population and aging infrastructure. Third, the American tax system is extraordinarily complex. Americans pay a wide variety of taxes imposed by three different levels of government. Some of those taxes are straightforward to understand and pay. But many, especially the federal income tax, are complicated. And one reason for this complexity is the tax expenditure system—the credits, deductions, and preferential tax rates that subsidize individual and business activity through lowering tax liability. The tax break system reduces taxes the most for the rich and is enormous, one reason tax revenues are low compared to peer nations. Fourth, race has played a role in tax policy throughout American history, from decisions about funding the state in the nation's earliest days to the contemporary era in which the public has become a factor in tax policymaking.

Blunted Progressivity

The successive waves of the Reagan, Bush, and Trump tax cuts reduced individual income taxes the most for top earners, and trimmed other taxes that are focused on the top of the economic ladder: corporate income taxes, capital gains taxes, and estate taxes. As a result, even as incomes and wealth have climbed in the upper economic reaches, effective federal taxes for the affluent and especially the truly rich have fallen substantially. Supporters of these cuts point to the share of all taxes—especially federal income taxes—paid by high earners, which are high indeed. And it is true that lower-income people have largely been removed from the federal income tax system by a high standard deduction and expanded EITC. But lower-income households also pay sales and payroll taxes, which hit them quite hard, along with other regressive levies such as gas taxes and local fees and charges. And there is a reason that high earners pay such a large share of income taxes: they enjoy a large share of total income.

The trend in state and local taxation is less uniform. Some states have increased progressivity with higher taxes on top earners (for example, as of 2024, California, New Jersey, New York, and Washington, DC, had "millionaire's taxes," meaning top rates that apply to incomes over $1 million). But elsewhere regressivity has increased. State corporate tax revenues have fallen over time while charges, which are typically regressive, have increased substantially.[38] In some states, supermajority requirements make it difficult to raise income taxes. At the local level, declines in state aid and property tax revenues due to Prop-13-style limitation measures have led governments to rely increasingly on fees, which are regressive and have a racially disparate effect (Lav and Leachman 2018). Collectively, state and local taxes have long been regressive, and have become more regressive over time.

Combining the average (or effective) tax rates for federal, state, and local levels of government—that is, total taxes as a share of pretax income—shows

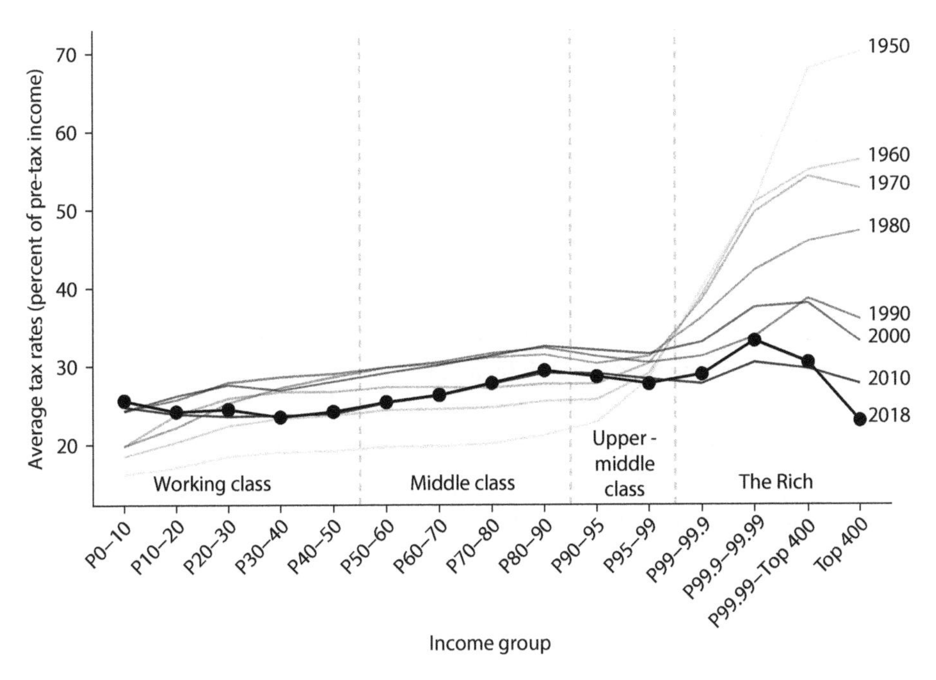

FIGURE 2.1 Average Federal, State, and Local Tax Rates by Income Group, 1950–2018
Note: Figure shows the average (effective) tax rate for all federal, state, and local taxes combined as a percent of pretax income. P0–10 indicates the bottom 10 percent of the income distribution, P10–20 the next 10 percent, and so on.
Source: Saez and Zucman 2020, figure 5.

how markedly progressivity has declined over the decades (figure 2.1). By 2018, the richest were paying the lowest tax rates of all, as economists Emmanuel Saez and Gabriel Zucman (2020) show. At the same time, those in the bottom half of the income distribution were paying more of their income in total taxes than they were in 1950, while those in the middle and upper-middle classes—between the fiftieth and ninetieth percentiles of income—were paying more than in the 1950s and 1960s.

Average tax rates for each income group are calculated by dividing the total taxes each group pays by its total income. Some critics argue that Saez and Zucman's conclusions hinge on their definition of income (they use market incomes), and that progressivity has declined less using other definitions and assumptions, such as how unreported income is allocated across income groups.[39] Much of this dispute among economists concerns arcane technical matters. But it is hard to imagine that incomes at the top have not soared over the last sixty years, since many other types of data reinforce that conclusion. It is also hard to imagine that the rich engage in less tax avoidance over time even as "IRS enforcement has gotten weaker and exotic tax-avoidance strategies have proliferated" (Karma 2024). The result of these two trends is decreased progressivity.

We do know that much of the progressivity of federal taxation is offset by the regressivity of state and local taxes. An analysis by the Institute on Taxation and Economic Policy (ITEP) using somewhat different data and methods shows how much progressivity has been blunted: the effective tax rate across all levels of government does not differ all that much across income levels. Federal taxation remains progressive; in 2024, the poorest quintile paid 3.6 percent of its income in federal taxes, rising to 25.5 percent among the top 1 percent. But state and local taxes are regressive, with the poor paying 13.5 percent of their income in state and local taxes, falling to 9.2 percent among the richest (figure 2.2a). In 2024, the combined effective rate of federal, state, and local taxes for the top 1 percent was just twice that of the poorest quintile (34.8 versus 17.1 percent), even though the average income of the top 1 percent was 160 times greater (over $2.5 million versus $15,400) (ITEP 2024).[40]

Federalism and the delegation of much of the nation's revenue raising to subnational governments is a major culprit in the undercutting of the system's progressivity. State and local governments face significant incentives to make their tax structures more regressive. One challenge for these subnational units is jurisdictional competition: a fear that high taxes will drive away businesses and affluent households. Social scientific evidence shows that these worries are exaggerated in legislators' minds—people, even millionaires, choose where to live for a variety of reasons well beyond taxes (job opportunities, location of family, community roots and standing, and recreational and cultural amenities)—but these fears of "millionaire flight" affect tax policy nonetheless (Young 2017).

Because state and local regressivity offsets so much of the remaining federal progressivity, the net result is that the share of total taxes that each income group pays is similar to the share of total income it earns (figure 2.2b).

Low Tax Revenues

Another major outcome of American tax policy and politics in recent decades is that US taxes are low in international comparison. The Organisation for Economic Co-operation and Development (OECD) is an international

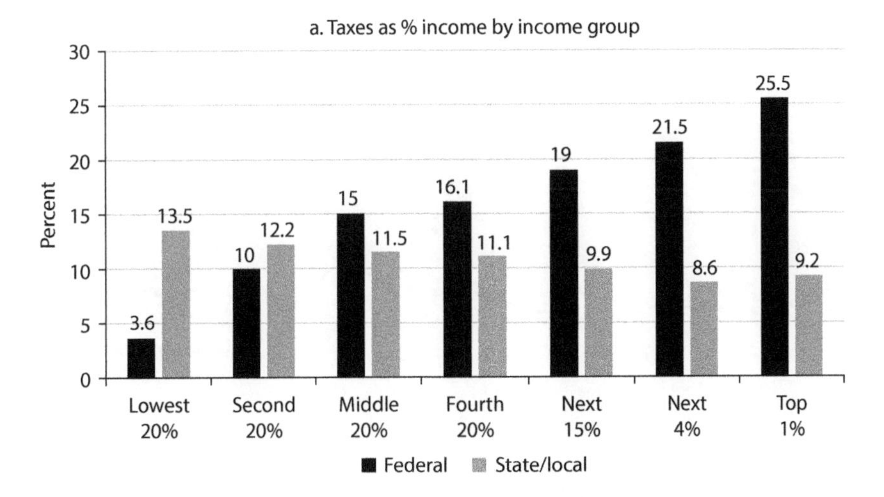

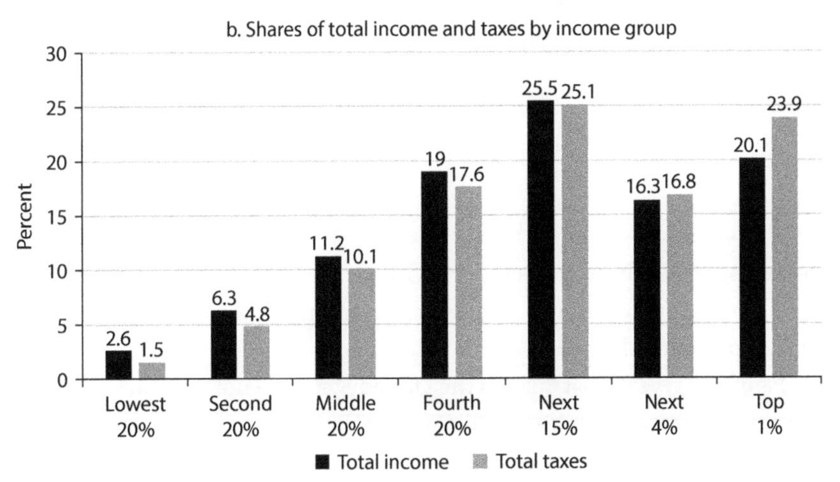

FIGURE 2.2 Federal and State/Local Taxes by Income Group, 2024
Source: ITEP 2024.

organization founded in the mid-twentieth century that collects policy and economic data across market economy democratic countries. Its data show that in 2022, the United States had lower tax revenues as a percentage of GDP than almost all other OECD countries (27.7 percent, compared to an OECD average of 34 percent). Only a handful of countries, mostly middle-income nations such as Chile, Ireland, Mexico, and Turkey, had lower tax revenues (figure 2.3). Countries whose economies and per capita income are more similar to those of the United States have far larger public sectors. Total taxes as a

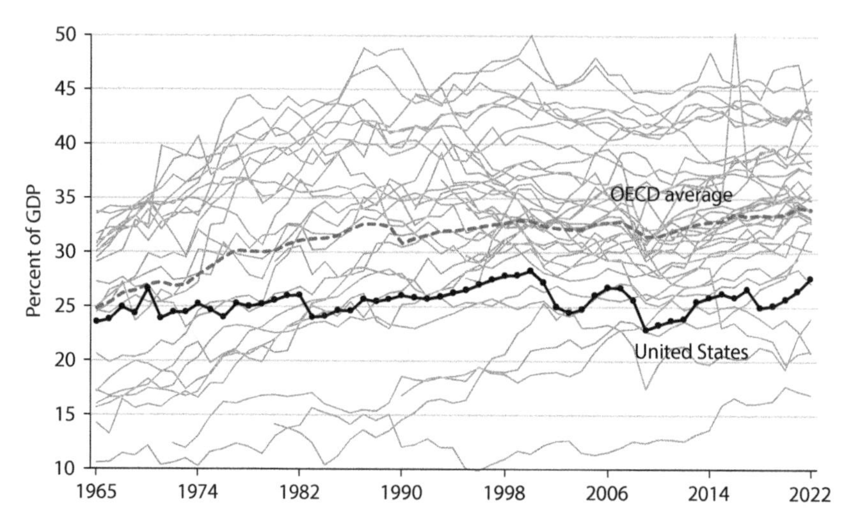

FIGURE 2.3 Total Taxes as Percentage of GDP: United States versus OECD, 1965–2022
Note: The solid black line indicates total taxes as a percentage of GDP for the United States; the dotted gray line indicates the OECD average.
Source: OECD 2023.

percentage of GDP are 33.2 percent in Canada, 35.3 percent in the United Kingdom, and 39.3 percent in Germany. Taxes top out at 44.3 percent in Norway and 46 percent in France.

Figure 2.3 reveals that taxes in the United States are not only lower but also have not increased over time, while peer nations' tax revenues have grown as a share of their economies. Back in 1965, US tax revenues were nearly the same as the OECD average; today the OECD average is one-quarter higher.

The main difference is that most other countries adopted a national-level consumption tax such as a VAT or a goods and services tax while the United States did not.[41] Even though progressivity has fallen in the United States, personal income taxes remain a key source of revenue. Figure 2.4a shows that the percentage of revenues coming from personal income taxes is quite high in the United States compared to other nations. At the same time, the percentage coming from goods and services taxes is quite low (figure 2.4b), largely because there are only state and some local sales taxes, no national sales tax or VAT. Thus a major reason for low revenues in the United States and a small public sector (the share of the economy composed of government) is the reliance on progressive taxation at the national level. The income tax is the largest

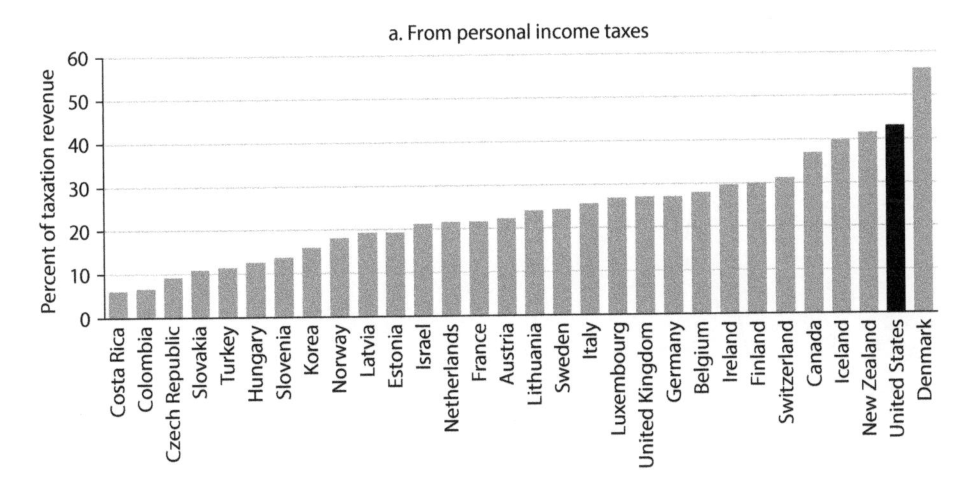

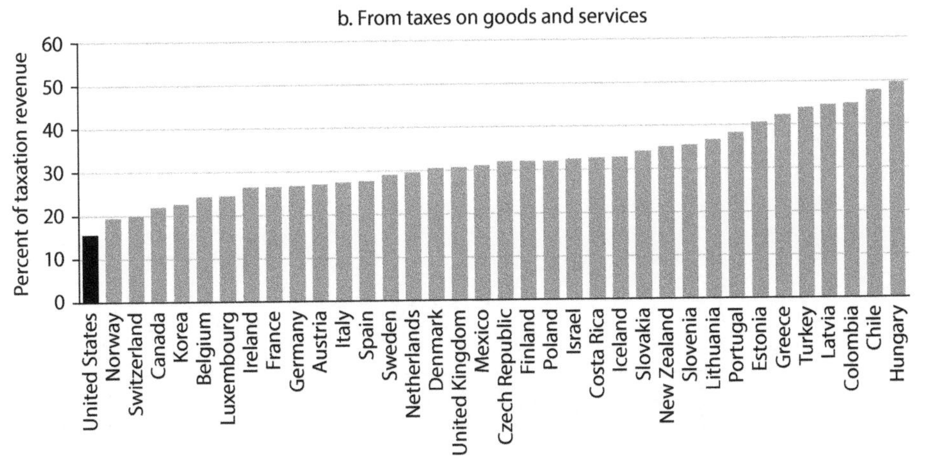

FIGURE 2.4 Percentage of Revenues from Personal Income Taxes and Goods and Services Taxes: United States versus OECD
Note: 2022 data.
Source: OECD 2023.

source of federal revenues, but as Eugene Steuerle (2004) points out, progressive income taxation is an inherently conservative form.[42] There is a limit to the amount of revenue that can be raised, as the tax imposes a zero rate (because of the standard deduction, the portion of income not subject to tax) and then low rates on the first portions of income earned by all taxpayers.[43] As implemented in the United States, the higher rates on upper incomes have been eroded by rate reductions or are effectively eroded by the many tax

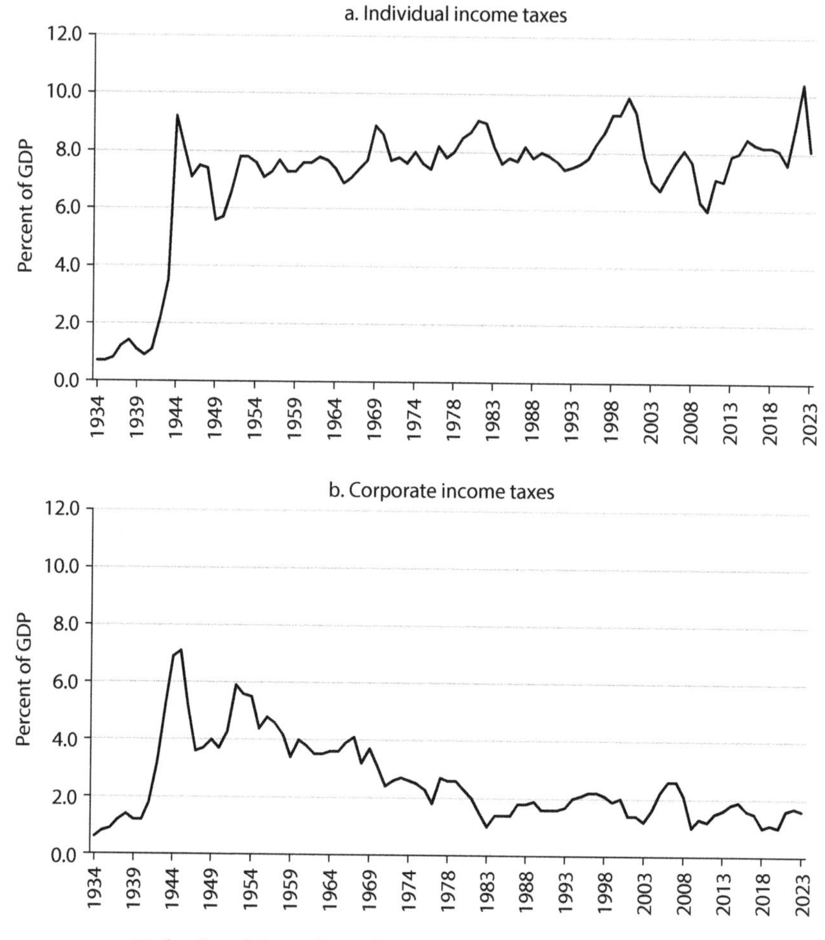

FIGURE 2.5 Federal and State/Local Taxes as a Percentage of GDP, 1934–2023
Source: OMB, n.d., tables 2.3, 14.1.

expenditures in the federal code. To bolster revenues and fund greater government spending, other countries adopted national-level consumption taxes such as the VAT in the mid-twentieth century as the limits to progressive income taxation became apparent. But the United States never did.

Not only has the United States never adopted a VAT, but revenues from the taxes that are collected have been mostly flat for years. Figures 2.5a–d show the trajectory of various taxes over time as a share of the economy. The individual income tax has tended to hover around 8 percent of GDP, despite the fact that income taxation is progressive and incomes in the upper brackets have grown

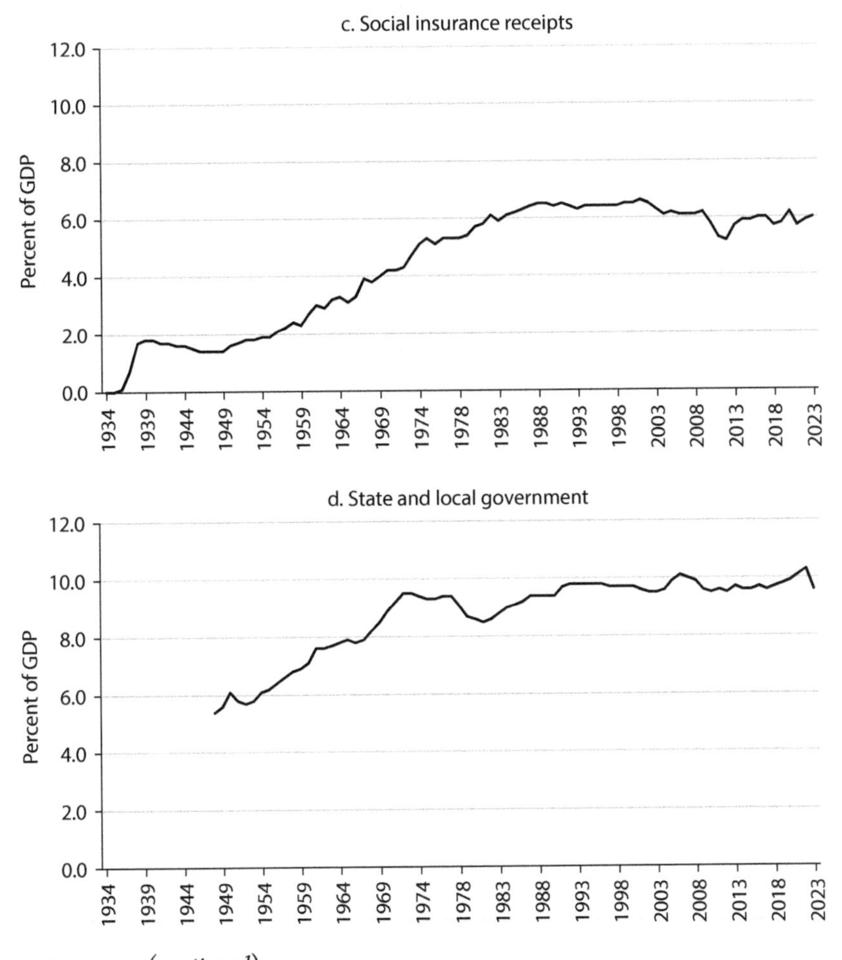

FIGURE 2.5 (*continued*)

dramatically, demonstrating how effective those earners at the top have been at blunting the tax's impact. Social insurance receipts grew at a rapid rate during the 1950s through the 1970s as Social Security expanded to cover most workers and Medicare was added in 1965. But the Social Security tax rate hasn't risen since 1990, and the share of total earned income on which the tax is imposed has shrunk because more income is earned above the wage cap. Nor has Congress taken any steps since the early 1980s to shore up Social Security's finances to cover the entire cost of baby boomer retirement, despite the popularity of the program and the public's professed willingness to pay higher taxes to fund the promised benefits (see Arnold 2022). As a result, social insurance receipts have been flat as a share of GDP for decades as well. State and local government revenues grew rapidly during the 1950s and 1960s, as noted earlier, but have hovered around 10 percent of GDP since the tax revolt, in part because forty-four states have at least one type of property tax limit in place, such as limits on property tax rates or the growth of assessed home values (many use several types of limits simultaneously) (Lav and Leachman 2018). Corporate tax revenues have fallen over time and now produce just 2 percent of GDP. Although it does not appear in figures 2.5a–d, it's worth mentioning that the federal gas tax has been the same 18.4 cents per gallon since 1993. Antitax forces have been successful at keeping American government small.

Tax Expenditures and Increased Complexity

A third phenomenon in American tax policy is the growth of the tax expenditure system. "Tax expenditure" is the formal term for credits, deductions, exclusions, exemptions, deferrals, and preferential tax rates in the individual and corporate income tax systems. These "tax breaks," to use the more colloquial term, subsidize and incentivize certain behaviors by collecting no taxes or reduced taxes on the relevant activity. Tax expenditures have been part of the federal income tax since its inception; the 1913 federal income tax included the deductions for state and local taxes as well as home mortgage interest along with the exclusion of state and local bond interest, which all survive in modified form to this day (Witte 1985). Because tax expenditures subsidize designated activities by taxing them less, they have a dual effect: they constitute "indirect" spending by government (as opposed to direct spending) and reduce tax revenues.

Tax expenditures also reveal what types of activities the government has chosen to support and whose behavior it has chosen to incentivize. In the individual income tax code, the home mortgage interest deduction subsidizes homeownership by allowing owners to deduct part of the mortgage interest they pay from their taxable income. The exclusion of employer-provided health insurance from taxation effectively reduces the premiums that workers pay for their health insurance (employers offering insurance get a break too). The deferral of taxes on IRA and 401(k) savings until withdrawal subsidizes retirement, since households' tax rates are usually lower then. The reduced (or "preferential") rate on long-term capital gains and qualified dividends subsidizes investing with a tax rate lower than that on earned income.[44] The CTC subsidizes the cost of raising children. The EITC enhances the income of low-wage workers (especially those with children) by refunding the income and (for some) payroll taxes withdrawn from their paychecks. In the corporate tax code, provisions around equipment depreciation, research and development, and the use of biofuels, to cite a few examples, lower tax burdens as well.

The above instances represent just a fraction of the scores of tax expenditures that riddle the federal tax code (and the income tax codes of many states). Although many Americans scorn the "loopholes" that allow corporations to minimize their taxes, more than 80 percent of this indirect spending goes to households. That's because tax expenditures have become a go-to way for lawmakers to pursue social and economic policy in the United States, particularly after the rise of the conservative movement in the Republican Party made passing new direct spending programs difficult. Tax credits or deductions can garner bipartisan support—from Democrats, because tax breaks can address some social need, and Republicans, because they do so by shrinking the size of government.[45] Another reason tax breaks are a common policy tool is that they typically only benefit people with a tax liability—that is, workers, who are viewed as more deserving than nonworkers, who in turn are suspect in American social policy discourse.[46]

Several features of the tax expenditure system are worth underscoring. First is its enormous size. The amount of federal revenues *not* collected because of tax breaks nearly equals—and at times has exceeded—the amount that *is* collected by the individual income tax (figure 2.6). Occasionally, tax expenditures are eliminated or reduced. The 1986 Tax Reform Act cut or modified a number of tax expenditures, broadening the tax base to enable the law's reduced tax rates; the 2017 TCJA limited the deduction of home mortgage interest to the first $750,000 of mortgage debt (down from $1 million), and capped the state and local tax exemption at $10,000 to pay for the corporate tax cuts (and penalize taxpayers in expensive blue states with high home prices and taxes who had not voted for Trump, observers argued) (Altig et al., 2020).[47] But such rollbacks are rare, and most high-value tax deductions have proven durable. Many also grow automatically, much like Social Security and Medicare entitlement spending (in an entitlement program, everyone who is eligible can file for the benefit, regardless of the cost to the nation's purse; similarly, everyone who is eligible for a tax break can file for it, regardless of the tax revenues lost). The Treasury Department did not begin to tally the value of forgone revenue until the late 1960s. By then, many of the biggest breaks were already entrenched.[48]

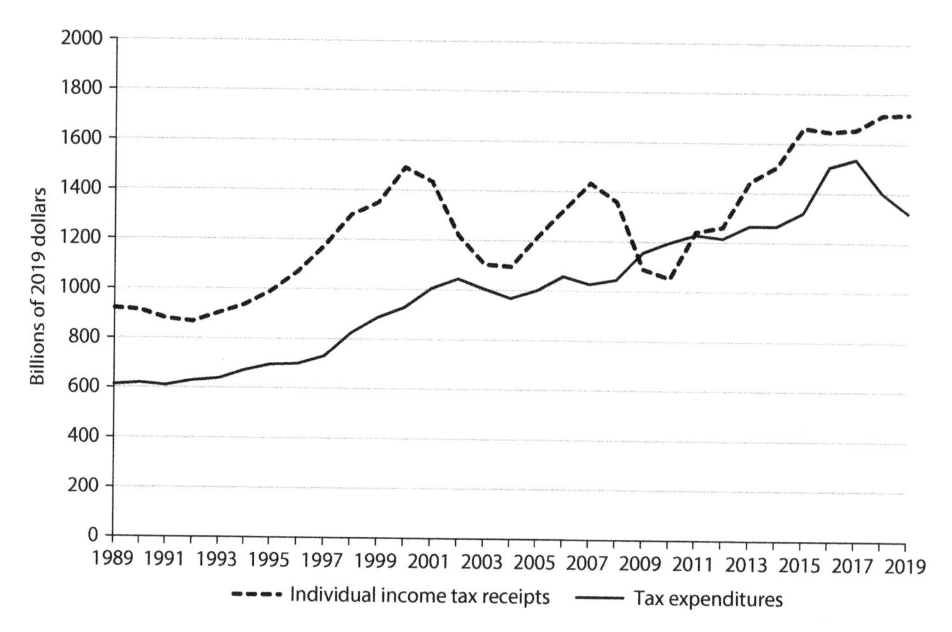

FIGURE 2.6 Value of Tax Expenditures and Individual Income Tax Receipts, 1989–2019
Sources: GAO, n.d.; OMB, n.d., table 2.1.

The second important feature of the tax expenditure system is that the affluent benefit the most, undermining progressivity. Many of the most valuable tax breaks are deductions from taxable income, not flat credits. In a graduated income tax system, the resulting tax savings rise with income. For example, an employee who contributes $6,000 toward their employer health insurance plan saves $720 if their income puts them in the 12 percent tax bracket, but $2,220 in the 37 percent bracket. The Urban-Brookings Tax Policy Center calculates that the top fifth of taxpayers received nearly 60 percent of the benefits of tax expenditures in the individual tax system in 2019, with the top 1 percent alone receiving almost one-quarter. Because the affluent are the main beneficiaries of favorable corporate tax policy, they benefit disproportionately from those tax expenditures as well (Berger and Toder 2019, table 2).[49]

Third, white taxpayers benefit more than Black taxpayers (Brown 2021). As will be discussed in greater detail in chapter 7, Black workers are less likely to hold jobs that offer tax-favored benefits such as employer-provided retirement and health benefits, and are less likely to participate in these plans when offered. Black homeowners have lower incomes and are less likely to itemize their deductions, and therefore take the home mortgage interest deduction less often than white homeowners. Black households are less likely to have capital gains income, which is taxed at a lower rate than earned income. Whites disproportionately benefit from the tax expenditure system, rendering Black households "overtaxed" on the same income on average. Moreover, those utilizing the tax expenditure system do not tend to recognize their tax breaks as government benefits (Mettler 2011). Whites disproportionately benefit from this "hidden" spending while in many cases thinking that Black households disproportionately benefit from direct spending funded by their tax dollars. Tax expenditures thus exacerbate the racialized politics of taxation.

Fourth, tax expenditures may undermine the legitimacy of the tax system. The purpose of the grueling and time-consuming task of filling out one's federal tax form is to reconcile what one owes with what one has already paid through withholding, which is rarely accurate in the United States. One reason is that the United States taxes households, not individuals. In two-income households, the second earner's tax rate begins where the first earner's ends, and it can be difficult for people to get the withholding correct. In addition, many tax breaks are deductions from taxable income rather than flat credits, again making it difficult to know enough about one's eventual tax liability to get withholding right. The compliance costs are enormous: American taxpayers average thirteen hours filling out their 1040 forms, the IRS (2023) estimates, and total compliance costs are in the hundreds of billions of dollars. Many other countries tax individuals rather than households and are more likely to provide tax breaks as flat credits, if they have them at all, making tax withholding more accurate (Campbell 2012a). Some of my graduate students and professional colleagues from other countries complete their tax returns in minutes on their cell phones.

The fallout may be reduced system legitimacy. Vanessa Williamson (2017) finds in taxpayer interviews that filling out their federal tax forms every April gives them a glimpse of the many, many breaks from which they cannot benefit, and reminds them that others are being taxed less.[50] Periodic revelations that corporations or the rich have used tax breaks to avoid income taxes altogether prompt outrage. An early such episode occurred in 1969, around the time the total revenue loss from tax expenditures was calculated for the first time. A Treasury Department report revealed that 155 high-income tax returns owed no taxes, prompting the creation of the Alternative Minimum Tax aimed at reducing the value of some tax breaks (which has been only intermittently successful). More recently, a 2021 ProPublica report based on IRS records similarly revealed that billionaires such as Jeff Bezos, Michael Bloomberg, and George Soros have often paid little or no federal income taxes (Eisenger, Ernsthausen, and Kiel 2021).[51] Between reduced tax rates, expanded tax expenditures, and extensive tax planning, the rich have been spectacularly successful at lowering their effective rates of taxation even as their incomes and wealth have soared.

The Enduring Role of Race

Tax expenditures are not the only tax provisions in which race is implicated. Race and tax policy have always been inextricably linked. From the early debates about how to fund the newly formed federal government without taking up the slavery issue, to the efforts of white taxpayers to reduce their tax liabilities through the tax expenditure system, taxes both reflect and have defined the racial order.

Tax policy has long been shaped by concerns among whites about who will be taxed and how the money will be spent. These worries became acute on the spending side when government began providing a wide array of benefits to ordinary people, from education in the nineteenth century to social welfare benefits in the twentieth. As political economists have long argued, diversity makes spending on redistribution and public goods more difficult.[52] Nowhere is this more so than in the United States, where racial antipathy among some white taxpayers has long been a resource to be tapped by advocates and lawmakers looking to redirect spending—or cut taxes—as chapter 6 will explore.

On the tax side of the equation, policy has been shaped to protect white taxpayers. These efforts range from the early choices to raise federal revenues from tariffs rather than property, as Einhorn argued, to many later provisions to limit property taxes in certain locales, exclude various employer benefits from taxation, and reduce top income tax rates, capital gains rates, and estate taxes, and so on.[53] The benefits of these as well as many other tax policies and reforms have disproportionately flowed to whites, who as chapter 7 will detail, are more likely to live in the places with property tax limits, benefit from tax-favored employer benefits, and enjoy the top incomes and assets whose taxation was lowered. Sometimes these policies were designed explicitly with race in mind; in other cases, the disparate racial effects were not noticed by white policymakers or were incidental to other goals. Either way, such policies shift the tax burden away from whites toward Black taxpayers.

Increased Politicization of Tax Policy and a New Role for the Public

Some of the features of tax politics and policy discussed so far have been with us for a long time, since the creation of the federal income tax, if not the beginning of the nation's history: the perennial efforts of the privileged to get their effective taxes reduced, outsized impact of tax expenditures, and role of race in shaping tax policy. What's new in the last four decades is the rightward movement of the Republican Party and its adoption of a steadfast antitax stance (Graetz 2024). The GOP had long stood for smaller, more efficient government. The tax revolt of the 1970s showed that a more vigorous antitax stance could be politically advantageous. It became clear that tax cuts win votes, while balanced budgets do not.

The Republicans' shift from being the party of fiscal responsibility to being the party of tax cuts proved a dilemma for Democrats. After the Bush tax cuts of the early 2000s, the Democrats' stance became preserving progressivity by keeping the Bush cuts in place for most taxpayers, but raising rates at the top of the income spectrum and maintaining the estate tax. The Democrats' message should resonate with voters, who want the privileged to pay more, as we will see in chapter 3. But the Republicans' message is simpler: tax cuts, full stop. And Republicans have kept the focus on the progressive income and estate taxes, which are unpopular among the public, to the great advantage of the privileged, who have capitalized on this sentiment to get their own taxes reduced. The great visibility of the progressive taxes and focus on tax rates has also shifted the conversation away from the tax expenditure system, which is vast and benefits the privileged disproportionately.

As tax policy has shifted from being the province of experts on Congress's tax-writing committees to being a central topic of electoral contestation, the public's role has grown. Public opinion is only one of many factors in tax policy—and probably not the most important—but it is a facilitating one. The public cares about taxes, as the tax revolt of the late 1970s demonstrated. It is far easier for lawmakers or economic elites to get what they want out of tax policy if the public is in agreement, as the great defanging of the estate tax has shown. But the public is also easily misled. Political elites, especially those seeking to cut taxes for the privileged, have great incentives to speak unclearly about taxes, and the very complexity of tax policy makes this easy to do (Graetz 2024). The remainder of the book examines how Americans think about taxes given the structures they face and information they have. It explores the degree to which individuals' tax attitudes are associated with their abstract preference for progressive taxation, material stakes in tax policy, partisanship, racial attitudes, and race. Large shares of Americans believe in progressive taxation, and think the rich and corporations do not pay enough, as we will see in the next chapter. Yet we will also see the difficulties individuals have in tying these abstract commitments—and their self-interest—to their preferences on specific taxes. The rest of the book will show how low information, partisanship, and racial resentment among whites complicate these relationships.

Implications for Public Opinion

The American tax system is enormously complex, with multiple types of taxes levied by different government entities across the federal system. National, state, and local governments all impose taxes (not to mention the thousands of special districts for water, fire, and other services that I did not even mention, and that are beyond the scope of this book). Earned income, unearned income, consumption, and wealth are all taxed somewhere. Overall, the system is progressive, based on an ability-to-pay principle, but the system has become much less progressive over time as the privileged have succeeded spectacularly in getting their effective rates reduced. The public has not served as an effective counterweight. In subsequent chapters, we will see that many Americans support progressivity as a general matter, and want privileged interests to contribute more, but have difficulty connecting these abstract preferences to specific policy attitudes. The great complexity of the American tax system renders the public susceptible to the antitax entreaties of the self-serving rich.

The privileged have been successful in attacking tax progressivity and reducing their effective tax rates for many reasons, including the permeability of the American policymaking process to organized interests, private financing of political campaigns, and so on, which give the organized and well resourced such great voice (Enns et al. 2014; Schlozman, Brady, and Verba 2018). Another factor is the role of the public. The complex, multiheaded American tax system has failed to generate sufficient public support.

The history of American taxation along with the themes of complexity, politicization, and racialization suggest a number of hypotheses about the nature of public opinion arising from the nature of the tax system. Because taxes are an economic issue, we might expect attitudes to vary with basic material stakes: that when and where people are taxed more, they have more negative attitudes. Mostly, however, measures of self-interest are not correlated with tax attitudes, and when they are, the results are mild and highly contingent. It may be that tax complexity makes it difficult for nonrich taxpayers to see their stake, and easy for economic elites and policymakers to obfuscate in ways that undermine connections between their objective self-interests and tax preferences. Given the usual strong influence of party identification on political attitudes, we might predict that tax opinions would vary by partisanship or political ideology. But that's not the case all the time either. In fact, we'll see that attitudes do not vary as often as we might expect, and the Republican Party's antitax message appeals strongly to independents and even Democrats as well. The long connections between race and taxes as well as the contemporary phenomenon of visible direct spending and invisible indirect spending suggest that racial resentment may play a role in whites' tax attitudes—and we will see that it does. And Black Americans, who are otherwise more liberal on average than white Americans and more supportive of government spending, may experience the tax side of government as especially coercive, an extension of the power arrayed against Black citizens in other ways by the state, and have more negative tax attitudes as a result.

The rest of the book examines the possible correlates of public attitudes: self-interest, partisanship, and ideology; racial sentiment among white taxpayers; and race itself, as reflected in the attitudes of Black and Hispanic taxpayers. It shows how both specific features and larger design elements of the US tax system influence these factors, undercutting some, and heightening others. Public opinion is far from the only factor in the policymaking process, but in the tax arena it proves to be an enabling one, twisted by privileged interests to secure tax policy in their interests, undermining prospects for ordinary Americans.

3

Self-Interest I

ATTITUDES ACROSS TAXES

THIS BOOK BEGAN with a series of puzzles. Why is it so hard to raise taxes in the United States? Why is support for the tax regime so low? Why does the progressive tax system fail to generate sufficient support? Although other scholars have explored other factors, I examine the nature of public opinion in contributing to the conundrums of American tax politics. Public opinion is not the only element behind tax policy, but it is a facilitating factor. It is easier to enact policies that the public supports or at least does not oppose. One goal of the book is to look at variation in attitudes across taxes and individuals to assess why higher taxes, or greater progressivity, lack public support, and in turn are difficult to implement.

This chapter starts the empirical examination of Americans' tax attitudes at the most basic point: the role of self-interest. Both common sense and standard economic models suggest that people think about taxes in cost-benefit terms, disliking taxes more that cost them more, and disliking taxes less when they cost less or deliver valuable benefits (although those are often less visible, as we will see). A long line of public opinion research shows that attitudes toward many issues do not vary with apparent self-interest. Taxes have been upheld as an exception because of their tangible natures.

This chapter considers preferences across taxes while the following chapter delves into preferences across individuals. I first define what self-interest looks like with regard to tax policy, and then stipulate what attitudes would be across taxes and different types of individuals if they were meaningfully shaped by material stakes. In the abstract, Americans do bring a self-interested stance to tax preferences. Many members of the public express a preference for progressive taxation and support for the ability-to-pay concept, in keeping with the self-interest of nonrich individuals, who are touched lightly by such taxes. Taxing the rich more would push the burden of public finance away from ordinary taxpayers toward the privileged.

When it comes to specific policy preferences, however, survey respondents frequently provide answers that are not in their objective self-interest. Their favorite taxes are the ones that cost them the most. They dislike—sometimes vehemently—the taxes that cost them less. Many Americans oppose taxes that would increase progressivity, such as the estate tax; support taxes that would lower progressivity, like a flat tax; and approve of tax breaks that primarily benefit the rich, such as the low capital gains rate and charitable giving deduction. In theory, ordinary Americans express support for the ability-to-pay principle: those with the most should pay the most to support government. But their preferences on individual taxes and tax breaks contradict their expressed principles. Many have great difficulty connecting these abstract preferences with their attitudes toward particular tax policies. A principle-policy gap characterizes the tax attitudes of the nonrich.

A number of factors may complicate the connection. One is partisan attachments, which could divert people from self-interested thinking (I take this up in chapter 5 and find that partisanship does not always structure tax attitudes in expected ways either). Another factor that may distract from self-interest is racial resentment, explored in chapter 6, which turns out to be the most potent influence on tax attitudes for white Americans. This chapter looks at three other phenomena that undermine the ability of many to connect their abstract preferences with their specific policy stances: low levels of tax knowledge, the distraction of the elite tax agenda, and obscuring tax designs.

The bottom line is that tax attitudes often do not correspond to people's apparent material stake. Among the rich they do: studies of the privileged show that they are knowledgeable about the tax system, clear-eyed about their costs and benefits, and vociferous in their determination to chip away at progressivity.[1] But among the nonrich—those who appear in the public opinion surveys on which this book is based—attitudes do not always correspond to objective self-interest. This wouldn't be a problem except that in some cases, the preferences of the nonrich are more in keeping with what would help the rich, not themselves. The inability of nonrich taxpayers to know and act on their own interests has helped the rich in their long quest to get their own effective tax rates reduced.

Self-Interest as a Possible Factor in Tax Attitudes

As Donald Kinder and Lynn Sanders (1996, 36) have documented, "The notion that citizens seek to advance their own material interests" figures prominently in political theory. Thomas Hobbes, David Hume, Adam Smith, and James Madison all rooted individual motivations regarding the public sphere in some notion of self-interest, the idea that "in forming political opinions, [individuals] fasten their attention securely on what is in it for themselves, supporting policies that advance their own material interests while standing against policies that threaten" (Kinder and Sanders 1996, 49). Evidence from the dawn of the behavioral revolution in political science bolstered this perspective. In the survey findings of the seminal *American Voter*, those with less income and education were more supportive of a government role in medical care, employment, and housing than the more privileged. Angus Campbell and his coauthors characterized this phenomenon as a form of "primitive self-interest."[2]

Increasing interest in importing models from economics into political science during the 1970s and 1980s spurred many scholars to look for attitudes congruent with self-interest. If individuals are utility-maximizing actors, as classical economic theory argues, their attitudes should vary with their objective, material stakes. But to analysts' surprise, such attitudes rarely appeared. In instance after instance, individuals who, to researchers' minds, appeared to have different material stakes in various issue areas, failed to express differential attitudes on public opinion surveys. Women and men did not differ in their opinions on women's issues, the elderly were not more supportive of Social Security spending than the nonelderly, the unemployed were not more favorable toward jobs programs than the employed, working women were no more likely to support the Equal Rights Amendment than homemakers, whites with children in public school did not have distinct opinions on busing, and so on.[3]

There was one exception to the dearth of self-interest effects: tax policy. Compared to other issue areas, scholars found much more evidence of the influence of material stakes and cost calculations emerging from individuals' demographic characteristics and lifestyles. Studies showed that smokers were more likely to oppose cigarette taxes than were nonsmokers (Green and Gerken 1989). The elderly and those without children were more likely than other voters to oppose school bond referenda.[4] Homeowners were more likely than renters to support California's Proposition 13 limiting the property tax (Sears and Citrin 1985). Residents of states and localities with higher taxes expressed more negative attitudes toward them.[5] Middle-aged workers at the height of their earning power had more negative attitudes about the progressive federal income tax than did the retired elderly or low-wage young.[6] On a survey about a variety of tax policies, homeowners in areas with steeper recent house price increases were more supportive of the home mortgage interest deduction, those who owned stock expressed more support for capital gains deductions, and those with college-age children were more supportive of a college tuition tax credit (Hawthorne and Jackson 1987). On another survey about balancing a state budget, lower-income people preferred tax increases to spending cuts and income tax increases over sales tax increases, while high-resource people preferred spending cuts and sales tax increases over income tax increases—all preferences congruent with the self-interest of those economic groups (Donovan and Bowler 2020).

What might set taxation apart? As Jack Citrin and Don Green argued, self-interest effects are most likely to be found in issue areas where the stakes are visible, certain, tangible, and large.[7] Taxes seem to fit the bill.[8] If self-interested thinking requires a cost-benefit calculation, taxes constitute a visible cost measured in a tangible metric, dollars and cents (later I'll examine whether the benefits arising from taxes ever matter). With taxes, political scientists Michael Hawthorne and John Jackson (1987) asserted, many people have real experience and genuine opinions. Taxes are also obviously linked to government; indeed, they are one of the chief ways in which citizens interact with government. As a result, on this government-related, economic issue, individuals might not only be better able to incorporate their material stakes into their attitudes but also be more likely to see self-interest as a "legitimate" basis for their preferences (Sears et al. 1980, 672).[9] That at least some attitudes seemed to correspond to material stakes came as a relief to researchers, as major theories in political science, such as pocketbook voting, are predicated on a clear view of self-interest. So too are major theories in political economy, such as the canonical Meltzer-Richard (1981) model, which assumes that redistribution preferences are based on one's location on the income spectrum and that lower-income ("lower productivity") people benefit more from higher taxes than do higher-income, more productive people.

But while taxes seem to be an area where such clear-eyed calculations of material stake are more likely for ordinary citizens, complications abound. Taxes may appear visible, certain, tangible, and large, but as will become evident, the stakes can be obscured by a variety of factors including low levels of information, elite agendas, and complex tax designs.

Defining and Measuring Self-Interest

Before searching for self-interest effects, a necessary starting point is defining and measuring "self-interest." Traditionally scholars defined it as individual-level, short-term material stakes in an issue (Kinder and Sanders include the material interests of the self and the immediate family). The narrow definition is meant to differentiate self-interest from other concepts: individual self-interest as apart from group interests; instrumental material stakes as apart from symbolic attachments of party identification, ideology, and racial sentiment that arise from early socialization; and short-term stakes based on current needs as apart from long-term stakes (because long-term stakes could morph into symbolic interests) (Sears and Funk 1990).[10]

In keeping with established practice, I too will define self-interest as short-term material stakes for an individual and immediate family. Both the short-term and material stakes parts of the definition will allow me to differentiate self-interest from other factors in attitudes, including party identification and ideology (chapter 5) and racial resentment among whites (chapter 6). As in most surveys, I do not have questions that allow me to distinguish between self-interest and group interest. Political scientist Jake Haselswerdt (2020) has run experiments in which he is able to differentiate the two effects and thus estimates that group interest (in his case, senior citizens' interests around Social Security) inflates the effect of individual self-interest by 20 percent. This suggests that in the few instances where I do find self-interest effects, the true individual self-interest component is probably even smaller.

Regarding measurement, many researchers have read interests off individuals' demographic characteristics, using income, education, race, and gender as indicators. David Sears and Carolyn Funk (1990, 249) have objected to demographic indicators because they "reflect some unknown mixture of the residues of much earlier socialization and current interests." They urge the use of policy-specific indicators instead (such as whether a household member was unemployed as an indicator of self-interest in unemployment policy or lacking insurance as an indicator for a stake in health reform) (Sears et al. 1980).[11]

I will use demographic indicators of self-interest in tax policy, for two reasons. The first is in keeping with the corrective issued by political psychologists Jason Wedeen and Robert Kurzban, who contend that self-interest has been measured too narrowly. They argue that ruling out demographic indicators, or assuming that group interest is distinct from self-interest, has "essentially defined out the possibility of self-interest being a major determinant of political views" (Wedeen and Kurzban 2017, 67). Not only did *The American Voter* define stakes through demographics, they note. More recent studies too have used demographics as a measure of self-interest, particularly on economic issues (see, for example, Krimmel and Rader 2017).

Second, I can sidestep the debate about whether demographic indicators must be eschewed for domain-specific ones because in tax policy, demographics *are* domain-specific self-interest indicators. Income, age, and marital status directly affect how much one pays in federal and state income taxes. Income determines the capital gains and dividend tax rates one pays (and the likelihood of having such unearned income). Homeownership and parental status help define stake in the property tax. Taxes are an area where "the personal impact of a policy issue clearly depends partly on the individual's social location," as Sears and his colleagues offered in their discussion of self-interest (Sears et al. 1980). I will use such indicators to assess whether attitudes vary according to how much one pays (and how much one benefits from taxes, although those considerations will prove murkier). My self-interest indicators are imprecise—I do not know in my survey data how much individuals pay in each tax assessed—but demographic characteristics indicate roughly who pays more and who pays less. Moreover, the fact that my demographic characteristics are imprecise for all respondents, yet some nonetheless have attitudes congruent with their (approximate) self-interest while others do not, is the pertinent political and economic point. If some are able to articulate and defend their material interests in the tax realm while others cannot, and if such awareness is greater among the more affluent, these differences will exacerbate inequality.

The Exception of the Rich

"Let me tell you about the very rich. They are different from you and me" (Fitzgerald 2007, 5). Another piece of business before assessing tax attitudes is to set aside the wealthy (and by "rich," I mean both high-wealth and high-income people). F. Scott Fitzgerald was right: the very rich are different. They know a great deal about taxes and have self-interested tax attitudes that they work hard to see realized in policy. The genuinely rich do not appear in my data. As is the case with virtually all ordinary nationally representative surveys, my data top out with the merely affluent, and miss the top 1 percent and richer subsets thereof. We know how this elusive group feels about taxes, though, thanks to the tenacious work of political scientists Benjamin Page,

Larry Bartels, and Jason Seawright (2013). They managed to secure interviews with eighty-three wealthy Chicagoans (mean wealth of $14 million), which revealed that the wealthy know quite a bit about economic and tax policies. They are knowledgeable about marginal tax rates and the costs of economic regulation. They are aware that economic inequality is high. At the same time, they have preferences that reflect their "narrow economic self-interest": they support the principle of progressive taxation, but at low tax rates, and strongly oppose redistribution and social policy spending. In line with the view of political knowledge scholars Michael Delli Carpini and Scott Keeter (1996) that knowledge is power, the rich also vote, make campaign contributions, and contact elected officials at extraordinarily high rates (Page, Bartels, and Seawright 2013, 54). In a follow-on book with Matthew Lacombe, Page and Seawright examine the public statements and political actions of the hundred-richest Americans over a ten-year period. They find that the very rich mostly declined to make public statements about taxes, but *all* of their financial contributions to tax policy organizations and advocacy groups supported antitax stances, especially reductions in progressive taxes: personal income, corporate income, capital gains, and estate taxes (abolishing the estate tax is a "favorite aim," the authors contend) (Page, Seawright, and Lacombe 2019, 2, chap. 2). The revealed preferences of the very rich square with their self-interest in minimizing taxes aimed at them.

Self-interested thinking is facilitated among the rich not only because of their high knowledge levels but also because their self-interest and ideological commitments typically line up. As political behavior scholar Julianna Pacheco (2014) has noted, among ordinary individuals, the effects of self-interest on attitudes may be muted because individuals' partisan and ideological identifications can point in different directions; think of lower-income Republicans whose income-based self-interest would drive them to support progressive taxes while their party identification would push them to oppose.[12] When self-interest and symbolic predispositions conflict, the latter often win out because they are easier for people to utilize in formulating their attitudes. But consider the rich: not only are they better equipped to know what their self-interest is and overcome the cognitive hurdles of self-interested thinking, but also they face fewer conflicts among attitude factors. Returning to the example of progressive taxes, self-interest would dictate that the rich should oppose progressive taxation because they would be hit hardest. The very rich are also predominantly Republican, and when they are Democrats, are more conservative than other Democrats, especially on economic issues, as Page,

Bartels, and Seawright find. Other scholars corroborate these findings. A survey of affluent Americans—the top 5 percent of the income spectrum—by political scientist Elisabeth Suhay and colleagues finds that the affluent are more likely than the general public to attribute economic success to individual characteristics rather than to systemic reasons and that this "tendency to individualize inequality" was more strongly associated with economic conservatism among the affluent than among the general public.[13] In a study using social media posts, political scientist Adam Thal (2022, 426) argues that status competition among the rich "causes them to become more economically conservative." Regardless of the source of the rich's economic conservatism, both self-interest and symbolic predispositions among them point toward opposition to progressive taxation. Compared to nonrich taxpayers, the rich are much less cross pressured. Moreover, the rich who are Democrats may espouse liberal policy preferences, but on economic policy, they can be safe in the knowledge that in the present neoliberal era, marginal income tax rates will never rise to the pre-1980s levels, as political economist Charlotte Cavaille asserts. It's easy to be a "bleeding heart" liberal, in her words, and pay lip service to redistribution, if the fight is about moving the top income tax rate from 37 to 39.6 percent. When 70 percent is simply off the table, such altruism comes "cheap" (Cavaille 2023, 197–98).

There is another way in which the rich have a clearer path to self-interested thinking than nonrich taxpayers: their cost-benefit calculations are easy because they do not think they benefit from taxes, only pay them. For the nonrich, benefits arising from government activity, to the extent to which they are visible, might complicate the calculation about how one feels about taxes: yes, one pays taxes, but one gets something in return too (property taxes are easy to hate, but maybe they are not so bad if one likes the public school one's children attend). But for the rich, few such cognitive complications ensue; they tend to believe they are self-made people who earned their money by dint of their own talents and hard work (or they are heirs who think their forebearers did). Interviews with the rich reveal that the government is typically seen as an obstacle, not a provider of policies and functions necessary to one's success, such as securing property rights, maintaining financial markets, or providing infrastructure and employees' educations.[14] Tax costs are high, and the benefits are zero. In addition, their knowledge is "one-sided": while the wealthy know quite a bit about taxes and regulation, they know less than ordinary citizens do about the benefits that taxes and regulations provide, especially in the social policy realm (Page, Bartels, and Seawright 2013, 67).

Possessing a great deal of knowledge about tax policy, and able to calculate their narrow economic self-interest undistracted by conflicting ideological commitments or considerations of benefits, the rich have a strong preference on taxes: they want them minimized, especially the progressive taxes that are aimed at them. In keeping with the notion of knowledge as power, the rich participate in politics at high rates, both in modes available to ordinary people (voting) and those that the nonrich cannot access (lobbying and making large political contributions) (Bonica et al. 2013). For example, during the debate over the 2022 Inflation Reduction Act, the Biden era health, climate, and tax legislation, there was a concerted effort among progressives in Congress to limit the carried interest loophole by which individuals in the hedge fund, private equity, and venture capital sectors pay taxes at the low capital gains rate rather than the income tax rate. After heavy lobbying by hedge fund interests, the provision was defeated (Rappeport, Flitter, and Kelly 2022). And the rich have a final advantage: as we will see in this chapter and the next, the nonrich are often confused by tax policy, sometimes even holding opinions that square more with the interests of the rich than their own concerns. In this way, the confused opinions of the nonrich can become a political resource for the rich in their quest to get their taxes reduced.

What Self-Interested Attitudes Would Look Like among the Rest of Us: Actual Tax Burdens

What might attitudes toward taxes be if regular, nonrich people think about them in a cost-based, self-interest-oriented way? Another task before searching for self-interest effects is to lay out a series of hypotheses about how attitudes toward different taxes should vary as the costs they impose vary (chapter 4 will examine hypotheses across different types of people). Among the nonrich, attitudes toward progressive taxes should be more favorable than those toward regressive taxes, as progressive taxes impose higher costs on the affluent and rich, while regressive taxes impose higher costs on middle- and lower-income households. The emphasis here is on the costs of taxes, as benefits are typically less visible and less likely to be influential on attitudes.

Table 3.1 calculates a progressivity score for each tax, in which the tax as a share of income for the lowest quintile is subtracted from the tax as a share of income for the highest one. Progressive taxes that take a larger share of the incomes of high earners compared to low earners have positive progressivity scores. These include federal and state income taxes along with the corporate

TABLE 3.1 Tax Progressivity Scores

	Taxes as a share of income		
	Lowest quintile	Highest quintile	Progressivity score (high-low share)
Federal income**	−11.1	15.4	26.5
State income	0.1	3.4	3.3
Corporate income	0.5	2.2	1.7
Property	4.2	2.8	−1.4
Federal excise (incl. gas)	1.7	*	−1.7
Payroll	9.4	6.5	−2.9
State sales and excise (incl. gas)	7.1	2.4	−4.7

Note: Taxes are arrayed by progressivity score (tax as share of income for the highest quintile minus the share for the lowest quintile). * Between 0.0 and 0.5 percent. ** Some low-income households qualify for "refundable" tax credits such as the EITC; when the amount of the credit exceeds the tax liability, the taxpayer receives a refund for the difference, resulting in a negative percentage. Data are for 2018–19.

Sources: Congressional Budget Office 2022, exhibit 13; ITEP 2018, 11.

income tax (which is not a subject of my surveys, but that is calculated here by attributing the corporate income tax to each income quintile). Note that these data do not include the estate tax, which would have a high score as the most progressive tax in the American system. Nor do they separately include investment taxes (capital gains and dividend taxes), which are calculated as part of one's federal tax return. Capital gains and dividend tax rates are lower than income tax rates on wages and salaries during the period of these data (formally, the low "preferential" rates are a tax break, although I collect attitudinal data on them as a tax). But because high-income people are much more likely to have these forms of unearned income, these taxes too would have positive progressivity scores (in 2015, for example, 42 percent of top quintile households benefited from the preferential rates on long-term capital gains and qualified dividends, getting 95 percent of the total benefit of that tax break) (Tax Policy Center 2013). Conversely, regressive taxes earn negative progressivity scores because they take a greater share of the income of low earners than high earners. These include the property tax, which is mildly regressive with respect to income, federal excise taxes (which include the gas tax), payroll tax, and sales tax (which includes state excise taxes in these data).[15]

Most Americans are not rich or even affluent (if we think of the top 20 percent as being somewhat affluent). Table 3.1 suggests what their aggregate attitudes about different taxes should be if they are thinking in a cost-oriented, self-interested way; the nonrich survey respondents analyzed here should embrace progressive taxation, which burdens them less, and resent regressive taxation, which burdens them more.

Abstract Tax Preferences

In their abstract preferences, my nonrich survey respondents do hold self-interested preferences, in two senses.

First, when asked how fair various types of tax systems are, respondents show a great preference for progressive taxation (table 3.2). In the 2012 CCES, I asked respondents to rate the fairness of each type of tax system after providing definitions: "A progressive tax system is one in which the tax rate a person pays increases as the amount of income that person makes increases. A flat tax system is one in which the tax rate is the same for all income levels. A regressive system is one in which the tax rate a person pays decreases as the amount of income that person makes increases. Please indicate how fair you think each tax system is." Two-thirds say that a progressive system is fair, compared to 16 percent who say a regressive tax system is fair (it is also worth noting that a majority, 55 percent, said that a flat tax is fair—a phenomenon to which I will return). In the 2019 CCES, I asked respondents which structure would be the fairest for the federal income tax, again defining each term: "Thinking about the federal income tax, which is most fair: a progressive system (high-income people pay a greater share of their income in tax than lower-income people), a regressive system (high-income people pay a smaller share of their income in tax than lower-income people), or a proportional system (people of all income levels pay the same share of their income in tax)?" Among the respondents who gave an answer, nearly two-thirds said a progressive system would be most fair for the federal income tax; one-third said a proportional system; and just 5 percent said a regressive system.

Other survey findings over the decades report a similar embrace of progressive taxation as a general concept. In a 1981 Harris poll, 58 percent of respondents said that the principle on which the federal income tax is based—"that higher-income people not only have to pay more in taxes but must pay a greater percentage of their income in taxes"—is fair, compared to 38 percent who say that principle is not fair. In NORC surveys in 1987, 2000, and 2008,

TABLE 3.2 Abstract Tax Preferences

2012 CCES	Fairness of each type of tax system	Percent
	Progressive system fair	65
	Flat system fair	55
	Regressive system fair	16
2019 CCES	Fairest system for the federal income tax (choose one)	
	Progressive	61
	Proportional	34
	Regressive	5
1981 Harris[a]	Principle that higher-income people should pay greater share of income in federal income tax	
	Fair	58
	Not fair	38
1987, 2000, 2008 NORC[a]	How much people with high incomes should pay in taxes	
	Larger share	60–68
	Same share	30–38
	Smaller share	1–2
2008 American Patriot Survey[b]	Agree making taxes progressive is a good expression of American patriotism	63
1977–92 Roper[a]	High-income families pay too little in taxes	72–80
1992–2016 Gallup[a]	Upper-income people pay too little in federal taxes	55–77
2004–16 Gallup[a]	Corporations pay too little in federal taxes	62–73
2009 CBS/*NYT*[a]	Change tax code so middle- and lower-income people pay less than now, upper-income pay more	65

Sources: [a] Bowman, Sims, and O'Neil 2017, 37–47. [b] Thorndike 2013. For question wording, see appendix.

three-fifths to two-thirds of respondents said that "people with high incomes should pay a larger share of their income in taxes than those with low incomes"; about one-third said the share should be the same. A 2008 survey found that two-thirds of respondents thought making taxes more progressive was a somewhat good or very good expression of American patriotism.[16] In the abstract, robust majorities support progressive taxation (as long as the question does not invoke "government redistribution," in which case support is lower).[17]

Second, a long-standing finding in surveys, echoed in the contemporary CCES, is that many Americans believe the rich and corporations do not pay enough. About three-quarters of Roper respondents between 1977 and 1992 said that high-income families "pay too little in taxes." Picking up where

Roper left off, Gallup found in surveys from 1992 to 2016 that three-fifths to three-quarters of respondents said that upper-income people were not paying their "fair share in federal taxes." Between 2004 and 2016, around two-thirds of Gallup respondents regularly said that corporations were not paying their fair share either. In 2009, two-thirds of CBS/*New York Times* survey respondents said that "the new tax code should be changed so that middle- and lower-income people pay less than they do now and upper-income people pay more in taxes than they do now" (Bowman, Sims, and O'Neil 2017, 37–39, 47).

This concern is reflected in CCES data. In the 2012 module, I asked respondents to rate the fairness of the share they pay for each of five taxes on a one-to-five scale as well as to rate the share paid by low- and high-income people. In the 2019 module, I asked respondents to rate the "fairness of the share each income group pays" in federal income tax as well as state and local taxes. In the surveys, higher values indicate the share is too high or unfair. As shown in figure 3.1a, respondents were more likely to say that the share they pay of each of the five taxes is unfair and the share paid by low-income people is too high, while the share paid by high-income people is perceived as lower. In figure 3.1b, respondents were much more likely to say the share of federal income and state/local taxes paid by high-income people is too low, while the shares paid by low- and middle-income people (the group with which many identify) are too high.

In an experiment embedded in the 2019 CCES, I asked respondents whether they would approve or disapprove of a tax cut "being contemplated" that would give most taxpayers a $500 rebate. I split respondents into three groups in which the "top 2 percent of earners" would receive the same $500 rebate, no rebate, or a $5,000 rebate. Approval was 60 percent in the scenario in which top earners got the same $500 rebate, 73 percent when top earners received no rebate, and just 44 percent when top earners received $5,000. These results suggest greater approval of scenarios in which outcomes are more progressive (that is, greater support when the rich get nothing, and less support when the rich get more than the nonrich).

In these contemporary and historical survey data, nonrich Americans express a preference for progressive taxation in the abstract. They like the concept of higher taxes on the privileged as a theoretical matter and think the rich should pay more. These hypothetical preferences are in keeping with their objective self-interest: for most taxpayers, especially those in the lower and middle quintiles of income, progressive taxes are far less costly as a share of income than regressive taxes, as table 3.1 hints at and figure 4.1 in the next chapter

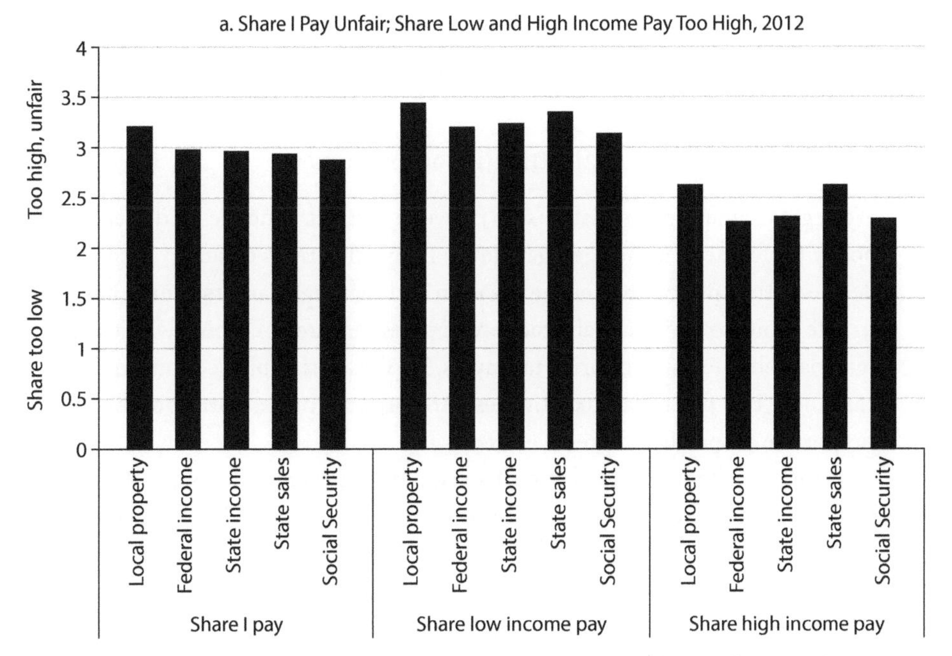

Note: Bars indicate mean score on 1–5 scale, with higher values indicating the share I pay is unfair, or the share low- or high-income people pay is too high.

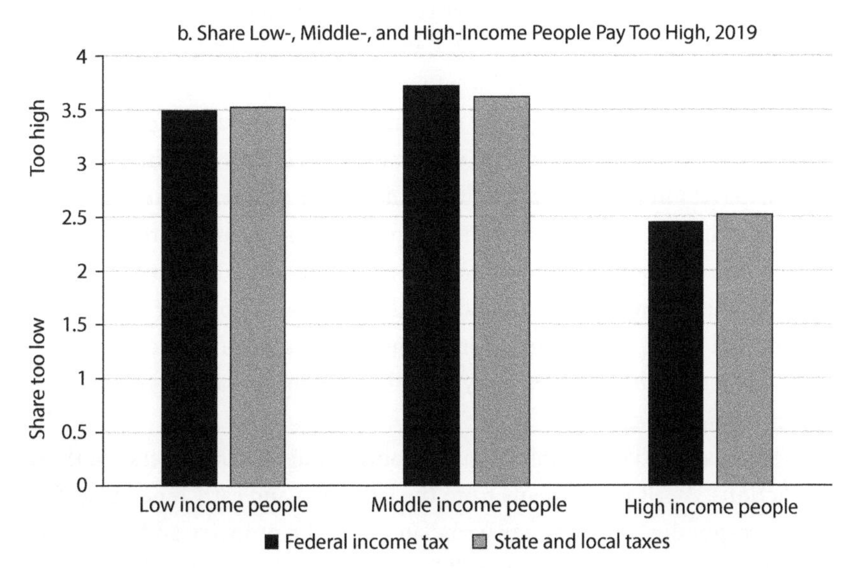

Note: Bars indicate mean score on 1–5 scale, with higher values indicating the share paid is too high.
Source: 2012, 2019 CCES.

FIGURE 3.1 Fairness of Tax Share Paid by Each Income Group

shows in greater detail. The question is whether people can connect these abstract preferences to their specific tax attitudes.

Actual Attitudes across Taxes

We begin examining the relationship between abstract principles and specific policy preferences at the aggregate level. Large majorities of survey respondents say they prefer progressive taxation and that high earners should contribute more tax revenues, abstract preferences that are in keeping with their material self-interest as nonrich taxpayers. Do these principled commitments carry over into particular tax attitudes? Are large majorities correspondingly supportive of specific progressive taxes?

Figure 3.2 gathers tax attitudes across decades and survey items. ACIR surveys from 1988 through 1994 asked respondents to rank which they thought "the worst tax is—that is, the least fair." The 2019 CCES asked respondents to rank the same five taxes from "the tax you dislike the most to the tax you dislike the least" (the 2012 CCES included the same item, and the responses are similar). My other 2019 CCES module included three additional taxes—estate, gas, and investment—and asked respondents about the fairness of each tax, assessing each separately rather than ranking them against each other. Another item in the 2016 and 2019 CCES modules asked respondents about the fairness of the amount they have to pay.[18]

If tax attitudes squared with the majority's preference for progressive taxation (which also comports with their cost-based self-interest), then the nonrich taxpayers in these survey data should prefer progressive to regressive taxes. Specifically, they should deem the regressive sales and payroll taxes the worst, most disliked, and most unfair, followed by the mildly regressive property tax. The progressive federal and state income taxes should be less disliked and viewed as less unfair, and the investment and estate taxes the least unfair of all. That is, regressive taxes (gray) should be to the left of progressive taxes (black) in figure 3.2.

Actual tax attitudes are inconsistent and frequently the reverse of these predictions. ACIR respondents from the late 1980s and early 1990s as well as CCES respondents from thirty years later rank the property and federal income taxes as the worst or most disliked, even though one is slightly regressive and the other progressive. Sales and payroll taxes were named much less often even though they are much costlier to the typical taxpayer (figure 3.2a, left two portions).[19]

The rightmost portion of figure 3.2a shows the results when respondents are asked about the fairness of each tax separately. Here, the estate tax is deemed unfair by the most respondents even though it is the most progressive tax (in violation of the abstract preference for progressive taxation), and none of these respondents will actually pay it (their material stake—the cost—is zero). The regressive gas and property taxes are seen as unfair by many, in keeping with abstract principles and actual costs, but even costlier sales and payroll taxes are deemed unfair by the fewest respondents, going against these principles.

Similar results obtain in open-ended questions from 2016 in which I asked respondents which tax they thought the most unfair and most fair, and why—a query meant to measure both fairness and salience.[20] About two-thirds of respondents named a specific tax as the most unfair, citing federal income and property taxes most often, followed by the estate tax, similar to the closed-ended responses (figure 3.2b; the results for 2019 were similar). About two-thirds named a specific tax as the most fair as well, with the sales tax leading the way, followed more distantly by federal income and property taxes. Again, many of these responses are the opposite of what the abstract embrace of progressive taxation and self-interest would predict for these nonrich respondents; they deem the regressive sales tax the most fair and the progressive federal income tax as the most unfair.

One difficulty with asking survey respondents about dislike toward or the fairness of taxes is that we do not necessarily know the direction of that evaluation (is a tax unfair because it is too high or too low?). Thus the 2016 CCES additionally asked, Should each tax be increased, decreased, or kept the same? Figure 3.3 arrays taxes by the ratio of the share desiring the tax to be decreased to the share wishing it to be increased.

The first thing to notice is that the ratio is greater than one for every tax, reflective of the nation's antitax orientation. Decreasers outnumber increasers, even for highly progressive taxes that only the affluent and rich pay, such as estate and investment taxes. The second thing to notice is that the pattern of responses across taxes again goes against the abstract principles and self-interest of these nonrich survey respondents. They should be more enthusiastic about decreasing regressive taxes than decreasing progressive taxes. That is, the ratio of decrease to increase should be greater for regressive taxes (gray) than for progressive taxes (black). But with two exceptions, that is not what we see. Instead of gray bars on the left and black bars on the right, we see respondents more eager to decrease the progressive state and federal income

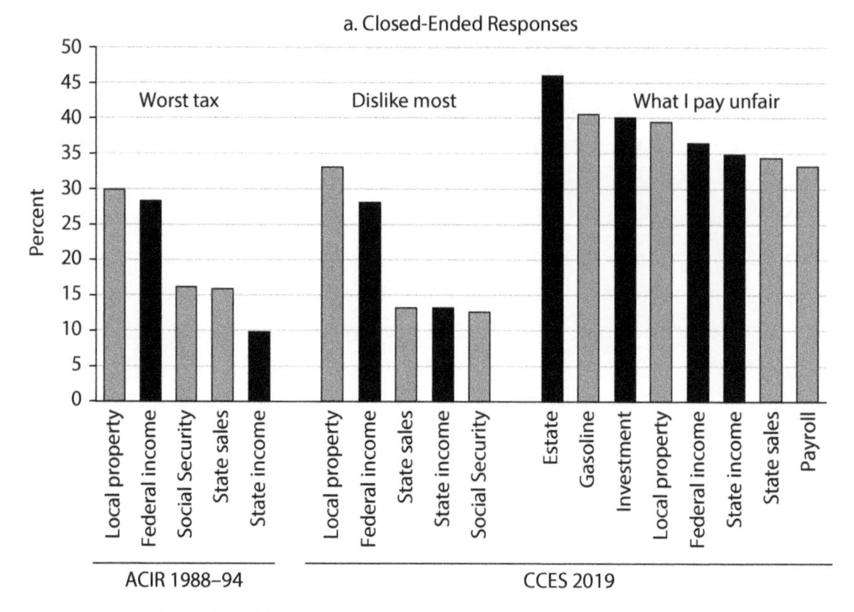

Note: "Worst" and "dislike" are relative rankings; the unfair evaluations are for each tax separately. ACIR results pooled for the 1988–94 period. Progressive taxes are black; regressive are gray.
Sources: ACIR in UNT Digital Library, n.d.; CCES 2019.

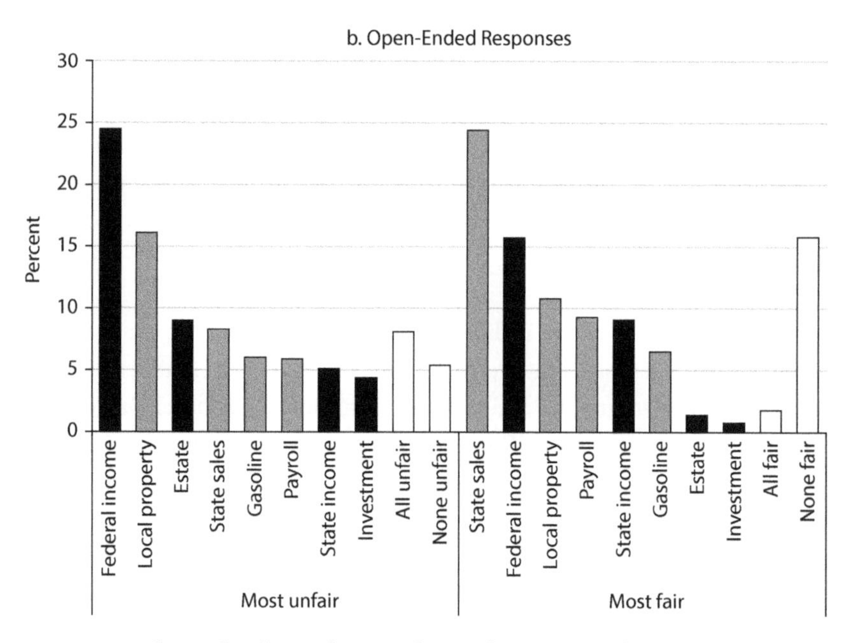

Note: Bars indicate the share of respondents who mentioned a particular tax as the most unfair or most fair. Progressive taxes are black; regressive are gray.
Source: 2016 CCES.

FIGURE 3.2 Tax Evaluations: Dislike and Fairness

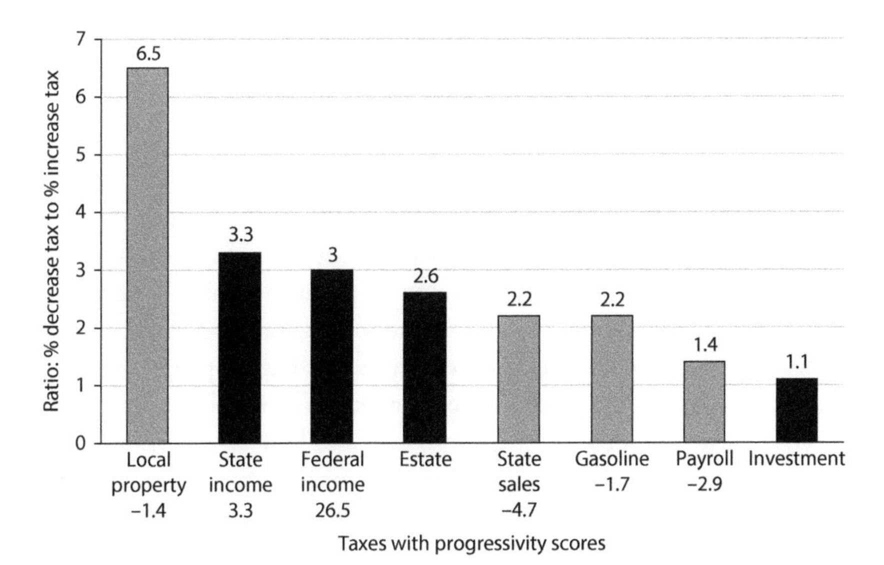

FIGURE 3.3 Tax Change Preferences: Ratio of Decrease to Increase
Note: Figure shows the ratio of the percentage of respondents wanting to decrease each tax to the percentage wanting to increase each tax. Progressive taxes are black; regressive are gray. Progressivity scores from table 3.1 shown below labels.
Source: 2016 CCES.

taxes as well as estate tax, and less enthusiastic about decreasing the regressive sales, gas, and payroll taxes, even though these taxes burden them more. These specific tax attitudes go against both self-interest and respondents' overall abstract preference for progressive taxation.

The two taxes where attitudes comport somewhat more with self-interest are property and investment taxes. The property tax is mildly regressive, hitting lower-income households more than the affluent. Survey respondents show a great deal of enthusiasm for reducing it, with decreasers outnumbering increasers by more than six to one. But this great desire for property tax reduction makes less sense when we consider that other regressive taxes are a greater burden for the nonaffluent, especially sales and payroll taxes, as shown in table 3.1 and figure 4.1 in the next chapter, yet there is less enthusiasm for cutting them. The one progressive tax that respondents have relatively more interest in increasing is the investment tax, which comports with self-interest in that the likelihood of owning assets that produce dividends and capital gains is far more common in the upper reaches of the income spectrum. Even here, though, the decreasers outnumber the increasers for a tax most of these respondents do not pay.

Actual Attitudes across Tax Expenditures

The analysis so far has examined the mismatch between abstract principles and self-interest, on the one hand, and specific attitudes, on the other, with regard to taxes. What about tax expenditures, the huge number of tax breaks that litter the federal income tax code? Do attitudes toward tax breaks comport with self-interest and the stated desire to tax higher-income people more?

Figure 3.4 shows the percentage of households receiving each major tax break along the bottom, with the columns indicating how the total value of each tax expenditure is distributed among income quintiles, in order by the share going to the highest quintile. This figure is somewhat analogous to table 3.1 in depicting the actual stakes behind each tax expenditure, except that this figure shows the magnitude of the breaks going to each income group (the benefits in the form of taxes refunded or not collected) rather than taxes paid as a share of income (the cost of each tax). If survey respondents are thinking about these tax breaks in self-interested or progressive principled ways, then they might be most eager to eliminate or reduce tax breaks going predominantly to the affluent. Thus respondents should be most enthusiastic about eliminating or reducing the investment tax break, since only 13 percent of households get this break and 95 percent of the total value goes to the top quintile. More households take the deduction for charitable contributions, about one-quarter, but its value is skewed too, with 82 percent going to the top quintile. Similarly, about one-quarter of households benefited from the home mortgage interest deduction, but two-thirds of the benefit went to the affluent.

We might predict less enthusiasm for cutting other tax breaks either because they are widely used or increase the progressivity of the tax system by refunding more tax dollars to middle- and low-income households. The top quintile gets two-thirds of the tax break for retirement savings, but the impulse to cut might be tempered by the fact that this is one of the more common tax breaks, benefiting 38 percent of households, second only to health insurance in its spread. We might imagine that there would be enthusiasm for expanding the CTC since one-quarter of households benefit from it (or did in these 2015 data, chosen to line up with my 2016 survey data) and the distribution of the CTC's value is fairly even across income groups. And if majorities of Americans say that a progressive system is the best for the income tax, then they should em-

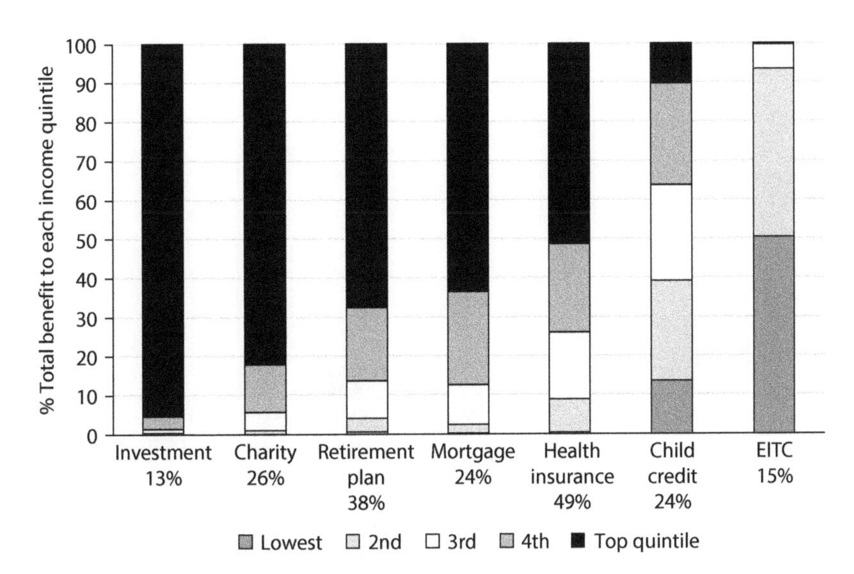

FIGURE 3.4 Share of Tax Expenditure Benefits by Income Quintile
Note: Figure shows the share of the total benefit from each tax expenditure going to each cash income quintile for 2015. The tax expenditures are arrayed by the share going to the top income quintile. Below each tax break label is the percentage of taxpaying units receiving it.
Source: Tax Policy Center 2013, tables T13–0079, T13–0081, T13–0083, T13–0087, T13–0095, T13–0264, T13–0265.

brace the EITC, whose benefits mostly go to the bottom two quintiles (the only major tax break to do so), making the system more progressive by refunding taxes paid by those households.

As with tax attitudes, tax break preferences do not always match these expectations. The 2016 CCES asked respondents which tax breaks they want to eliminate, reduce, or keep. Figure 3.5 arrays them in order of the desire to reduce or eliminate them. Note that the modal answer for every tax break is to keep it in place, even though most of the benefits of most of these tax breaks go overwhelmingly to the affluent, in violation of abstract principles embracing progressive taxation.[21] Respondents do express the most enthusiasm for eliminating or reducing the value of the lower tax rate on capital gains along with the deduction for charitable contributions, which would make the tax system more progressive. But they also express a fair amount of enthusiasm for eliminating or reducing the value of the EITC and CTC, changes that would make the tax system less progressive.

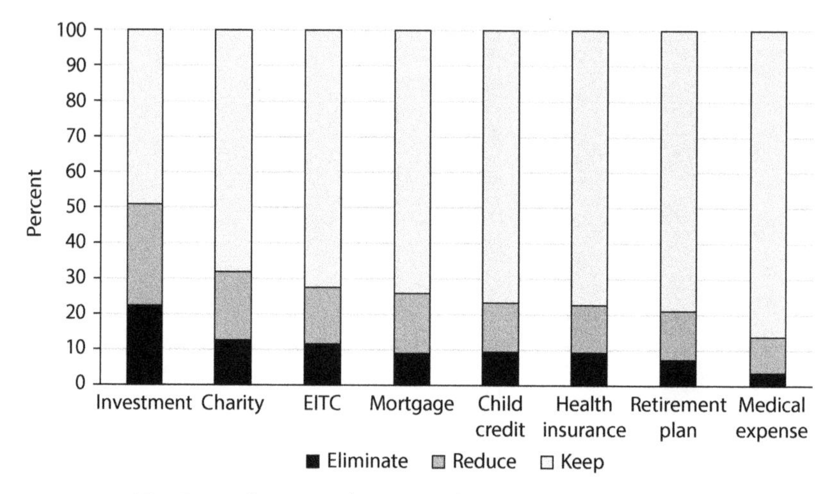

FIGURE 3.5 Tax Expenditure Evaluations: Eliminate, Reduce, or Keep
Note: The figure shows the share of respondents who want to eliminate, reduce, or keep each tax expenditure, among those giving a response.
Source: 2016 CCES.

Principle-Policy Gaps across Taxes

At the aggregate level, there are multiple mismatches in both tax and tax expenditure opinions between principles and self-interest, on the one hand, and specific policy attitudes, on the other. What about at the individual level? Do the individual survey respondents who favor progressive taxation in theory express more support for specific progressive taxes? Are those who favor flat or regressive taxation more skeptical about progressive taxes? (The focus in this section will be on tax attitudes as I do not have tax break attitudes in the same datasets in which I have abstract preferences.) Most individual-level analyses of self-interest appear in chapter 4. Here we can assess the correspondence between abstract and specific preferences across taxes.

The match—or mismatch—between abstract and specific preferences can be evaluated with CCES data from 2019. Recall that in 2019, just under two-thirds said a progressive system is the most fair for the federal income tax. If their specific preferences matched their abstract ones, this group should be more likely to deem the progressive federal income tax fair compared to those who favor a proportional or regressive income tax system. Progressive income tax preferers might reasonably be expected to deem other progressive taxes fair as well, compared to proportional/regressive preferers: estate, investment, and state income taxes. Conversely, those who favor a proportional or regressive system (combined because of the small share preferring a regressive system) should be more likely to say regressive taxes are fair. In short, black bars (progressive taxes) should be taller for progressive preferers and gray bars (regressive taxes) should be taller for proportional/regressive preferers in figure 3.6 (note that although previous figures focused on tax unfairness, here I flip to tax fairness to match the system fairness item).

These expectations are met for progressive taxes, but not for regressive ones. Those who favor a progressive system are more likely to consider the four progressive taxes fair, in keeping with their abstract preferences. But they don't differentiate among types of taxes; they are more likely to regard the four regressive taxes as fair too, relative to the proportional/regressive preferers. Among those who prefer a progressive tax system, the four most fair taxes are the progressive state income and investment taxes, but also the regressive payroll and sales taxes. Among proportional/regressive preferers, the four most fair taxes are the regressive payroll and sales taxes, but the progressive federal and state income taxes as well. In sum, attitudes toward individual taxes line up with some abstract preferences yet not with others. Moreover, it seems that those who prefer a progressive income tax system have a greater taste for taxes in general than those who prefer a proportional or regressive system: the progressive preferers rate every tax as more fair than do the proportional/regressive preferers.

So far, respondents' principled stances on taxation do not always match their specific policy attitudes, and the mismatches are more pronounced for regressive taxes. But perhaps using an item about the federal income tax is not the best way to measure abstract preferences. The 2012 CCES included a more comprehensive abstract item, asking respondents how fair they think each type of tax *system* is: progressive, flat, or regressive. As with the abstract federal income tax item, a large majority said a progressive system is fair. The 2012 data also include a set of items on possible tax changes regarding the taxation of estates, capital gains, and income. Unlike the fairness evaluations shown in figure 3.6, respondents' preferences on these reforms are more in line with their abstract preferences, as figure 3.7 indicates. That is, compared to those who prefer a flat or regressive tax system, those who prefer a progressive system are less supportive of reforms that would make the tax system less progressive, expressing less support for taxing no estates, having capital gains taxes that are lower than taxes on earned income, decreasing the income tax for high earners, and extending the Bush tax cuts for all households regardless of income.

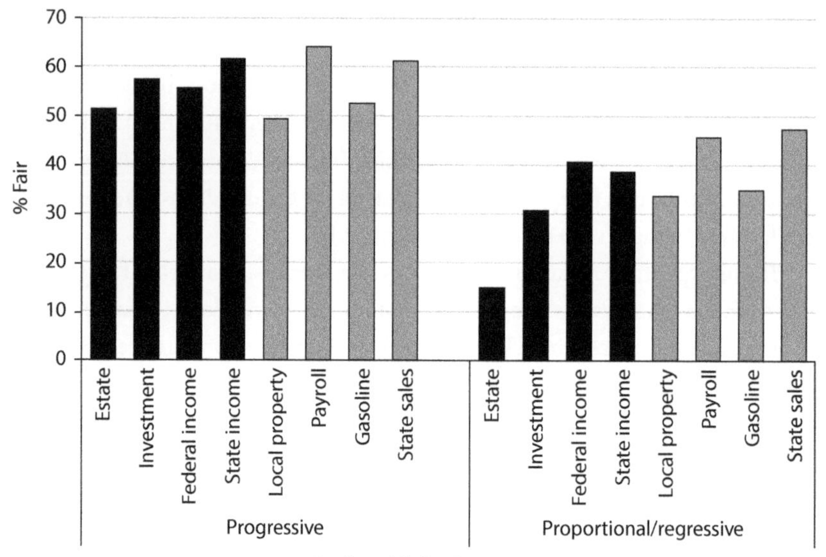

FIGURE 3.6 Tax Fair by Abstract Income Tax Preference
Note: Figure shows the share deeming each tax fair among those saying a progressive federal income tax system is the most fair compared to those saying a proportional or regressive system is most fair. Progressive taxes are black; regressive are gray.
Source: 2019 CCES.

The relative levels of support for these policies are in keeping with differences in abstract principles. Yet the absolute responses often stray from abstract principles. Note that over half of those who prefer a progressive tax system do not want any estates to be taxed. If you favor progressive taxation, you should probably favor the most progressive tax on the books. Similarly, note that only 13 percent of those who prefer a flat or regressive system want the income tax on high earners to be decreased, which would help achieve their abstract goal of flat or regressive taxation. Thus stances on particular tax policies frequently do not comport with abstract preferences for progressive or regressive taxes.

One more example of the mismatch between abstract principles and particular policy preferences: in the 2012 CCES, respondents were also asked how a state should raise taxes if needed. "What share of the tax increase should come from increased income taxes and what share from increased sales taxes?" On a scale where zero indicated all new revenues coming from sales taxes and a hundred indicated all from income taxes, flat/regressive preferers averaged forty-three and progressive tax preferers averaged forty-nine. Relative to each

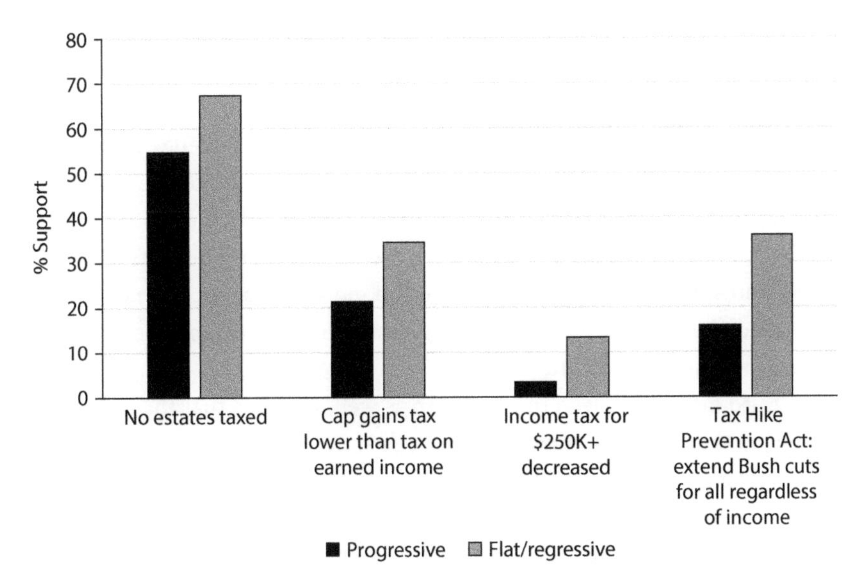

FIGURE 3.7 Tax Proposal Support by Abstract Tax System Preference
Note: Figure shows the percentage of respondents supporting each policy among those who deem a progressive tax system fair compared to those who deem a flat or regressive system fair.
Source: 2012 CCES.

other, these preferences conform to the groups' abstract preferences: progressive tax preferers want more revenue to come from income taxes. But note that the average response of both groups is below fifty—that is, on the regressive sales tax end of the scale. Not only do flat/regressive system preferers lean toward the sales tax as a means of raising state revenue, but so do progressive tax preferers, in violation of their abstract preference.

Explaining the Principle-Policy Gaps

For the types of nonrich respondents who appear in surveys, regressive taxes are costlier than progressive ones. If attitudes turned on objective self-interest, most people would be more supportive of progressive than regressive taxation. In the abstract they are, with sizable majorities saying the rich pay too little and that progressive taxation is their preferred system. When it comes to attitudes on specific taxes, however, these principled and self-interested stances break down, and a principle-policy gap emerges.[22] Often these mismatches take the form of less support for progressive taxation and more support for regressive taxation than we would expect.

Low information is one factor that may contribute to the mismatch between abstract and specific attitudes. Taxes are extraordinarily complex policies, and the principle-policy gap may arise from a lack of information or misunderstanding about how taxes work. Low tax knowledge may not be surprising in light of a second factor that may contribute to the principle-policy mismatch: tax designs. Specific tax parameters and the procedures for paying taxes may heighten or obscure perceived costs and benefits as well as affect perceptions of procedural justice and individual agency, which in turn may affect the connection between stakes and principles, on the one hand, and specific tax attitudes, on the other.

A third factor may lead to confusion as well, which is that the federal income tax looms large in taxpayers' thoughts. Even though for most nonrich taxpayers it constitutes a relatively small share of income, and is less costly than regressive sales and payroll taxes, it is disliked to a pronounced degree. The constant attacks on the income tax by economic elites who seek reductions appear to keep the tax front and center in the minds of nonrich individuals, distracting them from their theoretical commitment to progressive taxation and their self-interests.

Low Knowledge Levels and Confusion across Taxes

In order for people to have tax attitudes that conform to their self-interest and widespread preference for having high-income households pay more, they need to understand the burden that different taxes pose to various income groups. In the next chapter, I will examine general levels of knowledge about the taxation of different types of individuals. Here I simply consider knowledge levels by tax: Do survey respondents as a whole know which taxes are progressive and which are regressive?

In the 2016 CCES, I asked respondents to identify taxes as regressive or progressive after first defining these terms: "Is each of these taxes **progressive** (high-income people pay a greater share of their income in tax than lower-income people), **regressive** (high-income people pay a smaller share of their income in tax than lower-income people), or **proportional** (people of all income levels pay the same share of their income in tax)."[23]

Figure 3.8 shows the percentage of respondents characterizing each tax as progressive (on the bottom), proportional, or regressive (at the top of each bar). The correct answer is indicated with diagonal lines. The taxes are arrayed from left to right by the share of respondents who categorized the taxes correctly (note that I indicated that the correct answer for the state income tax in states

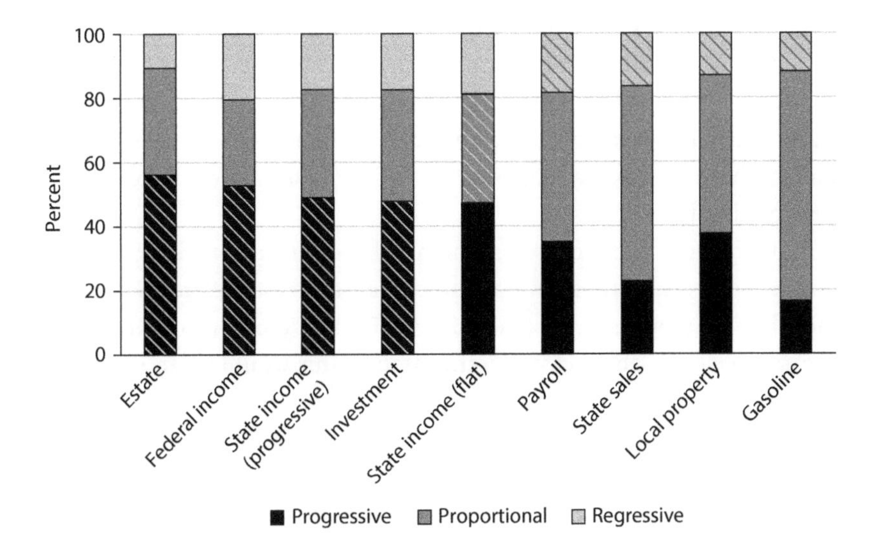

FIGURE 3.8 Tax Incidence Knowledge
Note: Bars show percentage of respondents saying, from bottom to top, that a given tax is progressive, proportional, or regressive among those giving a response. Correct responses indicated with diagonal bars. Taxes arrayed by the proportion of correct responses.
Source: 2016 CCES.

with only one rate is "proportional," although arguably these systems are still progressive since even states with a flat income tax rate exempt some income from taxation).

Clearly, regressive taxes are more difficult for respondents to characterize than progressive taxes. The modal response for the four progressive taxes was correct; among those giving a response, the largest share was able to identify the federal and state income, estate, and investment taxes as progressive. In contrast, the modal answer for the four regressive taxes (payroll, sales, property, and gas) was "proportional." Nearly half of respondents said that payroll and property taxes are proportional rather than regressive, and 60 percent or more said that sales and gas taxes are proportional. In other words, large shares of respondents said that "people of all income levels pay the same share of their income in tax," even though these taxes, especially sales and gas taxes, are regressive, as table 3.1 showed.

It may be that people confuse rates with shares of income; we all pay the same rate for sales, gas, and payroll taxes (up to the wage cap). In open-ended comments on the CCES, where I asked respondents what they think the least and most fair taxes are, and why, many cited the sales tax as the fairest because "everyone pays the same." There might be confusion about the property tax as well. Because housing and accompanying property taxes often constitute a greater share of spending for lower-income people, the property tax is slightly regressive.[24] But it might be perceived as progressive since the absolute amount that high-income people pay for their typically more valuable properties would be higher.

Unfortunately I cannot assess whether those who know the incidence of various taxes are better able to connect their abstract preferences to their specific policy preferences (the 2016 CCES that contains the incidence question lacks an abstract preference item). This would be an important question for future work. It is clear from the data that I do have in hand, however, that nonrich people have a difficult time with the mathematical notions of regressivity and progressivity, even when offered definitions. These are crucial and basic concepts in public finance—concepts that economists and policymakers readily understand. But for ordinary people, we can see the potential for confusion between tax rates and taxes as a share of income, and between the absolute cost of taxes compared to their cost relative to income. There may be less confusion about progressive taxes because both the rates and cost of taxes as a share of income rise with income. The math behind regressive taxes is confusing, in contrast, as we "all pay the same rate," but the total cost ends up being a larger share of income for lower-income households. That progressive taxation is easier to understand conceptually may help explain why mismatches between abstract preferences and specific tax opinions are more common with regressive than progressive taxes.

Low knowledge levels may help explain tax expenditure attitudes as well. The 2016 CCES asked respondents, "For each of these tax breaks, what kind of people (low income, middle income, or high income) get the biggest tax reduction on average?" Large percentages do not know; on average, CCES respondents were less likely to provide an answer to the tax break incidence question than to the direct federal spending items, suggesting that the designs of tax breaks do undermine people's knowledge.[25]

Figure 3.9 shows the responses for respondents who answered the question, arrayed by the percentage saying that middle-income people get the largest tax reduction, and correct responses indicated with diagonal lines. About three-quarters of respondents know that the tax break for charitable giving and the preferential tax rate for investment income both go disproportionately to high earners. These high knowledge levels could help explain why

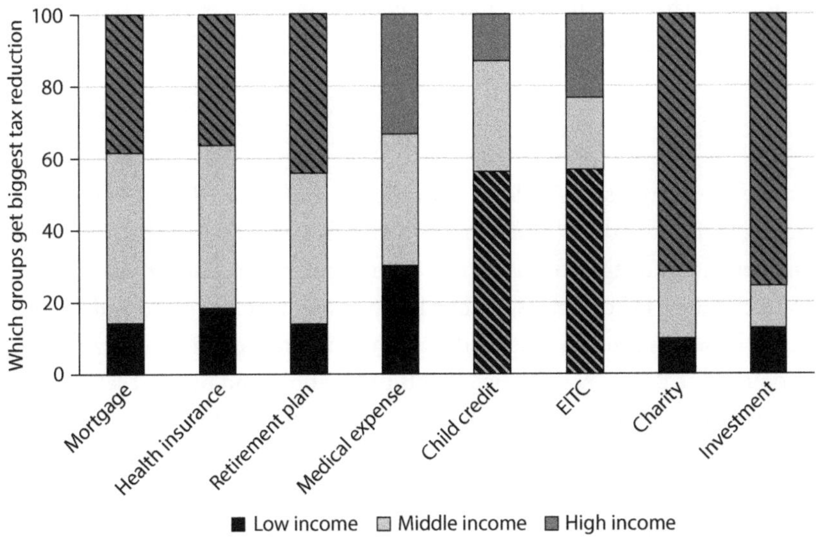

FIGURE 3.9 Tax Expenditure Knowledge
Note: Bars show the percentage of respondents saying, from bottom to top, that low-income, middle-income, or high-income people get the biggest tax reduction on average. Correct responses indicated with diagonal bars (I do not have information on the distribution of the medical costs deduction). Tax expenditures arrayed by the proportion saying middle-income people get the biggest tax reduction.
Source: 2016 CCES.

these are the two tax breaks respondents are most enthusiastic about reducing or eliminating (figure 3.5).

Large shares of respondents erroneously believe that middle-income people get the biggest tax reduction from the home mortgage interest deduction as well as the tax breaks for employer-provided health insurance and retirement plans. These misimpressions may underlie the enthusiasm for keeping these tax breaks (figure 3.5). In reality, the affluent garner the lion's share of these tax breaks.

Just over half of respondents were correct in saying that low-income people are the biggest beneficiaries of the EITC. A similar share thought the CTC too goes mostly to low-income groups, which is incorrect; it is more evenly distributed across income groups than is the EITC. We will see in chapter 6 that racial resentment is strongly associated with attitudes toward both of these tax breaks; perceptions about which income groups benefit, along with the strong relationship between income and race in the United States, may contribute to the desire to reduce them.

Tax Designs

Tax designs may also impede the consideration of material stakes or abstract principles in individuals' preferences on specific taxes. They may obscure costs and benefits or distract from abstract commitments to tax the privileged more by introducing other factors, such as feelings about what is taxed and the processes by which taxes are imposed. Table 3.3 summarizes the characteristics of various taxes that may influence tax attitudes above and beyond self-interest and abstract preferences. Definitive tests of the effect of these features on tax attitudes awaits future research; here I offer what evidence I have from the closed- and open-ended responses on the CCES.

What is taxed, controllability, and agency. Self-interested individuals should hold more negative attitudes toward taxes that cost them more. A dollar is a dollar, after all. Tax attitudes, though, may turn not just on how much one pays but also one's feelings about what is taxed. Income taxes and the payroll taxes for Social Security and Medicare are applied to the earned income of workers, while capital gains and dividend taxes are imposed on the unearned income from investments—a form of income far more common among the affluent and rich. Sales and gas taxes are consumption taxes that collect revenue from people when they spend money. The property and estate taxes are both on wealth, with the former on the wealth of homeowners, and the latter on the value of estates left by the deceased above an exemption. People may have views about what is appropriate for government to tax—what forms of income, consumption, and wealth the government ought to tax as a general matter, and what should be taxed given the forms of income and assets they enjoy as well as the patterns of consumption that mark their lives, not to mention their political commitments (as we'll see in chapter 5).

One puzzle is the great dislike of the estate tax. As shown here and in other accounts, the estate tax is one of the taxes deemed most unfair, with great enthusiasm for seeing it reduced or eliminated.[26] These attitudes contradict both individuals' personal costs, which are zero, and their abstract desire for the rich to pay more. But it may be that people simply dislike the taxation of wealth. In the open-ended CCES comments, many of those citing the estate and investment taxes as unfair said they constitute "double taxation"—a perception (fanned by elite discourse) that the money behind that wealth was

TABLE 3.3. **Characteristics of Select Taxes, from Perspective of Nonrich Taxpayers**

Characteristics	Federal income	Social Security	Sales	Gasoline	Property	Estate
What is taxed	Income	Income	Consumption	Consumption	Wealth	Wealth
Controllability	No, unless work less; rich control, but not others	No, unless work less	Controllable	No, unless drive less	Perceived as not controllable	Rich control, but not others
Process: How tax is imposed and paid	Withheld, totaled each year	Withheld, not totaled	Perceived small amounts, not totaled	Perceived high amounts, not totaled	Lump sum (or escrowed)	Lump sum at death
Administrative burden	High	Low	Low	Low	Low	High
Procedural justice	Rich perceived to manipulate	Rational	Rational	Rational	Particularistic	Rich perceived to manipulate
Benefits	Not visible: general revenues	Visible and desirable: earmarked tax	General revenues, but "help my state"	Not used as intended	May be visible and desirable (e.g., kids and schools)	Unknown

Note: Based on responses to closed- and open-ended comments on 2016 and 2019 CCES.

already taxed as ordinary income, and should not be taxed again as a capital gain or in an estate. "It is ridiculous to punish a family again for assets they have already paid taxes on," was one such respondent comment on the 2016 CCES. Similarly, several who said that the property tax is the most unfair maintained that it was akin to paying rent on a house one owns. "It's like paying taxes on the same product again and again," one respondent wrote. In the experience of the nonrich, wealth is what accumulates when one does not spend all of one's income (which is taxed). It seems unfair to tax that income twice. For the rich, however, wealth often accumulates not through the accumulation of unspent income but rather through inheritance or "unearned" gains in the value of an asset. These gains can escape taxation altogether unless subject to the estate tax. Yet these processes are outside the experience of many ordinary taxpayers, and so they are vulnerable to elite rhetoric about double taxation.

Another type of "double taxation" concern arises because every level of government in the United States imposes taxes, and some survey respondents complain about their income being taxed by both the federal and state government, or about state governments taxing both income and consumption. Some say the state income tax is the most unfair because of "having to pay twice on the same income." Another respondent wrote, "I consider the sales tax the most unfair as my disposable income has already been taxed by income taxes." Also, several respondents said the state income tax is the most unfair because not all states have one or the rates vary so much across states.

Individuals' personal sense of agency may affect tax attitudes as well. In other policy areas, the degree to which individuals feel they have personal control or face unyielding government coercion has a strong effect on policy and government attitudes.[27] Taxes vary in the degree of personal control. Wage and salary workers, for example, can only pay less in federal income, state income, or payroll taxes if they work less (or if they work under the table). In contrast, CCES respondents feel that sales taxes are more controllable: one has no control over the rate, but can avoid being taxed by spending less. The sales tax is the fairest because "I can control what I buy," wrote one CCES respondent. "Don't wanna pay the tax, don't buy the item," noted another. Perceptions of controllability and coercion may help explain why people dislike income taxes so much, but are relatively sanguine about sales taxes, even though they are costly for most of the nonaffluent.

In theory, gas taxes work the same way; people could pay less gas tax if they drove less, but that may not be an option for those who must drive to work, shop, and take children to school. This coercion—forced to pay a tax on fuel one must use in everyday life—may help explain why the gas tax is disliked more than the sales tax even though they are both regressive consumption taxes. Gas taxes "kinda get you where you live. You have to have transportation," remarked one CCES respondent. Gas "is necessary for everyday living," wrote another and therefore taxing it is unfair.

The property tax, by several measures the most loathed next to the federal income tax, may feel coercive too. If one's income falls because of retirement or job loss, one can reduce one's sales tax obligations by spending less, and one's income tax goes down automatically. But one's property tax stays the same, insensitive to income. Many respondents, elderly and nonelderly, cited concern over senior citizens and their difficulties in paying property taxes on a fixed income. As one 2016 CCES respondent observed, property taxes are the most unfair "because you can't afford your home once you retire."

Process by which taxes are imposed and paid, administrative and financial burden, and procedural justice. Another way in which policy designs could affect tax attitudes concerns the way in which taxes are imposed by government as well as paid by individuals and households. The modes of tax calculation and payment could obscure or highlight costs; make taxes seem easier or harder to pay, in the administrative and financial burden senses; or affect how people feel about the process of paying taxes and whether they are treated fairly.

First, the way in which taxes are tallied may influence the perception of costs, fanning an impression that a given tax is more or less costly than it actually is. Taxes for which the total annual amount paid is never known may appear to impose lower costs than those which are tallied up each year. Perhaps sales taxes are among the least disliked because the amount paid annually is never totaled, unless one diligently saves and sums up receipts from every transaction over the entire year. Similarly, a reason that the payroll taxes that support Social Security and Medicare are among the more popular taxes, even though they are costly for most workers, may be that payroll contributions are never totaled either. One can see the annual total on one's final December paycheck stub or W-2 form when preparing income tax returns, but one is never required to look at that number. That the cost of Social Security is obscured is evidenced by the fact that three-quarters of Americans pay more in annual Social Security taxes than in federal income taxes, but three-quarters believe the opposite is true.[28] In contrast, one sees an annual bill for federal and state income taxes, and a quarterly bill for the property tax, making the costs more visible and painful.

Second, the mode of administration may matter for cost perceptions. Taxes imposed in lump sums, such as property taxes, may seem costlier than those paid a portion at a time, such as sales taxes, which are taken in small amounts with each transaction, or income and payroll taxes, which are withheld by employers from paychecks, with the money never passing through the worker's hands.[29] The lump sum of the property tax may evoke the "peak-end" rule from psychology, which asserts that people evaluate an experience based on the moment of peak intensity or the final moment (Kahneman 2011). As for withholding, its potent effect was demonstrated in a 1968 IRS survey that found that 70 percent of respondents said they didn't mind paying income taxes as long as they did not have to pay an additional amount when they filed their return—a figure that was much the same decades later in the 2012 CCES (Hansen 1983).[30] Indeed, in his autobiography, conservative economist Milton Friedman lamented his role in establishing income tax withholding years earlier: "It never occurred to me at the time that I was helping to develop machinery that would make possible a government that I would come to criticize severely as too large, too intrusive, too destructive of freedom" (Friedman and Friedman 1998, 123). Similarly, the visibility of the property tax is diminished for those who have the mortgage holder pay it (Cabral and Hoxby 2012). In the 2016 CCES, those who pay their own property taxes rather than having them escrowed through their lender are slightly more likely to want property taxes decreased (58 to 51 percent). One reason the elderly may dislike the property tax—in the 2016 CCES, those aged sixty-five and over are more likely than those under sixty-five to say the property tax is unfair (60 versus 51 percent), and more likely to say it should be decreased (60 to 50 percent)—is that three-quarters of them own their houses free and clear, and therefore are more likely to pay the tax themselves (Campbell 2003, 42).

A third aspect of administration that affects evaluations of cost may be whether a tax is calculated by the government or taxpayer, with the latter constituting an administrative burden that affects the "cognitive load" associated with a given tax (Martin and Gabay 2008).[31] Consider the contrast between payroll and income taxes. Both are withheld from paychecks, but income taxes additionally, infamously, require the completion of a tax return by April 15 each year. A tax return is not necessary for Social Security and Medicare because payroll tax withholding is precise, imposed as a percentage of earned income. The story is completely different with the income tax, where withholding typically does not match actual tax liability, as explained in chapter 2. Hence the annual ritual of the income tax return, which is necessary to reconcile what one owes with what one has already paid in.

The CCES surveys provide some evidence of the attitudinal toll that filling out the federal tax return takes. Those who do their own taxes by hand using tax forms are much more likely to say that both federal and state income taxes should be decreased, even though they have lower average incomes than some other taxpayers: 54 percent of self-preparers ($43,000 average income) say the federal income tax should be decreased, compared to 43 percent of those who use an outside preparer or software ($67,000–$69,000 average income), and 35 percent of those who use a friend or family member ($26,000 average income); the figures are similar for the state income tax.[32] The survey data also show evidence for the complaint that Vanessa Williamson discovered in her taxpayer interviews that self-preparers are exposed to the deductions they cannot access: they are more likely than those using an outside preparer to say that what bothers them the most about the tax system is that some wealthy people do not pay their fair share (45 to 33 percent). Those using software were least likely to say that the complexity of the tax code bothers them the most, presumably because the software takes care of the intricate details, while those asking a friend to do it were most likely to say so. Thus the difficulty of filling out tax forms may affect tax attitudes above and beyond one's actual material stake.

Fourth, how taxes are imposed and paid may affect taxpayers' perceptions of procedural justice, a sense of the fairness of a process and quality of one's experience, which can influence attitudes beyond the end result itself (Tyler 1998). The policy feedbacks literature has shown how some programs, such as Social Security, are carried out according to well-defined, rational rules, while others, such as means-tested programs that grant greater discretion to administering bureaucrats, can result in capricious or arbitrary implementation, violating people's sense of procedural justice (Soss 1999). Treatment at the hands of government programs sends "interpretive messages" to individuals about their apparent worth to the polity, which shapes their feelings about government and political efficacy (their belief that government cares about people like them).[33]

Taxes too may be determined through a fixed, rational procedure or in a particularistic manner. Ordinary taxpayers cannot influence the amount they pay for most taxes. Property taxes are different: assessments are set by local assessors on a building-by-building basis and are open to appeal by the owner—a design that can make property taxes seem arbitrary. Respondents wrote that the property tax is unfair because "I don't think that they are fairly applied" and "assessments are not done properly." Assessments are also publicly available, so one can see whether one's neighbor pays less. One 2016 CCES respondent observed, "As a homeowner I have seen my property tax more than double in the last eighteen years and those [who] live a mile from me pay half the amount." Some scholars argue that seemingly capricious property valuations fanned the fires of the property tax revolt of the late 1970s.[34] Thus one reason property taxes are so loathed may be that they appear inconsistent and unjust. And there are two sides to the coin: if you win an assessment appeal and get your property tax lowered, it's personal agency; if your neighbor wins an appeal, it's a violation of procedural justice.

Concerns about procedural justice may help explain another regularity in tax sentiment: a feeling that the rich do not pay enough and can manipulate the tax system to minimize their taxes in ways ordinary taxpayers cannot. Most workers cannot influence how much federal income tax they pay because their employer reports their income to the IRS and withholds income tax. High-income, high-wealth individuals have much greater ability to shift their sources of income toward lower rates and less third-party reporting (such as corporate executives who request compensation in the form of stock options rather than income because the tax rates are lower on capital gains than on earned income). The privileged also have access to tax lawyers and a plethora of tax breaks that do not apply to regular workers. The "middle class does not have foundations to donate to and taxes are taken from our paychecks; the rich don't get paychecks," worried one respondent. "Rich people can easily reduce or evade, with the assistance of tax professionals the amount of tax they should pay," said another. A number of respondents complained that the affluent pay lower effective rates than the middle class: "Proportionally, poor and middle-class people pay more than rich people," asserted one respondent. The tax planning and avoidance in which the rich engage appear to violate regular taxpayers' sense of procedural justice.

The attraction of "everyone paying the same" may be a response to these justice concerns as well. One puzzle has been the popularity of the sales tax despite its high cost for many people. But part of its appeal may be that the rich cannot manipulate their share as much as with the income tax. The sales tax is the fairest, said 2016 CCES respondents, because there are "no loopholes to not pay"; instead, "it applies fairly to all citizens no matter their class," and more simply, "everyone bumps into it" and "no one can evade it." Another sentiment is that the uniform rate makes the sales tax egalitarian. Respondents said the sales tax is the fairest tax because "everyone has to pay the same per dollar spent," "everyone pays equally," and "everyone pays the same amount based on their purchases." Of course the appeal of "the same rate" ignores the fact that the tax is regressive as a share of income. Paying the "same rate" nonetheless remains an appealing concept.

One last note before turning to the benefits of taxes. The appeal of everyone "paying the same" may help explain support for a flat tax. Periodically there are proposals to replace the graduated rates of the federal income tax with one flat rate. Even when such proposals are paired with a reduction in tax breaks, they would favor upper-income groups, whose effective tax rates would likely fall. Yet there is a strong appeal for "flat taxes" among the public. Williamson found this in her interviews with taxpayers. It is evident in the 2012 CCES in which 65 percent of respondents said that a progressive tax system is fair, but 55 percent said a flat tax system is fair. And in the 2016 CCES, 40 percent of respondents said they would favor a change in "the current tax system so that everyone would pay the same income tax rate," with support rising to 59 percent among those who believe that the rich would pay more under such a system.[35]

One part of the appeal of taxing everyone "the same" is that everyone pays taxes in this scenario. In the open-ended comments on the CCES, there are concerns that both the rich and poor do not pay enough. Especially in the income tax, not only do the rich shift income and use sophisticated tax avoidance strategies to minimize their share, but also the poor are allegedly not taxed because of the standard deduction and the EITC (even though they pay other taxes). A flat income tax means everyone would have "skin in the game," to the satisfaction of some respondents.

Visibility and desirability of benefits. Finally, a third way in which tax designs could affect tax attitudes beyond cost considerations alone is the visibility and desirability of the spending that tax dollars enable. Benefits can be difficult to discern. As political scientists Kate Krimmel and Kelly Rader (2017, 730) put it, cost-benefit analyses are "tricky" because "unlike market goods and their prices, the relationship between public goods and taxes paid is more remote." Citizens "inevitably pay for some services that do not benefit them."

Whether benefits affect attitudes may depend on the size and visibility of such benefits, their traceability to the taxes that fund them, and their distribution—who pays and who benefits, as some groups are perceived as more deserving than others (Cook and Barrett 1992). The inability to see benefits arising from one's tax dollars, or a feeling that benefits are going to others of whom one does not approve, may undermine the linkage from self-interest and abstract preferences to specific tax attitudes.

Payroll taxes most closely tie costs and benefits, especially in the Social Security program, which is solely funded by the payroll tax (Medicare is additionally funded by general revenues and monthly premiums from recipients). A decades-long public relations campaign by Social Security's framers successfully established the link between payroll tax contributions and earned benefits in that program (Derthick 1979). Despite the fact that confidence in the Social Security system varies over time with the fiscal health of the program, and that many Americans realize that current payroll tax receipts fund current benefits, most Americans still believe Social Security represents a contractual obligation between government and worker, and that they will receive their contributions back in benefits when they retire (Jacobs and Shapiro 1998).[36] Since Social Security constitutes nearly all the income for the bottom 40 percent of seniors, and more than half the income for the next 40 percent, payroll taxes provide a highly visible and desirable benefit, and therefore are regarded more positively than other taxes for which the benefits are less clear, such as the income tax (Federal Interagency Forum on Aging-Related Statistics 2020). Social Security is the fairest tax, one CCES respondent wrote, "because I can understand where it goes" and "it comes back to you in the end." These visible and tangible benefits may help explain why the payroll tax is among the least disliked in the American system despite its high cost to many taxpayers.

Sales taxes are also perceived by many as providing visible benefits close to home, with CCES respondents saying it is the fairest tax because "it's reasonable and it goes to the state," and "I see it being utilized." Property taxes too provide highly visible services, such as fire and police protection along with public schools. "You can really see where your money goes," wrote a 2016 CCES respondent who deemed the property tax the most fair. But the personal linkage between what one pays and how much one benefits is more opaque than with Social Security, and some taxpayers may feel that they do not benefit at all, such as those without school-age children (Tedin, Matland, and Weiher 2001). "My house taxes are way too high. Have to pay for school and I have no kids in school," wrote one 2016 CCES respondent. Another suggested a user fee approach to school finance rather than community finance, saying that "school taxes" are the most unfair "because only homeowners have to pay this tax in Georgia. Anybody that has children going to school should be paying for that." One reason the gas tax may be so unpopular is that it doesn't appear to produce the benefits promised. Numerous CCES respondents said that the tax was high yet the roads they use are in poor condition. The gas tax is the most unfair, one respondent pointed out, because "I thought it was supposed to go for upkeep of roads and highways, and look at them." For other taxes, the benefits are simply unclear. That's especially true of federal and state income taxes, which go into big general revenue pots that pay for many government programs and functions, making the linkage between one's taxes and what the government does quite diffuse.[37] Some 2016 CCES respondents wrote that the federal income tax is the least fair because "we have nothing to show for it," "don't see any benefits," and "get very little in return." Moreover, general revenues fund social assistance programs, the opinion about which is highly racialized, fueling the unpopularity of these taxes, as we will see among white taxpayers in chapter 6 (Gilens 1998, 1999). Some claimed that the federal income tax is the least fair because "our tax dollars go to people who don't work," and "too many poor people do not pay enough and I'm left floating their bill too." Perceptions of waste abound as well, as Williamson found in her interviews with taxpayers. CCES respondents wrote of tax dollars that are "wasted and spent on crap," "squandered," and "mismanaged by corrupt and incompetent bureaucrats."

Taken together, tax designs can help explain deviations between how much various taxes cost people and what they think of them. For many nonrich taxpayers, regressive taxes are more costly than progressive ones, and many of these taxpayers embrace progressive taxation as a general concept. And yet they are more likely to say various progressive taxes are unfair and should be decreased, and are relatively sanguine about costly regressive taxes. Tax designs help make these patterns understandable. People feel that sales taxes are controllable, go to the state where benefits are more visible than with the federal government, and are "the same for everyone" with no loopholes for the wealthy. Since the amount one pays is never totaled, there is little chance for people to know how much of a burden sales taxes constitute. Payroll taxes have a positive profile too: never totaled, no administrative burden associated with paying them, and earmarked for a visible, desirable benefit that seems personalized, with your tax dollars going to you ("you get it back in the end") and not someone else supposedly less deserving. The dislike for gas taxes underscores the importance of some of these characteristics: it is never totaled either, but it feels less controllable to people than the sales tax because people have to drive, and the earmarked benefits do not seem to materialize, because roads are in poor condition.

In contrast, the three most unpopular taxes are estate, income, and property. Design features can help explain these patterns as well. In contrast to the advantageous characteristics of several of the regressive taxes, just about everything with the federal income tax seems designed to irritate: ordinary workers cannot control the amount they pay, the administrative burden is high, tax breaks for the privileged make it unjust, and the benefits are hard to see. Estate and property taxes too are unpopular. Both tax wealth, which strikes people as double taxation because surely that wealth derived from income that was already taxed. And the property tax arrives in a lump sum, making the cost particularly salient, and some do not want the benefits provided, such as those without school-age children.

Although I cannot systematically test whether various design features result in attitudes that stray from objective costs or abstract commitments, the anecdotal evidence suggests that they do. They help make it apparent why people do not like taxes that are in their economic self-interest or comport with their abstract commitments.

The Great Salience of the Federal Income Tax

The federal income tax looms large in the above analyses; it is at or near the top of the list for the worst and most disliked tax as well as the tax most in need of a decrease. When asked, "What is the most unfair tax?" in an open-ended format, where respondents have to come up with the answer on their own rather than being shown a list, they come up with the federal income tax. Clearly the federal income tax has great salience for many. Perhaps this helps explain why nonrich taxpayers for whom the income tax is less costly than other taxes dislike it so much; it's simply on their radars in a way that other taxes are not.

Further evidence of the salience of the federal income tax comes from the 2012 CCES. A series of questions found that when people feel squeezed financially and think taxes are to blame, they cite the federal income tax as the culprit, both for themselves and for others. Specifically, I asked respondents, "A lot of people feel squeezed financially these days—that their take-home income is not enough to meet their needs. Do you feel squeezed financially?" A large majority did: 70 percent, compared to just 21 percent who said no. Among those who felt squeezed, most said it was because their incomes are too low: 62 percent, compared to 38 percent who said taxes are too high (itself an interesting answer, suggesting that there are not large majorities of Americans who think their financial insecurity is due to excessively high tax levels, as fiscally conservative politicians might assert). Among those who did say that taxes are the culprit, I asked, "Which tax is the biggest problem?" The federal income tax was cited most frequently at 45 percent, followed by the property tax at 24 percent. For those who didn't feel squeezed, I asked their impressions of people who do feel squeezed. These respondents also cited low income more than high taxes, 70 to 30 percent. But again, when asked which tax is the biggest problem, the federal income tax headed the list by a significant margin, followed more distantly by the property tax.

Another indication of the great salience and dislike of the federal income tax comes from a 2012 CCES item that asked whether federal income taxes had gone up, down, or stayed the same for low-, middle-, and high-income people as well as people like the respondent, compared to 1980.[38] In reality, average federal income tax rates fell for all income groups over this period, as figure 3.10 shows. But 71 percent say middle-income people pay more in federal income taxes as a share of income now than in 1980, and 63 percent say that people like them pay more now (figure 3.11). Almost two in five say taxes for low-income people have gone up even though they have fallen tremendously because of expansions of the EITC and other policies. Majorities of respondents do recognize that average tax rates have fallen for high-income people, but most do not think taxes have fallen for other income groups or people like themselves. We can imagine that one reason that people dislike the federal income tax so much is that they (erroneously) think it has increased for people like them over the last four decades.

The great salience of the federal income tax is probably driven by elites' agenda and rhetoric. For this book, I have not done an extensive analysis of the volume and content of elite rhetoric about taxes. In previous work I found that the number of references to taxes, often federal income taxes, rises over time in party platforms as well as presidential nomination and general election speeches; concomitantly, an increasing share of all likes and dislikes about the parties that ANES respondents give concern taxes as well (Campbell 2009). More work linking tax rhetoric and public opinion is needed. I suspect that the nonrich focus on the federal income tax because they hear so much about it. Keeping the income tax front and center is a great help to the privileged—another way in which the nonrich serve as their allies in their quest to get their taxes reduced.

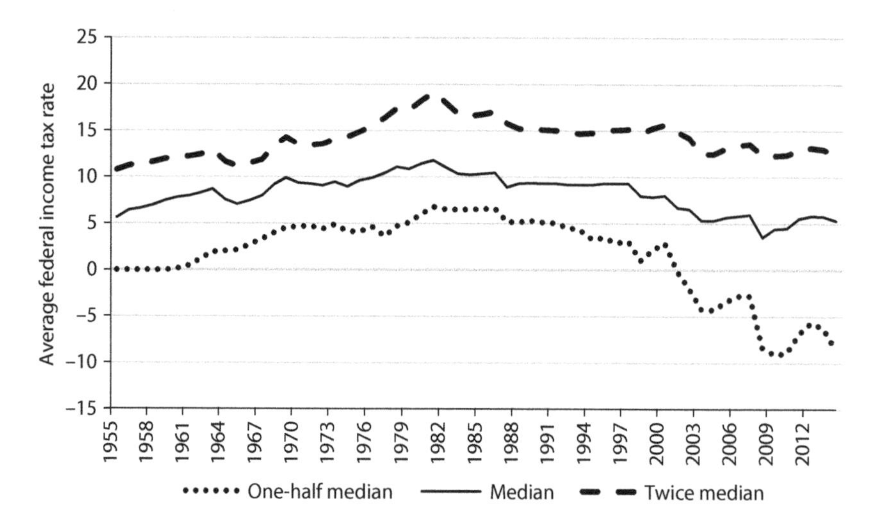

FIGURE 3.10 Average Federal Income Tax Rate by Income Level
Note: Figure shows the average (effective) federal income tax rates for four-person families at one-half median income, median income, and twice median income.
Source: Tax Policy Center 2015.

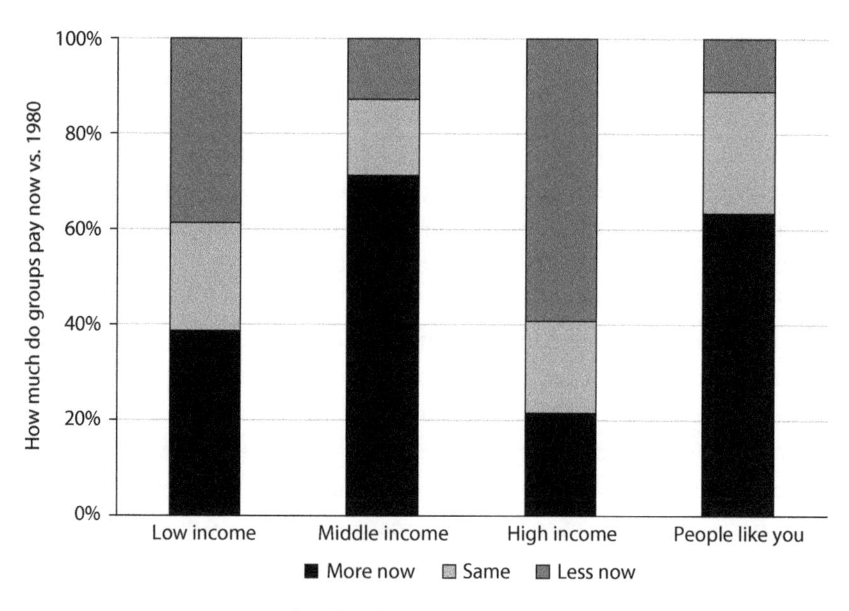

FIGURE 3.11 Perceptions of Federal Income Taxes Now versus 1980
Note: Figure shows the proportion of respondents saying how much of their income each income group (low-, middle-, and high-income people, and "people like you") pays in federal income tax now, compared to 1980.
Source: CCES 2012.

The Dearth of Self-Interested Attitudes across Taxes

Public opinion researchers have long pointed to taxes as a policy area where individuals' attitudes more often correspond to their material stakes—their objective self-interest—than is the case in other policy areas. Taxes seem to bear all the marks of a policy in which those with a personal stake would have distinctive attitudes: taxes are tangible, sizable, and measurable. They are also one of the most common interactions individuals have with government.

At first glance, it seems like those earlier researchers were on to something. On surveys, large majorities of nonrich people express support as a general matter for progressive taxation, which burdens higher-income households more and the nonrich less. Such a preference for a policy that means lower costs for oneself is a self-interested stance. But when it comes to the opinions of the nonrich on taxes—which they dislike, regard as unfair, and want to decrease—their opinions are not consistently patterned in a self-interested way. They dislike progressive taxes and think they are unfair, while they like regressive taxes that burden them more and think them fairer. Among the nonrich, there is a principle-policy gap: support for progressivity in the abstract, but support for regressivity when it comes to specific tax attitudes. Tax breaks show a similar pattern: majorities say they want the privileged to pay more, but majorities also want to retain every tax break, even those that disproportionately benefit the privileged.

Part of the problem is knowledge. Although a fair number of survey respondents can identify progressive taxes as progressive, more mischaracterize regressive taxes as proportional—the idea that "everyone pays the same." Regressive taxes are tricky because indeed, everyone pays the same rate. But they take a larger share of income for those lower on the income spectrum. Even with that definition right in front of them, large numbers of respondents still give a response based on tax rates. In contrast, more individuals correctly characterize progressive taxes as progressive, in part because it's an easier task: as income rises, both the tax rate and the tax as a share of income rises. With regressive taxes, the tax rate is the same for all, but the tax as a share of income falls as income rises.

Another issue is tax design. Particular design elements hide or highlight costs, enable or reduce personal agency and control, and increase or ease the administrative burden of tax payment. Some people get out of paying some taxes, like the privileged who capitalize on tax breaks or homeowners who seek lower assessments. Some taxes are linked to obvious and valuable benefits, while others are not. These features seem to influence tax preferences above and beyond objective cost, and help explain why the nonrich survey respondents examined here dislike taxes that burden them less or not at all, while being relatively favorable to some taxes that cost them dearly, like payroll and sales taxes.

These attitudinal patterns are consequential because they aid and abet the case of the rich in their quest to get progressive taxes reduced. Many ordinary Americans dislike the estate and federal income taxes. Indeed, many see the federal income tax as the main problem in tax policy. Yet in reality, the bottom quintile of households does not pay a federal income tax at all due to the standard deduction, EITC, and other provisions. For the next two quintiles, sales taxes are more costly than federal income taxes, and for all quintiles except the highest, payroll taxes are more costly than federal income taxes (this will be clearer in the next chapter, which examines attitudes across individuals). But those costs are never totaled each year, while filling out the federal income tax return is an annual, time-consuming ordeal. And the national conversation is often about the federal income tax. Even though effective rates have fallen for every income group since 1980, most Americans only recognize the decreases the affluent have enjoyed. Federal income taxes for low- and middle-income people have fallen too, but many think they have increased.

This pattern of attitudes across taxes begins to explain one way in which public opinion has aided the long campaign of the rich to get their own taxes reduced. The nonrich dislike the same taxes as the rich. They are not class opponents; they are unwitting allies attacking the same taxes the privileged attack: the estate and income taxes. The next chapter looks at whether patterns of attitudes across individuals also fail to conform to self-interested stakes.

4

Self-Interest II

ATTITUDES ACROSS INDIVIDUALS

A SECOND WAY of examining self-interest as a correlate of tax attitudes is to look across individuals, not just across taxes as in the previous chapter. We will see that individuals with different stakes in the tax system, who pay different costs, do not necessarily have different attitudes. Sometimes tax preferences are correlated with material stakes, but often they are not.

We will also see that individuals' tax attitudes are not consistently correlated with their abstract tax preferences either. Large majorities of Americans prefer progressive to regressive taxation. Individuals are able to connect these commitments to tax attitudes for progressive but not regressive taxes. That is, those who prefer the concept of progressive taxation are more likely to say various progressive taxes are fair. But they deem various regressive taxes fair too, contradicting their abstract preference. Regressive taxes are clearly more difficult for people to understand.

Part of the problem is a lack of tax knowledge. The nonrich score low on their knowledge of taxes in general and their ability to correctly characterize progressive and regressive taxes. Even among the more highly educated and knowledgeable, significant relationships between markers of self-interest and tax attitudes are infrequent. Also concerning is the fact that more economically vulnerable groups—women, younger people, and Black and Hispanic Americans—tend to have lower levels of tax knowledge. Taken together, the findings of this chapter and the previous one indicate that tax attitudes are infrequently related to ordinary people's material stakes.

Actual Tax Burdens across Individuals

Figure 4.1 shows how much taxpayers in each income quintile pay in each tax as a percentage of their income. These are the same data that appeared in table 3.1, in which I used the shares paid by the top and bottom income groups to calculate a progressivity score, but filling out the picture for all income groups. The figure highlights several phenomena. First, harking back to the previous chapter's discussion of different types of taxes, it illustrates in visual form the progressivity or regressivity of different taxes. Among the taxes shown here (the figure does not include the estate tax, for example), the federal income tax is the most progressive, with effective tax rates climbing dramatically with income. The bottom quintile on average gets money back from the federal government, largely due to tax credits such as the EITC, while the tax is the costliest for the top quintile, taking 15 percent of its income on average. State income and corporate taxes are progressive too, but in a much more modest fashion. The other four taxes are all regressive, costing lower-income taxpayers more as a share of income than higher-income taxpayers. The sales tax (here combined with state excise taxes including state gas taxes) is the most regressive, with low-income households paying more than 7 percent of their income compared to 2 percent for the top quintile.

If tax attitudes corresponded to the cost of taxes as represented in figure 4.1, then we might expect the following patterns. Most broadly, the share of respondents who say the federal income tax is unfair should climb with income and the share saying the sales tax is unfair should fall with income.

More specifically, one noticeable feature of this figure is how costly the payroll tax is for most income groups and how costly the sales tax is at the bottom of the income spectrum. If people are thinking about taxes in a cost-based manner, we might expect those in the lowest quintile to have the most negative attitudes toward the payroll tax, which costs them 9.4 percent of income, followed by sales (7.1 percent) and property taxes (4.2 percent). In contrast, they should be most positive toward the federal income tax since on average, all that they pay is refunded to them, and then some. People in the second quintile and third quintile (the middle of the spectrum) similarly should have the most negative attitudes toward the payroll and sales taxes, which remain the costliest for those groups (9.1 and 4.8 percent of income, respectively), followed somewhat distantly by the federal income tax, which costs the middle quintile half as much as the sales tax, or 2.4 percent of income. Even for the fourth quintile, the payroll tax is still the costliest at

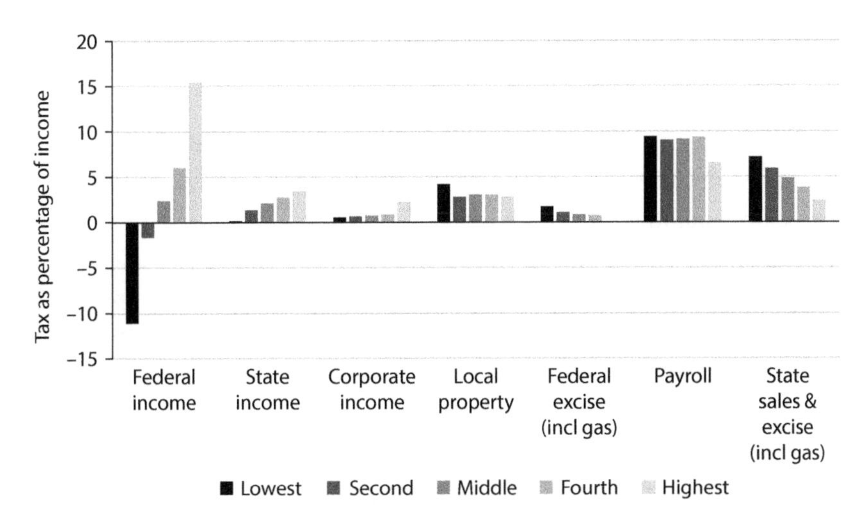

FIGURE 4.1 Taxes as a Share of Income, by Income Quintile
Note: Taxes are arrayed by progressivity score (tax as share of income for highest quintile minus share for lowest quintile from table 3.1). Data are for 2018–19 to match the survey data in hand.
Sources: Congressional Budget Office 2022, exhibit 13; ITEP 2018, 11.

9.3 percent of income, followed by the federal income tax at 6 percent and sales taxes at 3.8 percent. Only for the highest quintile is the federal income tax the costliest. Note that two other taxes discussed in the attitudinal data do not appear here. The estate tax applies to very few; in 2019, the year of the figure 4.1 data, the tax applied to 1,900 estates out of the 2.85 million Americans who died, or less than 0.1 percent. This is the most progressive tax in the American system and should be the most popular as the vast majority of people do not pay it, and as we saw in chapter 3, large shares of Americans support progressive taxation in the abstract. The tax rate on capital gains and investments is lower than on earned income. Technically, this preferential rate is a tax expenditure, with nearly all of this benefit (95 percent) going to the top income quintile, as figure 3.4 showed. Most people neither pay capital gains taxes nor benefit from the preferential tax rate. It's hard to predict what people think of it. Most do not pay it, so they should be relatively favorable toward the tax, which costs them nothing; on the other hand, they may dislike the fact that it provides a lower rate to privileged taxpayers.

Another set of expectations arises from the degree to which income should differentiate people's opinions. We would expect the largest differences by income in opinions on the federal income tax, as effective rates vary the most.

Effective sales tax rates vary by income too, but much less dramatically than income tax rates, and in the opposite direction with the larger burden on low-income groups. Differences across income groups might be more muted for other taxes that impose similar burdens on all groups, such as the payroll tax—similar for all except the top quintile—and property tax—similar for all except the bottom quintile.

From a pure tax cost perspective, the proverbial middle-class American—and lower-income ones—should hold the most negative attitudes toward the payroll tax, followed by sales taxes. They should be least exercised by federal income, state income, and gas taxes. Actual attitudes, as we'll see, are essentially the opposite of these predictions.

Tax Attitudes by Income and Other Self-Interest Measures

Figures 4.2a–b array responses to two tax questions by income: How fair is the amount you have to pay (unfair is shown)? And should the tax be increased, decreased, or kept the same (decrease is shown)? The four progressive taxes appear on the left and the four regressive ones on the right.[1] In the 2019 CCES, I also asked about the fairness of each tax in general (not shown); the pattern is almost identical to that shown in figure 4.2a for the fairness of one's own burden.

First consider federal and state income taxes compared to gas and sales taxes. As expected, lower-income people are more likely than higher-income people to say the amount they have to pay in gas and sales taxes is unfair (figure 4.2a) and should be decreased (figure 4.2b). These patterns reflect the greater burden these regressive taxes impose on lower-income groups, congruent with the cost-based self-interest of these groups. But lower-income people are also more likely to say federal and state income taxes are unfair, and are even more likely to say they should be decreased, even though they pay far less than higher-income people both absolutely and relative to income. The mismatch between the steep rise in the federal income tax burden by income in figure 4.1 and the fairly steep decline in unfairness evaluations as well as desire to decrease the tax in figures 4.2a–b is especially striking. If burdens drove attitudes in a cost-based way, income should most sharply differentiate attitudes on the federal income tax. It does, but in the opposite of the expected direction.

Payroll tax attitudes do not reflect actual tax burdens either. For the bottom four quintiles, the payroll tax is the costliest. And yet it is the tax every group least wants to decrease, with preferences no doubt reflective of the

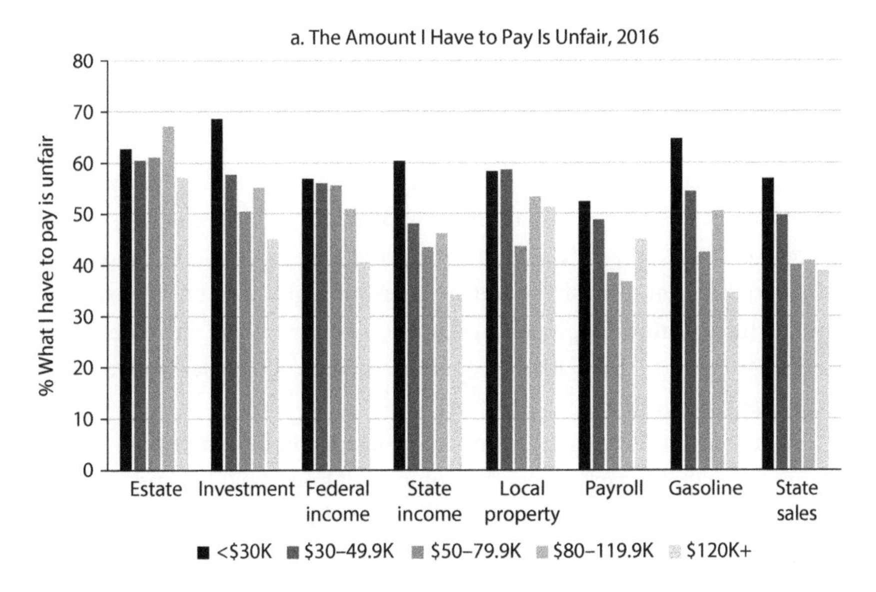

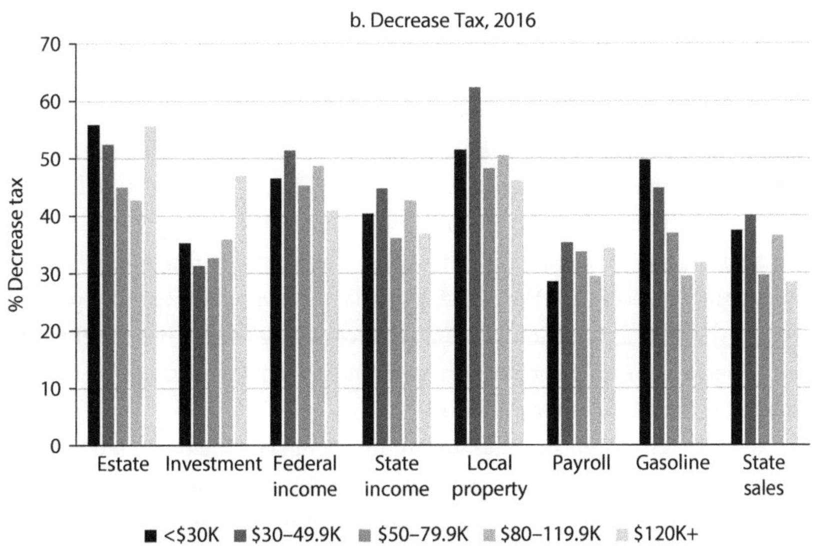

FIGURE 4.2 Tax Evaluations by Income
Source: 2016 CCES.

value of Social Security benefits rather than the cost of the tax. Also notice that far more people want to decrease the property tax than the sales tax even though the sales tax is costlier to most income groups. The top income group most wants to decrease the estate tax, followed by the investment tax—preferences that square with their self-interest (although not really the estate tax, since virtually no one pays it). But the tax low-income people most want to decrease? The estate tax as well. If we were to flip the data in figure 4.2b to show which taxes each income group wants to decrease the most, only the pattern for the top income group begins to square with self-interest: as taxes are arrayed from most progressive to most regressive, the desire to decrease them falls almost monotonically. Yet no such cost-based pattern exists clearly for other income groups. Federal income and estate taxes are high on the list for cutting, even though these taxes cost these groups little or nothing, compared to the costlier payroll and sales taxes. What's going on? Payroll taxes provide a visible benefit; sales taxes seem to escape people's notice.

Income is not the only indicator of self-interest in the tax system. Marital status can matter as well: depending on overall household income, and how similar or different income is across spouses, married couples can enjoy a federal income tax bonus compared to single filers of similar income.[2] So could having children: before the Trump tax cut of 2017, the federal income tax included an extra exemption for each child.[3] Seniors aged sixty-five and over can take an extra deduction on their federal income tax. Homeowners may feel more negatively toward the property tax than renters, for whom the property tax is paid by the landlord and hidden in their rent. Senior citizens may feel aggrieved by the property tax as many live on a "fixed" income as well as own their houses free and clear, which as mentioned earlier, means they have to pay their property tax rather than having it escrowed through their lender, heightening its visibility. We might also imagine seniors being more positive toward the payroll tax as most are no longer paying the tax but are enjoying Social Security benefits, or being more likely to deem the estate tax unfair as it looms larger than for younger folks.

Nevertheless, when attitudes toward the eight taxes are predicted by these self-interest indicators, few are correlated with fairness evaluations. Figure 4.3 finds that once all factors are taken into account in a multivariate analysis, none of these measures of self-interest are correlated with evaluations of the fairness of various taxes, with three exceptions. Those in the top income quintile are more likely to say property taxes are unfair, *perhaps* in keeping with self-interest (the affluent generally pay more in property taxes absolutely, although less as a share of income). But this finding is fragile; in the 2019 data, those in the top quintile are less likely to say property taxes are unfair. Second, married people are less likely to deem the payroll tax unfair than single or widowed people. It could be that respondents know that Social Security is

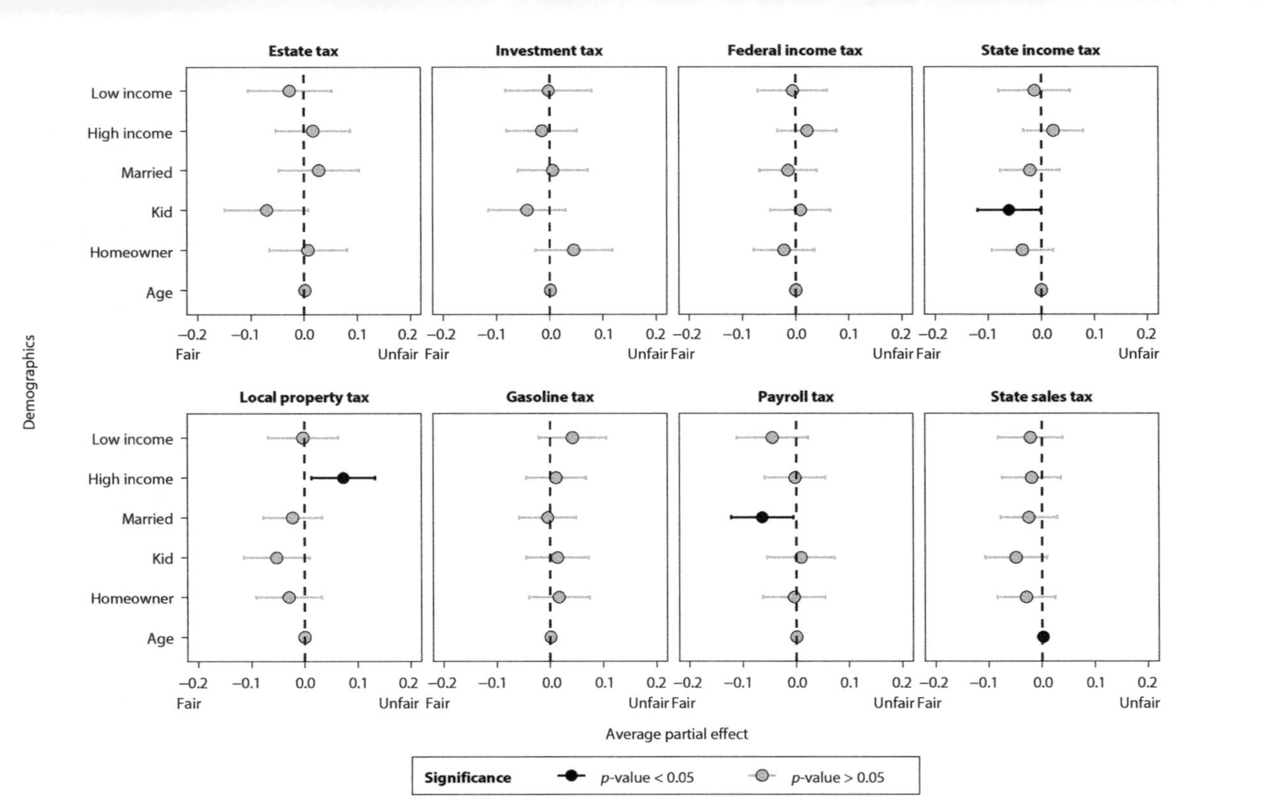

FIGURE 4.3 Tax Unfairness and Self-Interest Measures
Note: "Amount I pay is very unfair" is coded high. Ordinary least squares model. Full sample. Low income and high income are approximately the bottom and top 20 percent of income, respectively; reference category is the middle 60 percent. Includes controls for race/ethnicity, education, gender, partisanship, ideology, and government trust.
Source: 2016 CCES.

designed favorably for married people: if one spouse does not work, they still get a pension in retirement based on the earnings record of the working spouse, and married people with work histories get to take a pension based on their own work record or their spouse's, whichever is higher. Again, though, this is a fragile finding; in the 2019 data, married people are not distinctive in their payroll tax attitudes. Finally, in an alternative specification in which age is entered not as a continuous variable but rather analyzed with a sixty-five-plus indicator variable, seniors are more likely than nonseniors to deem the estate tax unfair. Otherwise, the affluent do not have distinct attitudes, nor do homeowners (even on the property tax), nor do the married, those with children, or people of different ages.[4]

A second set of attitudes to examine for evidence of self-interested thinking concerns preferences on the future of taxes: Should each be increased, decreased, or kept the same? The basic self-interest indicators do not explain much variation here either (figure 4.4). Homeowners want to see property taxes decreased more than do renters, but otherwise none of the other measures of self-interest are statistically significant.[5]

Finer Measures of Self-Interest

The indicators of self-interest examined so far are relatively gross. Few have proven statistically significant. Perhaps finer-grained hypotheses are more likely to pan out. These more specific situations are more akin to some of the studies cited earlier in which tax attitudes did correspond with self-interested stakes.

Instances in Which Attitudes Correspond with Self-Interest

High- and low-income people and the federal income tax. This analysis involves perhaps not a finer measure of self-interest but rather an alternative outcome. Beginning in 1947, Gallup asked survey respondents whether the federal income taxes they have to pay in a given year are too high, too low, or about right; the GSS added this question in 1976. Since the late 1970s, those in the top income quintile each year have been more likely than others to say that their federal income taxes are too high, above and beyond other demographic and political covariates, while those in the bottom quintile have been less likely to say that their federal income taxes are too high (see appendix, figures A.2 and A.3). In one sense, the results comport with actual burdens and therefore

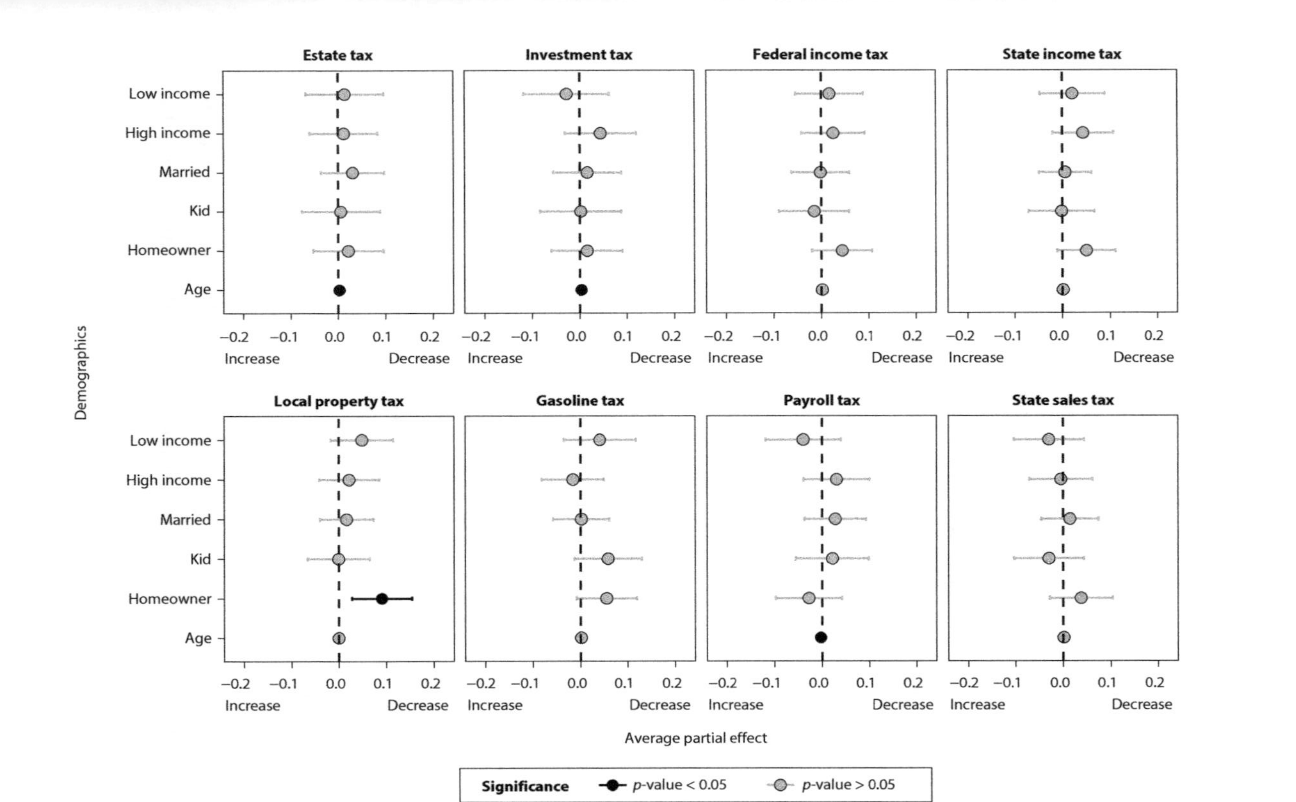

FIGURE 4.4 Tax Change Preferences and Self-Interest Measures
Note: "Tax should be decreased" is coded high. Ordinary least squares model. Full sample. Low income and high income are approximately the bottom and top 20 percent of income, respectively; reference category is the middle 60 percent. Includes controls for race/ethnicity, education, gender, partisanship, ideology, and government trust.
Source: 2016 CCES.

self-interest: respondents in the top quintile really do pay more in income tax, while those in the bottom pay less.

On the other hand, before the late 1970s, when top earners paid even more than they do today, they were not more likely than others to say their federal income taxes are too high in most years. They only became distinctive in their attitudes once cutting income taxes was on the nation's agenda. Thus these results are congruent with a self-interest effect in the time period when taxes were in the news but not before then. Perhaps the booming postwar economy dampened antitax politics, or perhaps people only think about their tax burdens when media coverage and elite rhetoric highlight them.[6]

Senior citizens and the federal income tax. Senior citizens get a greater deduction on their federal income taxes. Because their federal taxes are therefore less than similar nonseniors, they should have more positive attitudes. Descriptively, in the 1976–2018 pooled GSS data, senior citizens are 12 to 17 percent less likely than younger people to say their federal income taxes are too high, overall and within each income quintile—a relationship that persists in the same item in the 2019 CCES.[7]

One- versus two-earner couples and the federal income tax. In his extensive research on taxes across types of households, tax law scholar Edward McCaffery (1999, 457; 1997) deems one-earner married couples "big winners" in the federal income tax system compared to two-earner couples. One-earner families enjoy "imputed income" that is not taxed—the value of all the home- and child-related services provided by the nonworking spouse that would be taxed if the couple had to pay a third party to supply such services. That the household, not the individual, is the taxable unit in the United States also leads to differential tax treatment of one- and two-earner couples. Primary earners in two-earner couples enjoy a zero-tax bracket, but secondary earners do not; their tax rate begins where the primary earner's income ends. Each dollar of their income is taxed at a higher rate than the comparable dollar earned by the primary earner.

McCaffery's observations suggest a number of hypotheses about patterns of tax attitudes across family types. Individuals in two-earner couples should hold more negative attitudes toward the federal income tax than those in one-earner couples. This should be true in general and for couples with children (and for those with children, the difference might be even greater given the additional untaxed imputed income related to childcare). These attitudinal differences should be larger at higher marginal income tax rates because the value of escaping taxation on the unpaid labor of the nonworking spouse is greater—that is, at higher incomes compared to lower ones, and in periods when top marginal tax rates have been higher.

Many of these hypotheses are upheld in the pooled GSS data. Across the 1976–2018 period, respondents from two-earner households are more likely than those from one-earner households to say that their federal income taxes are too high, 68 versus 64 percent. Two-earner couples with children are more likely to say their federal income tax is too high than one-earner couples with children, 67 to 63 percent. Both of these differences are statistically significant at $p < 0.001$, and remain in multivariate analyses controlling for income, education, gender, age, race, partisanship, and ideology. Also, married respondents were more likely than singles to deem the federal income tax too high in eras when the top marginal tax rate was higher, and the gap between single- and dual-earner couples was larger during those times. Taken together, these findings suggest one area where attitudes do correspond with material stakes: where taxes differ because of patterns of work and marriage, tax evaluations differ as well.[8]

One- versus two-earner couples and the payroll tax. Marital status may also be correlated with attitudes toward the tax funding Social Security. Two-earner couples are penalized compared to one-earner couples because spouses can earn a retirement pension based on their employed spouse's earnings record, regardless of their own work history. Thus in a two-earner couple, the second earner's Social Security contributions are a "pure tax," as McCaffery (2009, 232) terms it: that spouse could have earned benefits even without working.

Determining whether individuals in two-earner couples hold more negative attitudes toward the Social Security payroll tax than those in one-earner couples is hindered by data availability: the surveys that include Social Security tax items—the ACIR, NPR, and CCES—do not ask about the employment status of spouses. But it is possible to approximate one- and two-earner household attitudes by looking at the attitudes of married women in the ACIR and CCES surveys because we know whether they were employed. If we assume that married women under sixty-five have working husbands (which is obviously only an approximation of reality, but necessary given the data available), then by comparing the attitudes of such women who work with those who do not work, we can approximate the attitudes of two- and one-earner households (at least among women).

In the ACIR data, pooled over the 1983–94 period, married working women under sixty-five are more likely than their nonworking counterparts to say that the Social Security tax is the worst one, 15 versus 11 percent, a statistically significant difference in the expected direction—the tax is a worse deal for two-earner households. In the 2019 CCES data, however, married working women are not more negative toward the Social Security tax; they are actually less likely to say it is the worst tax and that what they pay is unfair (12 versus 19 percent), and less likely to say that the tax is unfair in general (42 versus 53 percent), going against expectations.[9] The lack of support for the hypothesis in the 2019 CCES data is confined to the Social Security tax; nonsenior married women who work are more negative toward the federal income tax than those who do not work outside the home—more likely to say it is too high (48 to 40 percent) and unfair—just as in the pooled GSS data and in line with McCaffery's observation that the federal income tax is a worse deal for two-earner couples.

It is not clear why Social Security attitudes differ by the number of earners in the ACIR data but not in the CCES data; one possibility is that Social Security was in the news less in 2016 and 2019 than it had been in 1983–94, when the program's long-term viability was threatened and highly publicized efforts to shore up its finances took place, including a payroll tax increase in 1990 (Campbell 2003, chap. 5). Perhaps greater media coverage exposed some of the more detailed workings of the program. Another possibility is that the composition of the stay-at-home population has changed over this period. These mixed findings suggest that the ability of individuals to recognize their material stakes in policy may be context dependent.

Homeowners, the property tax, and escrow. Figure 4.4 indicated that homeowners are more likely than renters to want the property tax decreased—a difference in contemporary data that echoes the finding of David Sears and Jack Citrin that homeowners were more likely than renters to support Prop 13, the 1978 property tax limitation measure in California. Both of these differences correspond to the material stakes owners and renters face.

Yet the property tax also provides evidence that tax designs can cloud perceptions of self-interest. The homeowners in the 2016 CCES who had their property taxes escrowed by their lender were more likely to say the property tax is fair than those who paid it directly, other demographic characteristics held constant. This suggests that escrowing reduces the visibility and hence the perceived cost of the property tax, muting the relationship between cost and property tax attitudes (Cabral and Hoxby 2012).

Regressivity of state tax systems. States vary considerably in the regressivity of their tax systems (ITEP 2015, 2018). One question from the self-interest perspective is whether upper-income groups have more positive state tax attitudes in states with more regressive systems that tax them lightly. The answer is yes. Using 2018 state tax rates, the ITEP calculated an index of state income tax regressivity by subtracting the effective income tax rate for the top 1 percent of state taxpayers from the effective rate for the bottom quintile. In most states, the income tax is progressive so that the measure is a negative number. The same index for sales taxes yields positive numbers for all states, indicating that the sales tax is regressive everywhere.

In a multivariate analysis in which the outcome is the fairness of the state income tax, an interaction term between the ITEP state income tax regressivity measure and income is statistically significant, indicating that higher-income people in states with more regressive income tax systems are more likely to say the state income tax is fair.[10] The same analysis for the sales tax finds the same relationship: higher-income people in states with more regressive sales taxes are more supportive of the sales tax, although this association does not quite reach standard levels of statistical significance. These findings are congruent with self-interest: higher-income people like state income and sales taxes more when they are taxed more lightly compared to lower-income people. Another finding in keeping with self-interest: respondents in states with higher sales taxes are more likely to say sales taxes are unfair in CCES data and select the sales tax as the worst tax in the ACIR data.[11]

Instances in Which Attitudes Do Not—or No Longer—Correspond with Self-Interest

Investors and the capital gains tax. Decades ago, political scientists Michael Hawthorne and John Jackson found that investors have distinct attitudes on the capital gains tax. In a multivariate analysis, they were more likely than those who did not "own shares in any publicly held corporations, investment companies or mutual funds" to say that exempting "half the profit (capital gains) from the sale of stock or property held more than 9 months [is] perfectly reasonable" rather than a "loophole" (Hawthorne and Jackson 1987).[12] The poll was conducted in May 1978, when Congress was debating a variety of tax changes. Ultimately the Tax Revenue Act of November 1978 increased the capital gains exclusion from 50 to 60 percent, reducing the effective capital gains tax rate to 28 percent.

Since the Bush tax cuts of the early 2000s, capital gains tax rates have been even lower, just 0, 15, or 20 percent depending on income, well below income tax rates. In turn, investors are no longer so distinctive in their attitudes. In the 2019 CCES survey, investors (measured as having "money invested in the stock market right now, either in an individual stock or in a mutual fund") actually have slightly more positive attitudes toward the capital gains tax than noninvestors and are less likely to say that the tax is unfair (59 percent among noninvestors and 54 percent among investors in the 2019 CCES)—a difference that is not statistically significant and disappears in a multivariate analysis. Nor is it the case that investors and noninvestors who say the tax is unfair have different reasons for doing so; in the 2016 CCES, majorities of both investors and noninvestors deeming the capital gains tax unfair want it decreased. The great decline in capital gains tax rates seems to have erased the distinctiveness of investor attitudes.

The self-employed and the payroll tax. Figure 4.2 indicated that despite the high cost of the Social Security payroll tax for most income groups, it is seen as the least unfair tax and the one least in need of reduction (at least at the income levels that ordinary surveys can access; Benjamin Page, Larry Bartels, and Jason Seawright (2013) have shown that the very rich wish to cut entitlement spending). From a cost perspective, however, there is one group that might have a dimmer view of the payroll tax: the self-employed. Employers and employees both pay into the Social Security system—6.2 percent of wages each—but the self-employed have to pay both shares themselves. Economists argue that in reality, all employees pay both halves because employers simply subtract their share from wages, but that is far less visible than the double tax for the self-employed, which they must calculate on their federal income tax returns. Because the Social Security tax is both more visible and greater for the self-employed, we would predict more negative payroll tax attitudes among these individuals.

This hypothesis is not upheld, though. The 2019 CCES identifies self-employed individuals, but they are no more likely than other workers to say the Social Security tax is the worst tax or that it is unfair. Nor do the self-employed evaluate the federal income tax—where their additional Social Security tax is figured—differently (unfortunately the 2019 CCES does not contain the "decrease tax" item). These nonfindings for the fairness evaluations obtain controlling for income as well, nor does it matter whether the respondents earned part or all of their income from self-employment.

Political scientists Alexander Hertel-Fernandez and Theda Skocpol (2015) find that the self-employed in the GSS are more likely than others to say that their federal income taxes are too high when tax reform is on the national agenda, as during the early Reagan years, the mid-1990s, and the mid-2000s. As with the findings on investors and capital gains opinion, this variation across time suggests that political context and national agendas may shape the ability of individuals to connect their tax attitudes to their objective stakes.

High-income seniors with taxable Social Security income. The taxation of a portion of Social Security benefits began in 1984, adopted in the 1983 Social Security Amendments to shore up the program's financing (Campbell 2003). We might imagine high-income seniors having more negative federal income tax attitudes compared to lower-income seniors, and that this gap might grow starting in 1984, but I do not detect such a pattern in the GSS data. Senior citizens, like nonseniors, become less likely to say their federal income taxes are too high after 1984 because federal income taxes do fall thanks to the Reagan and Bush tax cuts. Higher-income seniors are slightly more likely to say their federal income taxes are too high than lower-income seniors, and the gap grows after 1984, but these associations are substantively small and neither is statistically significant.[13] Therefore the taxation of Social Security income among affluent seniors does not produce distinctive attitudes in line with cost-related self-interest. The effect may be too subtle, or my measures too imprecise to capture which seniors are subject to higher federal income tax.

Table 4.1 summarizes the results of the search for relationships between self-interest and tax attitudes thus far in this chapter. The top panel enumerates the relatively limited instances in which attitudes square with the self-interest hypothesis—cases in which those who pay more have more negative attitudes toward a tax while those who pay less are more positive. The bottom panel lists the findings that are not congruent with a self-interest hypothesis because the attitudes of those who pay more and those who pay less are indistinguishable. Across the situations I have analyzed, the number of instances where self-interest fails is greater than the number in which it can be detected, although that is a function of cases I can test with the available data. Also worth noting is that several of the historical instances of a self-interest relationship listed in the top panel have since faded; as federal income and capital gains tax rates have fallen over time, the differences between income groups have shrunk.

Across income groups, we do observe self-interested attitudes with regard to two regressive taxes, the sales and gas taxes, in that lower-income people find them more unfair than higher-income people, and are more likely to want them decreased. Most of the other instances in which attitudes correspond to cost, however, reflect not just income but more particular circumstances as well. Many of the non-self-interest findings in the lower panel concern

TABLE 4.1 Summary of Self-Interest Associations

Tax	Data	Outcome	Relationship to tax attitudes	Notes
Self-interest findings				
Federal income	GSS 1976–2018; CCES 2019	Too high	Seniors less "too high"	
	GSS 1976–2018	Too high	Two-earner vs. one-earner couples	Fades over time
Capital gains	Roper 1978	Exclusion reasonable	Investors distinct	But not in CCES
Social Security	ACIR 1983–94	Worst tax	Married vs. unmarried women	But not in CCES
Property	CCES	Unfair	Escrow vs. pay directly	
	CCES	Decrease	Homeowners want decrease v. renters	
Sales	CCES	Unfair	Low income more unfair than high income	
	CCES	Decrease	Low income want decrease	
State tax systems	CCES	Unfair	High income more fair in regressive states	
Gasoline	CCES	Unfair	Low income more unfair than high income	
	CCES	Decrease	Low income want decrease	
Non-self-interest findings				
Federal income	CCES	Unfair	Low income more unfair than high income	
	CCES	Decrease	No difference by income	
	GSS 1976–2018	Too high	High-income seniors not distinct after 1984	
	CCES	Unfair	Seniors not distinct	
State income	CCES	Unfair	Low income more unfair than high income	

Tax	Data	Outcome	Relationship to tax attitudes	Notes
	CCES	Decrease	Top income not distinct	
Capital gains	CCES	Unfair	Investors not distinct	
	CCES	Decrease	Investors not distinct	
	CCES	Unfair	Top income not distinct	
	CCES	Decrease	Top income not distinct	
Estate	CCES	Unfair	No difference by income	
	CCES	Decrease	Top income not distinct	
	CCES	Unfair	All respondents: Most unfair across taxes	
	CCES	Decrease	No difference by income	
Social Security	CCES	Unfair	Married women not distinct	
	CCES	Unfair	Self-employed not distinct	
Property	CCES	Unfair	Homeowners not distinct	
	CCES	Unfair	Top income more unfair (regressive tax)	

Note: CCES data are from 2016 and 2019.

progressive taxes; attitudes do not vary as much as expected with income and therefore costs. That is, lower-income groups think regressive taxes are unfair and should be decreased, but they also feel that way about progressive taxes that touch them lightly. This pattern of attitudes helps the rich and affluent; higher-income groups that pay more for these progressive taxes disfavor them, but so do lower-income groups that pay less. These patterns make the politics of progressive taxes one-sided and help those who wish to reduce them; low- and middle-income people want these taxes decreased too even though payroll and sales taxes cost them much more.

Tax Principles and Tax Attitudes

In the previous chapter looking across taxes, we discovered that many Americans have an abstract preference for progressive taxation. One question for this chapter is whether these abstract preferences are correlated with specific tax attitudes at the individual level. Are those who say progressive taxation is the fairest way to tax more likely to say that progressive taxes are fair? So far in this chapter we have found that objective measures of self-interest such as income are not correlated with tax opinions. We might wonder in turn about people's abstract principles: who prefers each form of taxation, progressive, proportional, or regressive; and are individuals able to link their abstract preference with their specific policy attitudes.

Who Adheres to Each Tax Principle?

The first question concerns who supports each principle of taxation. Majorities of Americans say they prefer progressive taxation in the abstract. As mentioned in table 3.2, among those giving a response to a 2019 CCES question about the most fair system for the federal income tax, 61 percent preferred a progressive income tax, 34 percent a proportional one, and 5 percent a regressive one. Figures 4.5a–b depict the demographic and political correlates of respondents choosing each system over the other two.[14]

We might expect that an individual's abstract preferences would be related to their individual stakes in tax policy, and that is apparent for those in the top income quintile; they are more likely than the middle 60 percent to say that a progressive federal income tax is not fair while a regressive system, in which they would pay less, is fair. Note, however, that the bottom income quintile does not have corresponding attitudes; all things being equal, this group does not distinguish among the systems, even though objectively a progressive system is in their interest. Also worth noting is that in the 2012 version of this question, which asks respondents to evaluate the fairness of each type of tax system separately, income is not a correlate of opinion at all (see appendix figure A.1). Thus the finding that high-income people have abstract preferences congruent with their material stakes is fragile. I find it in the 2019 survey item that asks them to choose one system as the fairest for the federal income tax, but not in the more difficult 2012 item, which asks them to evaluate the fairness of progressive, proportional, and regressive taxes separately.

In contrast, figures 4.5a–b reveal that partisanship and ideology are highly correlated with abstract preferences (that is also true for the 2012 item). Compared to Democrats and liberals, Republicans and independents as well as moderates and conservatives are all more likely to say a regressive system is fair for the federal income tax and a progressive system is unfair. Among whites, those who are more racially resentful prefer a regressive system, which squares with other findings in chapter 6. Therefore abstract preferences for different tax systems are related to the symbolic factors of partisanship, ideology, and racial resentment. The ability to link one's abstract preference and one's objective stake in tax policy is only apparent for high-income people, at least for the federal income tax.

Are Tax Principles and Tax Attitudes Correlated?

The next question is whether individuals are able to connect their abstract preferences to their tax attitudes. So far, this chapter has examined correlations between indicators of self-interest, such as income and tax attitudes, and found little relationship. But large shares of Americans say they prefer progressive taxation. Is there a relationship between this abstract preference and tax attitudes?

Returning to the 2019 CCES, I examined the relationship between an abstract preference for each type of system for the federal income tax and evaluations of the fairness of each of the eight taxes in the CCES (in the 2019 data, the tax items ask how fair each tax is, not how fair is the amount you pay, which appears in the 2016 data). The findings are available in the online appendix, tables OA.12–OA.19, and reveal that people are able to connect their abstract preferences and specific tax attitudes for progressive taxes, but not for regressive ones. That is, above and beyond controls for demographic and political variables (government trust is not available in this dataset), those who say a progressive system is the fairest in the abstract are more likely to say each of the four progressive taxes is fair (federal income, state income, estate, and investment). And those who say a regressive system is the fairest in the abstract are less likely to say these progressive taxes are fair.

Respondents, though, are less able to match their abstract preferences and specific attitudes when it comes to regressive taxes. Those who prefer a progressive system are also more likely to say three of the four regressive taxes are fair (payroll, sales, and gas). And those who prefer a regressive system are less likely to say the gas tax is fair, going against their stated principles.

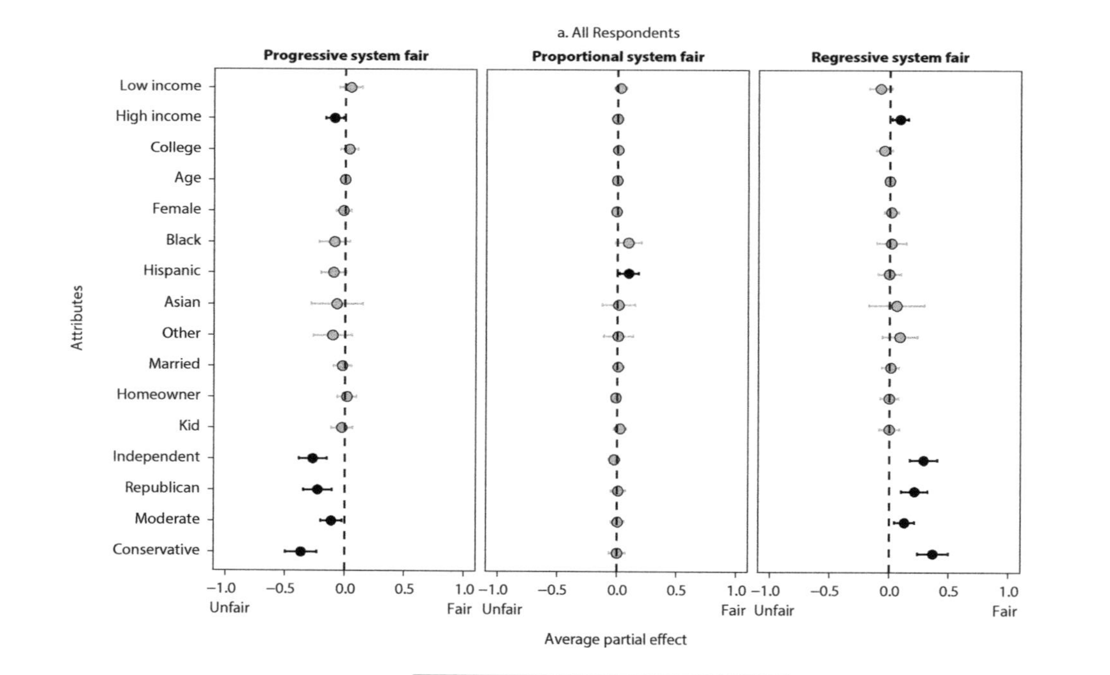

FIGURE 4.5 Correlates of Abstract Federal Income Tax Principles

Note: Each outcome is preference for that system over the other two for the federal income tax. Logit model. a. All respondents. b. Whites only, adding symbolic racism as a correlate. Low and high income are approximately the bottom and top 20 percent of income, respectively; reference category is the middle 60 percent. Reference category for party is Democrat; for ideology, it is liberal. Government trust not available in this dataset.

Source: 2019 CCES.

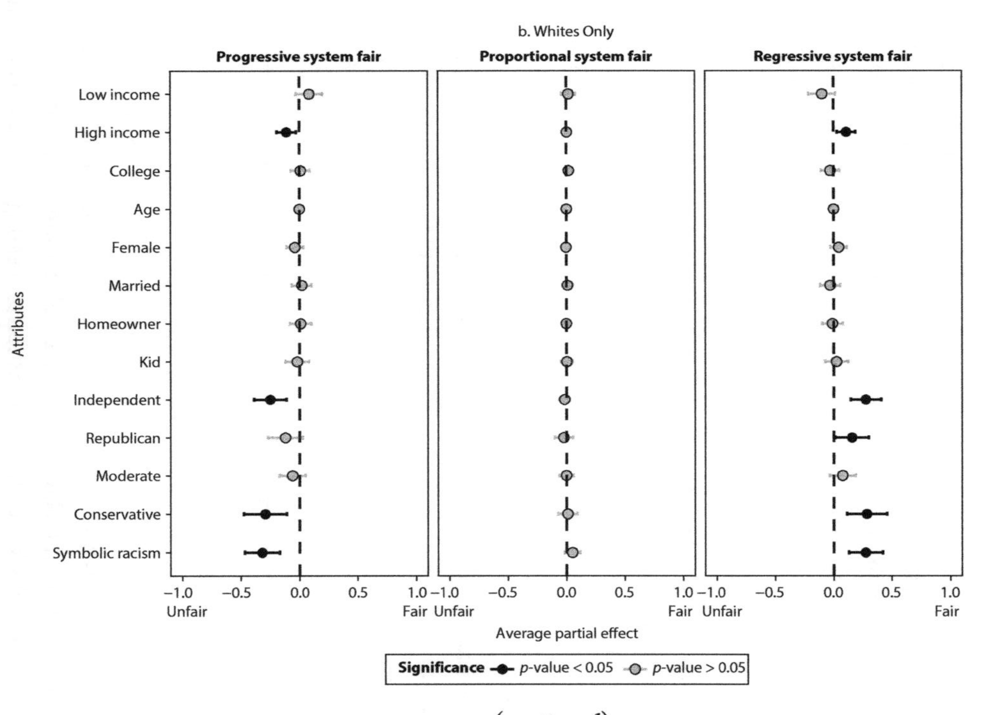

FIGURE 4.5 *(continued)*

A similar analysis can be conducted with the 2012 CCES item asking respondents to evaluate the fairness of each tax system separately (progressive, flat, or regressive) after receiving definitions of each. They were also asked about the fairness of the share they have to pay for five taxes. As in the 2019 results, respondents were able to link their abstract preferences for progressive taxes but not for regressive ones (online appendix, tables OA.7–OA.11). Those who thought a progressive system was fair were more likely to say their share of federal and state income taxes were fair. But they were more likely to say their share of the payroll tax for Social Security was fair too, even though it is a regressive tax. And those who said a regressive tax system was fair were more likely to say that payroll and sales taxes are unfair even though they are regressive.

In sum, attitudes across individuals toward taxes of all types do not correlate with measure of self-interest such as income. For regressive taxes, abstract commitments and specific tax attitudes do not line up either. We can begin to see how nonrich Americans might be vulnerable in the tax policymaking realm if they are unable to think about taxes in a self-interested way or connect their abstract commitments to preferences across all types of taxes.

At least for progressive taxes, the issue isn't abstract preferences: respondents are able to match their theoretical system preferences to specific attitudes. But that linkage breaks down for regressive taxes. This makes sense in that regressive taxes are more difficult for people to understand, as first hinted at in chapter 3, and as we are about to explore further at the individual level.

Tax Knowledge and Self-Interest

Objective measures of self-interest like income are not correlated with tax opinions. Perhaps another barrier at the individual level is tax knowledge. Some scholars, such as Christopher Achen and Larry Bartels (2016), argue that ignorance undermines individuals' ability to recognize their stakes in public policy. Moreover, making self-interest calculations is cognitively difficult, requiring "effortful, systematic information processing."[15] One reason why the symbolic predispositions of party identification, political ideology, and racial sentiment are often more highly correlated with attitudes is that they are easier to use, providing accessible heuristics and requiring only "shortcut" processing. In contrast, the cognitive piece of self-interested thinking is difficult because it rests on political and policy knowledge: Do individuals have the information necessary to recognize their interests?

Knowledge is important in order for citizens to have a voice in democratic governance. In their seminal work on political knowledge, Michael Delli Carpini and Scott Keeter (1996) link knowledge to both self-interest and political power. They contend that knowledge is a resource that enables individuals to realize their "true interests" and make them heard in the political system. Indeed, they push back on Anthony Downs's argument in his *Economic Theory of Democracy* that it is rational to be ignorant about politics. If that is true, then why are the most privileged members of society also the most knowledgeable? Given their higher education levels and social networks, they can more easily access information. But they recognize that it is useful as well. The greater knowledge levels of the rich are not merely about opportunity for information acquisition but also about the instrumental uses of such knowledge for political and policy gain.

Delli Carpini and Keeter (1996, chap. 4) measure general political knowledge with a series of questions about political actors and institutions, and find large differences across societal groups. Higher-income, male, and white respondents score higher in formal political knowledge than their lower-income, female, and Black counterparts. In their view, this variation arises because political knowledge is both an individual trait and one that is structurally determined, arising from "the interaction of ability, motivation, and opportunity" (Delli Carpini and Keeter 1996, 8). Regardless of personal interest, some, more than others, have opportunities to learn about political institutions and the workings of the political system in the family, at school, at work, through personal networks, in the media, and so on. They also note that some groups that score low on general political knowledge have pockets of expertise—such as women, who score higher on questions regarding local government, presumably because of interest in public schools and other local matters, and Black respondents, who displayed higher levels of political knowledge in cities with a high share of Black elected officials (Delli Carpini and Keeter 1996, chap. 4). Thus understanding the lack of a relationship between many measures of self-interest and tax attitudes requires an examination of tax policy knowledge along with its variation across different types of individuals.

Who Is Knowledgeable about Taxes?

The rich and the experts around them know a great deal about the tax system. What about everyone else? I placed items on the 2016 and 2019 CCES that measure general knowledge about tax policy as well as knowledge of the incidence of progressive and regressive taxes. In keeping with Martin Gilens's (2001) notion that people may be information specialists, these are policy-specific knowledge items to allow us to assess how well people are informed about this particular issue area.

Figures 4.6a–c portray how tax knowledge varies across various societal groups among respondents who provided answers to the knowledge questions. Figure 4.6a shows the mean results for general tax knowledge. The 2016 CCES included two such items: whether Americans pay more or less in taxes than Europeans (they pay less), and whether the payroll tax is part of the federal income tax (it is not). Much as Delli Carpini and Keeter found with general political knowledge, more privileged groups are more knowledgeable about taxes. General tax knowledge scores climb with education and income, with those who declined to share their income, presumably economically privileged individuals, knowing the most of all. In addition, male, older, white, and Asian respondents provide more correct answers than their female, younger, and Black or Hispanic counterparts. Those who are married or own their homes are more knowledgeable as well in these bivariate data. On these general tax questions, differences by party identification and ideology are muted.

In the 2016 CCES, I asked an additional set of tax knowledge questions about the incidence of progressive and regressive taxes, after first defining these terms, as described in chapter 3. As that chapter demonstrated, progressive taxes are easier for respondents to characterize correctly, and regressive taxes much more difficult, despite having the definitions in hand. Figures 4.6b–c show that this pattern appears for every demographic and political group.

Perhaps because the regressive tax items are more difficult, the knowledge gradients across the demographic groups are more in the expected pattern for regressive taxes compared to the progressive taxes, more effectively separating the knowledgeable from the less knowledgeable. The ability to correctly characterize progressive taxes as progressive is not necessarily greater among more privileged groups. In contrast, all groups were much less able to correctly characterize regressive taxes as regressive, but the ability to do so was greater among men, Asian respondents, the more educated, the top income quintile, and homeowners. Although I will be exploring the influence of partisan and ideological self-identifications on tax attitudes in the next chapter, it is worth noting here that knowledge of tax incidence is far greater among Democrats and liberals than among Republicans and conservatives.[16] Republicans and conservatives tend to characterize regressive taxes as "proportional," which

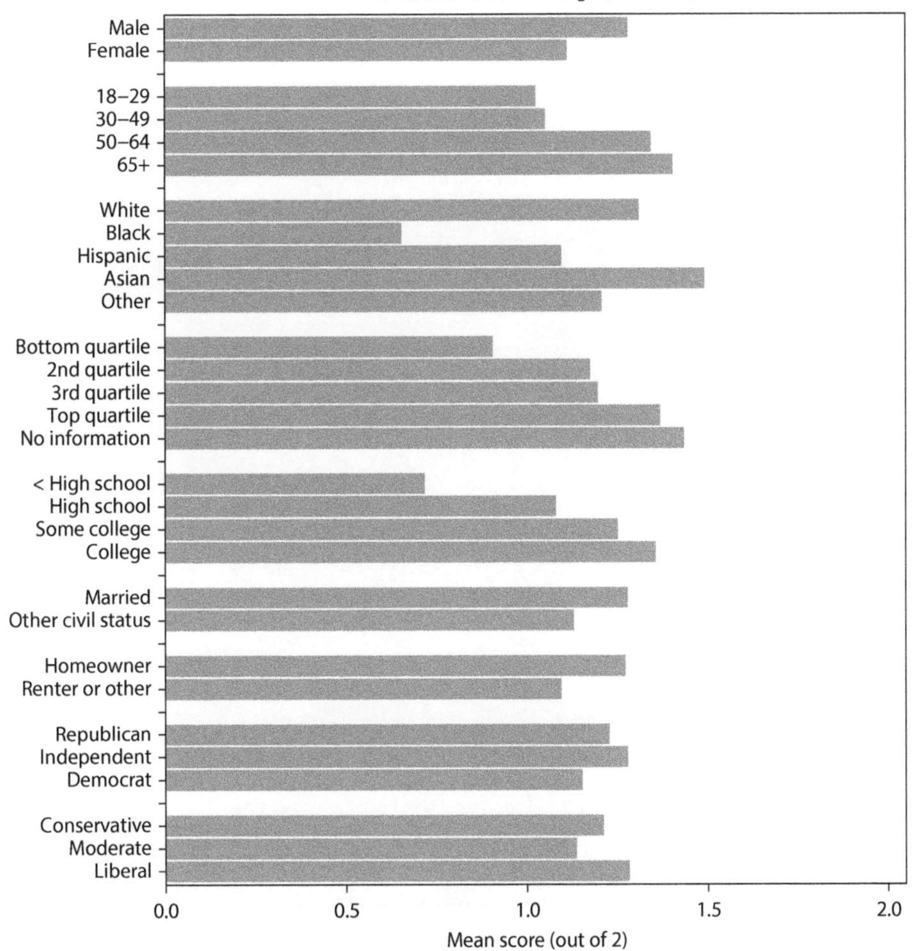

FIGURE 4.6 Tax Knowledge among Demographic and Political Groups
Note: General tax knowledge measures mean correct scores on two tax policy items. Knowledge of progressive tax incidence counts the number of progressive taxes respondents correctly characterized out of four (estate, investment, federal income, and state income), while the regressive incidence does the same for four regressive taxes (property, payroll, sales, and gas).
Source: 2016 CCES.

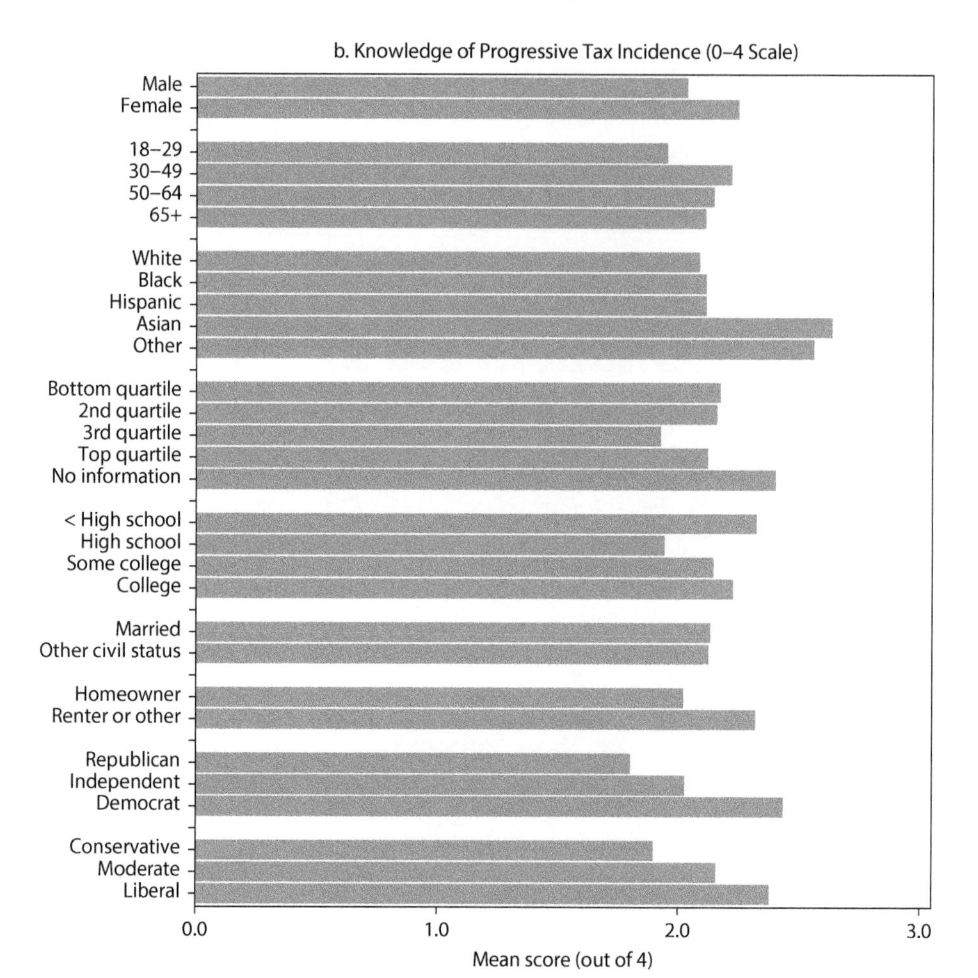

FIGURE 4.6 (*continued*)

may reflect an ideological commitment as much as a factual statement. The modal answer on incidence for the regressive sales and gas taxes is "proportional" rather than the correct "regressive" for both Democrats and Republicans, but Republicans are 15 percentage points more likely to say so, and college-educated Republicans just as likely to characterize these taxes as proportional, indicating that an ideological commitment is at play and not just ignorance.

The descriptive data in figures 4.6a–c are quite useful for showing which societal groups are more and less knowledgeable about taxes, according to these formal knowledge questions. Yet these measures of social position are

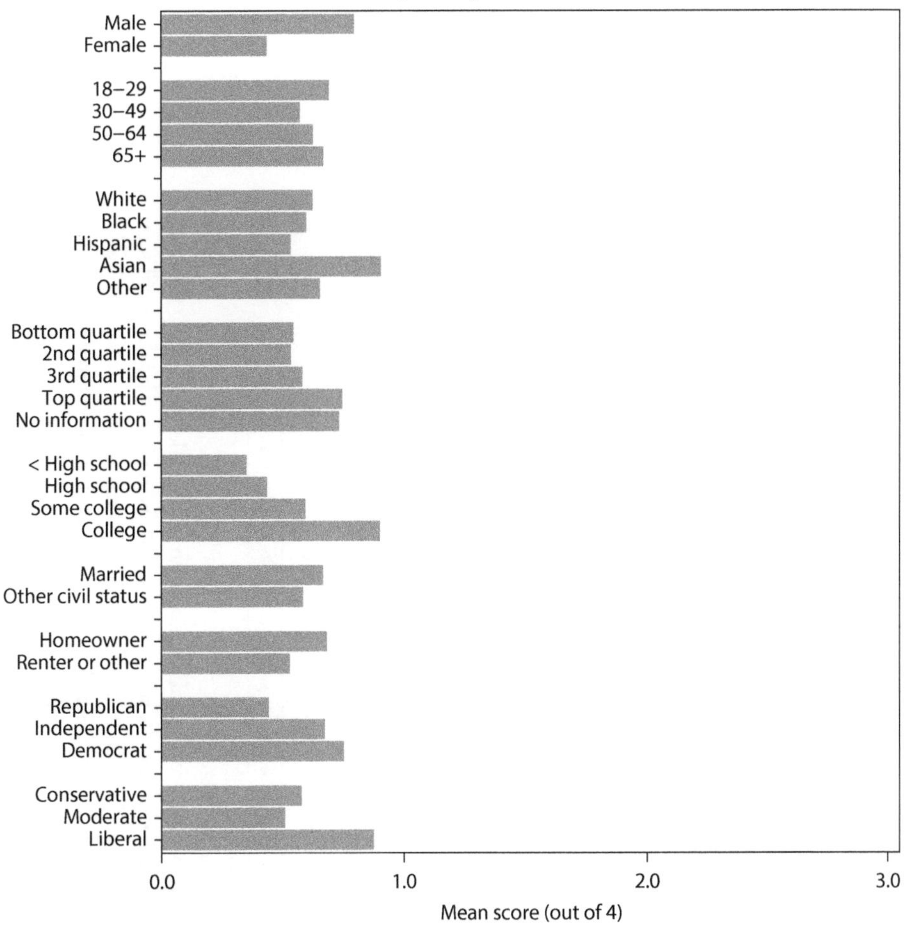

FIGURE 4.6 (*continued*)

correlated: homeowners are a little more knowledgeable than renters, but perhaps that is because they have higher incomes or are older. A multivariate analysis allows us to see the relationship of each demographic and political variable to tax knowledge, holding the other factors constant. In figure 4.7, the outcomes are indexes of the number of correct answers, which range from zero to two for general tax knowledge, and zero to four for progressive and regressive taxes, which I analyze separately as further analysis indicated that they load on different dimensions and have different sets of explanatory factors, as we will see. Figure 4.7 shows the results from ordinary least

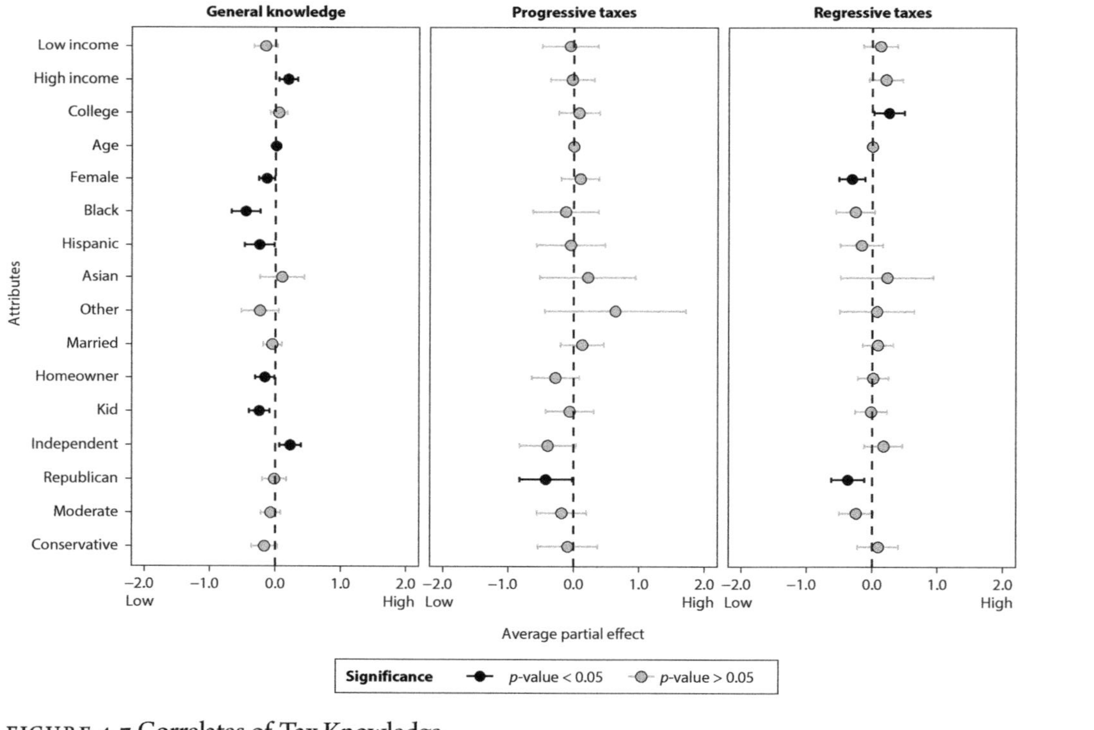

FIGURE 4.7 Correlates of Tax Knowledge

Notes: Figure shows the average partial effect of each variable on tax knowledge (having the correct versus the incorrect response) from ordinary least squares models, as measured by three different indexes (don't know responses are excluded). High income is a dummy variable indicating those approximately in the top 20 percent of income and low income indicates approximately the bottom 20 percent versus the middle 60 percent. The reference category for race/ethnicity is white; for party it is Democrats, and for ideology, it is liberal. Model also includes government trust.
Source: 2016 CCES.

squares regression, but alternative models such as a count model (negative binomial) or models with different coding schemes for the outcome yield largely the same results. Those who did not answer the knowledge questions are excluded.

All things being equal, general knowledge is greater among high-income people (the top 20 percent) relative to the middle 60 percent of respondents and among independent respondents compared to Democrats (the reference category), while lower among women, Black and Hispanic respondents, homeowners, and those with children under eighteen in the home compared to men, whites, renters, and those without children present. These correlates are similar to those of general political knowledge: more privileged groups—higher income, men, and whites—know more.

The story is a bit different when it comes to characterizing taxes as progressive or regressive. On the incidence of the four progressive taxes, knowledge is greater among Democrats than among independents and Republicans. No other factors are statistically significant. On the incidence of the four regressive taxes, knowledge is greater among the college educated and lower among women, Republicans, and moderates compared to their male, Democratic, and liberal counterparts.

An additional way of assessing tax knowledge is to examine which groups were more or less likely to respond to the tax knowledge questions at all. In order to minimize guessing and avoid an inflated measure of knowledge, the survey items include a don't know response. Therefore we can examine the correlates of declining to answer the knowledge items compared to providing an answer, whether correct or incorrect. A multivariate analysis (not shown) reveals that nonresponse was most common among lower-income, lower-education, and female respondents. In the case of some taxes, younger respondents were also more likely to decline to answer the knowledge questions, and older respondents were more likely to answer, perhaps because they have more experience with a variety of taxes.

Thus patterns of knowledge about taxes follow much the same patterns that Delli Carpini and Keeter found for general political knowledge: high-income, male, and white respondents often display more formal tax knowledge than lower-income, female, and Black or Hispanic respondents. Tax knowledge and a willingness to answer tax questions at all are greater among more privileged societal groups.[17] These relationships persist in different specifications and different codings of the knowledge variables. It is worth noting too that inequalities in tax knowledge accumulate; high-income white males are much more knowledgeable than low-income Black females, just as Delli Carpini and Keeter (1996, chap. 4) found for general political knowledge.[18]

Privileged groups have more tax knowledge most likely because the cost of information acquisition is lower for them. High-income, male, and white individuals are more likely to work in occupations that expose them to political news and informed coworkers. There is evidence that taxes are "a man's world," which may help explain women's lower levels of knowledge.[19] And we should keep in mind that the truly rich, who very much have tax attitudes congruent with their self-interest, do not appear in these survey data. Like other researchers who have examined preferences, policy outcomes, and inequality with survey data, I can examine the attitudes of the affluent—the top 10 or 20 percent of the population—compared to the rest, but not those of the top 1 or 0.01 percent.[20] The merely affluent are more diverse and less knowledgeable than the very rich, and so we should not be surprised if they do not always have attitudes that line up with their self-interest. But they will be more likely to display attitudes congruent with self-interest than those below them on the income spectrum.

Are Self-Interest and Tax Attitudes More Highly Correlated among the Knowledgeable?

Given the great differences in levels of tax knowledge across individuals, and the linkages between knowledge and ability to think about public policy in cost-based, self-interested terms, we might wonder whether attitudes toward taxes are more congruent with actual tax burdens among the more knowledgeable compared to the less knowledgeable.

Respondents can be divided by knowledge in a number of different ways. Figures 4.8a–b and 4.9a–b show results dividing by education, as education strongly differentiated respondents in their levels of tax knowledge, as revealed in figure 4.6, and using education preserves more cases. (I also ran models dividing respondents by level of general tax knowledge in different permutations—defining high knowledge as two correct, or one or two correct; don't knows included or not included—and the results are similar to those dividing the sample by education.)

Generally, the various measures of self-interest are not necessarily correlated with tax attitudes more often among high-knowledge respondents. College-educated homeowners are more likely than renters to say the investment and gas taxes are unfair (figure 4.8b), and property and gas taxes should be decreased (figure 4.9b). Those who are college educated and low income are also

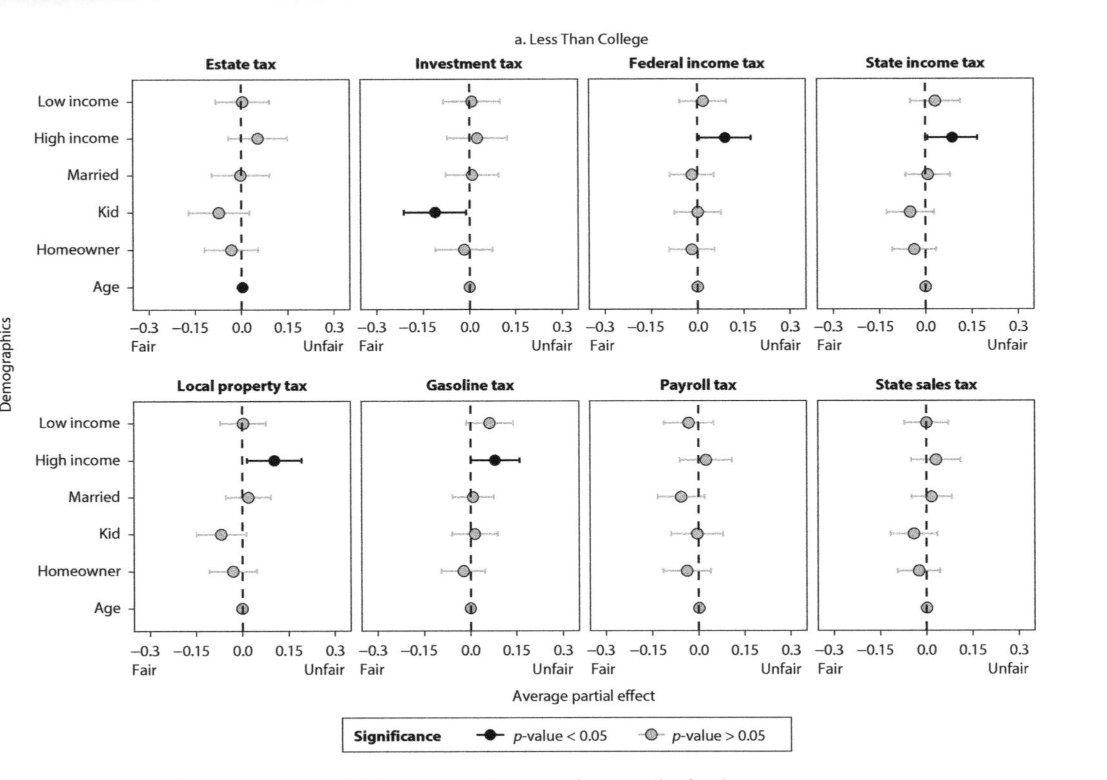

FIGURE 4.8 Tax Unfairness and Self-Interest Measures by Level of Education
Note: "Amount I pay is very unfair" is coded high. Full sample, divided into groups by level of education. Ordinary least squares model. Includes controls for income, education, gender, age, race/ethnicity, marital status, child, homeowner, partisanship, ideology, and government trust. Low and high income are approximately the bottom and top 20 percent of income, respectively; reference category is the middle 60 percent.
Source: 2016 CCES.

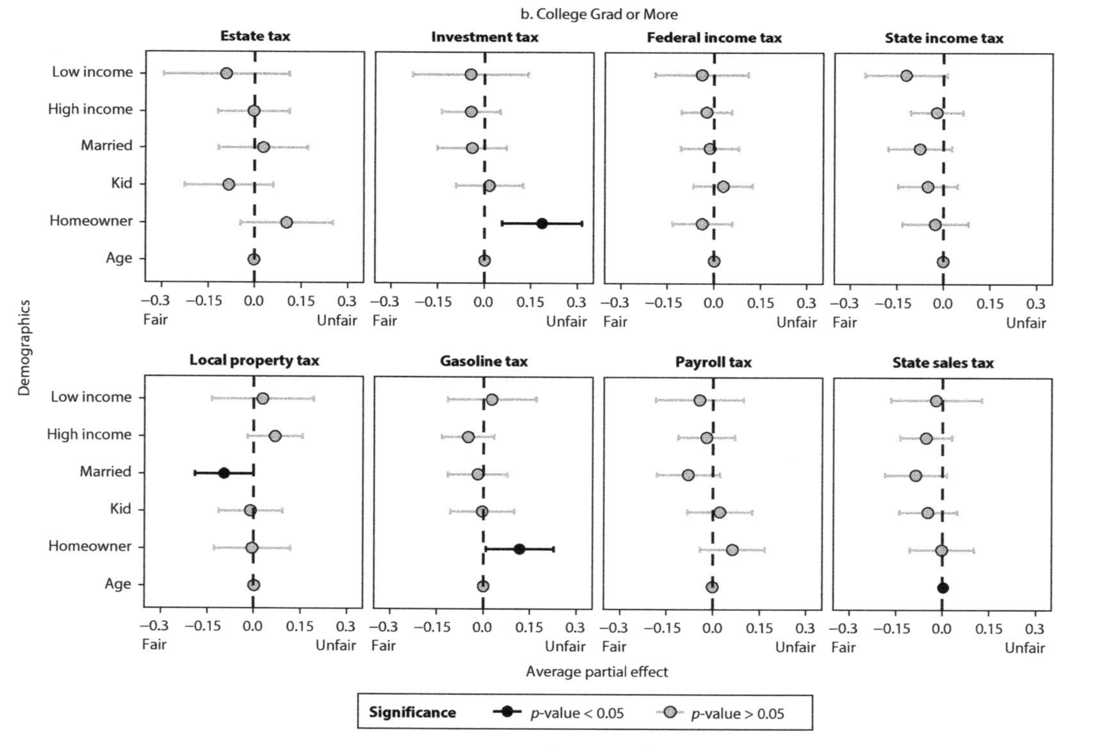

FIGURE 4.8 (*continued*)

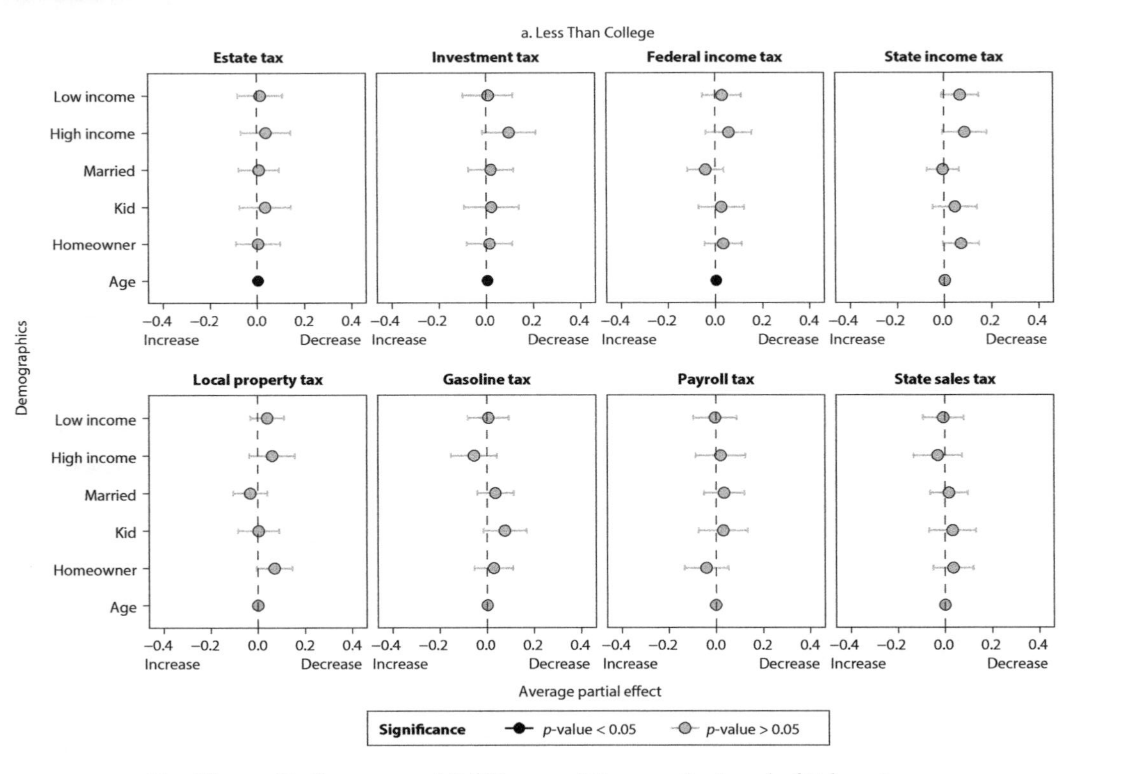

FIGURE 4.9 Tax Change Preferences and Self-Interest Measures by Level of Education
Note: "Tax should be decreased" is coded high. Full sample, divided into groups by level of education. Ordinary least squares model. Includes controls for income, education, gender, age, race/ethnicity, marital status, child, homeowner, partisanship, ideology, and government trust. Low and high income are approximately the bottom and top 20 percent of income, respectively; reference category is the middle 60 percent.
Source: 2016 CCES.

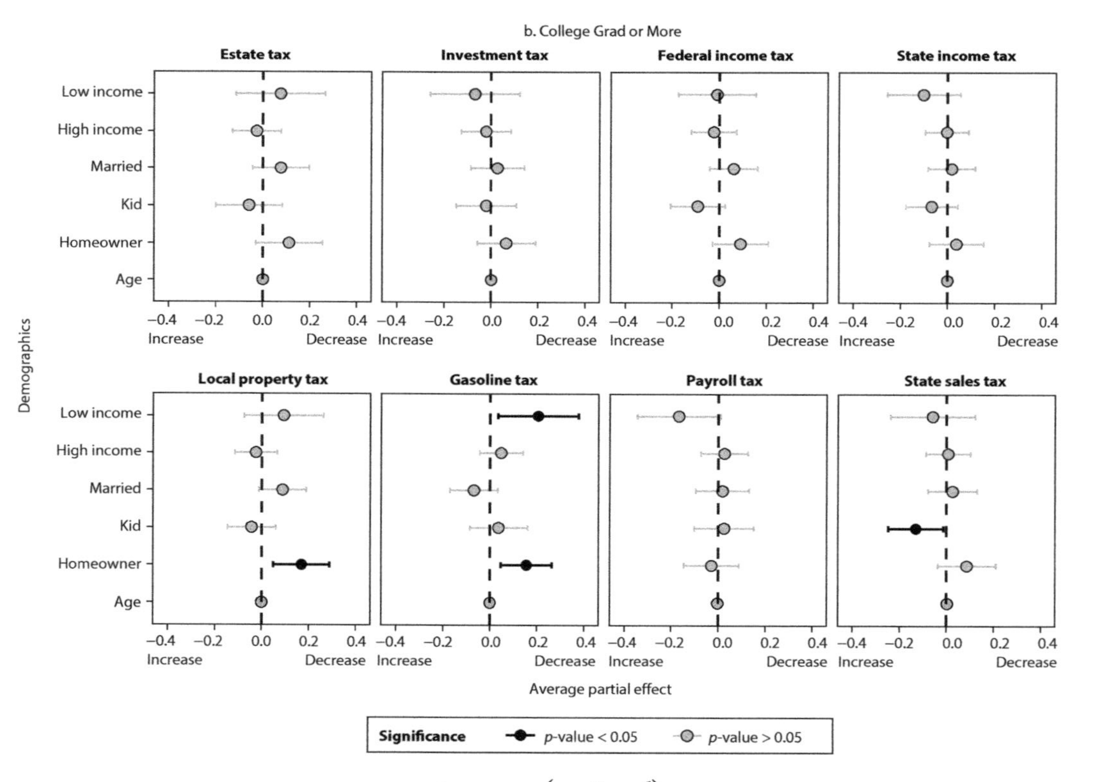

FIGURE 4.9 (*continued*)

more likely than middle-income people to say the gas tax should be decreased (figure 4.9b). These are all self-interested stands, but they are fairly infrequent. It's not as if self-interest is suddenly highly correlated with tax attitudes among the more knowledgeable. And in some cases, correlations were stronger among those without a college degree, where high-income respondents were more likely than middle-income people to say federal and state income, property, and gas taxes are unfair (figure 4.8a).

Nor do that many correlations appear when using the general tax knowledge index to divide respondents into high- and low-knowledge groups (not shown). In a few instances, those with higher knowledge levels display more self-interested attitudes, such as high-knowledge homeowners who want the property or gas taxes decreased. Interestingly, in the few instances where self-interest indicators are correlated with tax attitudes, it's around property and gas taxes, and rarely the federal income tax. In sum, tax attitudes are not necessarily more congruent with self-interest among the politically sophisticated. Self-interest instead remains a relatively rare correlate of tax attitudes, despite the seeming relevance of cost calculations for tax attitudes.

The Dearth of Self-Interested Attitudes across Individuals

Ordinary, nonrich people have abstract preferences that are congruent with their material self-interest: not being rich themselves, they think the rich and corporations should pay more, and support progressive taxation as a concept. But when it comes to their specific attitudes, we find great dislike of taxes that fall on them rather lightly, if at all (income and estate), and a relative embrace of taxes that are quite costly (payroll and sales). Attitudes do not correspond with costs across many types of individuals. There are a few exceptions where perhaps the costs are more salient or the indicators of self-interest more precise, but mostly the self-interest hypothesis fails, despite the fact that it is the cornerstone of many political economy models.

The ability of the nonrich to connect their material stakes to their attitudes is undermined by low levels of knowledge. Even among relatively more knowledgeable people—those who are college educated or score higher on tax knowledge—significant correlations between the markers of self-interest and tax attitudes are not particularly common.

The case of regressive taxes is especially interesting. Given how costly they are for many households—in the middle-income quintile, the sales tax costs twice as much as a share of income as the federal income tax, and even more in the bottom two quintiles—it is remarkable how few people say they are unfair and should be decreased. As I speculated in the discussion about tax designs in chapter 3, one reason may be that the cost is hidden because the tax is imposed just a bit at a time, the annual total is never known, and many feel they can control their spending and therefore how much tax they pay. The findings in this chapter suggest another reason: low knowledge. Relatively few people correctly categorize sales taxes as regressive, viewing them as proportional instead, which may make them seem less costly. Moreover, understanding around regressive taxation is clearly less than around progressive taxation, as people are better able to connect their abstract preferences to progressive taxes, but less able to do so with regard to regressive taxes, especially the sales and payroll taxes.

One concern is that some groups have less tax knowledge than others: women, younger respondents, and Black and Hispanic respondents. Privileged groups know more: male, higher income, and white. These knowledge differentials may render more vulnerable taxpayers susceptible to manipulation by political and economic elites eager to secure tax policies in their own interests, not in the interests of these less privileged groups. Everyone has a stake in tax policy, but if one cannot translate one's stake into policy positions, one is going to have little voice and may be subjected to policies not in one's economic interest.

Finally, the lack of a correspondence between the cost of many taxes and taxpayer attitudes is a great boon to the rich. The nonrich dislike the same taxes the rich do. All, regardless of income, are focused on the federal income, property, and estate taxes. The nonrich do not think the rich pay enough, but then hold tax attitudes that facilitate tax reductions for the rich.[21] Self-interest may have appeared in some specific cases to be associated with tax attitudes, both in previous work and here, but its influence is not apparent across the board. The next chapter examines another possible correlate of tax attitudes: party identification and ideology.

5

Partisan Identification and Ideology

CHAPTERS 3 AND 4 revealed that individuals' attitudes toward taxes often do not vary with their apparent material stakes. This chapter turns to the leading alternative to self-interest in public opinion: symbolic attachments. If self-interest is rarely a factor in individuals' tax attitudes, surely party identification and ideology are. They are among the strongest influences on political attitudes, especially in the current era of pronounced partisan polarization. Political scientist Richard Johnston (2006, 347) called party identification "probably the most highly leveraged measure in all of political science."

This chapter shows, however, that tax attitudes do not always vary with party identification and ideology. These factors are not always a significant factor in the tax context—a truly unusual finding. Frequently Republicans and conservatives hold more antitax attitudes than Democrats and liberals, but sometimes they do not, both at the descriptive level—what partisans think—and in multivariate analyses controlling for differences in demographic characteristics, when ordinarily the influence of party and ideology persists. Republicans and Democrats do not differ in their ranking of various taxes as "the worst" or "most disliked." They also do not differ in their evaluations of the fairness of regressive taxes such as the payroll tax for Social Security and sales taxes (and Republicans are not more likely to say the gas tax is unfair, although they are more likely than Democrats to want it decreased).

Republicans mainly differ from Democrats in their attitudes toward the progressive federal income, estate, and capital gains taxes. That these are precisely the taxes that have been the focus of Republican tax cutting at the national level suggests that partisans may differ more in tax attitudes when some type of political cue is available. Subsequent findings show that Republican responses are more distinct when "Bush" or "Trump" are mentioned in the question wording. Over time, Republicans are not consistently more likely than Democrats to say that their federal income taxes are too high; they say so chiefly when a Democrat occupies the White House. At the same time, tax attitudes rarely vary by ideology. That partisanship has a stronger relationship with tax attitudes than does ideology, all things being equal, suggests that individuals need partisan cues to figure out their tax attitudes, even though taxes get at the heart of the size of government, on which ideological stances are supposed to turn.

The muted differences among partisans have significant political effects. If Republicans and Democrats differed in their tax preferences, then the Republican Party would gain few votes from outpartisans with an antitax stance. But if antitax sentiment is present among identifiers of both parties (and quite evident among independents, as we will see), then there is much for Republican politicians to gain from pledging to reduce taxes.

Party and Ideology in Public Opinion

Existing work in political science suggests that party identification and ideology would strongly influence tax attitudes, for reasons arising from both politics and the nature of public opinion.

Politically, taxes are at the core of political elites' partisan and ideological disagreements about the size and role of government. These partisan differences have not always been as strong. For much of the twentieth century, tax policymaking was a nonpolitical, technocratic exercise.[1] In the immediate postwar era, Republicans extolled small government but also fiscal responsibility; Eisenhower declined to cut taxes during the 1950s in order to maintain a balanced budget.[2] It was Democrat John F. Kennedy who oversaw the first major postwar tax cut, in 1962. In the contemporary era, actual practices may not seem so distinctive either, since federal spending is high under both parties, and both champion low taxes for most taxpayers—with Democratic politicians differing mainly in wishing to raise taxes exclusively on the rich.

Rhetorically, though, the United States still has one small government party, and one party more supportive of government spending and redistribution. Among politicians and policymakers, taxes are a heavily partisan issue—one that looms large in the contrasts they try to draw with the opposite party. Reagan made tax cuts a centerpiece of the Republican agenda and important party-building tool.[3] Even though the party has since strayed from Reagan policy in other arenas, especially foreign policy, low taxes remain Republican orthodoxy.

Tax policy at the federal level since the 1980s has toggled between cuts under Republican presidents and partial restorations of progressivity at the top of the income spectrum under Democratic presidents, as chapter 2 showed.

Among the public, the Republican Party firmly "owns" the tax issue. Republicans are perceived as better at handling taxes (and many other economic issues), while Democrats are viewed as better able to handle social welfare issues, whether such "issue ownership" is measured with closed-ended survey items or open-ended questions on the likes and dislikes associated with each party.[4] The strong differences in the images of the parties with regard to tax policy suggest that partisanship and tax attitudes should be correlated among the public.

Another reason to predict that tax attitudes might differ significantly by partisanship and ideology is that spending attitudes do. Conservative and Republican members of the public are less supportive of government spending, especially on redistributive programs, than their liberal or Democratic counterparts (Rudolph and Evans 2005). Since taxes fuel spending, we might expect tax attitudes to have the same structure.

Beyond these political reasons predicting a strong relationship among partisanship, ideology, and tax attitudes is the nature of public opinion itself. A robust literature argues that "symbolic" political attachments such as party identification, ideology, and racial resentment have strong influences on individuals' attitudes due to their deep origins, easily understood connections to political objects, and low cognitive demands. As the previous two chapters described, basing attitudes on self-interest is cognitively difficult, requiring individuals to calculate how a policy would affect their material well-being—a complex operation often undercut by ignorance of and inattention to political matters.[5] In contrast, symbolic attachments are more accessible and easier to connect to politics. These "general predispositions" or "stable affective preferences" emerge early in life. Most people have meaningful party attachments, regardless of their level of political sophistication, and frequently use these attachments to make sense of the political world (Erikson and Tedin 2019). Party identification acts as a "perceptual screen" through which individuals view issues (Campbell et al. 1960). Scholars contend that it even rises to the level of a social identity that shapes issue attitudes (Green, Palmquist, and Schickler 2002). Head-to-head comparisons of party identification and self-interest find that partisan attachment is a much stronger correlate of attitudes—one that may even prevent people from making rational, stakes-oriented judgments, including on economic and estate tax policies, when self-interest and partisanship may not line up (Achen and Bartels 2016).

Partisanship is a powerful enough influence that it can displace factual information. For example, when their copartisan occupies the White House, individuals are more likely to say that the economy is performing well, and give more favorable answers to questions about inflation and unemployment rates.[6] In some of these responses, partisanship may be substituting for factual information. But there is partisan cheerleading too, as when high-information partisans give different answers to factual questions when their copartisan is in the White House, not out of ignorance, but out of a desire to profess "what they should *want* to be true" (Achen and Bartels 2016, 18).[7] Evidence suggests that increased polarization among political elites (that is, greater ideological distance between the politicians and activists of each party along with greater ideological homogeneity within each party) increases the effect of partisanship on public opinion and decreases the effect of substantive information (Druckman, Peterson, and Slothuus 2013).

I will examine the role of another symbolic attachment, racial resentment among white individuals, in the next chapter. Here I will concentrate on political ideology and especially partisan identification. Taxes concern the size and role of government, about which the political parties differ at least rhetorically. The symbolic attachments of partisanship and ideology operate automatically as well as quickly, and provide accessible, politically predigested superstructures from which particular issue attitudes derive (Sears et al. 1980, 671). For all of these reasons, we might expect party identification and ideology to play a large role in structuring tax attitudes.

Party, Ideology, and Tax Attitudes

Although existing work might predict large attitudinal differences across partisan and ideological groups, the findings with regard to tax attitudes are mixed and contingent. Compared to the previous chapter's examination of self-interest and tax attitudes, which did not produce consistently distinctive attitudes about taxes based on apparent material stakes, attitudes differ more commonly by party and ideology. Yet the results are often modest and situational rather than large and consistent, as is usually the case with symbolic predispositions. Partisan and ideological differences are muted in the relative rankings of taxes—everyone ranks the same taxes as the worst—but emerge when survey respondents are asked to evaluate taxes separately. No doubt these descriptive differences matter for politics—Republicans and Democrats, conservatives and liberals, really do have different feelings about taxes—but when we ask the social scientific question of whether these elements are still correlated with tax attitudes independent of other factors, their influence largely disappears for regressive taxes. All things being equal, Republicans and Democrats do not differ in their views on the fairness of regressive taxes along with the degree to which they want them decreased (although Republicans are not too keen on the gas tax). Partisan differences reappear when it comes to progressive income, estate, and capital gains taxes; Republicans are more likely to deem such taxes unfair and seek their reduction.[8]

Relative Ranking of Taxes: Muted Differences

Sometimes the tax attitudes of Democrats and Republicans, liberals and conservatives, are not all that different from each other. Surveys spanning nearly four decades find that individuals of differing partisan attachments and ideological commitments tend to rank the same taxes as "the worst" or "most disliked." Ire is directed the most at the federal income and property taxes—and by similar percentages.

In the pooled 1983–1993 ACIR data, nearly 40 percent of Democrats, independents, and Republicans alike deemed the federal income tax the worst, and around 30 percent said the property tax was the worst.[9] Just over 10 percent of each group said the state income tax was the worst, with around 20 percent deeming sales taxes the worst. In the 2003 NPR Taxes Study a decade later, partisans similarly differed little in answer to a question asking them which taxes they most dislike to pay, with slightly larger differences between Democrats and Republicans on the sales tax (with the former 6 percentage points more likely to say they most dislike it). When the CCES repeated the most disliked item in 2019, the results once again were muted across partisan groups. Partisans (and ideologues, not shown) rank taxes similarly—and have done so for four decades. From both ends of the political spectrum, disapproval is directed the most at federal income and property taxes.

Separate Evaluations: Partisan Differences Emerge

Although we might anticipate partisan differences in tax opinions, Democrats and Republicans both have a dim view of the federal income or property tax compared to other taxes. The similarities between political groups, however, may be due to the question wording in the above surveys; asking respondents to choose one tax as the worst or rank them by level of dislike may constrain

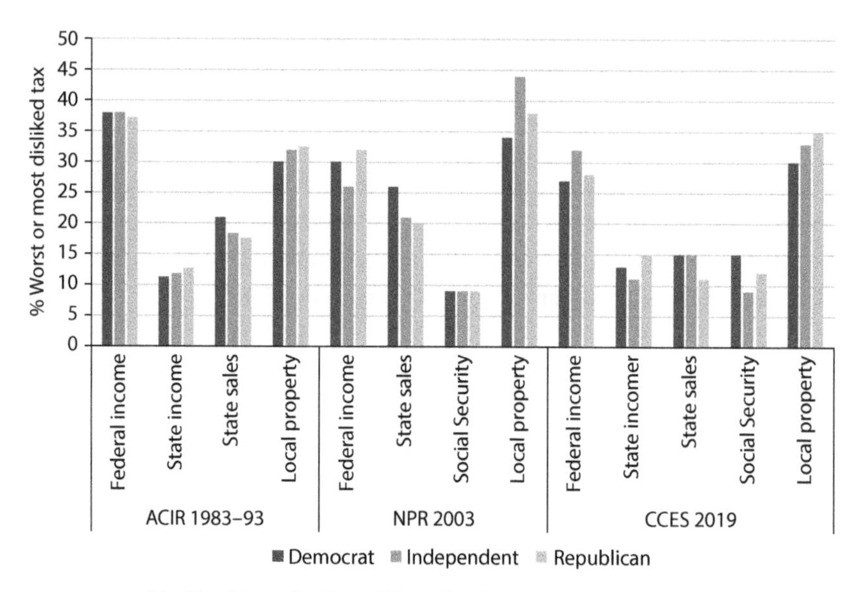

FIGURE 5.1 Tax Rankings by Party Identification
Note: ACIR: "Which is the worst tax—that's the least fair?" NPR and CCES: rank in order of "dislike the most." For complete question wording, see the appendix. The ACIR data are pooled, 1983–93, and the independent category includes partisan leaners.
Sources: ACIR in UNT Digital Library, n.d.; 2003 NPR Tax Study; 2019 CCES.

responses. To get at the possibility that respondents of different political orientations may have different absolute feelings about taxes, 2016 CCES items asked respondents to evaluate taxes separately: How fair is what you pay for each tax, and should each tax be increased, decreased, or kept the same? In 2019, I also asked, How fair is each tax generally speaking? (not shown; similar answers to fairness of what respondents pay). Figures 5.2a–b show that partisans differ more when evaluating taxes separately than when ranking them as the worst (figure 5.1). For example, although almost identical shares of Democrats and Republicans ranked the federal income tax as the worst or most disliked, Republicans are 25 percent more likely than Democrats to say the federal income tax is unfair, and 30 percent more likely to want it decreased. Differences between conservatives and liberals are also larger for these evaluations compared to the ranking results (not shown).

When each tax is evaluated separately, the more pronounced antitax stance of Republicans is noticeable. Among Republicans, unfair evaluations outnum-

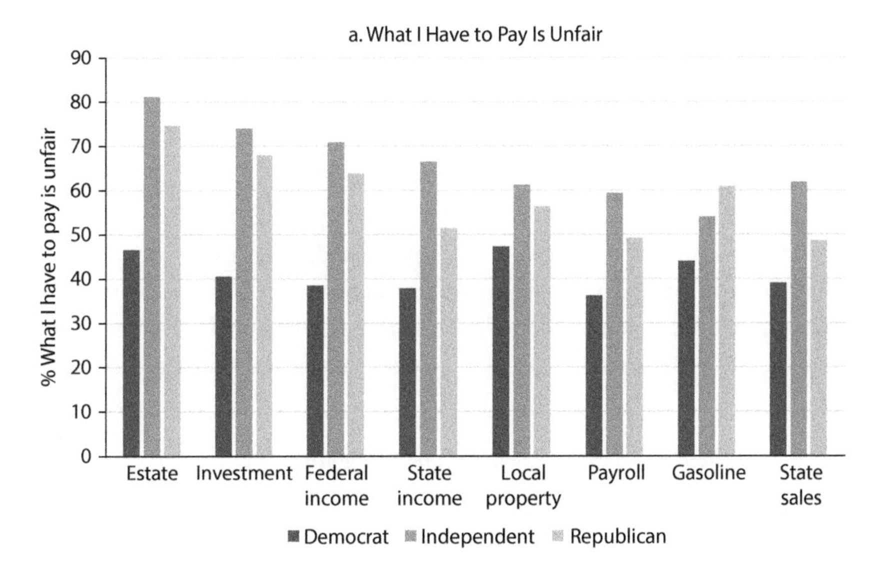

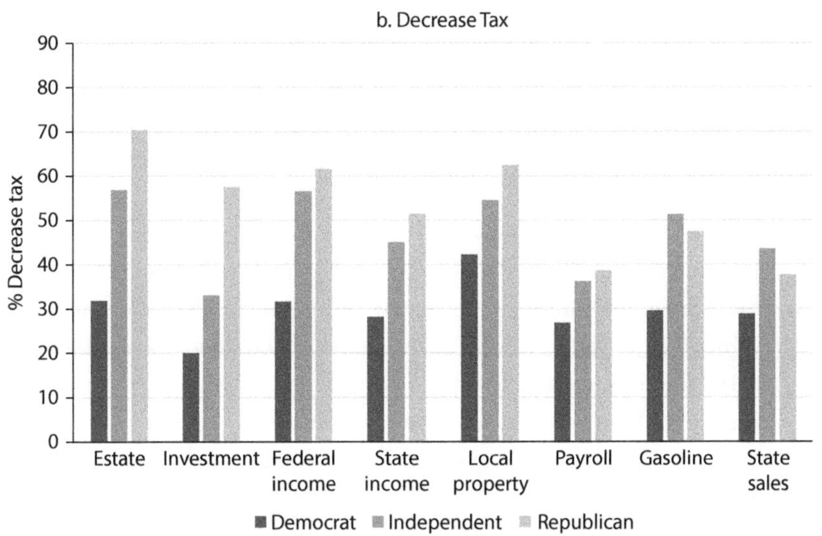

FIGURE 5.2 Tax Evaluations by Party Identification
Note: The top panel shows the percentage of respondents saying what they have to pay for each tax is unfair (rather than fair) among those giving a response. The bottom panel shows the percentage of respondents saying each tax should be decreased (rather than increased or kept the same) among those giving a response. The taxes are arrayed from progressive to regressive (see chapter 3).
Source: 2016 CCES.

ber fair ones for six of the eight taxes included in the CCES; among Democrats, fair responses outnumber unfair responses in all eight instances. Partisans are the most distinct regarding progressive taxes; the difference in the share of Republicans and Democrats saying each tax is unfair or should be decreased is the largest for the estate, investment, and federal income taxes. Conversely, partisan differences are smaller for the regressive payroll and sales taxes.

In their absolute evaluations of taxes, partisan differences are pronounced. That said, the three taxes that Democrats most want to decrease—property, estate, and federal income—are the same three that Republicans most want to decrease. Democrats are just 30 to 40 percent less likely to want to do so.

The Role of Partisanship Controlling for Other Factors

Republicans differ from Democrats when evaluating taxes separately. But Republicans also differ demographically from Democrats: they have higher incomes on average, are older, and are more likely to be male, white, and less trusting of government. Are Republicans still distinctive in their tax attitudes controlling for these demographic and political differences? Previous research has shown that across many issue areas, partisan differences are so strong that they appear even in multivariate analyses. The question here is whether that is true for tax attitudes as well.

Figure 5.3 shows the average partial effect for party identification and ideology in evaluations of the fairness of what respondents pay for each tax in the 2016 CCES, controlling for a variety of demographic characteristics and government trust. The outcomes range from very fair to very unfair (coded high). The findings indicate that partisan differences are more pronounced for progressive than for regressive taxes, all things being equal. Compared to Democrats, Republicans and independents are more likely to say what they pay for three of the four progressive taxes is unfair (federal income, estate, and capital gains taxes; the coefficients for state income tax do not achieve statistical significance). By contrast, partisan differences are not statistically significant when it comes to regressive taxes, with the exception that independents are distinctive in saying the payroll tax is unfair.

Unfairness evaluations differ even less across ideological groups. Conservatives are more likely than liberals, the reference category, to say gas and property taxes are unfair; otherwise ideological groups do not differ from each other on their fairness evaluations, all things being equal. Among whites only (not shown), ideology is not statistically significant at all.

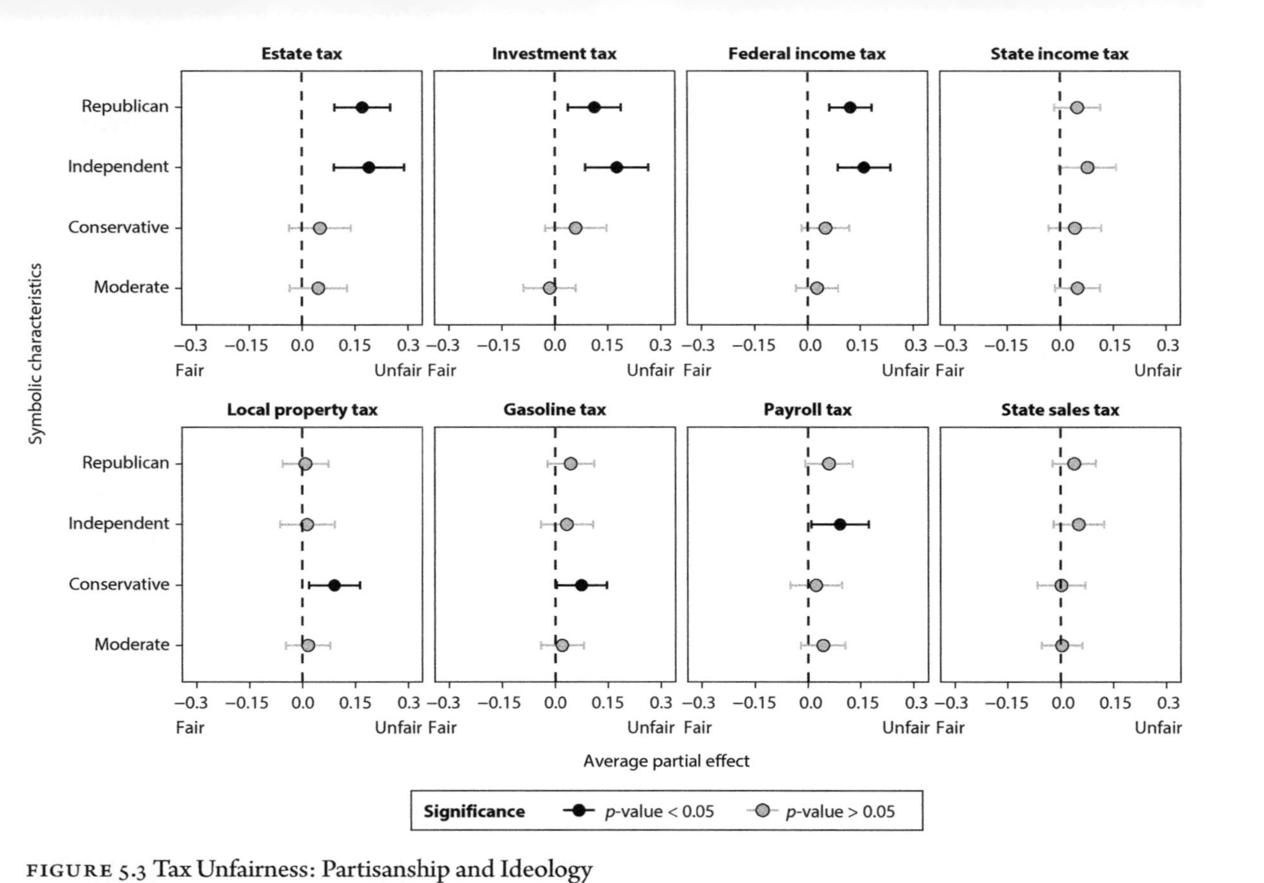

FIGURE 5.3 Tax Unfairness: Partisanship and Ideology
Note: "Amount I pay is very unfair" is coded high. Full sample. Ordinary least squares model. Includes controls for income, education, gender, age, race/ethnicity, marital status, children, homeowner, and government trust. Reference category for partisanship is Democrat; for ideology, it is liberal.
Source: 2016 CCES.

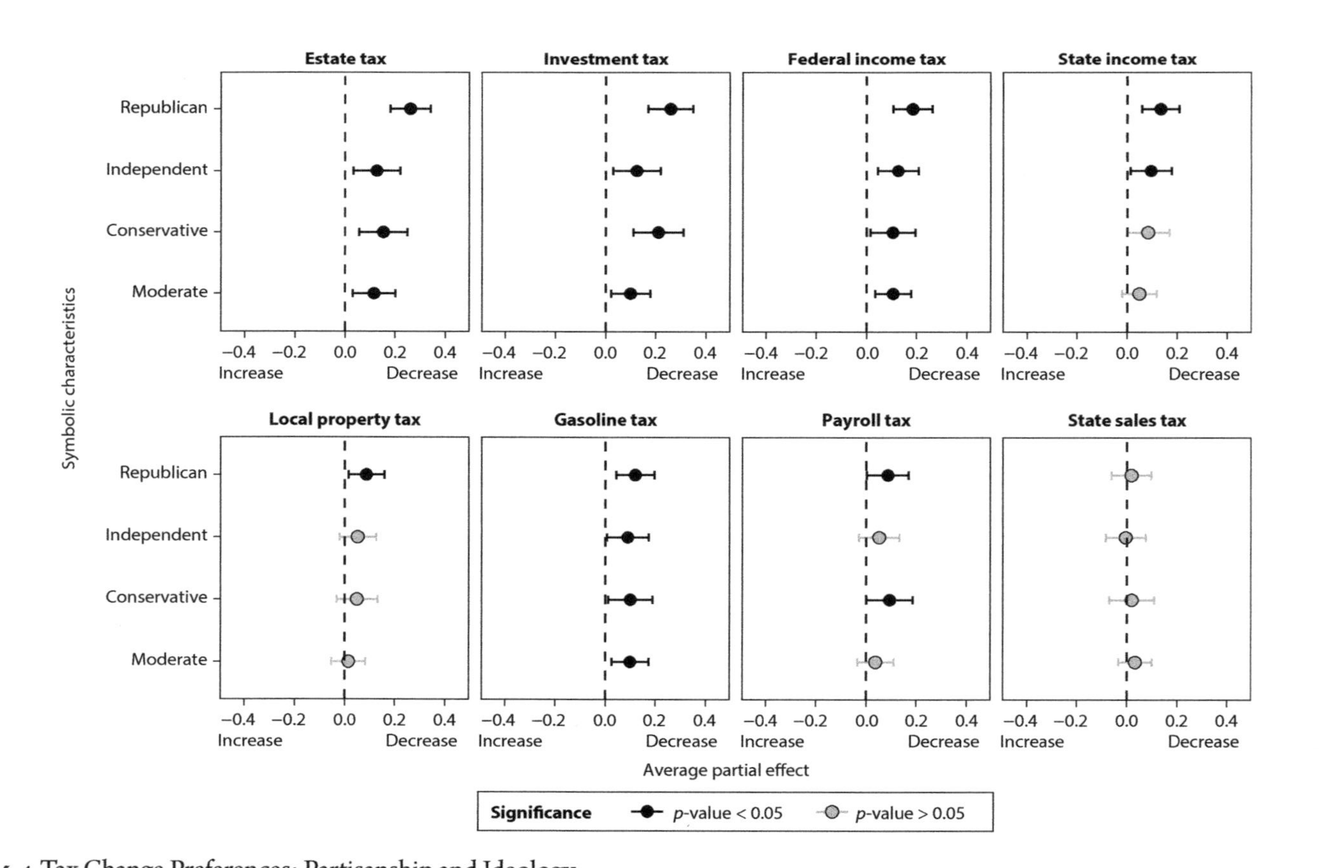

FIGURE 5.4 Tax Change Preferences: Partisanship and Ideology
Note: "Decrease tax" is coded high. Full sample. Ordinary least squares model. Includes controls for income, education, gender, age, race/ethnicity, marital status, children, homeowner, and government trust. Reference category for partisanship is Democrat; for ideology, it is liberal.
Source: 2016 CCES.

When the question shifts from the fairness of taxes to whether they should be increased, kept the same, or decreased, the Republican antitax stance is more pronounced. In figure 5.4, the preference for decreasing each tax is coded high. Compared to Democrats, Republicans are more likely to want all the taxes decreased except the sales tax; independents are more likely to want all the progressive taxes plus the gas tax to be decreased. Compared to liberals, conservatives and moderates say three of the four progressive taxes should be decreased, as should the gas tax, and among conservatives, also the payroll tax.

Republicans and Democrats differ in their tax attitudes, descriptively as well as when demographic factors and government trust are taken into account. The differences are nonetheless larger—and the absolute levels of dislike much higher—with regard to progressive taxation, especially the estate, investment, and income taxes, which burden high-income and high-wealth households the most. Republicans don't like most taxes, but are less eager to cut regressive taxes that are costlier to low- to mid-income households.

The Tax Attitudes of Low- and High-Income Partisans

Republicans differ from Democrats more regarding progressive taxes than regressive ones. This may make sense in that the focus of Republican elites since the Reagan era has been the reduction of progressive taxes, especially income, investment, and estate taxes. But is the association between partisanship, ideology, and tax attitudes found across the income spectrum? For higher-income Republicans, partisanship and income point in the same direction regarding progressive taxes: they should be more likely to say such taxes are unfair because both their political party has railed against them for decades and they would personally benefit from reductions in these taxes. In other words, they are not conflicted. Lower-income Republicans, however, are cross pressured: their partisanship would drive them to oppose progressive taxation, but their self-interest would be better served with increased progressive taxation. These contradictory pressures should manifest as a weak or nonexistent association between partisanship and tax attitudes.

If we divide the CCES sample in half by income, we find that Republican and conservative distinctiveness on progressive taxation is confined almost entirely to the upper half, as predicted. Figures 5.5a–b show the multivariate results for the unfairness of each tax where the sample has been divided in half by income ($55,000 is the dividing line in these data). Among lower-income respondents (figure 5.5a), Republicans and conservatives do not have different preferences compared to Democrats and liberals, with the one exception that

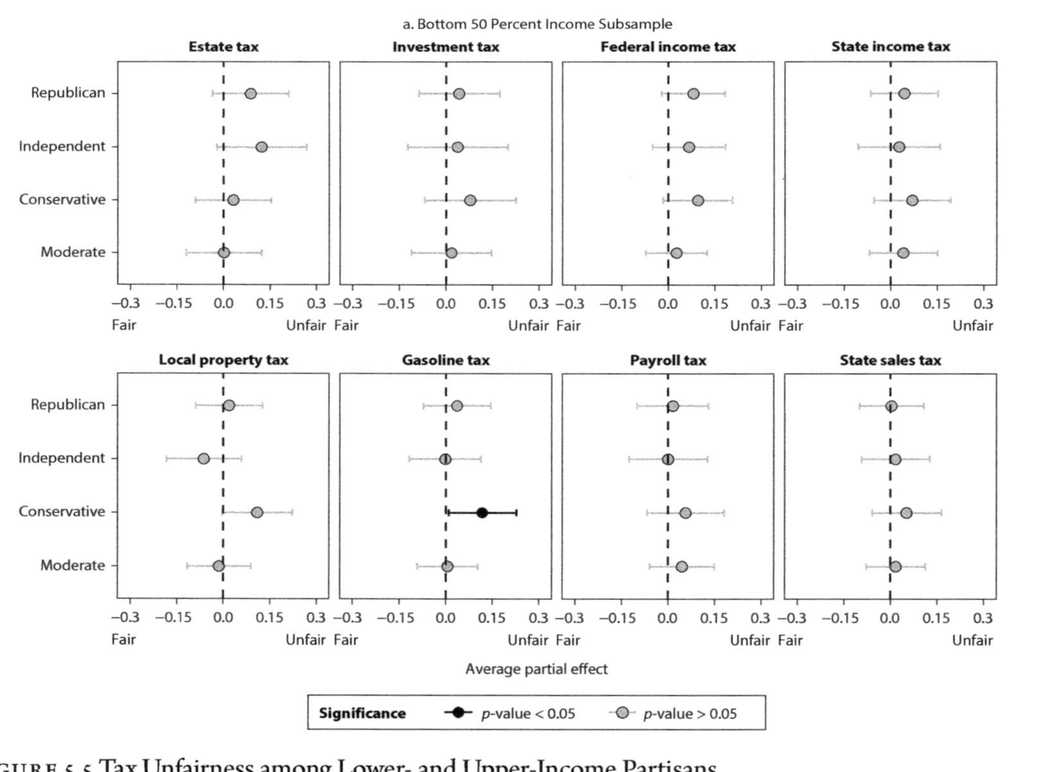

FIGURE 5.5 Tax Unfairness among Lower- and Upper-Income Partisans
Note: "Amount I pay is very unfair" is coded high. Full sample, divided in half by income at $55,000. Ordinary least squares model. Includes controls for income, education, gender, age, race/ethnicity, marital status, children, homeowner, and government trust. Reference category for partisanship is Democrat; for ideology, it is liberal.
Source: 2016 CCES.

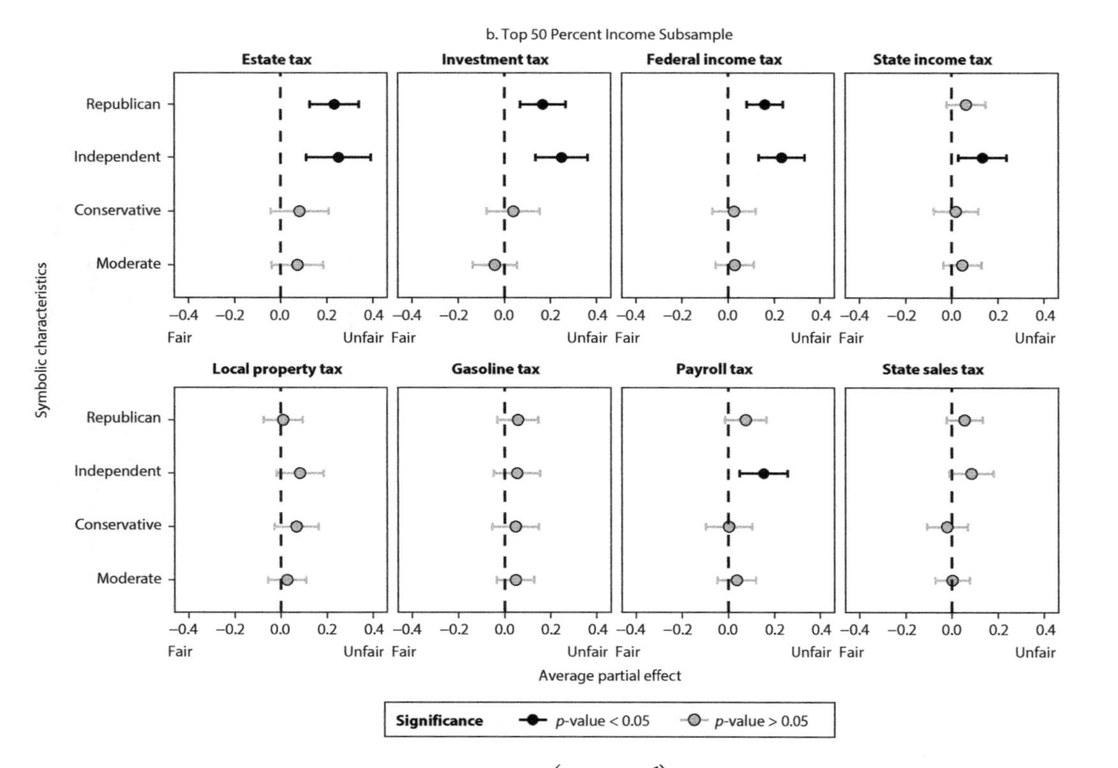

FIGURE 5.5 (*continued*)

conservatives are more likely to say the gas tax is unfair. Otherwise it is only upper-income Republicans and conservatives who are more likely than Democrats to say three of the progressive taxes are unfair (figure 5.5b).

Similarly, the desire to see progressive taxes decreased is more evident among higher-income Republicans and conservatives. In the bottom half of the income distribution, Republicans differ from Democrats in desiring decreases in the estate and property taxes, and conservatives differ from liberals in wanting the investment tax decreased (figure 5.6a). Otherwise, the Republican and conservative preference for decreased progressive taxation is limited to upper-income respondents (and the gas tax remains a target as well) (figure 5.6b).

Thus another way in which partisan differences in tax attitudes are contingent is by income: the expected attitudinal differences between party identifiers are most evident in the upper half of the income spectrum, where Republicans are more likely than Democrats to say progressive taxes are unfair and want them decreased. There are few partisan differences in the bottom half of the income spectrum, where Republicans face cross pressures between their partisan commitments and material interests. Those in the bottom half may also have difficulty connecting their partisanship to their tax attitudes due to lower information levels, since information and income are correlated. And even the distinctiveness of higher-income Republicans is confined to progressive taxes; except for the gas tax, which they dislike, they do not differ from Democrats in their preferences on regressive taxes. In sum, Republicans do not always differ from Democrats on their tax attitudes; these partisan groups have distinctive attitudes mostly around progressive taxes, not the regressive payroll and sales taxes, and only among the upper half of the income distribution.

The Tax Attitudes of Political Independents

The negative tax attitudes of political independents stand out to a striking degree—especially those of upper-income independents. Throughout this book, the results shown are for pure independents (leaners were coded with their party).[10] Majorities of pure independents say every tax is unfair—even more than do Republicans, except for the gas tax (figure 5.2a). Large shares want most taxes decreased, again more than Republicans in some cases (figure 5.2b). After accounting for demographic differences and government trust, independents remain more likely than the Democratic reference group to say the payroll tax and all the progressive taxes are unfair (with the bare exception of the state income tax; figure 5.3). Independents are also more likely to want

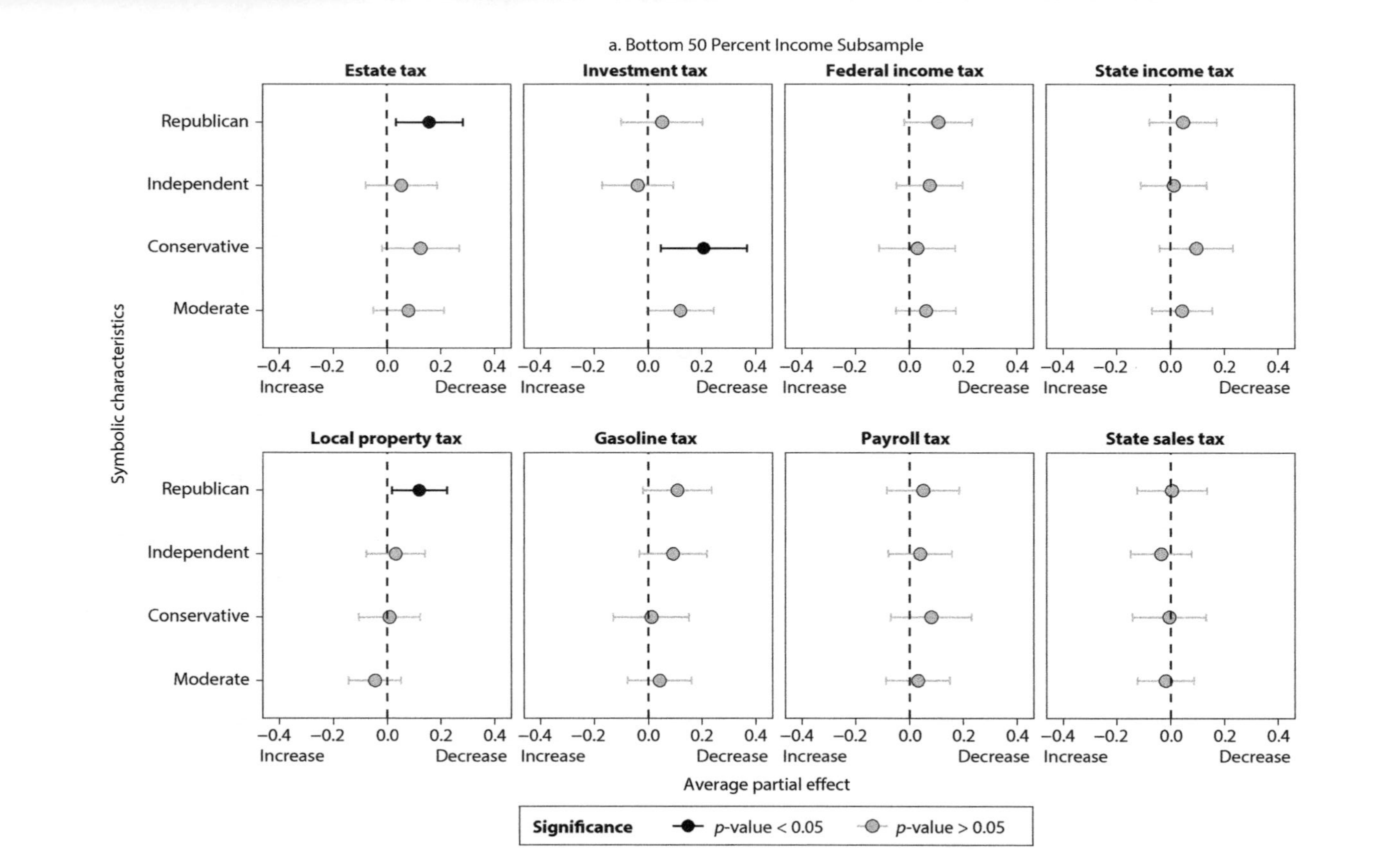

FIGURE 5.6 Tax Change Preferences among Lower- and Upper-Income Partisans

Note: "Decrease tax" is coded high. Full sample, divided in half by income at $55,000. Ordinary least squares model. Includes controls for income, education, gender, age, race/ethnicity, marital status, children, homeowner, and government trust. Reference category for partisanship is Democrat; for ideology, it is liberal.

Source: 2016 CCES.

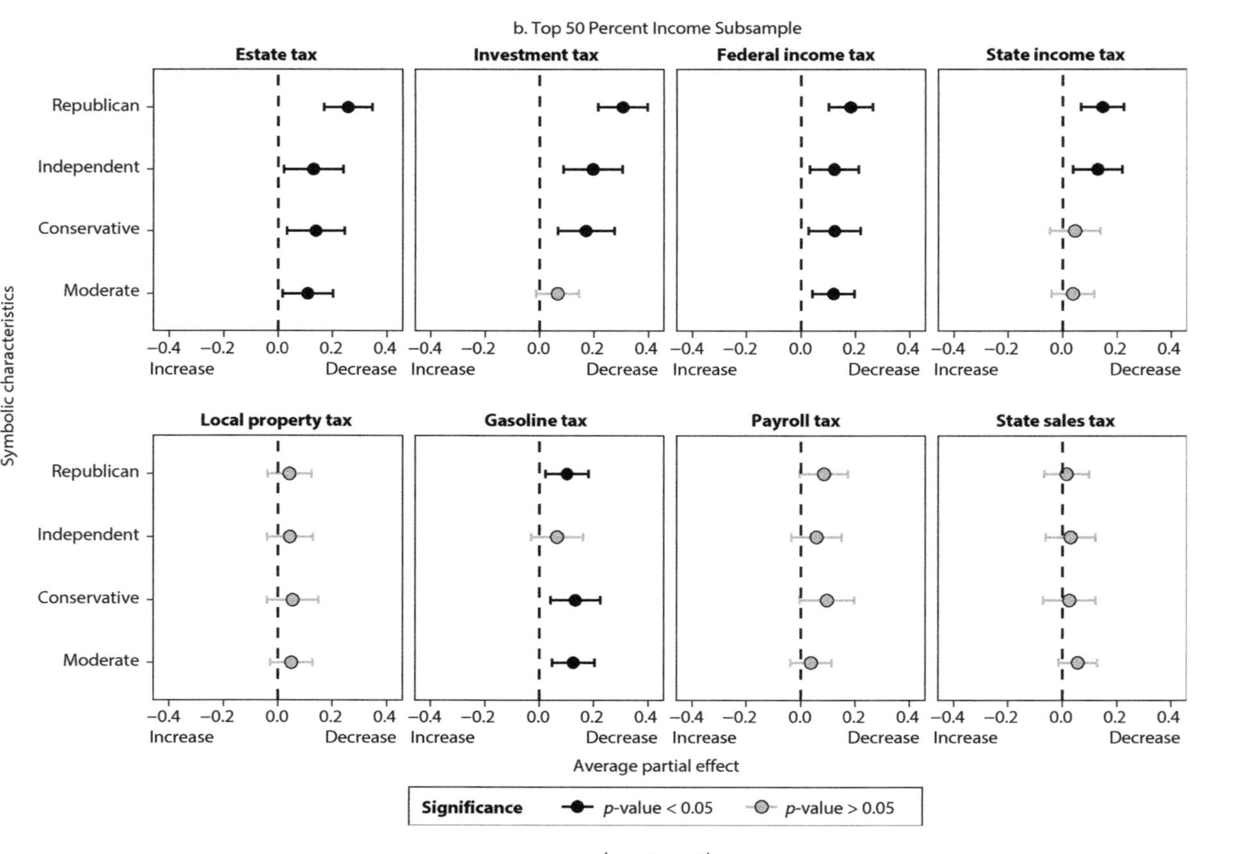

FIGURE 5.6 (*continued*)

all the progressive taxes plus the gas tax decreased (figure 5.4). As with Republicans, these differences are confined to upper-income respondents, as figures 5.5a–b and 5.6a–b show. In the lower half of the income spectrum, independents' unfairness and decrease attitudes are not distinctive. But upper-income independents resemble their Republican counterparts in their dislike of progressive taxes; they are more likely than Democrats to say every progressive tax is unfair and should be decreased.

Pure independents' tax attitudes—especially those of upper-income independents—stand out compared with their other political attitudes. In their update of *The Myth of the Independent Voter*, David Magleby, Candice Nelson, and Mark Westlye (2011, 252–53) argue that pure independents are quite moderate. On average, they place themselves in the middle of both the traditional seven-point ideology scale and a four-item index of economic policies the authors construct (slightly to the right of the middle, if one looks closely, but certainly not as far right as Republican leaners and partisans). John Petrocik (2009, 572) similarly finds that pure independents have policy preferences in the middle between the gradations of partisans and leaners. One hint that taxes might be different: a Pew analysis of 2018 data finds that pure independents are closer to Democrats on social and racial issues as well as immigration (same-sex marriage, marijuana legalization, the belief that more change is needed for equal chances for Black Americans, opposition to a border wall with Mexico, and the belief that immigrants strengthen the country), but closer to Republicans on sentiments toward government (smaller government providing fewer services, and government regulation does more harm than good) (Pew Research Center 2019).

Another hint that taxes might be different: tax knowledge. Magleby and coauthors argue that pure independents are more likely to choose middle responses on ideological and issue scales because they are less educated and less politically knowledgeable than partisans or leaners.[11] But pure independents are more knowledgeable about taxes—at least those who answer the tax knowledge questions in my CCES modules. Recall from chapter 4 that Republicans and Democrats do not differ on the two-item general knowledge index in the 2016 CCES, while Republicans are less knowledgeable than Democrats about the incidence of progressive and especially regressive taxes. Strikingly, independents score higher than partisans on the general knowledge index and are just as knowledgeable as Democrats on both tax incidence indexes.

Why might independents hold such negative attitudes toward taxes? One possibility is the role of government trust. Independents have long been established as having lower trust in government than partisans; perhaps their low levels of trust manifest strongly around one of government's most coercive functions, taxation (Wilkes 2015, 361). But that cannot be the whole answer, as the multivariate analyses presented here include government trust as a correlate, indicating that independents are more likely to say taxes are unfair or should be decreased above and beyond their levels of government trust.

A second possibility is raised by recent work in social psychology that shows that the political preferences of independents are based more in negativity than are those of partisans (Siev, Rovenpor, and Petty 2024). For example, independents' feeling thermometer scores in regard to candidates and parties are more negative toward the opposing side than positive toward the favored side relative to partisans. Independents are also more likely to vote against rather than for candidates. These pronounced negative relationships are found among both leaners and pure independents. Most relevant for tax attitudes, the researchers find that independents agree more with negatively framed political appeals, while partisans are more responsive to positively framed appeals. Perhaps independents express more negative attitudes toward taxes because they are drawn to the predominantly negative tone used in American discourse around taxes (Williamson 2017). Exploring why independents have such strongly negative views of taxes is an important area for future research.[12]

The skepticism of independents toward taxes is politically consequential. A fairly significant share of respondents are pure independents: 8 to 12 percent in recent ANES surveys, and 15 to 18 percent in the 2016 and 2019 CCES surveys (the partisanship questions are worded somewhat differently in the two sets of surveys and hence the differing shares). Even if their more antitax attitudes are more pronounced among upper-income independents, these attitudes constitute another advantage for the Republican Party. Descriptively, majorities of Republicans think most taxes are unfair and should be decreased; a fair number of Democrats agree. And the fact that pure independents are even more hostile to taxes than Republicans means the party has quite a few allies to call on in their perennial efforts to cut taxes, especially progressive ones.

The Role of Party Cues in Heightening Partisan Differences

Republicans are not always more likely than Democrats to say that taxes are unfair or should be decreased. Instead, the association between partisanship and tax attitudes is strongest for three progressive taxes (federal income, estate, and investment taxes), and sometimes the gas tax, and strongest among upper-income Republicans. That the partisanship–tax attitudes correlation is strongest for the taxes that have been the main targets of Republican tax-cutting efforts over the years suggests that particular elite cues and contexts may strengthen these relationships among nonrich taxpayers. The following analyses examine additional types of cues—from question wording to the political environment—to show other ways in which partisanship is a contingent rather than consistent correlate of tax attitudes.

A look at question wording shows that Republicans and Democrats are more distinctive in their tax attitudes when partisanship is cued. In the 2003 NPR Taxes Study, several questions about attitudes toward the current tax system do not contain an explicit partisan cue: Are federal income taxes too high? How fair is the federal tax system? How complex is the federal income tax? What is the worst tax? (For question wording, see the appendix). With just a few exceptions, these attitudes are not structured by partisanship or ideology; that is, Republicans and independents mostly do not have different opinions than Democrats on whether taxes are too high, fair, or complex, or what the worst tax is, and conservatives and moderates do not have different opinions than liberals (figure 5.7, left panel). The two exceptions are that Republicans are more likely than Democrats to say the federal income tax is too high and less likely to say it is unfair (perhaps because this question was asked in 2003, in the immediate aftermath of the Bush tax cuts, and when a Republican occupied the White House). Otherwise, partisanship and ideology do not shape these general attitudes toward the federal tax system.[13]

In contrast, Republicans and conservatives are consistently distinctive in their attitudes toward politically cued items (figure 5.7, right panel). The survey included questions about various aspects of the Bush tax cuts and other tax policies that were being discussed at the time in a highly politicized context: whether the Bush tax cuts should be sped up or made permanent; whether the estate or death taxes should be eliminated (half the sample was asked each version; the analysis here combines the responses, which were nearly identical); and whether the tax on dividends should be eliminated. Each of these proposals was strongly identified with the Bush administration, and the survey items about speeding up or making permanent the tax cuts invoked Bush's name. For all four of these politically cued items, Republicans and conservatives hold distinctive attitudes compared to Democrats and liberals. On speeding the Bush tax cuts along with eliminating the estate and dividend taxes, independents are distinctly supportive as well.

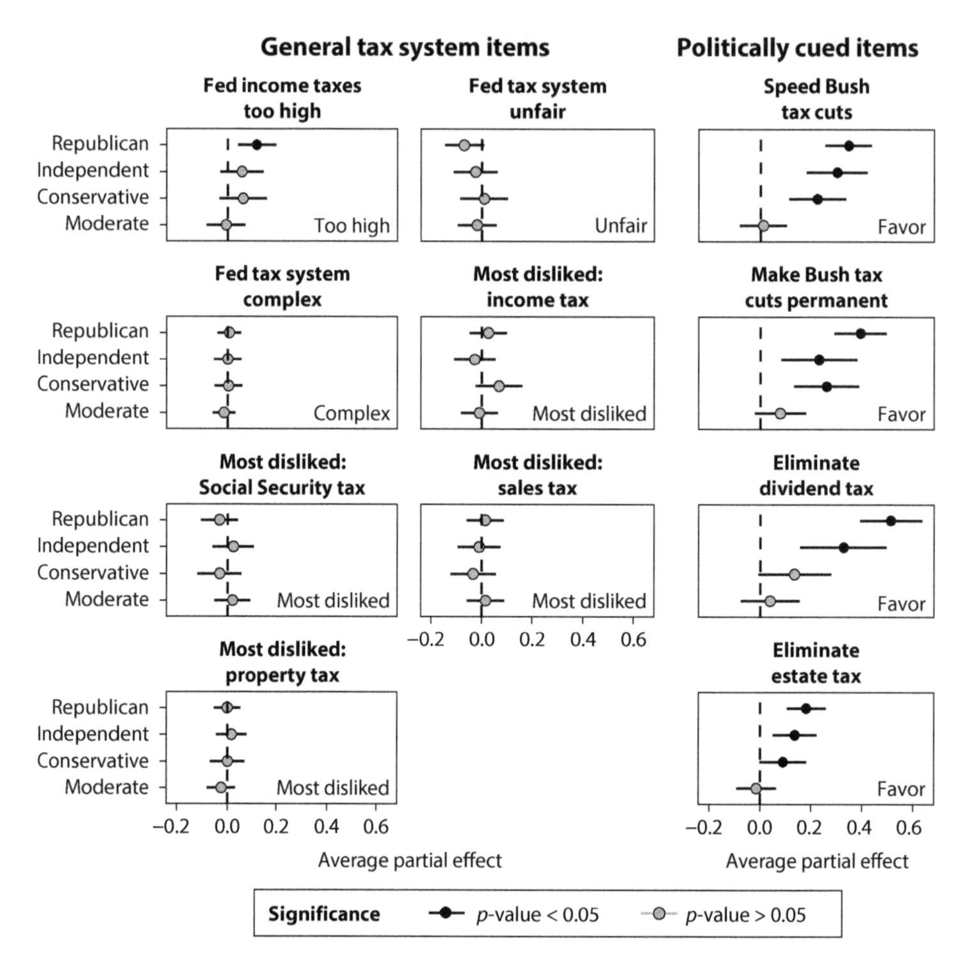

FIGURE 5.7 Partisanship and Ideology in General Tax Attitudes versus Politically Cued Items
Note: Full sample. Average partial effects are calculated from logit models. Includes controls for income, education, gender, age, race/ethnicity, marital status, children, homeowner, and government trust. Reference category for partisanship is Democrat; for ideology, it is liberal. In this survey, the independent category includes pure independents and leaners.
Source: 2003 NPR Taxes Study.

The influence of political cuing is also evidenced in an experiment embedded in the 2019 CCES. The survey asked respondents whether they approved of the 2017 TCJA and whether their taxes had gone down as a result. Half of the respondents were asked about the "new tax bill . . . which affected taxes beginning in 2018," and half were reminded that the bill was passed "by Congress and signed by President Trump." There are partisan and ideological differences in the results, but they are larger for the half of the respondents for whom Trump's name was mentioned in the question wording.[14] With no mention of Trump, 5 percent of Democrats, 22 percent of independents, and 39 percent of Republicans approved of the TCJA. But for the half of the sample for whom Trump was invoked, approval was the same among Democrats and independents, but jumped to 62 percent among Republicans, with similar results by ideology. Moreover, mention of Trump increased the share of Republicans and conservatives saying their taxes had gone down because of the law, by about 10 percentage points, while responses were mostly unmoved among the other partisan and ideological groups. Figure 5.8 shows the conditional average treatment effect of the Trump cue, which increased the TCJA approval among Republicans, but not independents or Democrats. There was no statistically significant effect of the Trump cue on perceptions that respondents' taxes had gone down because of the TCJA, suggesting that approving of the law had more to do with partisan cheerleading than tangible changes in respondents' taxes.[15]

Perhaps Republicans needed the Trump cue because of the TCJA's design. The Bush tax cuts of the early 2000s reduced taxes the most for the affluent, but did cut taxes for the nonrich, most visibly by sending rebate checks of $300 to $600 to those who had filed a tax return for 2000. In contrast, the TCJA contained few provisions for nonrich taxpayers. It was chiefly a tax cut for businesses, which may help explain why only 20 percent of the CCES respondents said their taxes went down because of the law.[16] The lack of visible relief for most nonaffluent taxpayers may also explain why it was remarkably unpopular. The website FiveThirtyEight compiled data showing that the TCJA was less favored on the eve of passage than the Reagan and Bush tax cuts of 1981, 1986, 2001, and 2003 had been, and even less popular than tax *increases* under George H. W. Bush in 1990 and Clinton in 1993 (Enten 2017). Political scientist Chris Warshaw compiled poll data showing that the TCJA was less popular than many pieces of major legislation from the previous three decades, including the TARP bank bailout during the 2008 financial crisis, Dodd-Frank financial reform bill, Clinton health care plan, and Affordable Care Act.[17] Given the low visibility and unpopularity of the TCJA, Republicans in the CCES apparently didn't "know" they were supposed to approve of the law without being reminded that Trump supported the bill.

A third source of cues that can increase the relationship between partisanship and tax attitudes arises not from question wording but instead from the

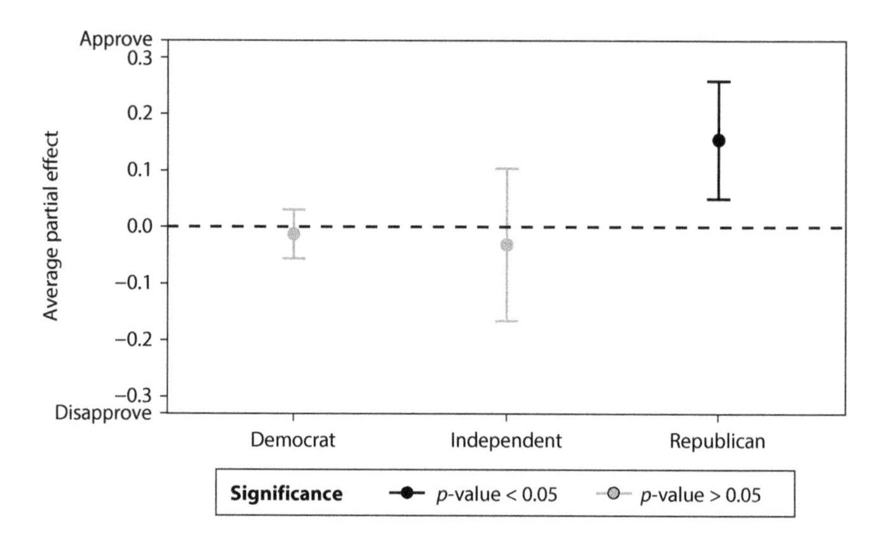

FIGURE 5.8 Trump Tax Cut Approval by Party, Cued versus Uncued
Note: Average treatment effect of receiving Trump cue among all respondents who gave an answer, linear model.
Source: 2019 CCES.

political environment itself. The Gallup and GSS item asking respondents whether the federal income taxes they have to pay this year are too high, too low, or about right allows an examination of partisans' attitudes over time. Figure 5.9 shows the average partial effect for Republicans compared to Democrats by presidential administration, with higher coefficients indicating a greater likelihood of saying one's federal income taxes are too high with controls for income and other demographic differences between the groups of identifiers. Democratic administrations are shaded.

We might expect Republicans, hailing from the small government party and more skeptical of the federal government, to be consistently more likely than Democrats to say their federal income taxes are too high. But that is not the case. Republicans mainly objected to the federal income tax during Democratic presidential administrations, including those of Harry Truman, Kennedy, Clinton, and Obama. Under GOP presidents Eisenhower, Gerald Ford, Reagan, the elder Bush, the younger Bush, and Trump, the difference between Republicans and Democrats is indistinguishable from zero, and Republicans were even less likely to say their taxes are too high under Nixon.

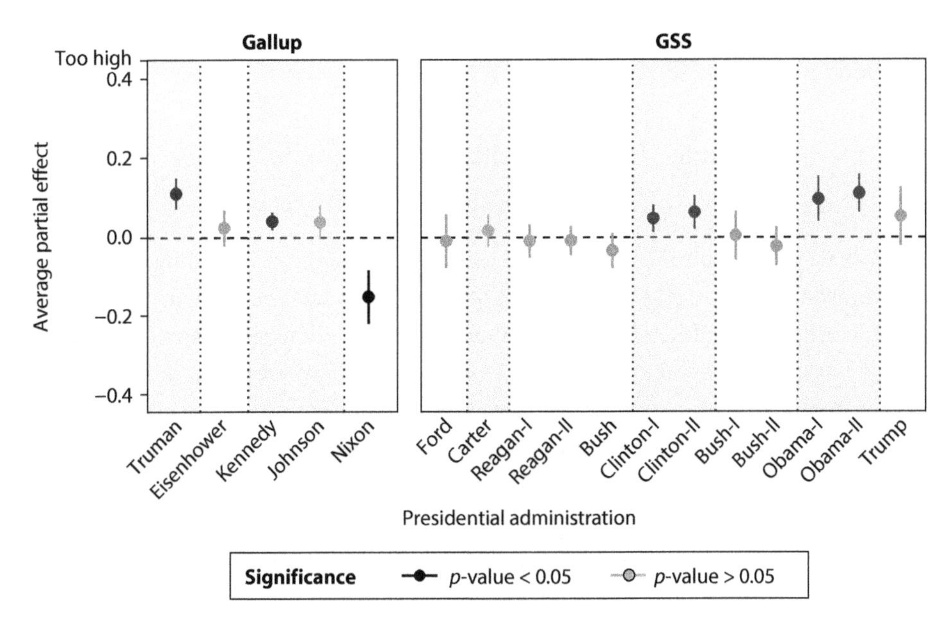

FIGURE 5.9 Federal Income Tax Too High by Party across Presidential Administrations

Note: "Federal income tax too high" is coded high. Full sample. Ordinary least squares model. Figure shows the average partial effect for Republicans compared to the reference category of Democrats. Democratic presidential administrations shaded. Gallup results on the left control for income, education, gender, age, race/ethnicity, and homeowner; GSS results on the right additionally control for marital status, children, "other" race group, and ideology. The results are largely the same when GSS covariates are limited to those available in Gallup. Government trust not included in these analyses. For the descriptive versions, see appendix figures A.4 and A.5.

Sources: Gallup 1947–73; GSS 1976–2018.

The descriptive data (see the appendix, figure A.5) reveal that most of the movement is among Republicans. Since the modern era of federal income tax cuts commenced during the Reagan administration, the percentage of Democrats saying their income taxes are too high has steadily slid, reflecting the actual decline in income taxes for most income levels (see figure 3.10). In contrast, the share of Republicans saying their income taxes are too high declines during Republican presidencies and rises during Democratic ones. These differences in the descriptive data may reflect underlying tax costs—Clinton and Obama especially did increase federal income taxes for high earners—but the multivariate analysis in figure 5.9 shows that Republicans during those presidencies say their income taxes are too high above and beyond such an income effect.

Lopsided Partisan Attitudes and the Challenges of Progressive Taxation

When public opinion scholars fail to find attitudes corresponding to self-interest, they typically turn to symbolic political attachments such as party identification and ideology. These attachments are strong correlates of other policy attitudes and behaviors such as vote choice. They would seem likely to be potent factors in tax attitudes as well, as taxes determine the size of government. Partisans would seemingly have strong views about who is compelled to support government spending through their tax dollars.

As with the findings regarding self-interest, however, party identification and ideology are not consistently correlated with tax attitudes. Republicans and Democrats alike think the federal income and property taxes are the worst, with state income, payroll, and sales taxes running far behind. But these survey items that ask respondents to compare taxes may compress responses. When asked to evaluate the fairness of various taxes separately, and say whether they want such taxes decreased, increased, or kept the same, larger differences between partisans emerge. That said, the differences are greater for progressive than regressive taxes, larger among higher-income respondents, and larger when survey items contain some political cue like a president's name or are asked during a particular presidential administration.

Once income and other differences between partisan groups are taken into account, Republicans and Democrats do not differ in evaluating how fair regressive taxes are or whether they should be decreased (except for the gas tax, which Republicans do distinctively want to see decreased). Where partisans differ is in their attitudes toward progressive taxes and tax policies that are clearly linked to Republican Party priorities and political figures. In line with the Republican agenda of lowering income, estate, and capital gains taxes, Republican identifiers are more likely than Democrats to say these taxes are unfair and that they should be decreased, both in the descriptive data and even after accounting for demographic differences as well as trust in government. Furthermore, Republicans were more likely to want the Bush tax cuts sped up or made permanent, and the estate and dividend taxes eliminated—taxes on wealth and unearned income that have been a particular target of their party's lawmakers.

Several implications of these findings are worth underscoring. The first is that attitudes do not always vary by party. Partisanship and ideology figure into tax attitudes more than do the self-interest considerations explored in the previous two chapters, but not as consistently as we might imagine given the usual strong effects of these factors on public attitudes and the centrality of the size of government to elites' partisan stances. Even though party and ideology are prominent explanations of the public's political attitudes and a "go-to" factor for public opinion analysts, their relationship to tax attitudes depends on both the particular attitude object and context. It appears that the complicated nature of American tax policy undercuts not just the influence of self-interest on tax attitudes but even that of party and ideology.

Second, there is far more partisan agreement on regressive than progressive taxes. Democrats' fairness perceptions do not vary all that much across the eight taxes included in the CCES surveys, but Republicans' views do differ, with the four progressive taxes much less popular than the four regressive ones. In multivariate analyses with controls for income, other demographic factors, and government trust, Democrats and Republicans do not differ in their attitudes toward the fairness of regressive taxes while Republicans are more likely to say the progressive taxes are unfair. Partisan differences are a little more pronounced when it comes to tax change preferences, with Republicans wanting all progressive taxes plus gas and property taxes decreased. Democrats and Republicans have similar attitudes on the regressive sales and payroll taxes. This suggests that it might be easier to increase revenues using regressive taxes, even though Americans have a commitment to progressive taxation in the abstract.

Third, even though Democrats and Republicans differ in some of their tax attitudes, especially support for progressive taxes, antitax sentiment cuts across partisan lines. Democrats are less likely than Republicans to say various taxes are unfair or want them decreased, but still represent a significant reservoir of tax hostility, with 30 to 40 percent of Democrats saying various taxes are unfair and 20 to 40 percent wanting different taxes decreased. Even more striking are the attitudes of independents, who, descriptively, are even more antitax than Republicans. These similarities across partisan groups are a boon to the Republican Party, which can win votes among Democrats and especially independents with antitax appeals. These data add to the findings of issue ownership scholars, who have also found taxes to be a particularly advantageous set of issues for Republicans. Democrats and Republicans are closer together in tax attitudes than in spending attitudes; political scientist

Patrick Egan (2013, 32) found that the difference in Democrats' and Republicans' views on lowering taxes was smaller than the partisan gap in views on spending for all the issues he examined (from social policy to the environment). And there is evidence of an electoral payoff for the GOP; in his seminal study of issue ownership, Petrocik (1996, 845) found that Democratic voters who are "preoccupied with Republican-owned issues" such as tax policy defect and vote Republican at high rates. Tax opinion in the United States is lopsided, with many Democrats and a large share of independents joining Republicans in their dislike of many taxes, to the advantage of the small government party. The similarity of Democrats and Republicans on taxes creates a political problem for proponents of a larger state.

Fourth, these findings add to the overall argument that the progressive tax system has a difficult time generating public support. Progressive taxes are more disliked than regressive ones, particularly among Republicans and independents. This is an especially propitious pattern for the nation's economic elite, who have many allies among the nonrich in their perpetual efforts to reduce their own taxes. Support for the American tax system, which is progressive overall, faces headwinds.

Finally, the effect of the political environment is consequential. Under Democratic presidents, Republican members of the public are sure to object to tax increases. Under Republican presidents, Republican identifiers might be willing to entertain them, if any Republican politician were brave enough to buck the party's firm antitax stance. Given how unlikely that is with the consolidation of the GOP around hostility to taxes, any tax increases will have to come at the behest of Democrats for the foreseeable future.[18] It is difficult to imagine the United States adopting a new category of tax, like a VAT, given overall tax antipathy and the fact that no new type of tax has been adopted since the New Deal. The tremendous unpopularity of the Clinton-Gore BTU tax proposal stands as a cautionary tale. But given patterns of tax attitudes by income and partisanship—the fact that attitudes are closer together on regressive taxes compared to progressive ones—one can start to see why most European nations depend so much on regressive VATs to fund their welfare states, and why, when tax revolts have erupted around the world, the issue has been not so much consumption taxes as property and income taxes.[19] As political economist Harold Wilensky (2012, 265) puts it, the formula for "stable public finance with the least political fuss" is a combination of progressive income taxes, payroll taxes, and consumption taxes, avoiding heavy property taxes, and acknowledging that "corporate taxes and taxes on the rich cannot yield huge sums." Americans like progressive taxation in the abstract and adhere to the ability-to-pay principle in theory. Clearly, though, there are limits both fiscally and politically to progressive taxation. The unusual reliance on income taxes in the United States helps explain why the public sector is small.

We have learned that tax attitudes, especially among the nonrich represented in the type of public opinion surveys reported in this book, are not structured much by self-interest. Attitudes toward progressive taxes and the gas tax are structured by party identification. But partisans do not differ much in their attitudes toward other regressive taxes. Given that self-interest, partisanship, and ideology have all failed to be consistent correlates, what does structure Americans' tax attitudes? The next chapter shows that the largest influence among white individuals is racial resentment.

6

Racial Resentment and Tax Attitudes among White Americans

THIS CHAPTER HELPS solve the puzzle presented by the previous three. They showed that tax attitudes are often not related to individuals' self-interest; those who pay more in a given tax because of their income or other characteristics are rarely more likely than those who pay less to say the tax is unfair. Attitudes do not vary by party identification and political ideology as consistently as we might expect either. Given that taxes are supposed to be an area where material stakes matter to attitudes, and given the strong influence of party and ideology on opinion in other issue areas, these scattered, intermittent results are striking.[1]

This chapter focuses on another possible factor in whites' tax attitudes: racial resentment. As first described in chapter 2 and explored in more depth here, tax policy in the United States has often been shaped by racialized considerations about who pays and who benefits. Throughout the nation's history, this has taken the form of whites' concern that their tax dollars are being spent on Black Americans. We might expect that at the individual level, those who harbor more racial animus might be more likely to think taxes are unfair and should be decreased. Decades of research show that racial animus has a strong effect on whites' preferences on government spending, especially for social assistance programs associated in the public mind with racial minorities.[2] This chapter examines whether racial animus is correlated with tax attitudes as well.

The answer in a nutshell: yes. The chapter chiefly delves into the role of racial resentment, or "symbolic racism," a measure of anti-Black prejudice that is based not on beliefs in the inferiority of Black people as a group (frequently called "old-fashioned racism") but rather racial animus combined with a feeling that Black individuals violate traditional values rooted in hard work and morality. The findings show that racial resentment is the strongest factor in whites' tax attitudes—far more influential than income, party identification, ideology, or other correlates that we might think would structure tax preferences. In their analysis of California's Prop 13, David Sears and Jack Citrin (1985, chap. 8) showed that the racially resentful were more supportive of property tax limitations. In a conjoint experiment, Cameron Ballard-Rosa, Lucy Martin, and Kenneth Scheve (2017) found a relationship between racial resentment and weaker preferences for progressive federal income taxation. Here we see that racial sentiment is associated with nearly every tax, with the racially resentful having especially negative views of progressive taxes: income, capital gains, and estate taxes. There is also evidence that the racially resentful have a particular affinity for flat and regressive taxes that burden lower-income groups the most. Given the strong relationship between race and both income and wealth in the United States, burdening lower-income groups means burdening nonwhite taxpayers disproportionately.

Those scoring higher on the racial resentment index are also more opposed to indirect tax spending on lower-income groups. Just as the racially resentful are less supportive of spending on welfare and other means-tested programs, so too are they opposed to tax expenditures that are tilted toward lower-income groups, such as the EITC and CTC. The "hidden" welfare state is not so much hidden as "obfuscated" in certain ways (McCabe 2018). Those who benefit from tax breaks may not view them as government programs, as Suzanne Mettler (2011) has shown, but many Americans are roughly aware of who benefits from which tax breaks. And attitudes of the racially resentful on indirect spending closely resemble their attitudes on direct spending: less support for provisions for the poor, greater support for provisions for the middle class such as the tax breaks for employer-provided benefits, and strong support for policies benefiting the rich such as a low capital gains tax rate.

Racial resentment is not the only way to measure anti-Black prejudice. Data availability limits my ability to assess the relationship between other measures of racism and tax attitudes, but the available evidence shows that there is an association there as well, especially for old-fashioned racism measures (less so with feeling thermometer and trait measures of racism). Racial resentment remains, however, the most consistent correlate. It may be that the particular ability of racial resentment to encompass notions of deservingness and perceived moral failings explains its close relationship with tax attitudes, in which some whites are clearly aggrieved by the possibility their tax dollars might go toward individuals of whom they do not approve. Taxes also present ripe opportunities for political elites to invoke race without explicitly mentioning it, a "dog whistle" politics rooted in moralism and concerns about who works hard or not, which is encapsulated in the racial resentment concept (Davis and Wilson 2022).

This examination of whites' tax attitudes and the role of racial resentment reveals two challenges to progressive taxation as well as the overall American tax-and-spend regime.

First, outside Social Security and Medicare, white taxpayers have a difficult time seeing how they benefit from taxes. Many, well beyond the rich, think that they only pay taxes and do not benefit (see Rosenthal 2021). Indeed, many believe that government confiscates their earnings and spends it in ways they dislike, such as funding social welfare benefits for nonwhites (Williamson 2017). In this way, taxes are heavily racialized in the United States, with whites framed as "taxpayers," and Black and Hispanic individuals as "tax eaters." Historians such as Camille Walsh (2018) and Molly Michelmore (2012) have traced the deep roots of the racialization of taxes, showing how such framings manifested after the Civil War and during the New Deal. The data here demonstrate that whites' self-conceptualization as beleaguered taxpayers forced to fund spending on others persists. We have long known how such racialized sentiments affect federal spending attitudes; the findings here indicate that they affect tax and tax expenditure attitudes as well.

Second, the role of racial resentment in whites' tax attitudes plays a central role in the failure of progressive taxation to generate robust support. White Americans have a particular dislike for income and estate taxes, despite saying that the rich do not pay enough. This chapter provides an additional clue about this mismatch between abstract preferences and specific policy opinions: the role of racial sentiment. Racially resentful whites oppose spending policies that they view as benefiting Black people; since income taxes are the chief component of general tax revenues, which fund both direct and indirect spending, their resentment over spending extends to the taxes that enable it. Opposition to the estate tax is more puzzling, as most will never pay it. But wealth is predominantly white in the United States, as legal scholar Dorothy Brown (2021) notes (more on her work in the next chapter), and we can imagine the racially resentful opposing the estate tax both because nearly all who pay it are white and its proceeds also go to general revenues, and therefore to direct and indirect spending on lower-income and Black recipients. Many Americans, including many whites, want the rich to pay more, but their resentment over the uses of tax revenues makes them vulnerable to appeals to cut progressive taxes. Elites who play on whites' racial resentments are able to break the link between a desire to tax the rich more and preferences on specific taxes that would tax the rich more. White grievance is a powerful political resource for the rich and their allies who want to diminish progressive taxation.

Racial Attitudes among White Americans

Why might racial and tax attitudes be connected in the minds of white Americans? Group theories of politics can help explain the linkages. An enormous amount of social scientific evidence shows that group-based thinking is widespread, automatic, and easy to trigger. Famous experiments in psychology by Muzafer Sherif, Henri Tajfel, and John Turner demonstrate that group thinking is so accessible to humans that in-group bias and out-group discrimination can be generated as easily as randomizing people into groups based on invented and trivial criteria (for example, Boy Scouts divided into The Eagles and The Rattlers, in Sherif's seminal experiment).[3] According to this "minimal group effects" paradigm, humans have a natural tendency, and even a psychological need, to "develop our sense of self in terms of the groups to which we belong and in contrast to the groups to which we do not" (Winter 2008, 33).

Group-based thinking is especially prevalent in politics.[4] The stakes of politics often involve competition among groups. Childhood political socialization teaches us early on to see the world in terms of politically relevant groups. Political actors shape and deploy group-based rhetoric in service of their policy goals. Group thinking produces group ideologies, as Nicholas Winter (2008, 34) puts it, or socially constructed stories that "explain, justify, and normalize the social relations among groups." These group ideologies arise from the "objective structure of group relations" as well as from "accidents of historical development." They are easily accessible cognitive structures that individuals use to think about and determine how to behave regarding political matters.

Among the forms group-centric thinking can take (class, religion, gender, and so on), racial sentiment is particularly potent in explaining political attitudes and behaviors in the United States.[5] Linkages between racial attitudes and public policy preferences are prevalent for issues that are explicitly about race, such as affirmative action, equal opportunity, and school desegregation, where "racially prejudiced whites line up on one side and racially sympathetic whites line up on the other," as Donald Kinder (2003) notes.[6] Racial sentiment also affects attitudes on issues that have become racialized over the decades, especially social policies such as welfare, Medicaid, and health reform.[7] A particular locus of anti-Black sentiment is cash welfare (Gilens 1996, 1999). Not only are whites who harbor more negative views about Black Americans less supportive of cash support for low-income families, but also welfare's racialization spills over into attitudes toward generalized government spending; attitudes toward both welfare and nonspecific "government spending" are structured by racial resentment apparently because when survey respondents are asked about "government spending," they think "welfare," and when they think "welfare," they think cash welfare, food stamps, and public housing.[8] One recent study finds that racial attitudes are four times more powerful than income (that is, self-interest) in explaining opposition to generalized federal spending. And among social policies, only the universal, contributory, and white-coded Social Security and Medicare programs are (mostly) immune to the racial sentiment effect (Winter 2006, 2008). Political economists have long argued that public goods provision is more difficult in heterogeneous societies.[9] Given the nation's fraught racial history, the United States is a predominant example, and poor provider of social policy.

Most of the studies just cited conceptualize racism in "symbolic" terms. There has been a theoretical and empirical debate about what form racism takes in the present-day United States. Some political scientists such as Paul Sniderman argue that old-fashioned racism remains extant, and racism is best measured with survey items on perceptions of Blacks' ability or intelligence, support for greater social distance such as opposition to interracial marriage, and support for policies upholding segregation. The more commonly used concept is symbolic racism, a "modern" form of racism developed by Sears, Donald Kinder, and their coauthors, also known as racial resentment.[10] Symbolic racism is

> usually described as a coherent belief system reflecting a unidimensional underlying prejudice toward Blacks, with four specific themes that are typically measured with corresponding survey items: the beliefs that Blacks no longer face much prejudice or discrimination, that their failure to progress results from their unwillingness to work hard enough, that they are demanding too much too fast, and that they have gotten more than they deserve (Sears and Henry 2005, 100).[11]

In the symbolic racism or racial resentment concept, racism is voiced as Black violations of American values such as hard work, with this version of racial prejudice less subject to the social desirability bias that impedes measurement using the old-fashioned racism survey items. By the racial resentment measure, Mike Tesler (2020, 119–20) notes, "America is a racially conservative country"; on a zero to one hundred scale from the most racially sympathetic to most racially resentful response, the average white American scores sixty. And that was in 2016, when recorded white racial resentment was lower than in any previous year, in apparent backlash to Trump's racially vitriolic campaign.

A great deal of evidence shows that this form of racism is potent in explaining white Americans' public policy attitudes. A key example is Winter's research demonstrating how the racialized notions of deservingness and hard work captured by the symbolic racism concept result in the encoding of different social policies as "white" or "Black," which in turn affects policy attitudes. He argues that decades of political discourse on welfare has linked the program symbolically to Blackness ("laziness, lack of personal responsibility, and perverse incentives"). In contrast, elite rhetoric around Social Security has highlighted an analogy to private insurance and a sense of an individual "earned right," tying the program to "work and just reward," the "white-linked attributes of the racial schema" (Winter 2008, 91–92). His survey experiments on program attitudes reveal the results of those differing political messages: Social Security is coded as white while welfare and other social policy spending is coded as Black in the minds of white Americans (Paul Kellstedt terms this process—fed by politicians and media cues—as the "fusing" of race and welfare state issues).[12] The result is that whites on different ends of the racial sentiment spectrum have very different opinions about spending programs.[13]

This chapter takes up the question of whether the strong relationship between racial resentment and spending among whites extends to taxes too—the flip side of the spending coin. Does the connection between racial resentment and property tax attitudes that Sears and Citrin found for Prop 13 exist for other taxes? Is taxpaying coded as "white"? And if attitudes toward direct spending are structured by racial sentiment, are attitudes toward indirect spending (that is, tax expenditures) any different?

The historical record strongly suggests a linkage between racial and tax attitudes. Journalists Tom Edsall and Mary Edsall (1991) made precisely these connections in their account of the rise of the modern Republican Party, *Chain Reaction*. They argued that Reagan used rhetoric linking taxes, spending, and race to unite a disparate coalition of social conservatives, working-class whites, and the party's traditional fiscal conservative and libertarian groups behind a racially resentful, antitax mantra. Economist J. Bradford DeLong (2022, 458) tells a similar story about that era in the more recent *Slouching towards Utopia*: neoliberal assertions about tax cuts and smaller government appealed to white males from the working and middle classes who were angry that they were falling behind economically while "the unworthy and minority poor got handouts." As DeLong notes, the neoliberal cure was tax cuts for the rich.

The association between taxpaying and whiteness has deeper roots than the economic anxieties of the 1970s, however. Historians provide much earlier examples of elites successfully fostering connections between taxpaying and race and fanning a two-way relationship in which white grievance was both fed and capitalized on by economic elites along with their political allies intent on cultivating antitax sentiment in the broader (white) public. As Kinder (2003, 38) writes, ethnocentrism—of which racial prejudice is one type—both "bubbles up from below but is also shaped and activated from above."

The connection between race and taxes goes back centuries, as we saw in chapter 2, with early choices to fund the federal government through tariffs rather than property taxes made to skirt the slavery issue (Einhorn 2006).[14] The active construction of whites as taxpayers also has a long history. Walsh shows how post–Civil War school funding debates framed whites as taxpayers whose hard-earned dollars were taken by government to fund benefits for undeserving Black students. The debate centered on the quality of schooling that children deserved given the amount of taxes their families could pay. Black families and desegregationists preferred a "threshold" approach to taxation in which citizens were entitled to equal resources as long as they reached some minimal level of tax participation. But the view that became dominant was the "consumer" approach favored by white families and segregationists, defining notions of "citizenship rights based on taxpaying status": those who paid more (whether the individual, family, or community) were entitled to more and better public goods and services (Walsh 2018, 9). This consumer approach helped racialize taxes, Walsh (2018, 5–6) explains, encoding taxpaying as white and receiving government services and benefits at a level less than one's actual fiscal contribution as Black. A late nineteenth-century Louisiana political slogan encapsulated the resentments: "The whites pay the taxes and the Negroes go to school" (Walsh 2018, 5). These debates cultivated a "mythology of white victimization" that would prove persistent: a sense of white entitlement to possessing income and assets as well as resisting government efforts to collect some of that income and property in the form of taxes.[15]

The codification of racial resentments into notions of fiscal citizenship continued in the New Deal era. Social policy was divided into two tiers: the social insurance programs such as Social Security, which were run by the federal government, and the social assistance programs such as cash welfare (then called Aid to Dependent Children), which were jointly run by the federal government and the states at the insistence of white southern lawmakers who did not want generous federal benefits flowing to the Black residents of their states. Many accounts highlight the implications of this social insurance / social assistance bifurcation for the differential well-being of Black and white Americans (social assistance has always been more meager) as well as the politics of social welfare spending (although some social assistance programs have proved durable, many are capped, wait-listed, or replete with sanctions).[16]

Michelmore (2012) explains the ramifications of the social insurance / social assistance divide for the subsequent politics of taxation. Social Security is rightfully lauded as one of the most popular government programs, most popular tax (see chapter 3), and most effective antipoverty program in the American welfare state (the senior poverty rate is half that of children) (Federal Interagency Forum on Aging-Related Statistics 2020). And the payroll tax did create an individual entitlement to benefits—a major reason for both the popularity of the tax and the program's political durability (Campbell 2003).

But there was another reason for using an earmarked payroll tax, Michelmore argues: fear of taxpayer hostility. Strikes against the property tax had sprung up during the Great Depression, as the economic crisis left people unable to pay (Leff 1983). The New Deal's framers feared the political consequences of funding the new economic security programs (Social Security and unemployment insurance) through an expanded income tax, which most workers at the time did not pay. Instead they chose a payroll tax for Social Security (and employer contributions for unemployment insurance) and then worked hard to sell an "annuity fiction": Social Security as an individual entitlement to benefits and the taxes as "contributions" analogous to a private insurance premium (Michelmore 2012, 6). The "social" part of social insurance—the fact that the program pools payroll tax proceeds and redistributes them from rich to poor and from those who die young to those who live longer—was downplayed.

The private insurance analogy proved politically successful. Over the decades, even as confidence in the system's long-term prospects has waned, and even as people recognize the pooled structure to some degree, the program remains popular.[17] Payroll tax financing, however—and the way it was sold to the American public—also undermined a broad sense of fiscal citizenship and helped racialize social policy funding, Michelmore contends. Elites' framing of Social Security's structure cemented the notion that the only good tax is a tax funding one's own benefits. Other taxes that might fund benefits for other people are suspect.[18]

Furthermore, the "other people" who might need social assistance were predominantly Black, again due to Social Security's design. The occupations in which Black people were concentrated were left out of the pension scheme in the beginning. Black workers also faced labor market discrimination and lacked access to jobs with employer-provided benefits that were adopted starting in World War II such as health insurance.[19] Lacking access to both the wage-based social insurance system and private system of employer-based benefits that sprang up around it, Black citizens were more economically vulnerable and in greater need of social assistance, funded by general tax dollars. These early policy choices meant whites became associated with the "legitimate" welfare state funded by the earmarked payroll tax, whose redistribution was hidden, while Black Americans became associated with the "illegitimate" welfare state of social assistance, funded by the visible income tax (these are the associations that fuel Winter's public opinion experiments decades later). As Michelmore asserts, whites became coded as taxpayers and Black Americans as tax eaters because government policies made them that way.[20]

Thus by the time Reagan was contemplating national office, these racialized social constructions around spending *and* taxation were widespread in the population, ripe for triggering yet again (Walsh 2018, 5). The 1970s were a propitious time for activating anxieties about tax levels, as chapter 2 noted. State and local taxes had risen dramatically between 1953 and 1973, from 7.6 to 12.1 percent of GDP, in part because property taxes surged as municipalities ended the practice of fractional assessment (assessing properties at less than full market value—a practice that overwhelmingly benefited white homeowners, as chapter 7 discusses).[21] Taxpayers did not much notice the increases while the postwar economy was booming and real incomes were rising, but after the 1970s' oil crisis, the economy slowed dramatically (Morgan 2007, 33). The new economic anxieties and increasing difficulty of maintaining a middle-class lifestyle were reflected in public opinion polls: between 1946 and 1972, survey respondents rarely cited the economy as the "most important problem," but did so three-quarters of the time between 1973 and 2004 (Smith 2007, 138–39). Politicians and political parties both fed and responded to these concerns, with the economy figuring more prominently in party platforms in the thirty years after 1976 than in the thirty years before; taxes becoming the most common topic in presidential advertisements between 1984 and

2004, among candidates of both parties; and taxes rising among all mentions of the "likes and dislikes" about the parties in ANES data.[22] As economic anxiety increased, taxes became a "symbol of all that was wrong with government" (Morgan 2007, 35).[23] Enterprising conservatives concentrated "on the most-hated elements of the tax system—income and property taxes—[as] a way to build a larger political movement against taxation and the growth of government," as Kimberly Morgan (2007, 35) has written.[24]

Moreover, the deep-seated cultural images of whites as taxpayers and Black Americans as program recipients allowed antigovernment conservatives to focus on taxes as a way to "tap racial resentments without making overtly racist statements" (Morgan 2007, 35).[25] When discussing Social Security, Reagan would refer to "our elderly" and "our senior citizens," while referring to "those people" when discussing welfare and food stamps (Winter 2008, 93). Media accounts portrayed welfare recipients as disproportionately Black, giving such statements purchase (Gilens 1999). "The meaning of 'taxes' was transformed," write the Edsalls (1991, 214). "No longer the resource with which to create a beneficent federal government, taxes had come for many voters to signify the forcible transfer of hard-earned money away from those who worked, to those who did not." Subsequent Republican politicians invoked similar rhetoric. In speeches lauding his tax cuts, George W. Bush (2001) regularly referred to tax revenue as "your money." Or as he put it in dozens of speeches during his 2004 reelection campaign, invoking other white-coded groups, "In order for this economy to continue to grow and for jobs to stay in America, we must be wise about how we spend your money, and we must keep your taxes low. Running up the taxes on the working people and the small-business owners and the farmers and ranchers of America would hurt this economic recovery" (Bush 2004).[26]

Perhaps the purest expression of white grievance around federal taxation came in a *Wall Street Journal* editorial titled "The Non-Taxpaying Class" (2002). The editors worried that there would be insufficient support for the Bush tax cuts because the nation had been divided into "two different taxpaying classes: those who pay a lot and those who pay very little." Tax revenue is being "increasingly squeezed out of top earners" while the "lucky duckies" at the bottom end of the income spectrum have a "growing number of absolutely legal escape hatches" such as the personal exemption and standard deduction, which reduced income taxes on those earning $12,000 to under 4 percent, and the EITC, which allowed low earners to "slip free" from the payroll tax. The editorial's main concern was that those who paid "little or no taxes" would not "care about tax relief for everybody else." Mitt Romney echoed this grievance at a private fundraising event for his 2012 presidential bid, lamenting that "47 percent" of Americans do not pay income tax and therefore would be unlikely to vote for him (Robillard 2021).

Contemporary interviews with taxpayers show the persistence of these historically fostered linkages between race and perceptions about who pays and who benefits. In her interviews with taxpayers, Vanessa Williamson (2017, chap. 5) reports that when people talk about government waste, they do not mean inefficiency but rather spending on programs of which they do not approve. Her respondents do not resent government spending overall, just spending for groups about which they are skeptical, such as the poor and immigrants.[27] In his interviews with citizens about their impressions of government, Aaron Rosenthal (2021) finds that the most visible aspects of government for white Americans are welfare and taxes (for Black Americans, it is the police).[28] Undergirding these attitudes is the consumer ethos that lives on, with taxpayers resentful when they believe they do not receive benefits commensurate with the taxes they have paid, while others receive benefits in excess of their contributions to the public purse.

Hypotheses about Racial Resentment and Whites' Tax Attitudes

What are the implications of these psychological processes and historical social constructions for the structure of whites' tax attitudes?

Given that racial resentment is strongly related to attitudes on means-tested social policies, we might predict that attitudes toward taxes that contribute to general revenues, the funding source for such policies, will also be structured by racial resentment. Thus those who score high on the racial resentment scale should be more likely than those who score low to say that federal and state income, estate, capital gains, and sales taxes are unfair. Given that wealth is associated with whiteness in the United States, the racially resentful should see taxes on wealth as more unfair, including property, estate, and capital gains taxes.

The association between racial resentment and tax attitudes may be a bit weaker for sales taxes, as we know from open-ended CCES items that people view the sales tax as more controllable than other ones (chapter 3); sensitivity around the extraction of personal resources to fund benefits for people of whom one does not approve may be lesser for the sales tax. Also, since Social

Security taxes are earmarked for that program and benefits are earned by working, there is less fear that those tax dollars will go to "undeserving" others. Hence racial resentment should have a more modest association with attitudes toward the payroll tax.

Moreover, I expect to find a relationship between racial resentment and attitudes toward a number of tax expenditures. Although scholars term the tax expenditure system the "hidden" or "submerged" welfare state, as long as survey respondents have some sense of which income groups benefit from which tax expenditures, we might expect racial resentment to bear the same relationship to indirect as to direct spending attitudes.[29] I anticipate that tax expenditures that benefit the poor will be the least supported by the racially resentful, while those benefiting the rich will be the most supported. Attitudes toward middle-class tax expenditures will be less structured by racial resentment, as is the case with spending on Social Security.

Finally, given the centuries-old framing of taxpayers as white, I expect the relationship between racial resentment and tax attitudes should exist as far back in time as the public opinion data allow.

To measure racial resentment, I will use the canonical symbolic racism measures, which are available in the GSS, ANES, and CCES. Depending on the particular survey, racial resentment will consist of a two- or four-item index of symbolic racism, with racially resentful views coded high for multivariate analysis purposes and white respondents divided into terciles for descriptive purposes. Since the average white American is moderately racially resentful, the questions here is, How do such individuals think about taxes? Finally, I will examine the relationship between other measures of racial prejudice to see whether they too structure tax attitudes.

Whites' Direct Spending Attitudes

Before exploring whether racial and tax attitudes are related, I first confirm that the strong relationship between racial and spending attitudes found in earlier research is present in these datasets as well. The 2016 CCES included items replicating standard GSS and ANES questions that ask whether federal spending in a variety of policy areas should be increased, decreased, or kept the same.

The descriptive data show that few white respondents want to decrease spending on the universal Social Security and Medicare programs, nor do they want to decrease infrastructure spending. Turning to social assistance and

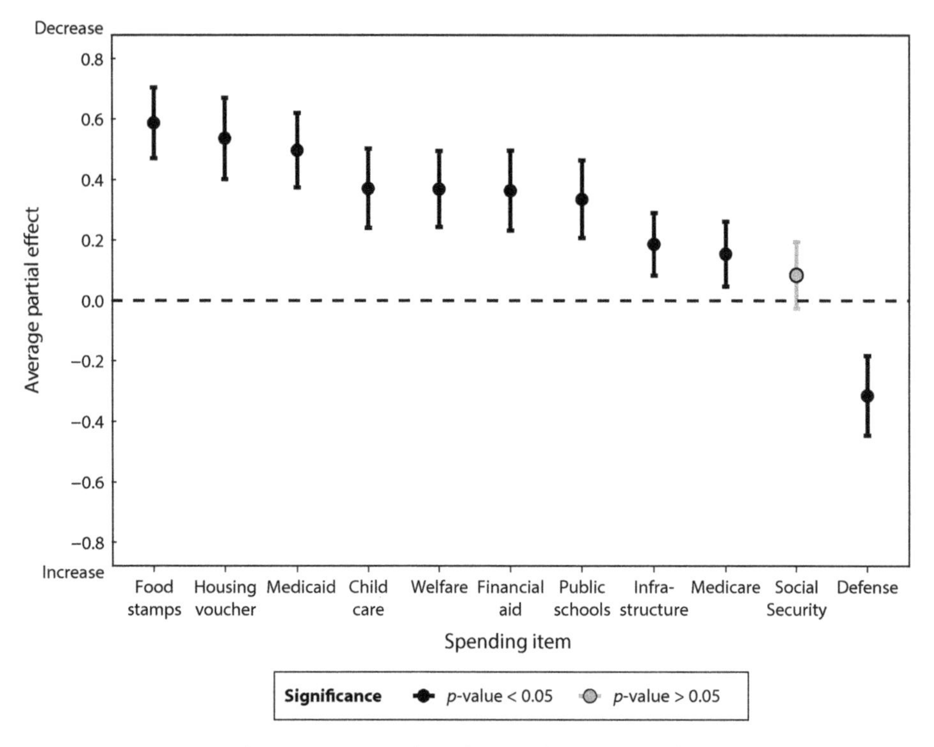

FIGURE 6.1 Racial Resentment and Preference for Decreased Federal Spending
Note: "Decrease spending" is coded high. Whites only. Figure shows the average partial effect of racial resentment from ordinary least squares analyses also controlling for education, income, gender, age, marital status, children, homeowner, partisanship, ideology, and government trust.
Source: 2016 CCES.

education, the strong relationship with racial resentment seen in previous research emerges, with those scoring higher in racial resentment much more likely to want spending on welfare, food stamps, housing vouchers, Medicaid, childcare, college financial aid, and public schools decreased.

Although the preferences of whites scoring higher and lower on the racial resentment scale differ substantially, the racially resentful may differ in other ways that explain these differences. Therefore figure 6.1 arrays the average partial effect of racial resentment from multivariate analyses controlling for demographic and political factors along with government trust. All things being equal, racial resentment is not correlated with spending preferences on Social

Security—much as Winter found—and is barely correlated with Medicare and infrastructure preferences, but is a strong factor in explaining preferences on defense spending (the racially resentful want more) as well as spending for means-tested and education programs (they prefer decreases). The association with racial resentment is particularly large for Medicaid, housing assistance, and food stamps. Even spending for public schools and college financial aid is structured by racial attitudes—despite Americans' beliefs in equality of opportunity—as are attitudes toward childcare spending.

These data confirm the findings of previous research that white Americans who are more racially resentful do not have distinctive opinions on Social Security and Medicare, but are more likely to want federal spending on means-tested social programs decreased, above and beyond their political commitments and any material stakes they might have, such as being lower-income themselves or having school-age children.[30] These patterns reflect Winter's (2008, 106) observation, evoking the Edsalls, that nearly "all social policy discourse invokes race implicitly to some extent."

The role of racial attitudes in spending is also seen in survey data that tap into the phenomenon that Williamson discovered in her in-depth interviews with taxpayers: that what people dislike about taxes is spending on people and programs of which they do not approve. The 2016 CCES asked respondents what bothers them the most when thinking about paying federal income taxes; figure 6.2 shows the results for white respondents who scored in the top third on racial resentment compared to those who scored in the bottom third. The two groups were similar in saying that what bothers them the most is the amount they pay (9 percent for the most racially resentful versus 5 percent for the least resentful), the feeling that the poor don't pay enough (8 to 5 percent), and the complexity of the tax system (12 versus 14 percent). Where they differ is in two other responses. What bothered half of the racially resentful the most, but only 9 percent of those scoring low on resentment, was "the way the government spends taxes." In contrast, what bothered two-thirds of low scorers, but only one in five high scorers, was "the feeling that some wealthy people don't pay their fair share." That the racially resentful do not like federal income taxes in part because of how the money is spent echoes not only Williamson's work but also Kate Krimmel and Kelly Rader's (2017) finding that the racially resentful express little support for "government spending" because when answering the corresponding survey item, they have social assistance programs in mind.

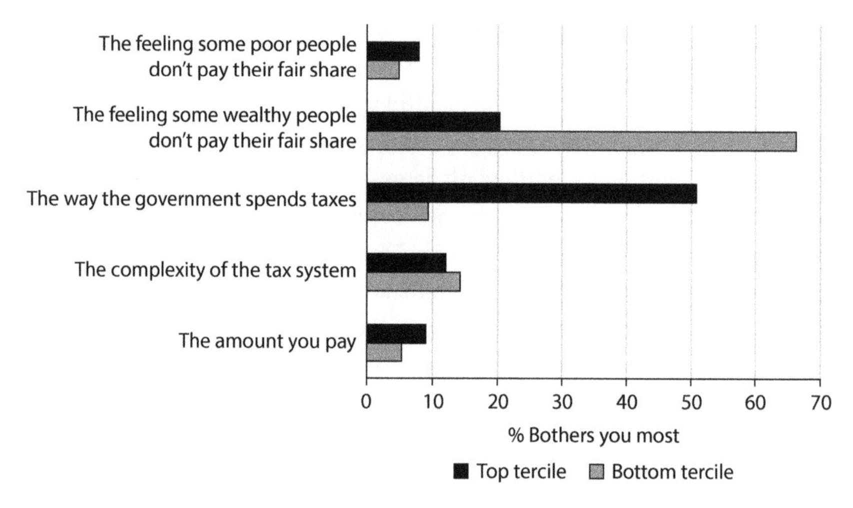

FIGURE 6.2 What Bothers You Most about Paying Federal Income Taxes, by Level of Racial Resentment

Note: Whites only. Figure shows percentage of white respondents in the top and bottom terciles of the racial resentment scale saying which feature bothers them the most about paying federal income taxes.

Source: 2016 CCES.

Whites' Tax Attitudes

In their landmark work, Sears and Citrin (1985) found that support for Prop 13, the 1978 California ballot initiative that sparked the property tax revolt, was greater among the racially resentful. The question here is whether other taxes have a similar underlying structure, especially those that contribute to the general revenues that fund means-tested program spending, associated in the minds of some white citizens with Blackness, and those that tax progressively and tax wealth, associated with whiteness.

Descriptively, whites scoring higher on racial resentment are more likely to say each of the eight taxes they have to pay is unfair. The strong association between racial resentment and the perceived unfairness of taxes remains even after controlling for demographic variables, other symbolic factors such as party identification and ideology, and government trust (figure 6.3). Indeed, racial resentment is the most consistent predictor of unfairness evaluations across the eight taxes examined. Only sales tax attitudes are not influenced by racial attitudes (barely failing to reach statistical significance). A similar pattern obtains for attitudes toward changing taxes (figure 6.4). Racially resentful

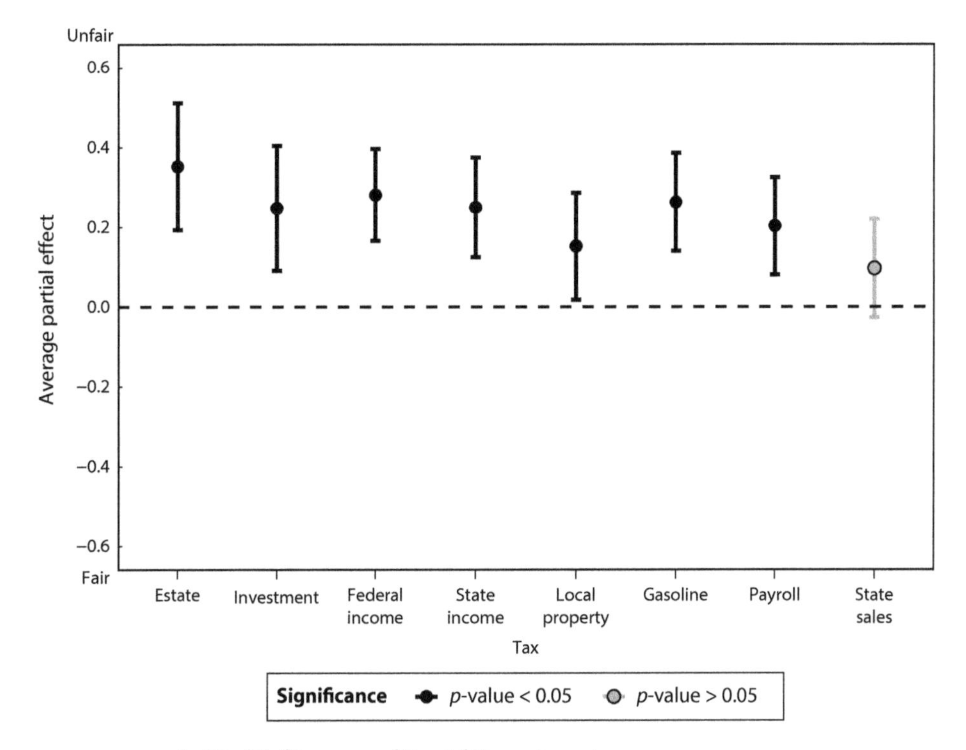

FIGURE 6.3 Tax Unfairness and Racial Resentment
Note: "Amount I pay is very unfair" is coded high. Whites only. Figure shows the average partial effect of racial resentment from ordinary least squares analyses also controlling for education, income, gender, age, marital status, children, homeowner, partisanship, ideology, and government trust.
Source: 2016 CCES.

whites are more likely to want every tax decreased (with the near exception of the sales tax). Perhaps most important, analysis also indicates that the association of racial resentment with both of these attitudinal outcomes is greater than that of any other variable. Notably, the relationship between racial resentment and these outcomes is larger than that of party identification or ideology.[31]

It might be surprising that racial resentment is associated with evaluations on the unfairness of the "payroll tax for Social Security and Medicare." One explanation is that attitudes toward Medicare spending are slightly more racialized than those toward Social Security (figure 6.1). The other is that Winter (2008) finds in the ANES data that Social Security is slightly racialized too,

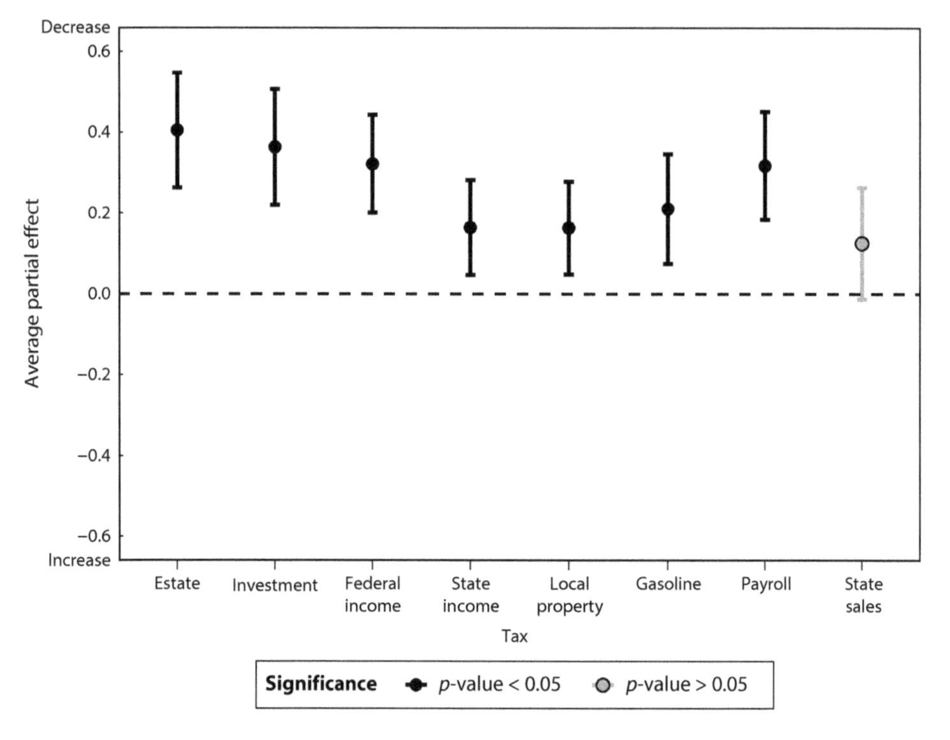

FIGURE 6.4 Tax Change Preferences and Racial Resentment
Note: "Decrease tax" is coded high. Whites only. Figure shows the average partial effect of racial resentment from ordinary least squares analyses also controlling for education, income, gender, age, marital status, children, homeowner, partisanship, ideology, and government trust.
Source: 2016 CCES.

although much less so than welfare, even if it is not racialized in a similar question in the CCES.

In figure 6.3, racial resentment exhibits its greatest relationships with whites' attitudes toward the progressive estate and income taxes. The particular dislike of progressive taxation among the racially resentful is also apparent in a different set of tax items from the 2012 CCES. This survey asked respondents about the fairness of progressive, flat, and regressive tax systems, after defining each type. In addition, the survey included items asking about eliminating the estate tax, whether capital gains should be taxed at a lower rate than earned income, and whether federal income taxes should be increased for high earners.[32] In figure 6.5, the outcomes are coded so that opposition to or the unfairness of progressive taxes is high.

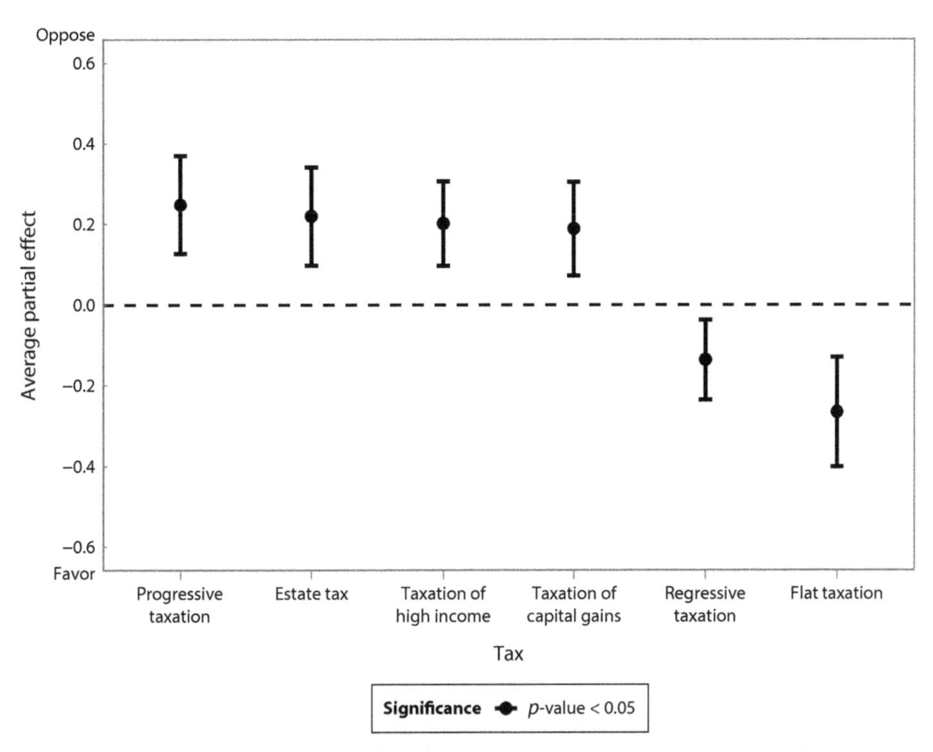

FIGURE 6.5 Opposition to Progressive Taxation and Racial Resentment
Note: Outcomes are coded so opposition to or unfairness of tax is high. Whites only. Figure shows the coefficient for racial resentment from ordinary least squares analyses also controlling for education, income, gender, age, marital status, children, homeowner, partisanship, and ideology. Government trust not available in this survey.
Source: 2012 CCES.

Controlling for demographic characteristics as well as party identification and ideology (government trust is not available in this survey), white respondents who are more racially resentful are more likely to say progressive tax systems are unfair (the coefficient on the far left), and more likely to say that regressive and flat tax systems are fair (the two coefficients on the far right). With regard to specific types of progressive taxation, racial resentment is a factor as well, with the racially resentful more likely to oppose estate taxation, higher income tax rates for families making more than $250,000, and high capital gains taxes. The racially resentful are more likely to oppose progressivity both as a system of taxation and with regard to specific progressive taxes. That is, those who harbor animus toward Black Americans support lower taxation for high-earning and high-wealth households, above and beyond their own income, party identification, and other factors.[33]

A Closer Look at the Estate Tax

The strong relationship between racial resentment and estate tax attitudes revealed in figures 6.3, 6.4, and 6.5 is worth underscoring. To many commentators, the estate tax represents one of the great puzzles in American tax politics: large percentages of survey respondents support estate tax repeal, even though the vast majority of Americans will never pay the tax (Graetz and Shapiro 2005). From a material stake perspective, this widely held attitude makes no sense. Nor does support for estate tax repeal comport with the preference among many Americans for progressive taxation as a general matter and their feeling that the rich pay too little. Previous scholars have noted that there is little relationship between estate tax attitudes and attitudes toward inequality—another puzzle, since the estate tax is the most progressive in the American fiscal tool kit and potentially an important means of redistribution. Larry Bartels (2016, table 6.1) shows that majorities of respondents in the 2002 ANES support estate tax repeal, even majorities of those with below-median incomes, those who want more government spending, those who say the income gap has increased and that it is a bad thing, those who say government policy contributes to differences in income, and those who say rich people pay less than they should in federal income taxes. Among those for whom all the above is true, an astonishing 63 percent support repeal.[34] He concludes that neither self-interest nor political values, including inequality concerns, seem to matter for estate tax attitudes.

Racial resentment may help solve the mystery of strong opposition to the estate tax, at least among white Americans. As figures 6.3 and 6.4 utilizing 2016 CCES data indicated, racial animus is a factor in estate tax attitudes, above and beyond demographic and political factors as well as government trust. Figure 6.5, using 2012 CCES data, finds the same pattern. The 2012 data allow for the addition of other correlates, including individuals' status as investors as another self-interest indicator and their beliefs about inequality. Even with these additional factors in the model, the strong association between racial resentment and estate tax attitudes persists.

Thus racial resentment is crucial in explaining estate tax opposition among white Americans. Estate tax attitudes do not turn on class-based self-interest or inequality attitudes. Instead, those who express animus toward Black

Americans oppose the estate tax more than other white Americans, all things being equal. Estate tax opinion among nonrich whites is less about economic class or inequality, and more about racialized perceptions of who pays and who benefits from American tax and spending policy. Despite the fact that only a tiny fraction of people ever pay it, there is not something special or puzzling about the estate tax. It displays the same attitudinal pattern as most taxes, especially progressive ones, in the American fiscal regime, in which racial resentment is a strong factor.

The Role of Racial Resentment over Time

The relationship between racial and tax attitudes is strong in contemporary data. We might additionally wonder whether dislike of taxes among the racially resentful has evolved over time. Was the relationship always there, or was this something fanned by either the racialization of welfare in the 1960s or Reagan's linking of federal government spending and taxes in the 1980s? Or as the historical accounts of Walsh, Michelmore, and Robin Einhorn suggest, does a relationship between attitudes about race and taxes date back to the New Deal or even earlier?

For the period beginning in 1976, the GSS allows an examination of the relationship between racial resentment, on the one hand, and government spending and federal income tax attitudes, on the other. These data allow us to see whether these attitudes were correlated before Reagan's presidency, although we cannot discern whether they were correlated before the 1960s.

For federal spending attitudes, the results for 1976 through 2018 mirror both contemporary findings in the CCES and Winter's using similar items in the ANES between 1992 and 2000: racial resentment structures welfare attitudes but not Social Security attitudes. The GSS asked respondents whether "we're spending" too much, too little, or about the right amount of money on a number of issue areas. All things being equal, racial resentment is a statistically significant factor in explaining attitudes toward welfare spending over the entire 1976–2018 span when measures of both are available. By contrast, racial resentment is not significant in explaining preferences on Social Security spending except in 2018, during the Trump administration, when the racially resentful were more likely to want Social Security spending increased, perhaps reflecting Trump's populist position that Social Security should be defended.[35]

For tax attitudes, the analysis uses the one tax item that appears in the GSS over time, asking respondents whether they think the federal income taxes

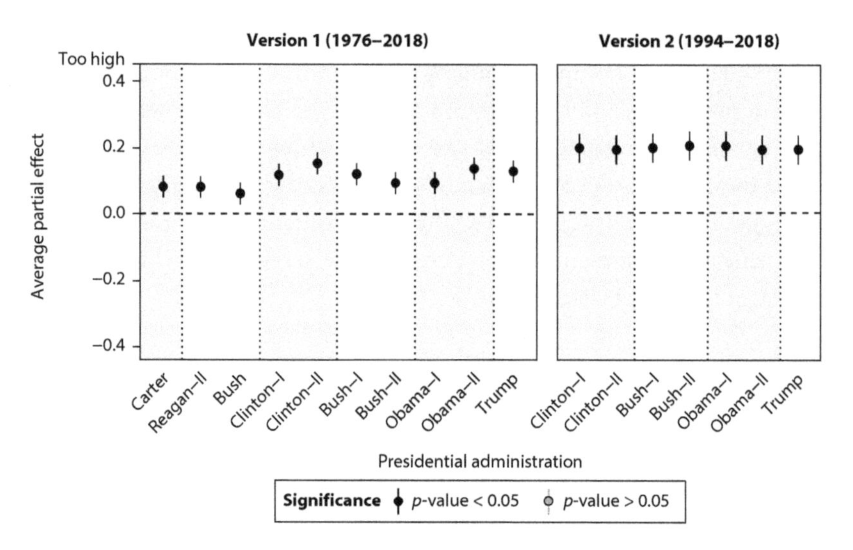

FIGURE 6.6 Federal Income Taxes Too High by Racial Resentment across Presidential Administrations

Note: Figure shows the average partial effect for whites scoring in the top tercile of racial resentment compared to those scoring in the middle or bottom terciles, controlling for income, education, gender, age, marital status, homeowner, children, partisanship, and ideology. Racial resentment measured by a two-item index 1976–2018 and a three-item index 1994–2018. Government trust not included in these analyses. Democratic presidential administrations shaded. For the descriptive versions, see appendix figure A.6.

Source: GSS 1976–2018.

they will have to pay this year are too high, too low, or about right. The data reveal that racial resentment is linked to federal income tax opinion throughout the 1976–2018 period.[36] Figure 6.6 shows the average partial effect of racial resentment, with the left panel depicting the results for the longer 1976–2018 period, when two racial resentment items are available, while the right panel displays the results for the shorter 1994–2018 period, when three items are available (for the descriptive results, see appendix, figure A.6).[37] The positive coefficients indicate that the more racially resentful are more likely to say their federal income taxes are too high.[38]

Although we cannot know whether this relationship predated the racialization of welfare during the 1960s, by Jimmy Carter's presidency in the latter half of the 1970s, more racially resentful whites were more likely than other whites to say their federal income taxes are too high, both in the descriptive data shown in the appendix and the multivariate analysis above and beyond their partisanship, ideological self-identification, and demographic characteristics.[39] Moreover, the data reveal the consistency of the relationship between symbolic racism and tax attitudes: even as partisans vary in their views (Republicans being more likely than Democrats to say their federal income tax is too high mostly when a Democrat is in the White House, as shown in chapter 5), the racially resentful are more likely to say their federal income taxes are too high regardless of party control of the White House.[40] The GSS data indicate that racial and tax attitudes are correlated not just in the CCES data of 2012, 2016, and 2019, when racial resentments were seething during and after the Obama presidency. Nor are they related only once there is a Black president, as Tesler (2016) found with health care reform attitudes. Instead, the relationship between racial and tax attitudes is long-standing, perhaps because, as the historians tell us, taxes have been structured around race for the nation's entire history.

Alternative Measures of Racism

Racial resentment among white Americans is strongly correlated with tax attitudes, one of this book's most important findings. These contemporary CCES and historical GSS results are both based on a particular measure of racial animus: symbolic racism. As noted, the now-classic symbolic racism index was created to capture the modern incarnation of racism, using survey items that are less subject to the social desirability bias and self-censoring that seemed to limit the utility of old-fashioned measures of racism rooted in biological superiority, desire for social distance, and other largely outdated sentiments.

One concern, however, may be that the association between racial resentment and tax attitudes is strong because the items making up the symbolic racism index may measure principled conservatism—an aversion to government—as well as racial sentiment. The question is whether racial and tax attitudes are still tightly correlated when alternative, "purer" measures of racial attitudes are used.

The CCES does not contain alternative measures of racism, but both the GSS and some ANES cross-sectional surveys do. First, the GSS includes several "old-fashioned" or traditional racism items, including questions measuring desire for social distance, notions of biological inferiority, and willingness to vote for a Black president. One pertinent ANES survey included a social distance item on segregation.

A second alternative measure of racism available in the ANES is rooted in stereotypes about racial groups. Respondents are asked about how hardworking or lazy groups are, or how intelligent. Using these items, whites' racial animus is measured by subtracting respondents' replies for Blacks from their scores for whites (a similar calculation can be made with the "feeling thermometers" for groups, which assess how warm or cold respondents feel toward various societal groups on a zero to one hundred scale). Those scoring higher are thought to harbor more racial animus than those scoring lower. A third measure of regard toward groups is "ethnocentrism," a more generalized animus toward racial/ethnic out-groups, not just racism toward Black individuals, as Kinder and Cindy Kam (2010) define it. Ethnocentrism among white respondents is calculated by subtracting average feeling thermometers or trait scores for Black, Hispanic, and Asian out-groups from whites' in-group feeling thermometers or trait scores. One downside of these stereotype-based measures of racial animus or ethnocentrism is that like traditional racism measures, they are susceptible to self-censorship arising from social desirability pressures. Also, because few whites rate other groups higher than their own, these scales are one-sided, measuring racial antipathy but failing to measure racial sympathy. In contrast, the racial resentment scale used in most of this book is better able to measure the entire racial attitude spectrum (Tesler 2020).

The findings indicate that tax attitudes are correlated with these alternative measures of racism, but the strength of the correlations vary. The relationships between federal income tax attitudes and the stereotype-based measures of racial animus in the ANES are weaker. The first set of dependent variables are 2004 items asking whether the respondent, the rich, or the poor pay more in federal income taxes than they should, less, or the right amount. A 2008 item asks whether people who make more money should pay a larger percent of their income in taxes than people who make less money, a smaller percent, or whether "the amount of money people make should not determine what percent of their income they pay in taxes." A third item in 2012, 2016, and 2020 asks whether income taxes should be increased on people making over $1 million per year. For most of these outcomes, racial resentment is a strong correlate. Yet the stereotype-based measures of racial animus are weak correlates. Their signs are generally in the expected direction, but only achieve statistical significance in a couple of instances (see online appendix, tables OA.37–OA.43).

The old-fashioned measures of racism have much stronger correlations with tax attitudes. In the 1972 ANES, respondents supporting segregation preferred flat taxation ("everyone should pay the same portion of their income" in taxes) to progressive taxation ("those with high incomes should pay even more of their income into taxes than they do now"; see online appendix, table OA.36). In the GSS, I pooled the years in which each old-fashioned racism measure is available, and found that all except the Black intelligence item are correlated with tax opinion. That is, white respondents who feel that Black people have less ability, oppose interracial marriage in general and for their relative, say whites should be allowed to live in a segregated neighborhood, and would not vote for a Black president are more likely to say their federal income taxes are too high, all things being equal (see appendix, figure A.7).

These findings indicate that racial resentment is not the only measure of racism that is correlated with tax opinions. White survey respondents who desire more separation between races and have doubts about Black people's ability also express more negative feelings toward the progressive federal income tax in the GSS, and those supporting segregation in the ANES prefer flat over progressive taxation. These findings square with the relationships reported earlier for symbolic racism: that those who score higher on the racial resentment index are less supportive of specific progressive taxes and progressive taxation as a general matter. It makes sense given the way taxes have been framed historically around race in the United States—that whites pay more than they benefit and Black Americans benefit more than they pay—that correlations between tax attitudes and the measure of racial animus based on perceived Black violations of white-coded values of individualism, hard work, and self-sufficiency would be particularly strong. Critics of the racial resentment measure might say that its relationship to tax attitudes arises from the fact that it measures not just anti-Black affect but opposition to government too, of which taxes are a visible manifestation. Purer forms of racial animus, however, such as support for segregation and other forms of social distance as well as beliefs in the biological inferiority of Black people, are also associated with antitax attitudes. These findings indicate that whites' feelings about Black Americans are key to their tax opinions, whether racism is measured in the modern, symbolic way with the racial resentment scale or the old-fashioned way, with items measuring explicit prejudice rooted in beliefs about the group-level social and biological inferiority of Black people.

Does White Identity Shape Tax Attitudes?

The findings show that whites' out-group attitudes toward Black Americans are strongly related to their tax attitudes. What about whites' in-group feelings? In *White Identity Politics*, political scientist Ashley Jardina (2019) defines a concept of white in-group solidarity and favoritism that operates separately from racial resentment. Jardina measures white identity with survey items asking, "How important is being white to your identity?" "To what extent do you feel that white people in this country have a lot to be proud of?" and "How much would you say that whites in this country have a lot in common with one another?" When these items are not available, she uses a white feeling thermometer. She examines whether those with strong feelings of solidarity with other whites have distinctive attitudes in a variety of policy areas.

Jardina finds that those for whom white identity is more important are more supportive of Social Security spending. In contrast, preferences on spending on means-tested programs are not correlated with white identity but instead with racial resentment.[41] Thus racial resentment, an out-group attitude, drives attitudes toward social assistance, but white identity, an in-group attitude, drives preferences on Social Security.[42] These findings square with Winter's conclusion that welfare is Black coded while Social Security is white coded. As Winter (2008, 9) puts it, "The racialization of welfare turns primarily on whites' views of blacks, whereas the racialization of Social Security turns on white Americans' feelings about their own racial group."

Might tax attitudes vary with white identity as well? The most plausible hypothesis emerging from the Jardina and Winter studies is that attitudes toward Social Security taxes may be associated with white identity. Unfortunately, I cannot test this hypothesis because the CCES data that measure payroll tax attitudes do not include a white identity item, and the ANES surveys that measure white identity do not contain a payroll tax item. With other taxes, hypotheses regarding associations with white identity are less clear. Perhaps white racial identity is related to attitudes toward the estate or capital gains taxes since wealth is coded as white in the United States. Yet we already know that racial resentment is strongly related to attitudes on just about every tax, especially progressive ones. It seems unlikely that white in-group identity is correlated with attitudes toward any tax except the payroll tax.

Our ability to examine whether white identity and any tax attitude is related is limited to the 2012 ANES, which contains two measures of white identity—the importance of white identity and a white feeling thermometer—as well as two types of outcome variables—an abstract item about the waste of tax dollars and three specific items about possible progressive tax reforms.

The findings show, yet again, a strong relationship between tax attitudes and racial resentment, but little relevance for white identity. For the abstract item about government spending and taxes—how much of the money the government collects in taxes is wasted—I find in a multivariate analysis that there is no relationship with white identity, while there is a relationship with racial resentment: the racially resentful are more likely to say the government wastes a lot of tax money, demographic and political variables as well as government trust held constant.

Nor is there much of a relationship between white identity and opinion on the three progressive tax proposals: support for a new tax on millionaires, support for closing the budget deficit with higher income taxes on those earning $250,000 or more, and support for closing the budget deficit with higher corporate taxes. At the bivariate level, there is no relationship between preferences on these three tax reforms and white identity (whether measured by the importance items or the white feeling thermometer).[43] In multivariate models also controlling for demographic characteristics, party identification, ideology, government trust, and racial resentment, white identity is only statistically significant in one of six cases (six cases because there are three tax questions, each with two measures of white identity): those who say white identity is more important to them are more favorable toward a tax on millionaires—a populist stance. Racial resentment is statistically significant in two of the six cases: the racially resentful are more opposed to an increased income tax on high earners, both when white identity is measured as importance and when it is measured with the feeling thermometer, in keeping with the findings above that the racially resentful are less supportive of progressive taxes.

These tests of the relationship between white identity and tax attitudes are incomplete because of the limited array of outcome variables. The evidence for a relationship is weak, however; white identity is not statistically significant in most cases, and the signs for the white identity coefficients are inconsistent. In contrast, the racial resentment coefficients are always in the expected direction (the racially resentful are more likely to think tax dollars are wasted and more opposed to progressive tax changes), even if only statistically significant in a few instances. The influence of white identity on tax attitudes awaits further work; at the same time, evidence for the influence of racial resentment continues to accumulate.[44] It seems that attitudes toward progressive tax reforms turn more on whites' attitudes toward Black Americans than sentiment toward their own racial group.

Sentiment toward the Wealthy

What about feelings toward the rich? Although many studies of redistributive policy analyze feelings toward the poor (that they fail to work hard and are undeserving), Kristina Jessen Hansen (2023) offers a microlevel theory of redistributive attitudes that focuses on feelings toward the rich. She finds with experimental and survey data in the United States and Denmark that those who like and admire the rich oppose increasing taxes on them, while those who envy the rich wish to increase their taxes.[45]

How do feelings about the rich stack up against racial resentment? In the 2012 CCES, I included a series of questions about the rich, asking respondents to indicate whether they thought each was "generally true or generally untrue of most rich people":

- They contribute generously to charitable causes
- They feel a responsibility to society because of the wealth they have
- They use their wealth mostly to protect their own positions in society
- They worked hard to earn the wealth they have
- They got where they are by exploiting other people
- Their spending gives employment to a lot of people
- Their investments help create jobs and provide prosperity

After a factor analysis indicated that these perceptions of the rich load on a single factor, I combined them into an index, reverse coding where necessary so that high scores mean positive feelings (Cronbach's alpha = 0.85). On the thirty-five-point scale, whites in the top third of racial resentment feel more positively toward the wealthy (average score twenty-four) than do those in the bottom third (average score eighteen).[46] The question is whether racial resentment continues to be correlated with attitudes on taxes on the rich even after controlling for these feelings about the rich.

The CCES data replicate Hansen's findings that those who feel more positively about the rich wish to tax them less (Campbell 2017).[47] In a multivariate analysis of white respondents, feelings toward the rich are correlated with attitudes toward estate, capital gains, and income taxes: whites who feel more positively toward the rich are more likely to want no estates taxed, a low capital gains tax, and reduced income taxes for those earning over $250,000. But racial resentment remains statistically significant for estate and capital gains tax attitudes, although not, all things being equal, with attitudes toward income taxes on high earners. Thus I confirm Hansen's finding that feelings about the rich are related to attitudes on progressive taxes. That's not the only thing going on, though. Racial resentment structures these attitudes above and beyond feelings about the rich.

Taken together, these CCES findings show that among white Americans, racial resentment has a strong relationship with tax attitudes. The racially resentful have a dim view of most taxes, especially progressive ones. Their skepticism extends to both specific taxes and progressive taxation as a general matter. They are also more supportive of the general notion of regressive taxation or flat taxes than are the racially sympathetic (with the exception of the gas tax, which earns their ire). These findings obtain above and beyond respondents' partisanship, ideology, income, government trust, and other factors, including, where I can test them, inequality attitudes, white identity, and feelings about the rich. They reveal that white Americans' tax attitudes are most consistently structured not by class or other markers of self-interest, or even partisan or ideological commitments, but rather by racial resentment. The opposition of the racially resentful to means-tested social spending and progressive taxes aimed at high-income and high-wealth households shows that the "consumer" view of taxation is alive and well. Taxes that ask more of the affluent and rich are not perceived as legitimate; the ability-to-pay principle (those who can afford more should contribute more to the public purse) has little sway with the racially resentful. Instead, both redistributive spending and progressive taxation are viewed as illegitimate because they violate the racially inflected consumer view that those who pay more should get more. That racially resentful whites are so opposed to progressive taxes helps diminish overall support for progressivity in the United States.

Whites' Tax Expenditure Attitudes

Racial resentment has a robust relationship with both spending and tax attitudes. What about indirect spending? The American tax code is replete with tax expenditures—the many credits, deductions, and preferential rates that subsidize various household and business activities, from owning a home to raising children to having employer-provided health insurance to purchasing equipment. The government does not collect taxes on the money used to secure these benefits (or collects less)—a form of "indirect" government spending, as opposed to the direct outlays that government makes when it provides Social Security, welfare, or Medicaid benefits, or pays contractors.

Mettler (2011) argues that tax expenditures for households are hidden because recipients getting tax breaks are less likely to say that they benefit from a government program than those benefiting from direct spending programs. But as chapter 3 shows, perceptions about which income groups get which tax breaks suggest that the hidden welfare state is not entirely hidden. The majority of respondents correctly assess that the EITC mostly benefits low-income taxpayers, and that the deduction for charitable contributions as well as the preferential rate on capital gains and dividends mostly benefit high-income households. Many respondents overestimate the shares of the home mortgage interest deduction as well as tax breaks for employer-provided health and retirement benefits that go to middle-income households (the breaks mostly go to top earners), but at least they recognize that low-income households rarely benefit from these breaks. One tax break where misperceptions are pronounced is the CTC: the majority of respondents think it benefits low-income households, whereas the actual benefits at the time the CCES surveys were conducted were fairly evenly distributed across the bottom four income quintiles.

Because income and race are correlated in the United States, we might imagine that there are racialized implications of this pattern of perception and misperception. We might predict that the racially resentful would be less supportive of tax breaks perceived as going mostly to lower-income (and therefore nonwhite) households such as the CTC and EITC, and more supportive of tax breaks perceived as going to affluent (white) households.

The evidence upholds these hypotheses, indicating that racial resentment structures white attitudes toward indirect spending through tax expenditures much as it does attitudes toward direct spending. Respondents in the 2016 CCES were asked whether they would like to eliminate, reduce the value of, or keep each tax break. Figure 6.7 shows the association between racial resentment and whites' tax break attitudes, holding other political and demographic characteristics as well as government trust constant. Positive coefficients indicate support for eliminating the tax break.

All things being equal, whites who are more racially resentful are more likely to want the EITC and CTC eliminated, just as they are more likely to want direct spending programs that are targeted toward lower-income groups to be reduced. Racial resentment is not a factor in attitudes toward the tax breaks that are perceived as going to the middle class (the breaks for employer-provided health insurance and retirement plans along with the home mortgage interest deduction).[48] These findings are akin to those on Social Security spending, also a "middle-class" program whose support does not vary with levels of racial resentment. Finally, the racially resentful are more supportive of the low preferential tax rate for investment taxes (the unearned income arising from capital gains and dividends), just as they were more skeptical of progressive taxation in general as well as income and estate taxes in particular.

Since many respondents correctly perceive high-income taxpayers as the main beneficiaries of the tax break for charitable contributions, we might have

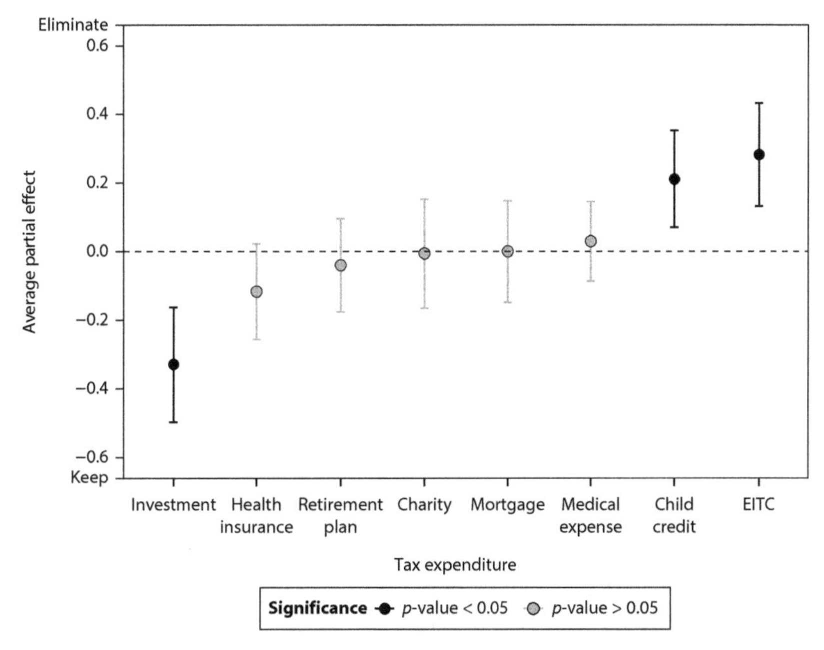

FIGURE 6.7 Desire to Eliminate Tax Expenditures and Racial Resentment
Note: "Eliminate break" is coded high. Whites only. Figure shows the average partial effect for racial resentment from ordinary least squares analyses also controlling for education, income, gender, age, marital status, children, homeowner, partisanship, ideology, and government trust.
Source: 2016 CCES.

anticipated that the racially resentful would be more supportive. Views on the charitable contribution tax deduction do not differ by level of racial resentment, however, perhaps because the break is more akin to the tax breaks utilized by many middle-class households such as those for employer-provided benefits. Many middle-class households make charitable contributions, even if they do not itemize deductions and get the break for doing so.

These findings indicate that tax expenditures display the same attitudinal structure as direct spending programs: racially resentful whites are more supportive of policies that help the privileged and more opposed to policies that help lower-income people. The CTC and EITC are racialized, similar to cash welfare and other income-targeted spending programs. The association might be a bit muted—Christopher Ellis and Christopher Faricy (2021) show that the effect of racial resentment on attitudes toward the EITC is less than for attitudes on the Temporary Assistance for Needy Families welfare program, and I find the same in the CCES data—but the relationship is there nonetheless. The dim view that many white Americans have of means-tested programs, situated in negative feelings about Black individuals, extends to tax breaks focused on lower-income people (the EITC) and the CTC, which is incorrectly perceived as centered on lower-income households as well.[49]

These findings help explain the lack of public enthusiasm for extending the pandemic era expansions of the CTC. In March 2021, Congress included a temporarily enhanced CTC in the American Rescue Plan pandemic relief bill. For the latter half of 2021, CTC eligibility was increased both up the income ladder and down to lower-income households that had previously been ineligible or only qualified for a partial benefit. The credit was also distributed monthly rather than as a lump sum at tax time. The enhanced credit was an immediate and enormous policy success, reducing child poverty by 30 percent (Turner 2022). Advocates had long sought these expansions, and thought that the credit's nearly universal nature—around 85 percent of all children under eighteen were covered—would ensure its popularity.[50] After all, for decades scholars had advocated modeling support for families on the universal Social Security program, which redistributes to lower-income seniors and nearly eliminates senior poverty in a hidden, nonstigmatizing way (Skocpol 1991). But a December 2021 Morning Consult poll showed that registered voters only approved continuing the enhanced credit for one year by 47 to 42 percent. And voters opposed making the expansion permanent, 51 to 35 percent (Yokley 2021). In the face of middling support, the enhanced credit expired at the end of 2021 after Congress declined to pass the Build Back Better plan, which would have made it permanent. A few states contemplated creating or enhancing their own CTC, but a federal expansion seemed unlikely (Thomson-Deveaux 2023). Why wasn't the credit more popular? One reason: the CTC was already racialized, considered in whites' minds as similar to welfare.[51]

Racial Resentment and Political Sophistication

So far the findings suggest that racial resentment and tax attitudes are highly correlated. We might wonder, however, whether this relationship varies across levels of political sophistication. For example, is the relationship stronger among whites who are less knowledgeable about taxes, with racism serving as a kind of heuristic guide for those who don't know much? Or is the relationship stronger among the knowledgeable, who are better able to link their tax attitudes to their racial affect? Both possibilities, especially the latter, have support in the literature.

I examined how the relationship between racial resentment and whites' tax attitudes varies across three measures of sophistication in the 2016 CCES (general tax knowledge, education, and income) and four attitudes (tax fairness, tax change preferences, federal spending, and tax expenditures; see online appendix, figures OA.1–OA.12 and tables OA.44–OA.55). Recall that general tax knowledge is measured with a two-item index (see chapter 3), but many respondents declined to answer the knowledge items, and so I use education and income as measures as well in order to preserve the number of cases. If racial resentment acts as a substitute for knowledge for the less politically sophisticated, then we would find that the relationship between racial resentment and tax attitudes is stronger for low-sophistication people than high-sophistication ones. Yet that is never the case: either the relationship is stronger among high-sophistication people (when sophistication is measured by general tax knowledge), or it is similar for high- and low-sophistication people (when sophistication is measured by education or income, which retains more cases). There are a few variations across taxes, but it is never the case that racial resentment is associated with tax unfairness or a desire to decrease a tax only among low-sophistication respondents.[52] For preferences on tax expenditures, the same patterns obtain. Either the correlation between racial resentment and tax expenditure opinion is greater at high-sophistication levels (when sophistication is measured by general tax knowledge), or the correlation is the same across sophistication levels (when sophistication is measured by education or income).

These findings indicate that racial resentment is a pervasive factor in white Americans' tax attitudes. It is not the case that racial resentment and tax attitudes are correlated only among low-sophistication respondents. Racial animus is not merely a shortcut or heuristic that those who know little about politics use to make sense of tax policy. Instead, racial resentment is a widespread correlate of whites' tax attitudes. Indeed, those who are more sophisticated by some measures are better able to line up their racial and tax attitudes. These findings underscore just how omnipresent racial resentment is in white Americans' tax preferences and opinions.

The Challenge of White Racial Attitudes for the American Fiscal State

Among white Americans, racial and tax attitudes are linked. The racially resentful do not merely have more negative attitudes toward the property tax, as Sears and Citrin showed. They do not just have more negative attitudes toward the federal income tax, as the Edsalls suggested. Racial resentment is a powerful correlate of attitudes toward every tax except the sales tax (by a hair), shaping attitudes above and beyond demographic indicators of self-interest, the other symbolic attachments of partisanship and ideology, and government trust. Racial resentment remains correlated with whites' tax attitudes when other factors are included in models as well: inequality attitudes, sentiment toward the rich, and white identity.

Racial resentment also influences opinion on tax expenditures, and not just attitudes toward direct spending, as has long been known. The racially resentful are less supportive of spending for lower-income groups whether it is direct, as through welfare, Medicaid, and food stamps, or indirect, through the EITC or CTC. Direct spending, indirect spending, taxes: they all have a similar attitudinal structure among nonrich whites. In refutation of the long-standing view that taxes represent a rare example of self-interested attitudes, tax preferences often do not vary by income or other indicators of material stake (chapters 3–4). Nor do tax attitudes differ between Democrats and Republicans, and between liberals and conservatives, as consistently as for many other issue areas (chapter 5). What does consistently structure whites' attitudes on both the spending and taxing sides of government activity is racial resentment.[53] Martin Gilens (1996, 593) found that whites' welfare attitudes are "inordinately shaped by highly salient negative perceptions of blacks." So too are whites' tax attitudes.

Furthermore, racial resentment and tax attitudes are correlated at all levels of political sophistication; racial resentment is not merely a shortcut used by low-information respondents. Racial resentment and tax attitudes have been correlated since the mid-1970s, the period for which we have data. Old-fashioned racism and tax attitudes are correlated too, going back to the early 1970s. The Edsalls were right: Reagan did mix together race, spending, and tax issues in white Americans' minds. But the historical record shows that these connections have much deeper roots in American history and governance. They are chronically available for activation when it advantages tax-cutting elites to do so.

The linkages between racial resentment and whites' opinions on tax expenditures are especially worth underscoring. Previous scholars' supposition that tax breaks are more politically feasible than direct spending programs because the public sees the beneficiaries as taxpaying workers who are more deserving than nonworking welfare recipients does not necessarily apply. There are limits to how "deserving" some white Americans think some tax break recipients are, especially the beneficiaries of the CTC and EITC.[54] True, the size of the racial resentment correlation is smaller for the EITC than for cash welfare, but the relationship is still there despite the supposedly protective policy design. Perceptions of who gets the CTC are simply wrong, as we saw in chapter 3, with respondents overestimating the share going to low-income households. What matters for white opinion, especially that of the racially resentful, is less the form of government spending, and more the identity of the real and imagined recipients. Spending on the middle class is not objectionable, whether direct (Social Security) or indirect (tax breaks for employer-provided benefits). But spending on lower-income (read: nonwhite) people, whether direct or indirect, is objectionable. What's key is that nonwhites are viewed as less deserving, little matter that tax break recipients must work to qualify for assistance. The racially resentful believe that nonwhites work less than whites and get more in benefits than they pay in—the old consumer approach to taxation rearing its head. The form of the spending is less relevant.

The tax expenditure system is therefore problematic not just because the middle class and affluent underestimate their government benefits, as Mettler has argued, but also because it is racialized. Put differently, only some aspects of tax expenditures are hidden. Racial and tax expenditure attitudes are linked because people do understand *somewhat* how the tax and tax expenditure systems work. They know approximately which income groups benefit the most from which tax breaks. They know that income and race are correlated in the United States, although they overestimate the share of the poor who are Black due to a news media that inaccurately portrays poor people as disproportionately Black, and codes the middle class and rich as white.[55] The level of understanding among nonrich Americans is not terribly high, but it is about as good as we would expect given tax complexity, media misportrayals, and elites' lack of clarity in discussing the system. What's key is that the level of knowledge is sufficient to enable racial resentment to operate. Indeed, the relationship between racial resentment and many tax attitudes is stronger among the more politically sophisticated.

We must add tax expenditures and taxes to the list of public policies that are ostensibly nonracial but around which whites' attitudes are structured by racial resentment.[56] The political implications are profound. Many white Americans, especially the racially resentful, do not see their own tax breaks as government programs but instead see—and resent—both direct and indirect spending on nonwhites. That the tax break system is actually tilted toward whites does not mitigate the racial politics of tax policy but rather exacerbates it. As Steve Teles (2013, 102) puts it, the tax expenditure system "perpetuates the national myth of radical individualism and independence while creating the impression that only other, less deserving people draw upon government largesse."

Tax breaks for the rich add to the problem and point to a second linkage worth underscoring: the racially resentful strongly support tax policy that helps the privileged. They are more likely than those who score low on racial resentment to think every tax is unfair and should be decreased, especially the progressive estate, investment, and federal and state income taxes. They are more likely to support regressive and flat tax systems, dislike progressive taxation as a general matter, and want investment taxes reduced as well as the CTC and EITC eliminated. Those who are racially resentful harbor positive feelings toward the rich. But even accounting for this favorable sentiment, the racially resentful disproportionately favor estate tax elimination and low rates for capital gains. That current policy has almost entirely defanged the estate tax and lowered tax rates on capital gains below those on earned income does little to alter these relationships. Continued hostility toward these taxes shows that when policies shift, attitudes often do not.[57] That these progressive taxes remain especially disfavored among the racially resentful also illustrates how policies are understood symbolically and shaped more by predispositions than by self-interest, as Sears (1993) argued.

The hostility of the racially resentful toward progressive taxation is particularly interesting given that the preferential capital gains tax has been a significant source of wealth accumulation at the top of the income spectrum and the ability to pass wealth onto children—frequently untouched by the estate or other taxes—has been a crucial mechanism of intergenerational privilege (Derenoncourt et al. 2022). The advantages arising from both of these policies accrue almost exclusively to white Americans.[58] The political and policy consequences of racial resentment are not just about undermining social policies for the poor. They are also about privileging the rich.

Indeed, racial resentment provides another reason why the progressive tax system fails to generate enough support. The racially resentful oppose both direct and indirect spending on low-income groups. They oppose nearly all taxes more than do the racially sympathetic, but especially the progressive income, estate, and capital gains taxes. These preferences, spurred by false narratives, help privileged whites in their perpetual campaign to get their taxes reduced. The nonrich racially resentful disapprove of spending and tax policies from which they would materially benefit, allowing racial resentment to become a powerful tool for undercutting progressive taxation to the benefit of the rich. As political economists Alberto Alesina and Edward Glaeser (2004, 218) put it in their book *Fighting Poverty in the United States and Europe*, "Racial conflicts can . . . be used strategically by political entrepreneurs interested not so much in 'hating blacks' but in preventing redistribution. By convincing even the not so rich whites that redistribution favors minorities, they have been able to build large coalitions against welfare policies." Group attitudes are more important for democratic politics than material interests, as Christopher Achen and Larry Bartels (2016, 18) argued, but the relevant groupings are not always partisan ones, as they asserted. With tax attitudes, it's racial groupings that matter, due to the long association between whiteness and taxpaying. Racial resentment has a corrosive effect on government's ability to fund itself, with many white Americans believing they are victimized by the nation's taxing and spending systems.

This chapter has shown that whites' racial attitudes are tightly linked to their tax attitudes and tax politics. Ironically, given the long history of white grievance, the real victims are Black Americans, as we will see in the next chapter.

7

State Coercion and Tax Attitudes among Black and Hispanic Americans

MANY WHITE AMERICANS harbor negative feelings toward government and its coercive powers. Taxes in particular are unpopular among white individuals and the focus of racially inflected white grievance. Many believe that the government extracts their earnings and spends that money not on them and people like them but instead disproportionately on the undeserving. Antitax politicians have ridden these sentiments to great electoral and policy success.

But what do Black Americans think of taxes? For the most part, we simply do not know. As historian Andrew Kahrl (2019, 191) has noted, the tendency of tax politics scholarship has been to concentrate on white taxpayers "to the virtual exclusion of African Americans, who are invariably cast as the object of white taxpayers' ire, and never as taxpayers in their own right." The same could be said of Hispanic Americans. The goal of this chapter is to focus on Hispanic and especially Black taxpayers to counteract this tendency, and explore how they feel about this crucial government function.

We might predict that Black Americans would be more supportive of taxes than white Americans. In their survey responses, Black Americans are more liberal on average than whites, and more supportive of a strong role for government and federal spending in a variety of areas, particularly social policy.[1] White Americans who share these characteristics are more favorable toward taxes; we might predict that Black Americans would be too.

Imposing taxes is one of the most coercive functions of government, however, and the Black experience of the state has been decidedly coercive over the course of American history. From institutionalizing slavery to abetting residential segregation to implementing highly punitive criminal justice and welfare systems, government has enabled and enforced systems of extraction, surveillance, control, and discipline that fall disproportionately on Black Americans. Joe Soss and Vesla Weaver (2016, 75) argue that political scientists have tended to focus on the "first face" of government power: the electoral and interest group processes by which citizens and organized groups contend for influence. More relevant for Black citizens, they say, is the American state's "second face" of power: the "practices of subjugation and repression" aimed at subordinate groups.[2] In this perspective, we might expect Black taxpayers, despite their support for government spending, to view the tax system as one more arm of a highly coercive government and have negative feelings about taxes as a result.

The findings in this chapter show that Black Americans are more likely than whites to say that a number of taxes are unfair and should be decreased, both in descriptive data and multivariate analyses controlling for differences in income, partisanship, government trust, and other factors. Moreover, the Black-white gap in tax attitudes is long-standing; Gallup and GSS data show that Black Americans have been more likely than whites to say their federal income taxes are too high over the entire public opinion record, going back to shortly after World War II. Even though most of the Black respondents in the survey data reported here are Democrats, they are much more likely than white Democrats to say every tax is unfair. Remarkably, their attitudes more closely resemble those of Republicans. And where government coercion has historically been the strongest, in the South, Black tax attitudes are even more negative. Raising revenues through taxation is a particularly coercive activity, and those citizens who have been on the receiving end of egregious government coercion in other arenas are not enthusiastic about coercion in this one. The fallout is that one of the few groups that embraces a strong role for government and supports government spending heartily dislikes taxes.

The irony of white anger over tax policy is that Black and Hispanic taxpayers are actually the victims of American tax policy. Critical tax theory, a movement in law and sociology, has revealed the many aspects of tax policy that are racially discriminatory, taxing Black and Hispanic Americans more than similar whites, at all levels of government.[3] The ways in which Black and Hispanic Americans earn, save, consume, hold assets, and even form families are typically less tax favored. In some cases, discriminatory policies were explicitly adopted as tools of racial repression. In others, white lawmakers writing tax policy simply ignored or were oblivious to the fact that provisions tailored to white lifestyles would result in the greater taxation of nonwhite households. The result is that Black Americans pay more than comparable whites, for both intentional and unintentional reasons. For all of whites' concerns about the long arm of government, Black Americans and other racial/ethnic minority groups have actually been the outsized victims of onerous tax policy.

I should underscore that I believe the mechanism behind Black and Hispanic taxpayers' more negative attitudes toward taxes is more their experience of the coercive state, and less their overtaxation in a self-interest sense. Black Americans have lower levels of formal tax knowledge on average than white Americans, as chapter 3 showed, and formal knowledge is typically needed for self-interest to influence attitudes. In other words, Black Americans may not explicitly know all the ways in which they are overtaxed. But they know that the government has historically and contemporarily held coercive power over them. They also likely recognize some disparate treatment, such as the high rates of audits for EITC claimants or overtaxation of Black homeowners in segregated neighborhoods, with the property tax deemed "the Black tax" in popular accounts.[4] Other disparities may be subtler, such as the lesser Black access to the tax expenditure system that the critical tax literature describes. Black taxpayers likely recognize some of these disparities, but also extrapolate from disparate treatment in other policy arenas to tax policy.

The economic ramifications of racialized tax policy are significant. By taxing Black and Hispanic Americans more, government reduces disposable incomes for these households, leaving them with less money for spending, savings, and asset accumulation. Taxes are one more policy in the long list of public policies designed by and for whites that undermine the economic prospects of nonwhites. The kicker is that in many cases, tax policy appears on its face to be race neutral, but in reality its effects are anything but. Overtaxing Black and Hispanic households is just one more way in which the state exercises power that reinforces white privilege and undermines the life prospects of nonwhites (Henricks and Seamster 2017).

The political implications of racialized tax policy are also profound. In previous chapters, we saw that many white Americans dislike taxes because they feel that government extracts resources from them to fund programs for nontaxpaying nonwhites, of whom they do not approve. In reality, nonwhites often pay higher taxes than whites because of the discriminatory nature of tax policy. The structural racism of the tax system means that some of the few groups in American society that embrace a strong role for government are punished at the hands of government because of the differential impact of tax policy across racial and ethnic groups. Tax policy thus undercuts overall support for government by harming otherwise progovernment groups.

The Black Experience of the State

We might imagine two sets of hypotheses about Black Americans' tax attitudes. On the one hand, Black individuals are more economically liberal than white Americans on average and support higher levels of federal spending, especially on social policies. Accompanying these more positive attitudes toward spending might be more positive attitudes toward taxes. On the other hand, the Black experience of the state is more negative. As taxes are one of the most coercive government functions, those who are frequently on the receiving end of heavy-handed government action may have more negative tax attitudes. As we will see, the data support the latter hypothesis: Black Americans are more likely to say most taxes are unfair and should be decreased compared to similar whites. Black taxpayers, who are typically ignored in analyses of tax opinion, harbor distinctive patterns reflective of their larger experience of the state.

General Government Attitudes among Black Americans

A long-observed pattern in public opinion research is that Black Americans have more positive attitudes toward the role of government and exhibit greater support for federal spending than white Americans. As political scientists Michael Dawson, Donald Kinder, and Lynn Sanders have shown with data from the 1980s and 1990s, and Zoltan Hajnal with data from 1972 through 2010, Black respondents are often 20 to 30 percentage points to the left of whites on survey items such as spending on government services and social welfare programs. They are more likely to support government health insurance, back increased spending for a variety of disadvantaged groups, and say the government should provide jobs and a good standard of living.[5] These differences have been apparent since the beginning of public opinion surveys; Eric Schickler (2016, 139) finds in survey data from the 1930s and 1940s that Black respondents were "well to the left of both southern and northern whites on economic policy."

These racial differences in preferences about the scope of government persist in contemporary CCES data, both in the abstract sense—generalized sentiment toward the role of government—and operational sense—preferences on government spending for specific programs.[6] As figure 7.1a shows, Black respondents are more likely than whites to describe themselves as liberal in the 2016 CCES data and to say government should provide more services even if it means an increase in spending (the two groups do not differ in their level of trust in federal government—a point to which we will return). Black respondents are also to the left of whites when it comes to operational items, that is, more likely to say that federal spending in a variety of areas should be increased (figure 7.1b). There is no difference between the groups for infrastructure as well as the big, universal Social Security and Medicare programs, where white support for increased spending is quite high and not racialized, as shown in the previous chapter. And whites are more supportive of increased defense spending. But for public school spending and means-tested programs, such as Medicaid, college financial aid, housing vouchers, food stamps, and welfare, the racial gap is particularly pronounced, with Black Americans much more supportive of increased spending, in line with decades of public opinion findings. Multivariate analyses show that Black respondents are still more liberal than whites and prefer more government services even after controlling for demographic factors. They also remain more supportive of increased spending on Medicare and all the means-tested programs.

Michael Dawson (1994, 182) explains that "the combination of blacks' low socioeconomic status and historical relationship to the federal government has led African Americans to be relatively pro-government." Among all survey respondents, those who are "progovernment" either because they are more liberal, identify as Democrats, support a larger abstract role for government, or favor increased federal spending tend to support higher taxes.[7] Since Black Americans exhibit these progovernment attitudes on average, we might expect them to support taxation to a greater degree than white Americans.

The Coercive State

On the other hand, there are significant reasons to predict that Black Americans might have more negative views of taxes than white Americans. One element may be Black awareness of economic disadvantage in American society. Black households have much lower levels of income and wealth than white Americans on average, due to many factors including the legacy of slavery along with historical and current patterns of segregation and discrimination in the labor market (Stewart et al. 2021). Black Americans are well aware of these economic

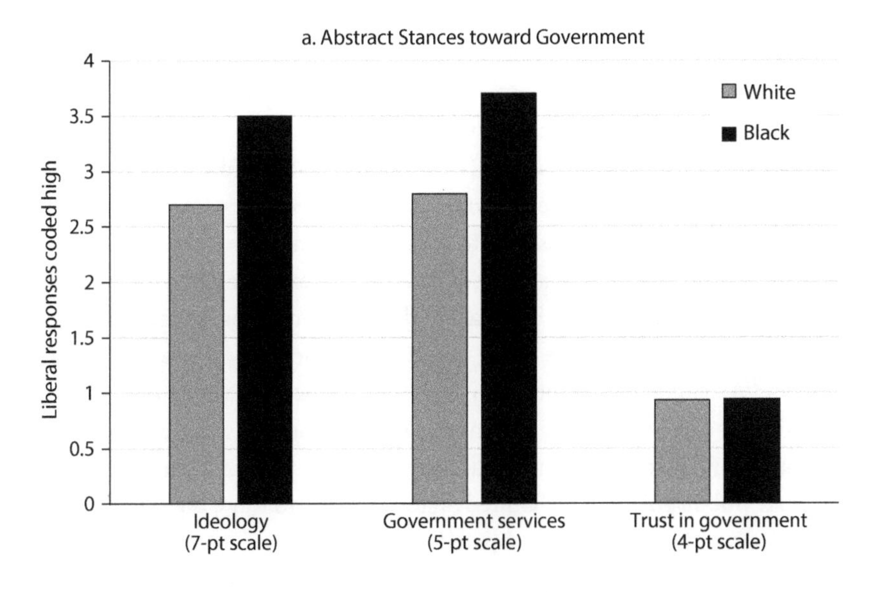

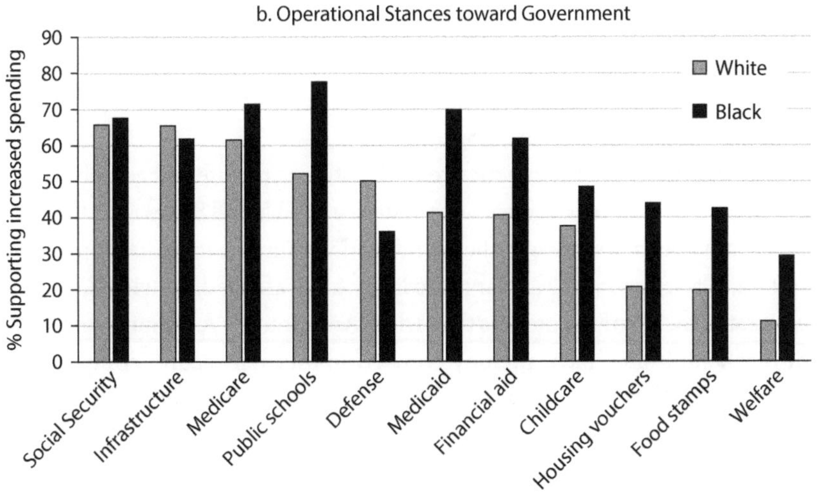

FIGURE 7.1 Racial Differences in General Orientations toward Government
Source: 2016 CCES.

disparities. For example, only 14 percent of Black adults told the Pew Research Center in 2021 that the economic system needs only minor changes or no changes for "Black people to be treated fairly," while 46 percent said it needs major changes, and 37 percent said it needs to be completely rebuilt (Edwards 2023). Dawson explains that awareness of economic disadvantage is associated with greater support for federal spending. But such disparities could manifest differently on the tax side of the equation: since taxes take away resources, those with less may be more negatively inclined.

A second reason that Black Americans may have distinctive tax attitudes is the Black experience of the state.[8] Handing over one's hard-earned money in the form of taxes is a coercive experience for everyone. But compared to white Americans, Black Americans tend to experience a more coercive state in general. In a variety of arenas, Black Americans have interactions with government that convey messages about how valued they are as citizens that are considerably more negative than the white experience, which may shape their tax attitudes.[9] As Jamila Michener (2019, 423) writes, "Race has been an enduring fulcrum around which elites and masses have arranged institutions, oriented discourse, and made decisions about how to prioritize, design, implement, and evaluate public policy in the United States." In myriad ways, the state actively constructs and controls "subordinated groups" at the intersection of race and class. For these groups, the relevant face of government is not the "first face" of electoral contestation or "combat" among organized interests but rather the "second face" of state power centered around control—"modes of coercion, containment, repression, surveillance, regulation, predation, discipline, and violence" (Soss and Weaver 2016, 74).[10]

The distinctive Black experience of the state is manifested acutely in the criminal justice and social assistance systems. The United States runs the largest criminal justice system in the world, and within this remarkably punitive system, Black Americans are far more likely to be arrested, convicted, and incarcerated for lengthy sentences than white Americans.[11] A stunning one-third of Black adult men have a felony conviction on their record, compared to 8 percent for the overall adult population (Sentencing Project 2018). The follow-on consequences are severe, with individuals with felony convictions facing barriers to employment, housing, social welfare programs, student aid, and the vote.[12] Contact with the criminal justice system disempowers citizens, undercuts their political efficacy, and undermines their sense of democratic citizenship, with such experiences sending the message that government does not care about them (Lerman and Weaver 2014). There are spillover effects on families and communities as well (Soss and Weaver 2017).

The social safety net system is also replete with practices that send negative messages to citizens about their apparent worth to government. Accessing social assistance programs such as cash welfare, housing aid, and Medicaid requires interacting with caseworkers who ask intrusive questions about one's personal life, and appear to have great control over whether one gets benefits and how much (Soss 1999). Such programs require recipients to reapply and prove eligibility again at intervals that differ by program and state, and that can be as short as every three months. The application and recertification processes are complex and confusing, with high administrative burdens often intentionally adopted to aid in gatekeeping and thwart enrollment (Herd and Moynihan 2018). Many means-tested programs impose work requirements on some or all recipients too, inflicting an additional layer of administrative burden, surveillance, and monitoring. Studies show that these practices lead recipients to believe the government does not trust them (Watson 2015).

In turn, such citizens do not trust government much. Black Americans tend to bear the brunt of practices that convey negative citizenship messages, with consequences for their feelings about government.[13] Although Black Americans on average are more liberal than white Americans, desire a greater role for government, and support more federal spending, they are not more trusting of government (figure 7.1a), even though white Americans who are similarly liberal, progovernment, and prospending do have higher levels of trust than other whites. This is one clue that the Black experience of the state has attitudinal consequences. And since trust is correlated with tax attitudes, as we learned in chapter 1, the low levels of government trust among this otherwise progovernment group gives a first hint that Black tax attitudes may be distinctive.

Tax Policy and Race

Black Americans have suffered economic coercion at the hands of the state as well. A long history of public policy in the United States has undermined economic prospects for many nonwhite groups, reducing incomes and opportunities for acquiring assets as well as magnifying the effects of private discriminatory practices. In some cases, government policy literally dispossessed the wealth of nonwhites (such as Native Americans stripped of their ancestral lands, Mexican Americans forcibly deported during the Great Depression, and Japanese Americans robbed of their assets when incarcerated in internment camps during World War II). In other cases, programs that led to generational wealth accumulation for whites explicitly excluded or sidelined nonwhites (Williams 2021).[14] The list is particularly long for Black Americans. Black freedpeople initially could not participate in the Homestead Act of 1862, whose promise of free land was a vehicle for financial security and wealth accumulation for millions of white families. Even after Black participation was later enabled, many of the recently emancipated lacked the money to travel to the claims office, buy tools and seed, and support themselves until a crop came in (Shanks 2005). Black participation in the Social Security retirement system too was delayed; occupations with predominantly Black workers were excluded when the law was enacted in 1935 and only added in the amendments of the 1950s (Lieberman 1998).[15] Access to the GI Bill, which provided World War II veterans with college, technical education, and low-interest mortgage, business, and farm loans, and contributed enormously to incomes and wealth in the postwar era, was tilted toward whites.[16] As mentioned, discrimination in the criminal justice system—excessive rates of conviction, sentencing, and criminal debt—has for decades undermined employment opportunities, incomes, and asset accumulation among the formerly incarcerated, who are disproportionately Black.[17] American public policy is replete with policy parameters and practices that have undercut economic opportunity as well as financial security for Black and other nonwhite citizens—including tax policy.[18]

A glaring example—and one in which taxes are implicated—is housing policy.[19] Private patterns of discrimination against Black homebuyers were intensified by early twentieth-century policies such as restrictive covenants on home sales, which reinforced segregation and were upheld by a 1926 Supreme Court ruling. When Black citizens could buy homes, they were forced into transitional or majority Black neighborhoods. They had to pay more because redlining meant such Black homebuyers were ineligible for federally backed mortgages with lower interest rates. Assessors would also overvalue such homes for taxation purposes, lowering disposable incomes. At the same time, the federal government and realtors used property appraisal guidelines that lowered home values when it came time for such homeowners to sell.[20] The high property taxes and poor public services in these neighborhoods—water and sewer services, roads, parks, and police and fire protection—also lowered resale values (and subjected Black children to underresourced public schools). Discriminatory housing policy provisions meant Black homeowners were hit coming and going, paying more and benefiting less from the main means of building wealth available to ordinary Americans.[21] Many of these practices, such as overtaxation and steering buyers of color to certain neighborhoods, continue to this day.[22] Moreover, newer practices target low-income and minority homeowners, such as tax auctions, which began in the 1990s, in which financially beleaguered cities raise revenues by selling property tax liens to private investors, who engage in predatory practices to collect the taxes or foreclose on the delinquent homeowners (Karhl 2017). For many Americans, especially at lower-income levels, the home is the main asset (Demsas 2020), but such practices undermine homeownership as a path to wealth for Black citizens. Indeed, the single-largest contributor to the Black-white wealth gap is homeownership (Brown 2021, 85).[23]

The property tax, to which I will return, is not the only tax that disfavors Black Americans. Many provisions in American tax policy discriminate on the basis of race as well as ethnicity and gender, even if such provisions do not appear to do so on their face.[24] We owe these observations to the field of critical tax theory. Examining "old, traditional tax issues from the perspective of feminism or critical race studies," critical tax scholars such as Beverly Moran, William Whitford, and Dorothy Brown have shown how tax provisions that adversely affect minority taxpayers "constitute, in effect, a form of discrimination" against them.[25]

Much of this scholarship concerns the federal income tax, a chief example of racially disparate tax policy. As Moran and Whitford (1996, 751) put it in their influential article, "A Black Critique of the Internal Revenue Code," the "Internal Revenue Code systematically favors whites over blacks." Tax expenditures are a major culprit. Black workers are less likely to hold jobs with employer-provided pension and 401(k) programs or to participate in them when available—programs that produce tax savings by deferring taxation until retirement, when one usually occupies a lower tax bracket.[26] Black Americans also hold relatively more wealth in vehicles, which are not a tax-favored investment, and less in real estate, stocks, and mutual funds, which are tax favored (because of the home mortgage interest deduction, large capital gains exclusion on home sales, and preferential tax rate on capital gains). The IRS does not publish data by race, but Tax Policy Center analysis shows that in zip codes with the highest rates of those claiming the home mortgage interest deduction, the population was 82 percent white and 5 percent Black. In those with the lowest rates of claiming, the Black population was almost three times higher, or 13.4 percent (Brown 2021, 71–72). Black homeowners suffer from an "appreciation gap" too, as Brown (2021, 79–80) puts it, benefiting less than whites from the exclusion from taxation of the first $500,000 in capital gain on a home sale.

Black (and Hispanic) households also rarely benefit from the low tax rate on unearned income such as capital gains and dividends; almost all of their income is taxed at the higher earned income tax rates. Survey of Consumer Finances data show that whites constitute 65 percent of families, but own almost 90 percent of corporate stock, nearly 90 percent of business assets, and more than three-quarters of all real estate. Black families own less than 2 percent of stock and business assets, and less than 6 percent of real estate holdings. The figures for Latinos, whose tax policy experiences are explored below, are even more modest: 0.5 percent of stock, 1.7 percent of business assets, and 5.3 percent of real estate (Hughes and Sifre 2021). Thus nearly all the unearned income arising from capital gains on asset sales and dividends paid on stockholdings goes to whites. Differences by race in asset types and sources of income remain even after controlling for income level (Moran and Whitford 1996).[27]

Black taxpayers are disadvantaged in subtler ways as well. In her seminal book *The Whiteness of Wealth*, Brown (2021) shows how the tax code interacts with patterns of family formation and earnings in ways that lead Black taxpayers to pay more.[28] The tax treatment of married couples provides one example. When the federal income tax was established in 1913, people were required to file as individuals, not as households as we do today. The ability of married couples to file a joint return originated in 1927 with a rich (white) Washington State shipbuilder, who decided to put half his income on a tax return for his nonworking wife in order to pay a lower tax rate. He figured he could do so because he lived in a community property state. But rather than getting charged with tax fraud for this illegal gambit, he took his case, with the help of a prominent law firm, all the way to the Supreme Court. The Court ruled in his favor, giving him and other married Americans "a permanent tax cut." This is the origin of the imputed income bonus (chapter 4) that one-earner couples enjoy because the stay-at-home family member's household services are not taxed—a benefit that grows with household income because of the graduated system of income tax rates (Brown 2021, 30–33).[29] As Brown (1997, 2021) points out, though, Black married women are more likely to work than their white counterparts, and so Black couples less often benefit from the advantages of joint filing. In addition, these advantages are greatest when one spouse earns much more than the other, and smaller when earnings are more similar—which is more common among Black households. She also shows how whites' marriage bonuses and Blacks' marriage penalties grow more common as incomes rise, and have been reinforced by tax changes such as the Bush and Trump tax cuts.

Adding insult to injury, Black taxpayers are more likely to be audited by the IRS, a group of academic and Treasury Department economists found (Elzayn et al. 2023). In the face of budget cuts, the agency has turned to automated systems, which although appearing race neutral, choose Black taxpayers for federal tax audits at three to five times the rate of non-Black taxpayers. The analysis demonstrates that the IRS's model is more likely to flag those who overclaim refundable tax credits like the EITC (who are more likely to be Black) than those who underreport taxes (who are more likely to be white). Lacking resources, the agency is less likely to examine complex returns, such as those with "substantial business income," which are more likely to be from white taxpayers. Also, the algorithm does not take into account the amount of money at stake. The result is that Black taxpayers are more likely to be audited over minor, low-value mistakes in misclaiming tax breaks, while white taxpayers with substantial business income, where much more tax revenue is involved, escape the IRS's scrutiny.

Racial discrimination in tax policy extends well beyond the federal income tax. And if at least some of the structurally racist provisions of the federal income tax code are inadvertent, or at least initially ignored the effects on nonwhites, the racial impact of other tax structures has often been far more intentional.

The sales tax in many southern states is one such example, as sociologists Katherine Newman and Rourke O'Brien (2011) maintain in their history of state and local taxation in the American South. A boom in government building projects during the roaring 1920s came home to roost during the 1930s, when many states struggled to service the resulting debt as revenues dropped during the Depression. In the South, the search for new revenues took a racialized cast as white property owners successfully pressured their state governments to create new sales taxes rather than increase property taxes. In doing so, they both minimized their own taxes (almost all property was white owned) and burdened the poor with regressive new sales taxes. The burden was concentrated among Black residents, who constituted a large percentage of the poor in the South, but could not voice their opposition, having been disenfranchised by Jim Crow. Newman and O'Brien proceed to argue that these regressive tax systems failed to raise sufficient revenue too, resulting in poor-quality public education, insufficient public investment, and low economic growth rates, disadvantaging all state residents, but especially Black residents, who already bore the weight of the high sales taxes.[30]

Property tax limitations have proven another durable form of racial disparity, with white Americans seeking to minimize their own property taxes, resulting in the higher taxation of nonwhites and less public investment, also harmful to nonwhites. Proposition 13, passed in California in 1978, as noted earlier, prompted a wave of property tax limitations by ballot initiative (they are now present in two-thirds of the states) (Martin and Beck 2017). But the history of such limitations is much older. An early example is the property tax limitation added to the Alabama Constitution in 1875, intended to protect white property owners from paying for Black students' education (Martin and Beck 2017). Race was implicated in the property tax revolt of the late 1970s and early 1980s as well, in two ways. First, an impetus for the property tax revolt was a series of good government reforms passed in state legislatures that had the effect of removing a form of white privilege: property underassessments. These laws standardized real estate appraisal, limited assessors' discretion, and enforced "common standards across jurisdictions." They came as welcome news for minority homeowners, promising "to bring a semblance of justice and equity to a system that historically rendered them susceptible to exploitation and abuse," as Kahrl (2018, 395) has written, but also meant higher bills for white homeowners as they lost the "informal privileges" that had been "bestowed on them by the state."[31] They made their dissatisfaction clear with the property tax revolt. Second, although Prop 13 is often upheld as a signal example of self-interest affecting voting behavior—support was stronger among homeowners than among renters—racial resentment also played a role, with the racially resentful more supportive of the tax limits than the racially sympathetic (Sears and Citrin 1985).

Sociologists Isaac Martin and Kevin Beck (2017) analyze data from 1986 through 2011, and find that tax limitation measures succeeded in lowering whites' property tax burdens compared to other racial and ethnic groups. Controlling for a host of characteristics, including income, state, and duration of residence, they find that Black homeowners pay higher property tax rates than white homeowners. The racial gaps are larger in states with property tax limitations in place and have grown over time as the effects of the limitation measures have accumulated. These property tax limitations are highly valuable; Martin and Beck calculate that nationwide, they saved homeowners $62.6 billion in 2011, almost as much as the value of the home mortgage interest deduction, which was $88.7 billion that year, and more than the value of federal housing assistance, which was $55.4 billion. A disproportionate share of the savings went to white homeowners because they own most of the housing wealth that benefits from such limitations.

White Americans also benefit disproportionately from assessment lags and appeals. Whites are more likely to own homes that are expensive or that rapidly increase in value, both of which tend to be underassessed and undertaxed because of lags in updating assessed values.[32] Moreover, white homeowners are more likely to appeal their property tax assessments, win their appeals, and get a larger reduction than Black and Hispanic homeowners (Avenancio-Leon and Howard 2020).

The result of these private and public actions is the greater taxation of non-white homeowners. The racially disparate effects have long been recognized; in 1973, the US Department of Housing and Urban Development (1973, 75) released a report finding that property taxes in Baltimore, Chicago, and Philadelphia had "a regressive impact" with the "burden of the tax bias [falling] most heavily on the properties occupied by low-income minorities." More contemporarily, an examination of twenty-six million home sales from 2007 to 2017 reveals that lower-value properties are pervasively overassessed for tax purposes, with the overassessments—and higher effective property tax rates—concentrated in Black neighborhoods (Berry 2021).[33] A 2020 study found that Black homeowners pay on average 13 percent more in property tax each year than similar whites (Black and Latino homeowners together pay 10 percent more) (Avenancio-Leon and Howard 2020). Overtaxed, Black homeowners are more likely to fall behind and fall victim to the tax auctions previously mentioned. Segregated patterns of homeownership—where Black citizens own homes—interact with differences in the tax treatment of expensive and inexpensive homes as well as differences across jurisdictions in achieving tax limitations to create differences in the effective property tax rates that Black and white homeowners pay. Such practices are particularly harmful to Black asset accumulation, as houses constitute a greater share of Black than white wealth (DeSilver 2013).

If property and sales tax differences across racial subgroups result from intentional efforts, we might wonder how such racial inequalities came to riddle the federal income tax code, which seems on its face race neutral. Moran and Whitford (1996) argue that one source is ignorance among members of Congress about the lived experience of Black individuals and families and the ways in which they would be differentially affected by various tax provisions. As white lawmakers over the decades adopted tax provisions that favored particular patterns of income, assets, consumption, and family configurations, there was little consideration of what such provisions might mean for other groups, especially Black Americans. "Our tax system, much like the rest of our law, was created by mostly wealthy, mostly male, mostly white individuals," legal scholar Sharon Nantell (1999, 64) notes.[34] Other observers cite the nature of the tax bar, which is also overwhelmingly white and prefers the view that the tax system is a "pristine revenue-raising machine" rather than one that institutionalizes certain values (Abreu and Greenstein 2018). As legal scholar Marjorie Kornhauser (1998, 1627) argues, "We must constantly be aware that the tax laws reflect social and political choices, not just economic ones, and that all these choices have different impacts on different groups." Both intentional and unintentional tax provisions are prime examples of public policies that first materialize and then institutionalize the power of dominant groups and discrimination against subordinate groups, as political theorist Clarissa Hayward (2013) puts it.

Regardless of their origins, these discriminatory tax policies reduce the disposable incomes of Black households and feed the enormous Black-white wealth gap. In 2019, Survey of Consumer Finance data revealed that median family wealth was $184,000 for whites, compared to $23,000 for Black families (Kent and Ricketts 2021).[35] Fifteen percent of white families were millionaires in 2019, compared to 2 percent of Black families, and even within this rarefied group, Black assets are less.[36] The racial wealth gap exists within every education level, where the median value of assets is much lower for Black families than white families, and the gap exists for every asset type: homes, businesses, stocks/bonds/mutual funds, and retirement accounts (Kent and Ricketts 2021). Moreover, progress in closing the racial gap slowed after 1950, and since the 1980s it has reversed. Most Black household wealth is tied up in housing, which has appreciated at one-fifth the rate of stock equity, which is predominantly owned by whites (Derenoncourt et al. 2022).

Almost all wealth in the United States is white. And a great deal of that wealth is taxed not at all or at low rates (Kahrl 2017). Not only are Black Americans and other nonwhite groups less likely to enjoy wealth and all of the beneficial nonmonetary effects of financial security, such as lower stress, favorable child development, and so on. Black and Hispanic Americans are also far less likely to enjoy the favorable tax policies aimed at high-income and high-wealth households—low capital gains rates and favorable estate tax provisions—while more subject to other tax policies that discriminate against them.

Attitudinal Hypotheses Arising from Racialized Tax Policy

Black Americans are often on the receiving end of the state's coercive powers. State-sanctioned forms of discrimination have undercut Black incomes and wealth over time. Racially disparate forms of surveillance, control, and punishment permeate Black experience with many forms of public policy. Tax policy, which constitutes a coercive face of government for all taxpayers, is designed to fall disproportionately on Black Americans for intentional and unintentional reasons that materialize in many types of taxes across all levels of government. Because Black Americans recognize that they are economically disadvantaged in American society and are aware of being on the receiving end of government coercion in other policy areas, we might expect them to have more negative attitudes about a particularly coercive form of government power: taxation.

I want to emphasize that this prediction about the distinctiveness of Black tax attitudes is not rooted in self-interest per se. Chapters 3 and 4 showed that Americans' tax attitudes rarely vary by objective measures of material stake. I can hardly argue that Black taxpayers know their self-interest with regard to tax policy while white taxpayers do not. Moreover, policy knowledge is important for the operation of self-interest as an influence on attitudes, and Black Americans on average have lower levels of formal tax knowledge than whites. Instead, the prediction of more negative tax attitudes among Black Americans arises from two pathways. One is the likelihood that Black taxpayers extrapolate from their other experiences of the state. In his interviews with welfare recipients, Soss (1999) finds that those dealing with intrusive, gatekeeping caseworkers who exercise arbitrary control over their benefits conclude that government in general is capricious, arbitrary, and punitive. Black taxpayers could similarly be expected to project from disparate treatment in some coercive policy areas (criminal justice and social assistance) to others (taxation), deducing that if they suffer punitiveness in one arena, they will suffer it in another. A second pathway is that Black taxpayers may project from more well-known instances of tax discrimination, such as the property tax, to others that are less visible, such as the racially disparate effects of some income tax provisions. Black Americans have long spoken of the property tax as a Black tax on homeownership (Kahrl 2018, 393). Researchers have shown that restrictive housing practices and the ensuing overtaxation were well-known in the Black community because of personal experience; the efforts of civil rights organizations to expose the role of federal government policy, and not just market practices, in undermining homeownership for Black Americans and enforcing segregation when they did achieve ownership (Thurston 2018, chap. 4); and the historical Black press, which contained abundant anecdotal evidence of discriminatory taxation (Kahrl interview, in "All Stick No Carrot" 2019).[37] One could reasonably surmise that ill-treatment in one area of tax policy extends to others as well.

Black Americans' Tax Attitudes

Although Black Americans profess more progovernment attitudes than whites in both the abstract size-of-government sense and operational federal-spending sense, their tax attitudes exhibit quite a different pattern. Descriptively, Black Americans are more likely than whites to say that a number of taxes are unfair. Each of the tax questions in figures 7.2a–c is arrayed by the size of the Black-white difference. The "share I have to pay" item in 2012 (figure 7.2a) elicits particularly large racial differences across the five taxes included. The gap is especially big for the state sales tax, but is also sizable for the federal and state income, Social Security, and property taxes.[38]

When asked about "the amount I have to pay" in 2016, Black Americans are more likely than whites to say that state and federal income as well as property taxes are unfair (figure 7.2b). These are the three taxes Black Americans deem most unfair with this question wording, and the three taxes for which the gap relative to whites is largest. Racial differences across the other taxes are more muted, and whites are slightly more likely to say what they have to pay in the estate tax is unfair.[39] Figure 7.2c shows that the taxes Black Americans most want to decrease are the property, federal income, state income, and gas taxes that they had deemed unfair. But whites are generally as or more likely to want each tax decreased.

For politics, the descriptive differences in Black and white opinion are typically what matter. Social scientists want to know, however, whether such differences persist after controlling for other factors that also differ across racial groups and that may also affect tax attitudes, such as education, income, party identification, and government trust. Figure 7.3 utilizes the same question on the fairness of the "amount I have to pay" as shown in figure 7.2b, combining data from the 2016 and 2019 CCES modules in which the same item appeared. The figure shows that above and beyond differences in demographic and political characteristics, Black respondents are more likely than whites to say each tax is unfair, with the results achieving statistical significance for federal and state income taxes as well as the payroll tax.

Even though descriptively, Black and white respondents were either equally likely to want each tax decreased, or whites were more likely to want decreases, after controlling for demographic and political factors as well as government trust, Black respondents are more likely to want all taxes except for property and payroll taxes decreased (figure 7.4). The confidence intervals are wider than in figure 7.3 because this item was only asked in 2016. Together with fig-

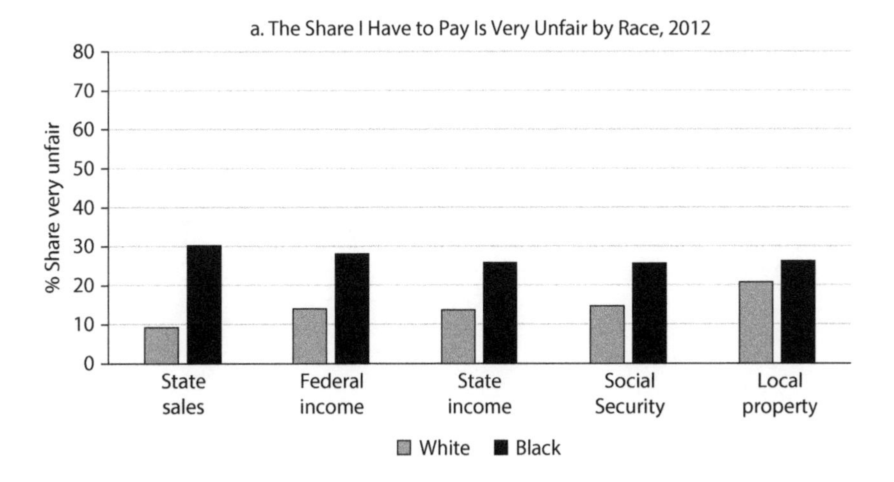

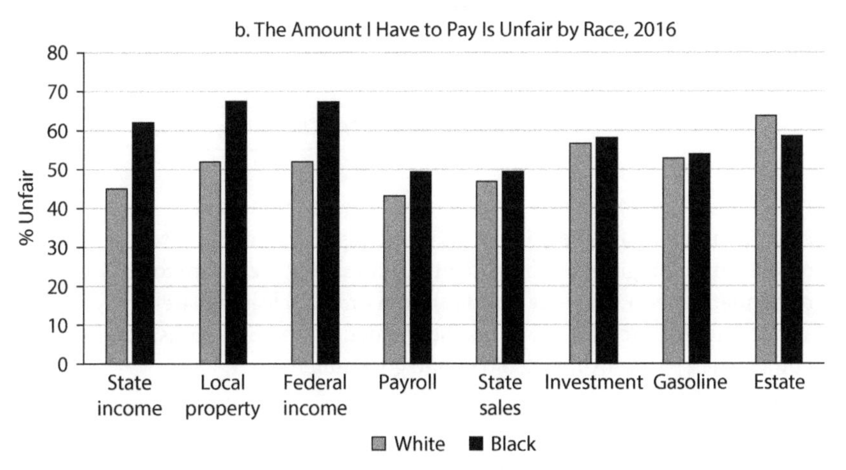

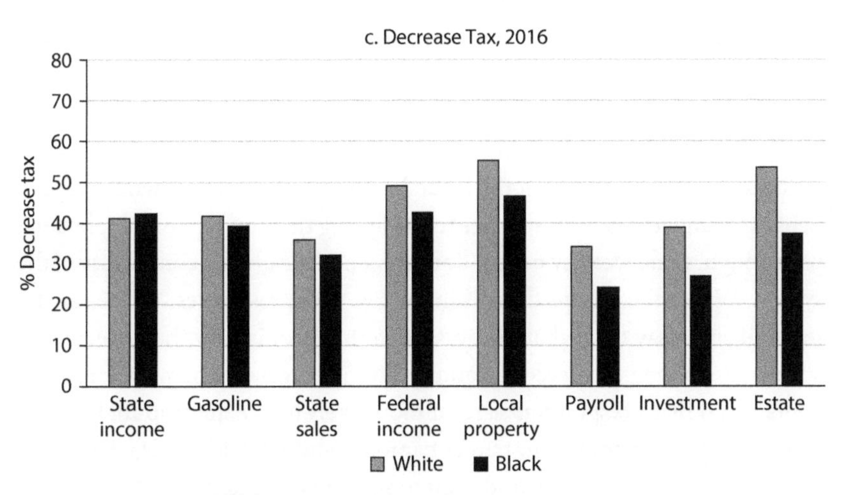

FIGURE 7.2 Racial Differences in Tax Attitudes
Source: 2012 and 2016 CCES.

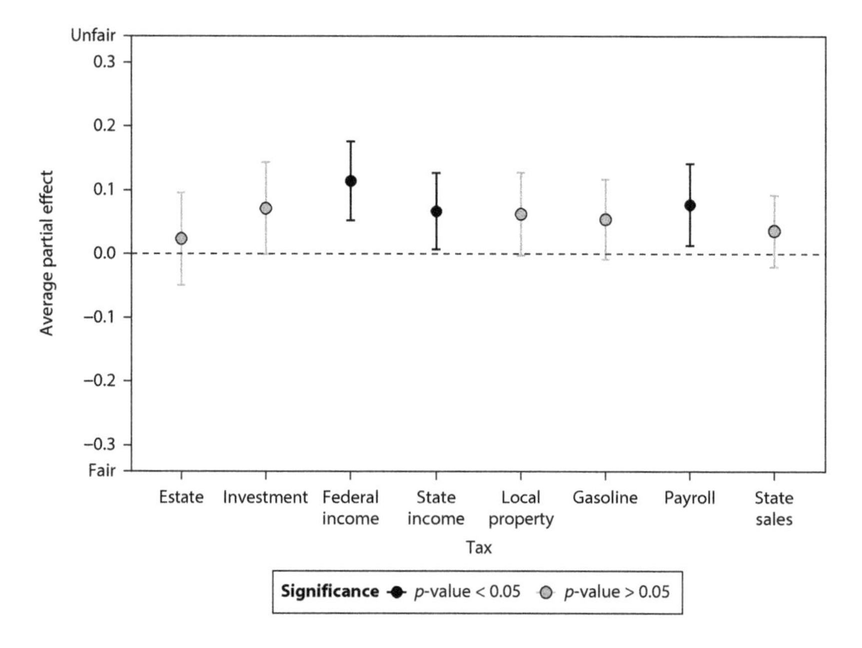

FIGURE 7.3 Tax Unfairness: Black versus White Respondents
Note: "Amount I pay is very unfair" is coded high. Progressive taxes are arrayed on the left, and regressive on the right. Figure shows coefficient for Black respondents (with whites as baseline) from ordinary least squares analyses also controlling for education, income, gender, age, marital status, children, homeowner, partisanship, ideology, and government trust.
Source: 2016 and 2019 CCES.

ure 7.3, it shows that Black Americans are more likely than white Americans to say that a number of taxes are unfair and should be decreased, even though they are more positively disposed toward government in general and federal spending, especially on social welfare policies.

It's also worth noting that in the 2016 CCES item asking respondents what bothers them the most about the federal income tax, Black and white respondents are similar in their responses to the feeling that some poor people don't pay enough, some wealthy people don't pay enough, and the complexity of the system. Where the groups differ is in the two other responses. Whites are far more likely to say that what bothers them the most is how the government spends the money (30 percent, compared to 13 percent among Black respondents). And Black respondents are far more likely to cite the amount they pay (29 percent, compared to 10 percent among whites). Clearly Black respondents feel that they pay a lot and want to see taxes decreased.

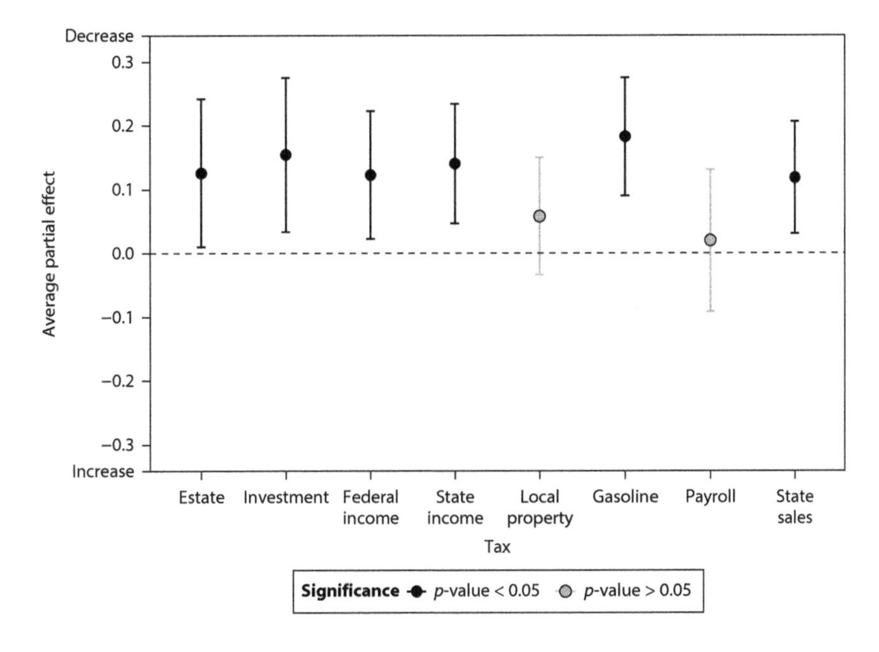

FIGURE 7.4 Tax Change Preferences, Black versus White Respondents
Note: "Decrease tax" is coded high. Ordinary least squares model. Figure shows coefficient for Black respondents (with whites as baseline) with controls for income, education, gender, age, marital status, children, homeowner, partisanship, ideology, and government trust.
Source: 2016 CCES.

Two things are striking about these findings. First, Black Americans are more likely to say many taxes are unfair and should be decreased even after accounting for racial differences in demographic and political characteristics. That means that Black and white Americans of similar types have different tax attitudes. It also indicates that Black taxpayers have an additional sense of unfairness that is not captured by differences in income, partisanship, and so on, or even government trust. That the differences cannot be accounted for by government trust is especially worthy of further research to probe the reasons behind Black Americans' distinctive tax attitudes.

Second, one reason that I was able to combine the 2016 and 2019 CCES data to increase the sample size in figure 7.3 is that an examination of the individual datasets revealed that Black respondents were more likely to say various taxes were unfair under both Obama and Trump. Especially for the federal income tax, Black Americans were more likely than comparable whites to say the federal

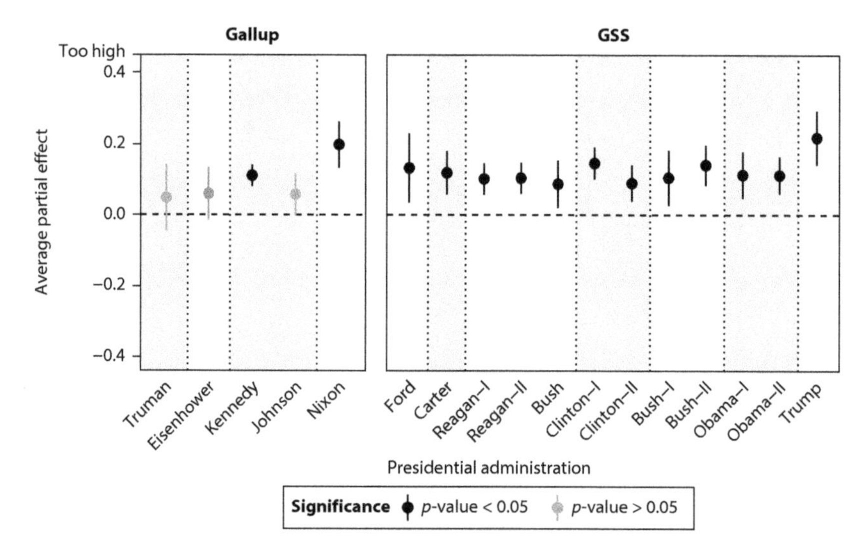

FIGURE 7.5 Federal Income Tax Too High by Race across Presidential Administrations
Note: "Federal income tax too high" is coded high. Full sample. Ordinary least squares model. Figure shows the average partial effect for Black respondents compared to the reference category of whites. Democratic presidential administrations shaded. Gallup results on the left control for income, education, gender, age, homeowner, and partisanship; GSS results on the right additionally control for marital status, children, "other" race group, and ideology. The results are largely the same when GSS covariates are limited to those available in Gallup. Government trust not included in these analyses. For the descriptive versions, see appendix figures A.8 and A.9.
Sources: Gallup 1947–73; GSS 1976–2018.

income tax was unfair both under the nation's first Black president and his successor, known for his racially incendiary language. The Black-white difference transcends particular presidential administrations.

Data from Gallup and the GSS confirm that the Black-white gap in federal income tax attitudes is a chronic phenomenon. Black respondents are always more likely than white ones to say their federal income taxes are too high, dating back to the immediate postwar period, both descriptively, shown in appendix figures A.8 and A.9, and after controlling for demographic and political differences, as portrayed in figure 7.5, which shows the average partial effect for Black respondents compared to the white baseline, all things being equal.

Nor does the gap depend on the partisanship of the president, as did the Republican-Democratic differences shown in chapter 5. Year in and year out, regardless of whether a Republican or Democrat occupies the White House, Black respondents are more likely than whites to say their federal income taxes are too high—even when the nation's first Black president called 1600 Pennsylvania Avenue home.[40]

Black Respondents versus White Republicans

The multivariate results in figure 7.3 showed that Black respondents are more likely than whites to say the amount they pay for every tax is unfair, with statistically significant results for several taxes. It's worth underscoring what this means with one more descriptive figure. Figure 7.6 depicts the percentage of Black respondents, white Democrats, and white Republicans who say the amount they pay in each tax is unfair, arrayed in order of the Black-white Republican difference. Nearly all the Black respondents are Democrats, but they are far more likely than white Democrats to say each tax is unfair. Indeed, their tax attitudes are more similar to those of white Republicans. For federal income, state income, and the property taxes, Black respondents are even more likely than white Republicans to say the taxes are unfair (67 versus 62 percent for the federal income tax, 62 versus 49 percent for the state income tax, and 68 versus 58 percent for the property tax).

Consider the political consequences. Black Americans are one of the few groups in American society that is relatively progovernment by a number of measures: more liberal, more Democratic, and more supportive of government spending. Yet many members of this group are also antitax—in some cases, even more so than white Republicans. This further helps Republican political forces hostile to taxes. Recall the finding in chapter 5 that not only do large shares of Republicans express hostility toward taxes, but so do even larger shares of independents and sizable minorities of Democrats. The Republican antitax stance picks up a lot of supporters from outside the party. Here we see that the antitax stance picks up significant Black support as well, especially the income taxes against which Republicans have long railed, and the property tax. Here is yet more evidence about the difficulty of raising revenues in the United States. Members of these groups may have different reasons for disliking taxes, but the point is that they all dislike taxes, which helps the antitax party and the economic elites perpetually seeking to cut their own taxes.

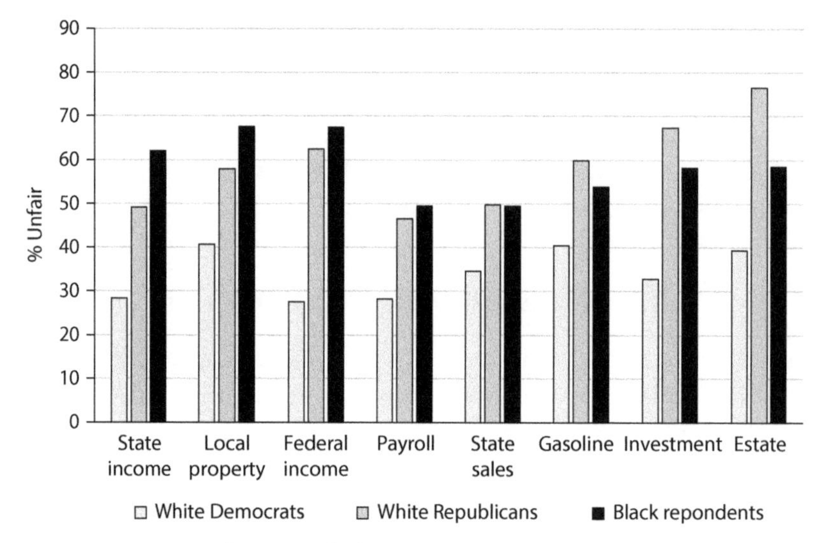

FIGURE 7.6 Tax Unfairness: Black Respondents versus White Democrats and Republicans
Note: The bars indicate the percentage of respondents in each group who say the amount they pay in each tax is unfair.
Source: 2016 CCES.

State and Local Taxes in the South

The survey results thus far support the hypothesis that Black Americans might have negative views of taxes in comparison with whites despite being more progovernment and supportive of federal spending because taxes are an extension of the coercive state, under which Black Americans have long suffered. We might further hypothesize that where taxes are more coercive, Black taxpayers would be even more likely to deem them unfair, which brings us to the American South.

Newman and O'Brien contended that southern state revenue systems were historically designed to saddle Black households with heavy sales taxes while homeowners, who were disproportionately white, enjoyed light property taxes. One question is whether these disparate impacts continue today and are reflected in public opinion.

Data on state and local tax structures gathered by the ITEP and Tax Foundation reveal that many southern states continue to burden lower-income taxpayers more than other states, although they are far from alone in having regressive tax structures.[41] That said, southern states still tend to rely heavily on sales taxes for revenue, with high sales tax rates and fewer exemptions than other states, along with low property tax rates.

Among the former Confederate states, four are heavily reliant on the sales tax for state revenue. Texas, Florida, Tennessee, and Mississippi rank numbers one, two, five, and seven in terms of states with the highest reliance on sales taxes (defined as retail sales tax collections as a percentage of total state tax revenue). Two more southern states are above median in their sales tax reliance (Arkansas and Louisiana), while the remaining five are below median in their reliance (South Carolina, North Carolina, Alabama, Georgia, and Virginia).

Sales tax *rates* may be more visible to residents, however, than overall state reliance on the sales tax for revenue. Four of the five states with the highest combined state and local sales tax rate are in the South (Louisiana, Tennessee, Arkansas, and Alabama). Except for Virginia and North Carolina (barely), all the southern states are in the top half of states in terms of their combined state and local tax rates. Five of the eleven former Confederate states impose state sales taxes on groceries, and five allow local sales taxes on groceries. Nearly all southern states lack a refundable credit in their income tax systems to offset sales, excise, and property taxes.

Southern states also continue to have light property taxes, to the advantage of whites who are more likely to own property. Average effective property tax rates (taxes paid as a percentage of home value) are low in the South, with Alabama, Louisiana, South Carolina, and Arkansas ranking numbers two, four, five, and ten in terms of states with the lowest effective property taxes. With the exception of Texas, southern states all have below-median effective property tax rates (Tax Foundation 2022).

These data indicate that southern state and local tax systems continue to reflect Newman and O'Brien's findings, although they are not the only states with high sales or low property taxes. In turn, CCES data reveal that southern Black respondents stand out compared to nonsouthern Black respondents as well as southern and nonsouthern whites in their attitudes toward these taxes. In the 2016 CCES, nearly half of Black southerners (46 percent) say that the amount they pay in sales tax is unfair, compared to 19 percent of white southerners and just 13 percent of Black respondents outside the South (the figure for whites outside the South is 22 percent). These are the top-line, descriptive figures; perhaps Black southerners are more likely to say the sales tax is unfair because they have lower incomes than other respondents or other characteristics related to tax attitudes. Figure 7.7 shows the average partial effect for

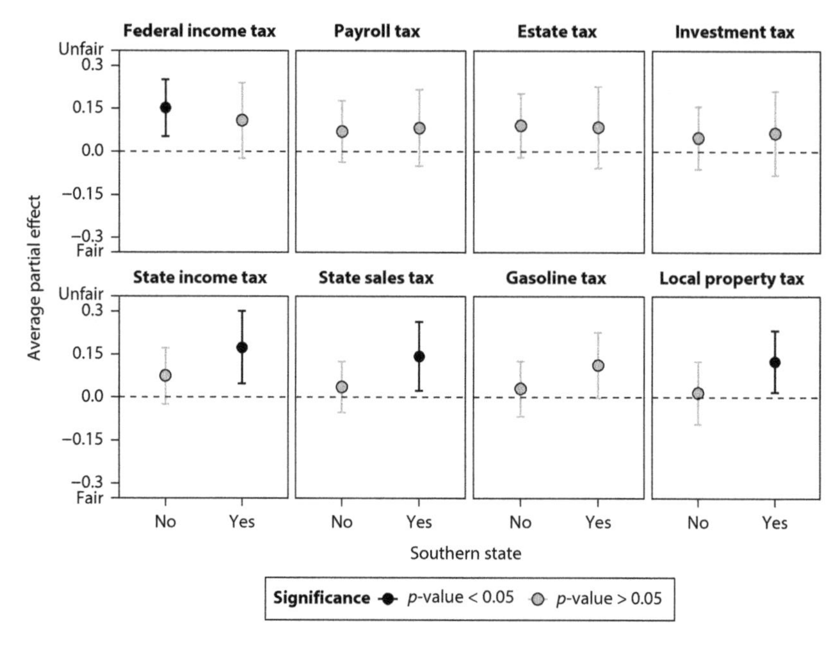

FIGURE 7.7 Tax Unfairness: Black Southerners and Non-Southerners
Note: South equals former Confederate states. "Amount I pay is very unfair" is coded high. Includes controls for education, income, gender, age, marital status, children, homeowner, partisanship, ideology, and government trust. Federal taxes arrayed on the top row, and state/local taxes on the bottom row.
Source: 2016 CCES.

non-South and southern Black respondents from an ordinary least squares analysis in which tax unfairness is coded high, controlling for income, education, age, and other demographic variables along with party identification, ideology, and government trust. The figure arrays federal taxes in the top row and state/local taxes in the bottom row (the gasoline tax is imposed by both federal and state governments).

For federal taxes, for which Black taxpayers would be treated the same whether they lived inside or outside the South, there is no difference in tax attitudes between southern and nonsouthern Black respondents (figure 7.7, top row). But for the state and local taxes arrayed across the bottom row, there are differences between those two groups. Southern Black respondents are more likely than white respondents (the reference category) to say that the sales tax is unfair, while there is no difference between nonsouthern Black respondents and whites. The pattern for the property tax is similar. The two findings conform to Newman and O'Brien's argument that Black citizens are particularly disadvantaged by southern policies of heavy sales and light property taxation (of white homeowners). Black southerners are also distinctly more likely to say that state income taxes are unfair, perhaps because southern states are less likely to have state EITCs or refundable credits to offset the high costs of sales and excise taxes. Southern Black respondents are more likely than other Black respondents to say the gas tax is unfair, although this difference is not statistically significant; in contrast to their high sales taxes, most southern states have low-to-modest gas taxes, although they are above the national median in Florida and North Carolina.[42]

Overall, many southern state and local tax systems are regressive, with high state and local sales taxes as well as no refundable credits in the state income tax, combined with low property tax rates that benefit white homeowners and no state-level estate or inheritance taxes, which also benefit whites who own almost all wealth. Black residents are disproportionately burdened by these regressive systems as they are overrepresented among lower-income groups, and these data show that this form of racially disparate state coercion is reflected in public opinion.

Hispanic Americans' Tax Attitudes

Black Americans are not the only group to suffer at the hands of a coercive state. Hispanic Americans too are subject to the punitive American criminal justice and welfare systems. Hispanic Americans are more likely to have criminal justice system contact than whites and more likely to be convicted; like Black Americans, they constitute a disproportionate share of the nation's prison population (League of United Latin American Citizens 2024). Furthermore, many Hispanic families and communities have suffered on the enforcement end of the nation's immigration system, with aggressive deportation policies threatening the lives of individuals, families, and entire communities, particularly in families and communities of mixed immigration status. The welfare system too can pose a minefield in which some states require Social Security numbers only for household members applying for assistance, while others require documentation for all household members. Especially when states do not stipulate clearly whether they will share collected information with US Immigration and Customs Enforcement, these requirements may have a chilling effect for mixed immigration status households.[43]

The tax regime also represents a coercive arm of the state for Hispanic Americans just as it does for Black Americans. There are fewer analyses in the critical tax theory and fiscal sociology literatures of the differential effects of tax provisions on Hispanic Americans compared to the extensive literature about Black Americans, as legal scholar Leo Martinez notes.[44] Moreover, the Hispanic population is quite diverse in terms of country of origin, generation in the United States, immigration status of households, incomes, and so on. Nonetheless, there are many ways in which Hispanic Americans too are differentially affected by tax policies and practices.[45]

Like Black Americans, Hispanic Americans are less likely to enjoy many of the tax breaks woven into the federal income tax (Martinez 2017). Homeownership is less common, and so, presumably, is taking the mortgage interest deduction; in 2019, 47.5 percent of Hispanic Americans owned homes—5 percentage points more than the Black homeownership rate, but far less than the 73 percent rate enjoyed by non-Hispanic whites ("Homeownership Rate by Race" 2023).[46] Hispanic Americans are more disadvantaged than Black Americans when it comes to tax-favored employer-provided benefits. Only 43 percent of Hispanic nonelderly adults have employer-sponsored health insurance, compared to 47 percent of Blacks and 66 percent of whites.[47] Two-thirds of Hispanic employees do not have access to an employer-sponsored retirement plan, compared to 43 percent of whites and 50 percent of Blacks (Harvey 2017). They are also less likely than whites to have capital gains income and benefit from that preferential tax rate (Brown 2013).

Furthermore, the tax code only recognizes some family relationships—provisions that may disproportionately affect Hispanic households (Brown 2021). For example, only certain relatives who support a child can file for the EITC (Abreu 2009). Also, households with mixed immigration status may not be able to claim the credit; the taxpayer seeking the credit, the spouse (if filing a joint return), and the qualifying child must all have Social Security numbers. The EITC cannot be claimed if any of those individuals instead have an Individual Taxpayer Identification Number, which is issued to noncitizens who cannot get Social Security numbers.

Similarly, Martinez (2017) notes that Hispanic families are more likely to rely on extended family for childcare and less likely to benefit from the dependent care tax credit. Hispanic couples are more likely than whites to include two earners, and so like Black married couples, are less likely to enjoy the untaxed imputed income that single-earner married couples do. Hispanic

Americans are also less likely to utilize the charitable contribution deduction; a tradition of "family-based self-help" along with donations to hometown associations and migrant organizations that transfer money abroad means that "Latinos bypass the Code mechanisms that reward such charitable behavior" (Martinez 2017, 107). With less access to the tax expenditure system, Hispanic taxpayers pay more federal income tax on the same income than do whites. Because state tax codes often mimic federal provisions, Hispanic families likely pay more state income tax than comparable whites as well.

Differential tax treatment of Hispanic Americans is not confined to the income tax. Martinez points out that undocumented workers pay Social Security taxes but never receive benefits, which may reduce perceptions of payroll tax fairness among Hispanic respondents overall.[48] Martin and Beck find that Hispanic homeowners report higher property tax rates than non-Hispanic whites, although the effect is smaller than for Black homeowners and not statistically significant. Given their geographic distribution, Hispanic homeowners also garner smaller savings from tax limitations than do white homeowners, and the foregone advantage is even larger for Hispanic homeowners than for Black ones. As well, Hispanic families have far less wealth than white ones; the median Hispanic family possessed $38,000 in wealth in 2019 compared to $184,000 for the median white family. Just about everything that characterizes the white-Black wealth gap characterizes the white-Hispanic wealth gap: compared to white households, Hispanic households own less wealth, have less wealth at every education level, are less likely to own various assets (homes, businesses, stocks/bonds/mutual funds, and retirement accounts), and the assets they do own are worth less on average. Just 3 percent of Hispanic families are millionaires, which is one-fifth the rate of white families (Kent and Ricketts 2021).

These findings suggest that on average, Hispanic Americans pay more for several taxes than similar whites. The tax system is a coercive force in the lives of Hispanic Americans, just as it is in the lives of Black Americans, and so we might hypothesize that Hispanic Americans will hold more negative tax attitudes than similar whites. As with Black Americans, I cannot attribute differences in Hispanic tax attitudes to self-interest itself. Many studies show that Hispanic survey respondents have lower levels of formal knowledge about politics based on standardized questions (although, like Black Americans, they have alternative information sources); the CCES results indicate low levels of tax knowledge as well (see chapter 3).[49] Instead, the hypothesized mechanism is coercion. I should also note that I will show results for all Hispanic respondents, even though some are noncitizens in the CCES, both because noncitizens pay many taxes and a notion of linked fate characterizes Hispanic public opinion.[50] Also, most of the Hispanic respondents in my datasets are Mexican or Latin American in origin, still diverse groups but including few Cubans, who may have distinctive tax attitudes.

Like Black Americans, Hispanic Americans embrace a larger role for government in the abstract and operational senses than do whites. In the 2016 CCES, Hispanic and white respondents did not differ on ideology, perhaps because of different understandings of the terms (Marisa Abrajano [2015, 46] shows that "being liberal in Latin America is to identify oneself as someone on the right of the political spectrum," the opposite of the United States, and so this item may be flawed for understanding Hispanic views on the abstract role of government). On the government services scale, however, Hispanics do score higher than whites. Hispanic respondents are also more supportive of federal spending than white respondents. Beyond Social Security and Medicare, where responses by ethnicity did not differ, Hispanic respondents are more supportive of increased spending on education and each of the means-tested social policies.

We may expect that Hispanic Americans' experience of a coercive state influences their attitudes toward tax policy, just as it did with Black Americans. Indeed, Hispanic respondents' tax attitudes stand in sharp contrast to their preferences for a greater role for government. At the bivariate level, Hispanic respondents are more likely than whites to say that the sales, payroll, and state income taxes are unfair. In multivariate analyses controlling for demographic and political variables, Hispanic respondents are more likely than the baseline of white respondents to say the amount they pay for nearly every tax is unfair (figure 7.8; 2016 and 2019 CCES data combined to increase the number of respondents).

Hispanic Americans are more likely than whites to want each tax decreased too, although the results only achieve statistical significance for the gas, payroll, and sales taxes (figure 7.9). As with Black Americans, the additional sense of unfairness and desire to get at least these three regressive taxes decreased are not explained entirely by differences in income, partisanship, or government trust. These attitudes are worthy of further exploration. And these data suggest yet again that the antitax stance of the Republican Party garners support from many groups beyond its white, male, and rural base.[51]

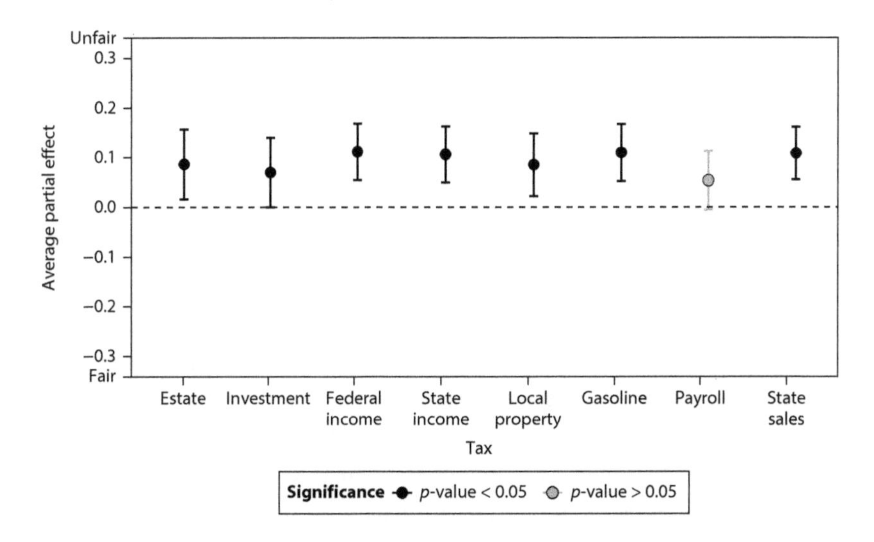

FIGURE 7.8 Tax Unfairness: Hispanic versus White Respondents
Note: "Amount I pay is very unfair" is coded high. Progressive taxes are arrayed on the left, and regressive on the right. Figure shows coefficient for Hispanic respondents (with whites as baseline) from ordinary least squares analyses also controlling for education, income, gender, age, marital status, children, homeowner, partisanship, ideology, and government trust.
Source: 2016 and 2019 CCES.

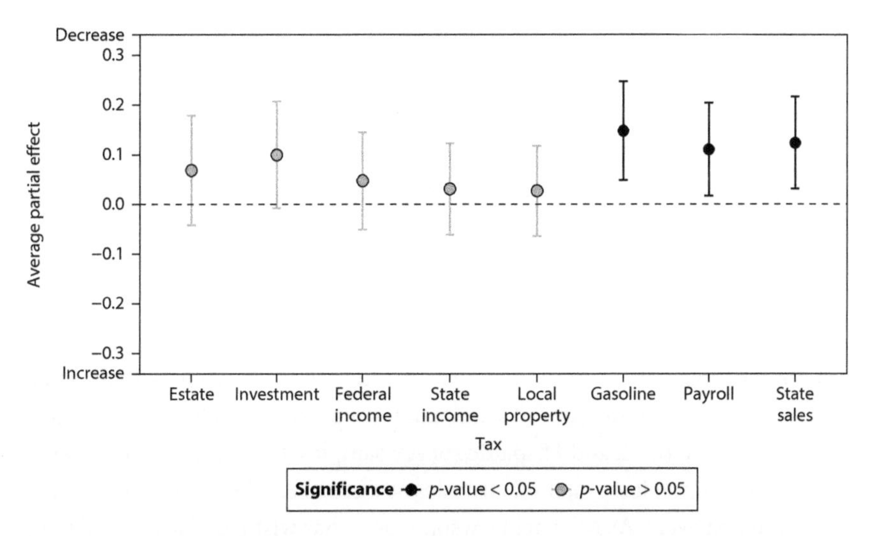

FIGURE 7.9 Tax Change Preferences: Hispanic versus White Respondents
Note: "Decrease tax" is coded high. Ordinary least squares model. Figure shows coefficient for Hispanic respondents (with whites as baseline) with controls for income, education, gender, age, marital status, children, homeowner, partisanship, ideology, and government trust.
Source: 2016 CCES.

The Attitudinal Fallout of the Racialized Tax System

Black Americans are one of the few groups in American society that generally support a strong role for government. On average, they are more liberal than white Americans, more likely to prefer an expansive role for government, and more supportive of federal spending, especially on education and social policies, including the means-tested programs of which many whites disapprove. And yet Black Americans are also less supportive of many taxes than white Americans. Depending on the question wording, they are more likely to say that a variety of progressive and regressive taxes are unfair, including federal and state income, property, gas, and sales. Even accounting for differences in income and other demographic factors, partisanship, ideology, and government trust, Black Americans are more likely than whites to say that all taxes are unfair, with the estimates achieving statistical significance for federal and state income taxes as well as the payroll tax. And all things being equal, Black taxpayers are more likely to want nearly every tax decreased. A look at the Gallup and GSS item about federal income taxes reveals that Black antitax sentiment is not a new phenomenon: since the late 1940s, Black Americans have been consistently more likely than whites to say their federal income taxes are too high, both absolutely and controlling for demographic and political differences, and through both Republican and Democratic presidential administrations. Remarkably, although nearly all Black respondents in these datasets are Democrats, they are far more likely than white Democrats to say each tax is unfair. Their tax attitudes resemble those of white Republicans more than those of white Democrats.

The Black experience of the state helps explain these skeptical attitudes toward taxation. Black Americans know that they are economically disadvantaged in the United States. They have been subject to the state's coercive powers in a variety of policy arenas both historically and contemporarily. They might reasonably have more negative attitudes about taxation, which is yet one more manifestation of the state's coercive powers. It's also worth noting that within the Black and Hispanic survey samples, tax attitudes do not vary much by income; instead, their attitudes as a group are distinctive from those of white taxpayers. As Michael Dawson (1994) has written, Black-linked fate, a particular form of group consciousness, arises because Black Americans, regardless of income, face the vagaries of American race relations in their everyday lives.[52] Or as Ismail White and Chryl Laird (2020) put it, all Black Americans are subject to racial apartheid in the United States, even those who might have different individual interests. In tax too, just as in other policy areas, race is more important than income or class differences within the group because Black Americans are subject to the state's coercive powers by virtue of being Black. Hispanic Americans have policy experiences distinct from those of non-Hispanic whites as well.[53] The state has long singled out Black and Hispanic people for differential treatment. There is no reason for these individuals to think tax policy is any different. And where state coercion has historically been the most severe, in the South, Black taxpayers are even more likely to say taxes are unfair.[54]

As it turns out, Black and Hispanic suspicion about state coercion is well-founded because tax policy actually is discriminatory. Public policy in the United States has long been racially stratified.[55] Taxes are no different. White Americans, especially the well-off, have successfully shaped the federal tax code to advantage their patterns of earning income, holding wealth, dividing household labor, and so on, in ways that end up penalizing Black Americans with different economic, financial, and household patterns. The racially unequal effects of tax policy do not end with the federal government. Subnational governments likewise have instituted tax policies that explicitly and implicitly discriminate against Black Americans. The racialized effects of these tax provisions mean that Black Americans literally pay more in taxes than whites at the same income level—a massive violation of horizontal equity, the tax principle of the same treatment for those in the same situation. As sociologists Kasey Henricks and Louise Seamster (2017, 169) put it, the United States is a "racial tax state."

That Black Americans score low in terms of tax knowledge is concerning. I rooted the explanation of differential Black attitudes toward taxes in distrust of a coercive state, not in self-interest, because of low levels of tax knowledge. Aside from affluent white men, most individuals know little about tax policy, as we saw in chapter 3. Black (and female) respondents are especially likely to avoid factual information questions and give incorrect responses when they do answer. Thus I cannot attribute Black respondents' negative tax attitudes to their knowledge that they are overtaxed compared to similar whites because they may not explicitly know that to be the case, especially for the more hidden discriminatory provisions. Instead, what's possible is for Black Americans to extrapolate from their negative experiences at the hands of government to the tax arena. The concerning part is that knowledge is power, to use Michael Delli Carpini and Scott Keeter's formulation, and if those who are discriminated against in tax policy do not explicitly know how or why, they cannot fight back.

Low levels of knowledge among the nonrich, of any race or ethnicity, benefit the rich, who capitalize on ignorance and inattention among the public to shape tax policy in their own interests.

The economic and political implications of the racialized tax system along with the pattern of attitudes across racial and ethnic groups that it engenders are profound.

First, tax policy helps create the racial wealth gap. Black and other nonwhite Americans have been stymied in their efforts to accrue wealth, for a vast number of reasons.[56] Many of these arise from private discriminatory actions, with government policy often playing an exacerbating role. Government action has undermined the life chances of nonwhites more directly as well. Scholars have long documented how a coercive state uses the welfare and carceral systems as tools for the construction and control of subordinated groups.[57] We must include the tax system, at all levels of government, in the catalog of coercive policies. The property tax and housing market are particularly egregious examples. Historian Andrew Kahrl (2019, 190) has a term for government policies that have elevated white homeownership and corporate profit while subjecting Black homeowners to segregation, overassessment, and foreclosure and tax auction proceedings: "stategraft." Other tax policies, such as numerous white-oriented federal income tax provisions and high sales taxes in states with large shares of minority poor, also undermine nonwhite disposable incomes and savings. If anything, tax policy is an even more insidious tool of Black and Hispanic oppression than welfare or criminal justice policy, as it is "seemingly innocuous," appearing to be technocratic and race neutral yet instantiating racism nonetheless.[58] Brown (2021) concludes that a harmful outcome of a set of tax institutions designed with only whites in mind is that Black citizens disproportionately pay into a system from which they do not reap the same benefits or gain the same opportunities to parlay public policy into prosperity and wealth accumulation.

A second implication of the intersection between race and tax policy in the United States brings together the findings of this chapter and the previous one: whites, who have designed a tax regime in their favor, believe *they* are the victims of tax policy. The nation's long and fraught economic, social, and racial history already inclines white Americans to see themselves as makers and nonwhites as takers. Decades, and even centuries, of elite messages have framed whites as responsible taxpayers and Black Americans especially as shiftless tax eaters. Overlaying these predilections are policies that further inflame the racialized politics of tax, especially tax expenditures. Tax breaks are a prominent vehicle by which privileged interests have reduced their effective taxes. They are also the delivery mechanism for some of the most significant government benefits for the middle class, particularly employer-provided health insurance and retirement plans. In both cases, they are tilted toward white Americans. And yet these benefits remain underappreciated by their recipients, who instead recognize only the direct spending that government does, which they believe is fueled by their tax dollars and which media have disproportionately portrayed as going to nonwhite people. The tax expenditure system exacerbates white Americans' tendency—especially pronounced among racial conservatives—to underestimate their government benefits while overestimating spending on Black Americans.

Examples of misplaced victimhood abound. Consider the estate tax, for which racially conservative whites have the most distinctive opinions. Estate tax opponents will often portray white farmers and their families as victims of the estate tax—a rhetorically useful feint, even if stories of families losing farms because of the estate tax are largely apocryphal.[59] But while virtually no white farmers have been hurt by the estate tax (a fictional harm), in 2022 white farmers sued to block debt relief for Black farmers in the pandemic-era American Relief Plan intended to compensate them for discrimination in US Department of Agriculture farm support programs (an actual harm).[60] Or consider tax breaks. Not only do white people benefit disproportionately. In addition, the high-value tax breaks for employer-provided health and retirement benefits are removed from one's gross income by one's employer, no taxpayer action required (the money is already subtracted from one's income on the W-2 form used to fill in line 1a of the 1040 tax return). The administrative burden of these benefits is zero. In contrast, the administrative burden is far higher for the few tax breaks from which Black and Hispanic taxpayers are somewhat more likely to benefit. For example, one must complete a separate, confusing form to secure the EITC, which is one reason why even low-income people in the United States use paid tax preparers (Tax Policy Center 2020a).[61] And employer-provided benefits hardly ever generate IRS audits while the EITC is a major source.

Third, racialized tax policy is an underappreciated instance of representational failure. Martin Gilens, Larry Bartels, and others have documented the extensive class biases in American public policy. There is representational bias not just by income and wealth but also by race. In part, the racial bias arises because whites hold most wealth in the United States and so the wealth bias in responsiveness is a racial bias in responsiveness as well. Furthermore, there is more direct racial bias in representation. In reference to the property tax, Kahrl (2019, 191) writes of "Black taxpayers' struggle to be heard," which "stands in stark contrast to white suburban homeowners," who have successfully secured property tax reductions for themselves. Examining eleven spending areas, Zoltan Hajnal finds that Black Americans lose out—fail to see their preferences realized in policy—more than any other group studied (by income, age, gender, urbanicity, and religion). Taxes, an instrument of white power, privilege, and dominance, are no different. In taxes, as in electoral politics and the other policy areas Hajnal (2020, 13) explores, "A key aspect of this story is not just that race matters but also that it eclipses the other important dividing lines in American society."[62]

Fourth, existing work on public opinion on taxes tends to focus on whites' attitudes. These data show that Black and Hispanic attitudes are distinct and important. I have barely scratched the surface of race and tax opinion. There is much more work to do, and this area deserves to be the focus of much future research.

Finally, back to one of the book's main themes: we see yet again how the progressive tax system fails to generate its own support. There is a general antitax disposition among both white and Black taxpayers, but for different reasons. White taxpayers, especially the racially resentful, are suspicious about how their tax dollars will be spent. Black taxpayers distrust the coercive side of the state. Whites do not like the system because they think they are victimized by it. Black and Hispanic Americans do not like the system because they are actually victimized by it. Either way, privileged interests gain allies in their fight against the tax system and then twist that antitax sentiment in the broader public to their own political advantage. Funding the American state is difficult indeed.

8

Conclusion

THE AMERICAN TAX SYSTEM is complex. Tax knowledge levels are low. Elites obfuscate, increasing the confusion. In this context, nonrich taxpayers face a difficult challenge. Many support the notion of progressive taxation, with higher-income people paying not just more but instead progressively more. This abstract commitment is also in the economic self-interest of the nonrich, as progressivity shifts the burden of funding government onto those with more, in accordance with the ability-to-pay principle. Following from this support for progressivity, large majorities tell pollsters that the rich and corporations should pay more.

But many nonrich individuals have a difficult time connecting these abstract predilections to specific policy preferences. Their attitudes toward particular taxes and reforms often do not follow logically from either their abstract views or material stakes. Nearly every income group deems the estate tax the most unfair and most in need of decreasing, despite the fact that fleetingly few pay it—and certainly none of the nonrich individuals who appear in these conventional survey data. The share of survey respondents saying that the progressive federal and state income taxes they pay are unfair falls with income rather than rises as it would if attitudes reflected actual tax costs as a share of income. The regressive payroll and sales taxes are the costliest for low- and middle-income households, yet perceived as the fairest and least disliked. Perhaps the relatively sanguine attitudes toward the costly payroll tax make sense, as it funds visible benefits in old age. Still, no such obvious benefits derive from the sales tax, which goes into the general revenues pot just like the despised income tax. In a few specific instances attitudes correspond with self-interest, but frequently not with the general markers of material stakes such as income. In contrast to what previous researchers have asserted, taxes are not necessarily an area where self-interest plays a strong role in attitudes.

When self-interest fails as an attitudinal influence in other policy areas, symbolic preferences such as partisanship and ideology typically loom large. Given that tax policy, and the size and scope of government implied, differentiate the political parties, at least rhetorically, and given the strong influence of partisanship and ideology in other policy areas, we might assume that Democrats and Republicans have quite distinctive tax attitudes. When there are cues that render party salient, attitudes differ. Yet in many ways the differences are muted. Democrats dislike the same taxes that Republicans do. Republicans are more likely than Democrats to say most taxes are unfair and should be decreased, but in multivariate analyses with controls for other factors, partisan differences persist only for progressive taxes. For regressive taxes, Republicans and Democrats do not differ in their fairness evaluations or desire to decrease them (except for the gas tax, which Republicans particularly loathe). Partisanship is not a consistent attitudinal factor when it comes to taxes, in part because majorities of Republicans have negative attitudes toward taxes, but so do large minorities of Democrats. And importantly, independents are even more likely than Republicans to say various taxes are unfair and should be decreased.

Among whites, a different symbolic consideration structures tax attitudes: racial resentment. Formal levels of tax knowledge are low, but people "know" enough to have impressions about who pays and benefits. Throughout American history, policy and rhetoric have framed whites as taxpayers, and Black Americans and other nonwhites as burdens on the state. Those who score high on racial resentment, or symbolic racism, the form of modern racism based on assessments of Black failure to adhere to the "American" values of hard work and self-reliance, have more negative attitudes toward income-targeted federal spending, as has long been known. Chapter 6 showed that racial resentment is correlated with attitudes toward the tax breaks targeted at low-income people as well. That the racially resentful would oppose spending on lower-income groups, whether direct or indirect through tax expenditures, is not surprising given previous research. Perhaps even more notable is that the racially resentful are opposed to the concept of progressive taxation and supportive of tax policies favorable to the rich: estate tax elimination, low income and capital gains rates, and tax breaks for charitable contributions. This racial resentment relationship obtains both in descriptive data and multivariate analyses above and beyond income and other demographic characteristics, partisanship, ideology, and government trust. It may be that the racially resentful oppose progressive taxes because they constitute general revenues and fund the means-tested programs that they oppose. Or perhaps the opposition arises from the racialized distribution of American wealth: not all whites are wealthy, but almost all wealthy are white (Wolff 2017, table 10.1).[1] Taxes that are progressive or imposed on wealth attack white privilege, drawing the ire of the racially resentful. Whatever the mechanism, the relationship between racial resentment and tax attitudes is strong. Furthermore, data from the ANES and GSS show that the relationship between tax attitudes and alternative measures of racism rooted in the desire for social distance between races and biological inferiority (sometimes termed old-fashioned racism) is strong as well. Race, racism, and taxes are inexorably linked in the United States.[2]

Another notable finding concerns the attitudes of nonwhites. Nearly every racial and ethnic group in the United States, at one point or another, has suffered at the hands of a coercive state, especially Black Americans. Tax policy constitutes one additional area in which state coercion and the disproportionate extraction of resources occurs, as legal scholars and sociologists of the critical tax theory school have detailed. Governments at all levels of the federal system overtax Black and Hispanic households relative to similar whites. Some of these practices are well-known, such as the differential property tax treatment of Black homeowners. Others are subtler, such as lesser Black and Hispanic access to tax breaks for employer-provided benefits along with other forms of indirect spending that are tilted toward the affluent, and therefore whites. But given experiences of coercion, repression, and predation in other policy areas, combined with what is known about discriminatory practices in the tax arena, nonwhites have strong reasons to expect differential treatment in tax policy more broadly. The attitudinal fallout is immense. On average, Black and Hispanic Americans, unlike whites, want a larger role for government and support greater federal spending, especially on social policies. Yet they are more likely than white Americans to say most taxes are unfair and should be decreased. Thus some of the few groups in American society that might be supportive of a large role for the state and the generous tax revenues needed to fund that role instead have negative views of taxes.

Asymmetries around Taxation and the Many Difficulties of Funding Government

Devising a tax system that provides sufficient government revenue as well as distributes the burden in some way that is widely deemed fair and acceptable is exceedingly difficult. Many aspects of taxation as a policy area interact with the patterns of public opinion revealed in this book and exacerbate them. Tax policy is riven with asymmetries that make policymaking in the public interest challenging. Some of these asymmetries arise from the nature of public opinion itself, some derive from tax policy, and many benefit the rich, who would like to undermine the cause of progressive taxation.

Progressivity as Self-Undermining

The federal tax system since the early twentieth century has centered on progressive taxes. It was established on the ability-to-pay principle—again, that those with more should pay more to fund the public sector, both because they can do so more comfortably and have benefited from many aspects of public policy. Many members of the public support the notion of progressive taxation as fair and desirable. But progressivity in the federal system has declined over time, with effective tax rates falling dramatically at the top of the income spectrum. At the same time, state and local tax systems taken together are regressive, and have become more so. Now the overall US tax system is only mildly progressive even as top incomes have soared. It raises less money than tax systems in other rich democracies.

Part of the difficulty is that progressive taxation has two self-undermining characteristics. The first is that by definition, progressive taxation imposes the greatest burdens on the most privileged, organized, knowledgeable, self-interested, and vocal elements of society. Progressive taxation focuses on those who are well aware of their economic stakes and have the resources and access to influence tax policy. Especially in a political system where private interests play such a large role via lobbying and campaign finance, the privileged have been successful in getting their taxes reduced through both lower rates and expanded tax breaks.

The other self-undermining challenge to progressive taxation follows from the first. The nonrich are less knowledgeable about taxes and less likely to recognize their material stakes in tax policy to begin with. These informational challenges are exacerbated by the very strategies that the privileged use to get their own taxes reduced, such as the extensive tax expenditure system. Although supportive of progressive taxation as a concept, many nonrich taxpayers deem most progressive taxes unfair and favor regressive taxes more than we would expect given their great cost for these income groups. The nonrich have the same preferences as the rich, except that for the rich, these preferences correspond to their material self-interest while among the nonrich they do not. Thus public opinion fails to pose a hurdle that prevents the rich from securing the policies they want to the detriment of everyone else.[3]

The asymmetry operating here that amplifies the self-undermining characteristics of progressive taxation is that public opinion is more top-down than bottom-up. Although there is some debate, and some room for a two-way relationship, the consensus among many public opinion scholars is that the public largely follows elites. Most people do not pay close attention to politics and government. Many do not have firm or detailed policy preferences (see, among others, Converse 1964). Many adopt the policy stances of politicians they like rather than support politicians who share their policy stances (Lenz 2012). Top-down opinion leadership favors the privileged and facilitates the realization of their preferences in policy. In the case of taxes, the rich know what they want, a permeable political system renders politicians open to their views, and then those views trickle down to the rest of the public in ways that often conflict with their objective stakes.

The normative problem is that democracy is supposed to provide a counterweight to the control of policymaking by the privileged. But if the public only believes in progressive taxation in the abstract and fails to translate that sentiment into attitudes on specific taxes, then public opinion does not serve its intended role in helping steer the outputs of democratic governance toward the preferences of the citizenry.

Visible Costs, Invisible Benefits

One reason that nonrich Americans have such difficulty in understanding their interests in the tax system is that some costs and many benefits are hidden by policy designs. Even if both costs and benefits were perfectly visible, losses are more salient than equal-size gains, as Daniel Kahneman and Amos Tversky's (1979) prospect theory tells us, and the cost of taxes would loom larger in tax attitudes than the benefits received. But the politics and designs of taxes make the cost-benefit asymmetry much worse. With the exception of Social Security, where the linkage is clearer, taxes paid are much more salient than benefits received. Benefits are even more obscured when they are delivered in the form of taxes not collected, as with tax expenditures.

In the absence of a clear linkage between taxes paid and benefits received, public opinion on taxes is malleable. And some taxes are the object of more political discourse than others. Those discussed regularly by economic elites and politicians (and disfavored by the rich) earn more ire among the public than those that are seldom mentioned. Hence the focus of the nonrich on income, estate, and property taxes, which are loathed even though they are not that costly as a share of income for these households, while those taxes that economic and political elites seldom mention, such as sales taxes, are much costlier to nonrich taxpayers, yet disliked much less. Given the opaqueness of the tax-benefit relationship for most taxes for most people, nonrich taxpayers might be forgiven for thinking about and disliking most the taxes they hear about the most.

The Asymmetries of Comparison

One reason for the misplaced preferences of the nonrich and the existence of the principle-policy gap in their thinking about taxes is that they extrapolate from their own experiences without realizing that the experience of the rich is completely different. Many nonrich people find the tax that they must pay on their own main source of wealth, the property tax, painful and unfair. In turn, they do not support the tax on the wealth of the rich, the estate tax, either. Many nonrich people focus on the federal income tax on their earned income and angrily perceive the rich as not paying enough. For the rich, however, earned income is often less important than unearned income, which is taxed at low rates or not at all—something that many of the nonrich do not realize (Wolff 2017, 646). And nonrich Americans pay the sales tax, and think that taxing consumption is controllable and fair. But they do not realize that regressive taxes hit them harder—next to the payroll tax, the sales tax is the costliest for middle-income households—and that sales taxes are a tiny burden for the rich, because their incomes are so high and they can only consume so much. Unable to think about taxes outside their own experience and context, it is difficult for many nonrich to understand taxes and the distributive implications of tax reforms that are in the interest of upper-income groups but not themselves.

The nonrich also have difficulty thinking about the tax system as a whole. To the extent to which people consider taxes at all, they do so in an individualized way rather than the system-wide way that would be necessary for inequality to factor into their attitudes (Strand and Mirkay 2020). Elite rhetoric tends to emphasize the individual—"you know how to spend your money better than the government does" and so on. There is little extant discourse in the United States about how public policy might address inequality, nor do political and economic elites offer a clear connection between taxes and inequality. And because of the pernicious role of race and racial attitudes, there is only anemic support among whites for addressing inequality through redistributive spending.

A related asymmetry that can undermine awareness of inequality and support for redistribution arises from the nature of social comparison. In a fascinating series of experiments, Meghan Condon and Amber Wichowsky (2020) explore the effects of cross-class comparison for political attitudes. They ask their experimental subjects to imagine a ladder that represents "where people stand in the United States," and think about the people who are worst or best off in terms of income, education, and job status. They find that looking up the ladder increases support for redistributive policy, but looking up is rare because it makes people uncomfortable. Looking down is far more common, but reduces support for redistribution because those lower on the ladder are perceived as less deserving.[4] In the tax arena, many nonrich want the rich to pay more. Yet among whites, tax attitudes are dominated by negative feelings about those who might benefit from government spending.

The Asymmetry of Taxes and Party

An asymmetry that permeates the politics of taxation is that people would rather not pay taxes—or pay less. In his study of party issue ownership, Patrick Egan (2013, 5) deems taxes a "consensus" issue: "Most Americans (including liberals) want to pay lower taxes in a simplified, transparent fashion." This asymmetry helps those in the small government party, the Republicans, who have long "owned" the low-tax mantle, and complicates the calculations of Democratic politicians, who would prefer to raise revenues and fund greater government activity. Taxes aside, a related asymmetry is that Americans are right of center in their views of government. There are more conservatives than liberals. On balance, Americans are skeptical of government and believe that it wastes a lot of money. Trust in government could hardly be lower. Large minorities of Democrats, majorities of Republicans, and even larger majorities of independents say a variety of taxes are unfair and should be decreased.

Funding government in this environment is extremely difficult and makes for an enduring political advantage for the GOP. One compelling example is Alexander Hertel-Fernandez and Theda Skocpol's (2015) analysis of the failure of Senate Democrats to push back on the renewal of the Bush tax cuts for high earners, which expired at the end of 2010. Rather than separate the tax cuts for the middle class from those for high earners, Democrats and President Obama acceded to the Republican demand to extend the cuts for all households. Democrats apparently feared that letting the Bush tax cuts expire for top earners—even though favored by many members of the public—would come back to haunt them in the form of future GOP election ads saying they had voted for a tax increase. They also feared the anger of small business, whose interest groups successfully pressured Democrats to keep the tax cuts in place for all. It might seem curious that businesses would care about individual tax rates, but after Reagan's tax cuts reduced personal income tax rates below corporate ones, many businesses reorganized themselves as "pass-through" corporations taxed in the individual system. The asymmetries of tax perpetually harm Democrats and perpetually advantage Republicans; all tax increases are bad, and all tax cuts are good.

The Asymmetries of Race and Racism

Tax opinion inexorably gets tangled up in American race relations (except when people can trace benefits to themselves, as with Social Security, or common tax expenditures for employer benefits and excess medical costs, where racial resentment does not rear its head). Racial resentment is a strong correlate of whites' opinions on direct spending, indirect spending, and taxes. The relationship between white racial resentment and tax attitudes is remarkably durable over time, and widespread, found across vastly different types of taxes. The asymmetry here is that many white Americans oppose taxes because of racial resentment, but are actually advantaged in the tax system over similar Black Americans. The rich harness nonrich white resentment over spending and taxes to their cause, securing lower taxes for themselves, while tax policy, designed at the behest of the privileged, simultaneously taxes Black Americans more. Some tax policies are accidentally discriminatory—a result of tax policy written by whites for whites, without consideration of disparate effects on other groups. Other tax policies are intentionally discriminatory—examples of the ways in which "constructed" identities such as race are "institutionalized" and perpetuated, as Clarissa Hayward (2013, chap. 1) writes. Either way, the American tax system is an instrument of white privilege even though many whites feel victimized by it.

Instead, the principal victims are nonwhites. Declining progressivity especially burdens Black taxpayers and other taxpayers of color by shifting tax liabilities from high-income and high-wealth people, who are disproportionately white, down the economic ladder (Strand and Mirkay 2020, 265).

Dorothy Brown (2021) notes that Black wealth and life chances—and the United States GDP—would be greater if Black taxpayers were not penalized in the tax system. A report by Citibank (2020) finds that closing racial gaps in education, wages, housing, and investments today would increase US GDP by $5 trillion over the next five years; had they been closed twenty years ago, $16 trillion could have been added.[5] Taxes are but one cog in a greater discriminatory system that penalizes Black citizens and undermines economic growth for the nation as a whole.

Worth underscoring is the particular harm of the tax expenditure system. Steve Teles (2013, 97) characterizes the American state as a "kludgeocracy" that "hides from view . . . the growing tendency of public policy to redistribute resources upward to the wealthy and the organized at the expense of the poorer and less organized." The tax system—especially tax expenditures—plays a central role, and in addition, has a racialized effect. An outsized share of the $1.6 trillion in revenue the federal government does not collect in taxes because of the many credits, deductions, and preferential rates in the system goes to white Americans. Black and Hispanic Americans benefit much less. And yet those largely white beneficiaries do not recognize that their benefits from this indirect spending represent government activity. At the same time, the racially resentful among them object to indirect spending aimed at lower-income people, which they believe is funded unfairly by their tax dollars and perceive as going disproportionately to nonwhite beneficiaries, just as with direct spending. The hidden welfare state literature has extensively discussed the upwardly redistributive nature of the tax break system; the racial politics has received much less attention.

The Difficulties of Funding Government

In their long fight to get their effective tax rates reduced, the rich have had many allies. Uninformed taxpayers, who resent progressive taxes even though regressive taxes are costlier to them. Large shares of partisans of all stripes. Racially resentful whites, who do not like how their tax dollars are spent. Black and Hispanic Americans, who are subject to many forms of state coercion, including overtaxation. So many types of people with so many reasons to dislike taxes, even those who generally support a greater role for government. Despite support for progressive taxation and taxing the privileged more, public opinion ends up being an aid to tax reduction for those at the top rather than a hurdle. There are plenty of reasons in the American political system that high-resource groups tend to achieve the public policies they desire. Malleable and permissive public opinion simply makes their political task that much easier.

The Future of Tax Policy

Taxes are likely to dominate American politics for years to come. In 2025, many provisions of the 2017 Tax Cuts and Jobs Act will expire, setting up a legislative battle. In 2029, the federal government's debt will reach 107 percent of GDP, more than the historical peak just after World War II. Under current law, it keeps on rising, with the interest payments consuming a growing share of the federal budget, increasing the pressure to cut spending or raise taxes (Congressional Budget Office 2024). In 2034, the Social Security trust fund, built up to finance baby boomers' retirement, will be exhausted. Because incoming payroll taxes only cover about 80 percent of the promised benefits, Social Security benefits will be cut by 20 percent automatically unless Congress acts (Arnold 2022). Other fiscal crises will arise as well, although many will be of the gradually accumulating type rather than the deadline or cliff type, on both the spending and revenue sides for governments at all levels: as the baby boomers retire, a shrinking workforce will produce lower tax revenues just as those aging boomers are in need of costly long-term care; a decaying transportation infrastructure needs investment; and a changing climate will usher in more frequent natural disasters and economic disruption, among other needs. Cutting spending will be difficult. Revenue needs will be great. Funding government will be as challenging as ever.

One could look at figure 2.3, which shows that US tax revenues have been flat as a share of the economy for sixty years, and think that perhaps more funding is necessary. But it is also difficult to imagine revenues increasing dramatically. Nearly all Republican lawmakers at the federal level, and quite a few at the state level, have signed Grover Norquist's no-taxes pledge. Democrats are unlikely to achieve commanding majorities in Congress, and Republicans now have self-sustaining and even veto-proof majorities in many statehouses, thanks to a combination of favorable partisan geography (Democratic voters are packed in cities; Republicans are more spread out in rural and suburban legislative districts) and partisan gerrymandering (Republican-led legislatures packing Democrats further).[6]

The fight over the future of Social Security will be especially interesting. Lawmakers have a limited number of choices, as Doug Arnold (2022) lays out in his insightful book about the history and future of the program. They can allow the 20 percent cut to occur, which seems electorally suicidal since the majority of seniors depend on the program for the majority of their income, and they are a widespread, highly informed, and mobilized constituency (Campbell 2003). Lawmakers could try to change Social Security parameters, but there isn't time before the 2034 trust fund exhaustion for the easier remedies like slowly raising the retirement age to have their effect. Completely changing Social Security by introducing individual accounts was shot down before under nonemergency circumstances and seems unlikely to garner greater support now. And so we're left with tax increases: either an increase in the tax rate, which hasn't changed since 1990, and/or a lifting of the wage cap on which the tax is imposed.

As Arnold notes, Republicans have backed themselves into a tough corner. They have pledged not to raise taxes, and their donors and the very rich are hostile to Social Security. But they have to get reelected too, and Social Security is the most popular government program funded by a popular (as taxes go) tax, as we have learned here. Social Security is also a crucial support for an older working-class constituency that now forms an important part of the Republican Party base. Polls show that Americans say they are willing to pay more to preserve Social Security. The solvency crisis will reveal whether that is just lip service.

The findings in this book suggest that increasing the rate on a regressive tax like the payroll tax may be easier than raising rates for progressive taxes, especially the federal income tax. It is difficult to imagine the privileged suddenly failing to secure tax policies favorable to themselves. Despite the widespread support for progressive taxation, there are many public opinion, institutional, and organizational barriers to greater progressivity, as I have documented.

These opinion dynamics may help explain why other countries have turned to a regressive consumption tax, the VAT, to increase revenues over the last many decades. Peer nations have progressive income taxes too, but overlaid is a VAT that can raise a tremendous amount of money. A VAT, as mentioned earlier, is a consumption tax that taxes the value that is added by each business in the chain of production (in contrast to a sales tax, a consumption tax that is added by the seller at the point of sale). Nearly every country except for some Persian Gulf states, some African countries, and the United States imposes a VAT. In the peer nations of Europe, the VAT raises about 7 percent of GDP, which is a little less than the personal income tax raises in the United States, around 8 percent of GDP (Campbell 2012a).

Adopting a VAT in the United States would face many challenges. Republican lawmakers would not want to add a new tax while Democrats would oppose its regressive nature. The forty-five states with sales taxes may object to another consumption layered on top (and we know that people are sensitive to "double taxation" by two entities). And even though sales taxes are among the least disliked in the United States, VAT rates are generally 20, 30, and even 40 percent, far higher than the single-digit sales taxes imposed in the United States (although they are more hidden as they are incorporated into the sales price, not separately itemized on receipts like sales taxes are). Another difficulty is that sales taxes are among the least disliked taxes because Americans are fonder of their state governments than the federal government; a federal consumption tax might prove more unpopular than state sales taxes.

Perhaps the biggest problem with a VAT is that I can imagine the United States achieving one-half of the European bargain but not the other. In Europe, regressive VATs are counterbalanced by redistributive social spending (Kato 2003). In the United States, it's easier to imagine the privileged getting their taxes reduced through replacing part of the income tax with a VAT without expanding government spending on education, infrastructure, or social policies, given representational barriers for lower- and middle-income people as well as the enduring role of racism in undercutting support for social spending.[7] That said, scholars have noted that VATs are relatively noncontroversial taxes once in place; tax revolts have sprung up not where taxes are higher but rather where progressive taxation is used more extensively.[8] In some ways, this book offers a microlevel explanation for this phenomenon: it is difficult to increase progressive taxes too much because it is relatively easy to get the nonrich on board with cuts to progressive taxes, and nonrich people don't mind regressive taxes so much.

Other policies may be more achievable, albeit still difficult. One would be tax expenditure reform. The United States ended up with an extensive tax break system for two reasons: seeking tax breaks is a central way privileged interests have sought to lower their effective taxes (in addition to securing lower rates), and implementing tax breaks has proven easier than passing direct spending programs in a nation where a small government and racialized politics dominates policymaking. Tax expenditures have many detrimental effects, as shown here. They rob the federal government of revenues. The affluent benefit the most, undermining progressivity. At the same time, their extensive use undercuts the legitimacy of the system and leads nonrich people to support reforms, such as a flat tax, that they think will stem tax avoidance by the privileged, but instead would probably raise their own taxes (see chapter 3). Tax expenditures penalize racial and ethnic minorities who end up paying more in taxes than comparable whites because they have less access to the tax break system (chapter 7). Tax expenditures also hide benefits, which go disproportionately to whites, while direct spending programs remain more visible and are portrayed in the media as going disproportionately to Black Americans, exacerbating the racial politics of taxation (chapter 6). Tax breaks may be politically expedient and desired by the privileged, but they create a number of economic and attitudinal distortions.

Peer nations have made other choices that make taxes simpler. Tax breaks are fewer and often in the form of flat credits rather than deductions from taxable income so that higher-income people do not disproportionately benefit to the same degree (OECD 2010).[9] Flat credits make tax filing easier too, as do provisions such as taxing individuals as opposed to households so that withholding more closely matches tax liabilities. More than three dozen countries have return-free tax filing for simple situations—a reform repeatedly blocked in the United States by tax preparation companies.[10] One problem with the great tax complexity in the United States, as Teles (2013) notes, is that it makes compliance with tax laws seem lower than it is, further diminishing the legitimacy of the tax system.[11]

Perhaps another path would be to try to harness the public's belief that the rich do not pay enough to bolster progressive taxation. Given the huge amount of income and wealth at the top of the spectrum, it is hard to imagine not trying to tap such sources in the search for more revenue. Some new tax targeted at the rich but less susceptible to their ability to shift their sources of income, such as a financial transaction tax, might work (Congressional Budget Office 2018).[12] But progressive reforms will face an uphill battle given the nature of public opinion revealed here and the great influence the privileged have over policymaking. Other alternatives aimed at the privileged are smaller bore, but more achievable. One move would be more stringent tax enforcement to address the tax gap, the difference between taxes owed and taxes collected, which the IRS pegs at nearly $700 billion per year (for comparison, defense spending in 2022 was $746 billion).[13] Greater IRS funding included in the 2022 Inflation Reduction Act was aimed at this problem, although this effort is vulnerable to Republican cuts. A reform directed at the structural racism embedded in the tax code would have the Treasury

Department calculate the impact of tax provisions, and proposed changes, not just by income but also by race and ethnicity.

Whatever tax changes come down the pike will probably have to come from lawmakers, not from the public. A main lesson of this book is that while the public wants the rich to pay more, the specific tax preferences of the nonrich resemble those of the rich rather than their own self-interested stakes. The toll of race means there is little sense of shared fiscal citizenship. The will and impetus to tax the rich is more likely to come from politicians, as when Clinton raised marginal income tax rates, and when Obama and congressional Democrats preserved the estate tax and financed the Affordable Care Act with progressive sources, such as increased Medicare and capital gains taxes on high earners. In recent decades, such instances of unified Democratic control of the federal government have been only sporadic and brief. I suspect that we will not see much movement in federal tax policy in the coming years, or much increase in tax revenues.

Interest and Participation in Tax Policy

Whatever tax reforms come onto the agenda, one concern is inequality in voice. We saw in chapter 4 that less privileged groups know less about taxes; people who are female, younger, Black or Hispanic, lower income, less educated, or renters know less about taxes than those who are male, older, white, higher income, more educated, and homeowners. Such groups express less interest in taxes too. Figure 8.1a shows that closely following news of taxes is more common among those who are more privileged: male, older, higher income, more educated, married, and homeowners. Republicans and conservatives express more interest than Democrats or liberals.

Similarly, these privileged groups as well as Republicans and conservatives are more participatory around taxes compared to the less privileged, Democrats, and liberals (figure 8.1b). Political participation is measured with a three-item index adding up whether respondents voted, contacted a government official, or made a campaign contribution with taxes in mind.[14] Politicians hear more from men, whites, the affluent, the married, and homeowners than from women, other racial and ethnic groups, singles, and renters. They also hear more from Republicans and conservatives. And what taxes do these tax-related participators focus on? Among voters and contributors, the federal income tax, by a wide margin. Among those who contact elected officials,

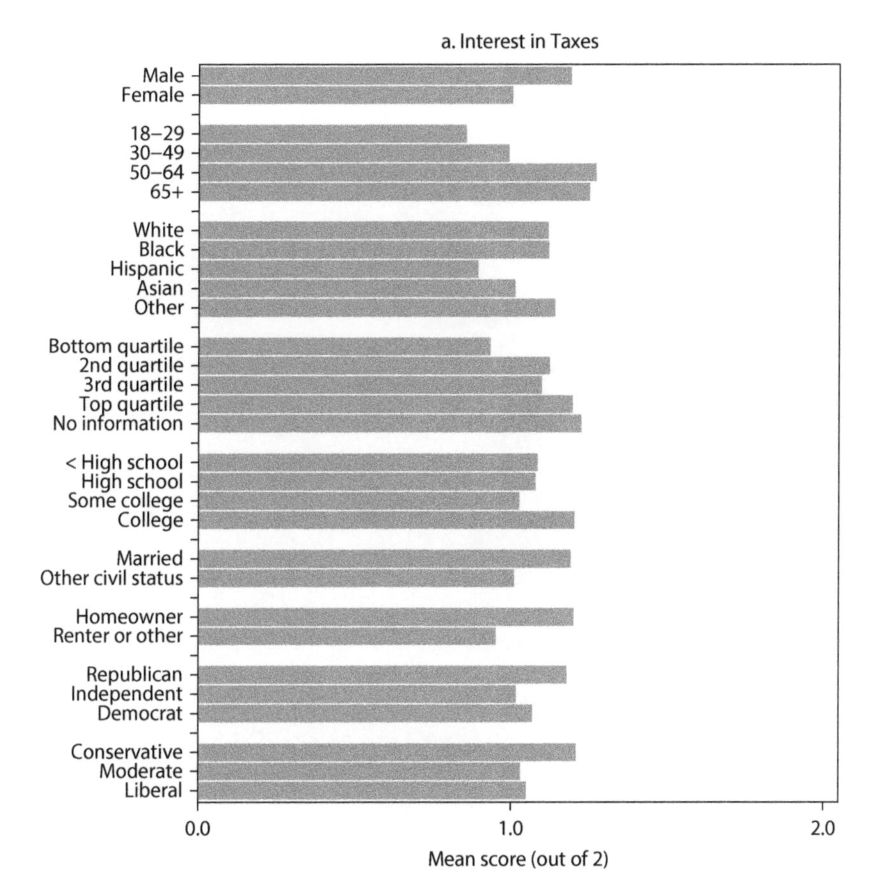

FIGURE 8.1 Tax Interest and Political Participation
Note: Tax interest is measured with a 0–2 scale, following news of taxes closely coded high. Tax participation is measured with a 0–3 additive scale for voting, contacting, or contributing concerning taxes.
Source: 2016 CCES.

the federal income tax and property tax in equal measure. It's safe to assume that those with voice are seeking reductions. Fewer people from less privileged groups participate around taxes, and even fewer participate around the regressive taxes that burden lower-income people more. Tax knowledge, interest, and participation are all the province of more highly resourced groups. They, and the politicians they elect, will be the ones driving the tax reform

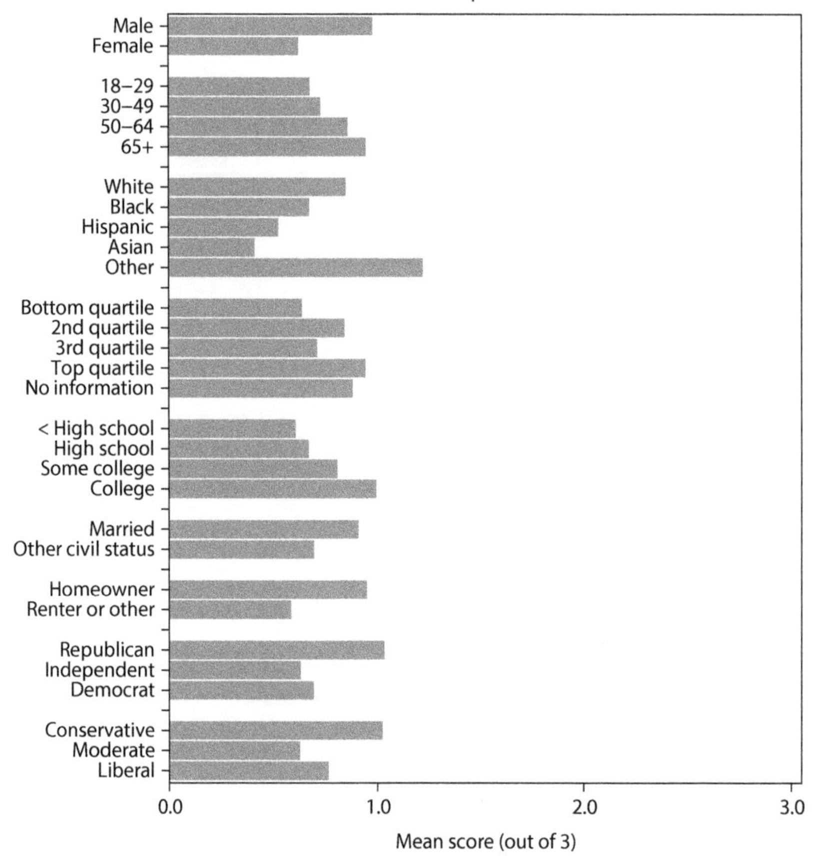

FIGURE 8.1 (*continued*)

bus unless the less privileged begin to realize their tremendous stake in the nation's tax policy.

Avenues for Future Research

In this book, I have tried to move beyond facile dismissals that Americans simply hate taxes—and beyond the short list of taxes previously studied—to explore the variation in and structures of attitudes across a wide array of taxes, individuals, and contexts. But there is much work to be done, and I hope this book will spur new activity around tax attitudes among political scientists and others who study public opinion. Many topics raised here deserve more research.

Contexts and Designs

Within the United States, there is much work to be done across states and localities. I have only scratched the surface of variation in tax attitudes across subnational units with differing institutional and policy configurations, not to mention differing social and economic contexts. Cross-national variation in tax attitudes deserves more attention as well. For decades, much of the most important scholarship on tax policy has been cross-national.[15] Yet for public opinion researchers interested in this area, cross-national data on tax attitudes are woefully sparse.[16]

The effects of tax design elements on attitudes also deserve further study. There is much to be learned about what types of taxes can garner public acceptance, for what purposes, and in what contexts.[17] This book has had a general policy feedback orientation, examining tax attitudes that arise as non-rich Americans respond to the tax policy landscape. My data only allow me to hint at possibilities that tax designs obscure costs or that people take umbrage at having their wealth taxed but less so their consumption. Many of the hypotheses raised here would lend themselves to more systematic policy feedback treatment, including causal analysis, looking at how specific policy designs have specific attitudinal effects.

Partisan Identification

As chapter 5 showed, sometimes attitudes do vary by party identification. More could be done to explore the conditions under which partisans emulate their parties' positions or not as well as the mechanisms linking partisanship and tax attitudes. What are the relative roles of information processes, partisan cheerleading, political trust, and other pathways? The vehemently antitax stances of independents are a particular area of interest.

Elite Rhetoric and Framing

The role of elite messaging could be studied in greater depth too. In discussing the messages white and Black taxpayers hear, for example, I have provided historical and anecdotal accounts, much like Nick Winter's (2008) exploration of race and gender messages around welfare and Social Security. The framing of different taxes around race (what types of income and assets are framed as white, what taxes are framed as white, and so on) would be a place to start.

I have not focused on perceptions of immigrants and their tax contributions, although Vanessa Williamson's (2017) in-depth interviews reveal that some taxpayers are quite concerned that immigrants do not pay taxes but do receive government benefits. More often than not the opposite is actually true, but the study of elite rhetoric in fanning these misperceptions would be valuable, especially as climate change and other disruptions drive more migration. More generally, systematic observational and experimental study of elite messages along with the ways in which their content, volume, timing, and context affect citizen attitudes would be most welcome.

At the intersection of both partisanship and elite framing, there is much work to be done on misperceptions and motivated reasoning. To what extent are tax misperceptions sincere (people having confidence in an unintentionally incorrect answer) or expressive (people intentionally report an incorrect answer as a form of partisan cheerleading) (Flynn, Nyhan, and Reifler 2017)? It would also be important to examine whether there is any possibility for the correction of misperceptions.

Attitudes of Black and Hispanic Taxpayers

Much more research is needed on the tax attitudes of various racial and ethnic groups. One place to start would be studying variation in tax attitudes among Black Americans, particularly across income. Many have argued that race is more important than class for Black attitudes because even high-income Black Americans face overt and covert discrimination and have a sense of linked fate, as the economic and social experience of race occurs across the income spectrum.[18] I did not have the sample sizes or indicators to test such hypotheses, but there is no doubt more to be learned. The representational angle deserves further study as well. Marisa Abrajano and Zoltan Hajnal (2015, 195–96) find that states with larger Hispanic populations collect more state revenues from regressive sales taxes and less from property taxes (whites are more likely to own homes) than states with smaller Hispanic populations, burdening Hispanic taxpayers. But the relationship is curvilinear: when the Hispanic population is large enough, state tax policy becomes more progressive. Both the mechanisms by which policy takes this form and the attitudinal manifestations deserve study. Another avenue for research on representation and tax attitudes is suggested by Christopher Clark's (2019, chap. 4) work, which finds that as the share of state legislators who are Black rises, per pupil education spending rises, but so do restrictions on eligibility for Temporary Assistance for Needy Families, both inside and outside the South. Clark argues that this effect is evidence of white backlash. Are there tax analogues to these effects? With new surveys on tax attitudes with Black and Hispanic oversamples, such effects could be investigated.

Another avenue for research would be exploring Black and Hispanic tax knowledge. Levels of formal tax knowledge among Black respondents are low, as chapter 4 showed. The formal tax knowledge questions test a narrow band of knowledge, however, just as traditional political knowledge items mainly assess knowledge of formal political institutions, which does not necessarily capture the knowledge of all communities. As Cathy Cohen and Matthew Luttig (2020, 806) put it in their study of Black political knowledge, "General political knowledge questions get at how *some people*, some of the time, interact, engage with, and understand politics and government."[19] When Cohen and Luttig add items to knowledge batteries asking about the operation of the carceral state, they find that the usual white-Black knowledge gap reverses, due to racial differences in lived experience. Again, could there be tax analogues to these effects? The literature on political knowledge asserts that citizens need to know the rules about "what the government is and does." Yet as Cohen and Luttig (2020, 806, quoting Barber 1973) point out, "What the government *does* as well as *the rules* it plays by often vary by community." Certainly that is true of tax policy.

So much tax scholarship has focused on white taxpayers, but it is crucial to know what other groups think of this central government activity. Most of the Hispanic respondents in my surveys were Mexican by origin, yet the Hispanic population is quite diverse by country of origin, income, occupation, and location. Asian Americans are even more diverse; on average, Asian households have higher incomes than white households, but this average hides tremendous variation. The tax attitudes of both of these growing groups deserve study. It would be important to study the tax attitudes of Native Americans as well. As US citizens, Native Americans pay federal income taxes, but whether they pay sales taxes depends on where they live. Tribes are sovereign nations, and states cannot force them to collect sales taxes, although some tribes impose their own on tribal lands.

Methods of Study

Because we know so little about tax attitudes, the data presented here have largely been descriptive. I have shown relationships among variables, but I have not demonstrated causality. These data can demonstrate, for example, that racial attitudes have stronger correlations with tax attitudes than do indicators of self-interest or partisan and ideological predispositions, but they do not show that racial attitudes cause tax attitudes. Now that we have a descriptive baseline, I hope other scholars will examine the causal relationships among variables where I have only been able to establish associations. Many aspects of tax policy lend themselves to experimental manipulation, as existing examples exploring whether people prefer tax breaks to direct spending reveal. I hope that researchers who specialize in experiments will capitalize on the wealth of hypotheses offered in this book and create corresponding experiments. Testing the implications for policy prescriptions would be welcome as well. That said, historical, descriptive, and causal data are all needed for a complete picture of the factors behind tax attitudes and preferences. Some factors do not easily lend themselves to experimental manipulation; experimental treatments may lack external validity too, failing to capture the reality of individuals' casual, complicated, and often distracted interactions with the tax system. And ultimately, political and economic elites control the policy agenda. We can test how individuals might react to a given tax proposal, but that proposal may never materialize in the real world or may be framed in a way that undermines what is known from scholars' experiments.

Taxes are a central function of government yet also one of the most controversial. They constitute one of the main interactions citizens have with the state, and in the United States, they are wrapped up in the political parties' pursuit of electoral advantage along with the nation's long and tragic history around race. Taxes are also constantly on the political agenda. Because they pose such a challenge for democratic governance—who is taxed how, for what purpose, and with what level of input and consent—they will continue to be a central concern for politics and policymaking, and I hope for those who study these areas.

APPENDIX

THE APPENDIX CONTAINS a description of the regression analysis, survey item wording, and supplementary figures. An additional online appendix at https://press.princeton.edu/ISBN/9780691137858 contains variable coding and descriptive statistics, regression results underlying the figures in the text, and additional supplementary figures.

Regression Analysis

In general, the reported models use the following specification for the full sample:

$$\begin{aligned}\mathbf{X}^T\beta = {} & \beta_0 + \beta_1\, female + \beta_2\, age + \beta_3\, age^2 + \beta_4\, black + \beta_5\, hispanic + \beta_6\, asian \\ & + \beta_7\, other\ race + \beta_8\, bottom\ income + \beta_9\, top\ income + \beta_{10}\, college \\ & + \beta_{11}\, married + \beta_{12}\, child + \beta_{13}\, homeowner + \beta_{14}\, independent \\ & + \beta_{15}\, republican + \beta_{16}\, moderate + \beta_{17}\, conservative \\ & + \beta_{18}\, government\ trust\end{aligned}$$

Some models include an additional covariate: South. The results displayed in chapters 5, 6, and 7 do not include the bottom income dummy, though this dummy's inclusion yields the same results. Table OA.1 in the online appendix reports the descriptive statistics of the variables used in the regression analysis. In analyses of Black, Hispanic, and Asian subgroups, the reference category is white (not white + other).

In the case of the models for the white subsample, the typical specification is:

$$\begin{aligned}\mathbf{X}^T\beta = {} & \beta_0 + \beta_1\, female + \beta_2\, age + \beta_3\, age^2 + \beta_4\, bottom\ income + \beta_5\, top\ income \\ & + \beta_6\, college + \beta_7\, married + \beta_8\, child + \beta_9\, homeowner \\ & + \beta_{10}\, independent + \beta_{11}\, republican + \beta_{12}\, moderate + \beta_{13}\, conservative \\ & + \beta_{14}\, government\ trust + \beta_{15}\, symbolic\ racism\end{aligned}$$

The additional covariate in this model (symbolic racism) is an additive index based on a scale of two to four items (depending on the data source). Metric analysis (interitem correlations, Cronbach's alpha, and principal component analysis) provides evidence of the adequate functioning of the scale.

In the cases of CCES 2016 and 2019, the variable "other race" combines the groups "Native American," "mixed," "Middle East," and "other." In the case of NPR 2003, the variable "other race" combines the groups "Asian" and "other." These coding choices are based on the small sample size of these subgroups in the data. Independent leaners are coded as partisans ("Democrat" or "Republican"); "independents" are true independents (midpoint of the scale). In the CCES, the income variable measures household income. In both CCES and NPR, the variable "top income" is calculated by coding one to 20 percent of respondents with the highest reported income (and zero otherwise). Likewise, the "bottom income" variable is calculated by coding one to 20 percent of respondents with the lowest reported income (and zero otherwise). The variable "college" assigns a one to respondents who are college graduates (four years) or report some postgraduate degree, and zero otherwise. The "South" variable assigns a one to respondents who live in Alabama, Arkansas, Florida, Georgia, Louisiana, Mississippi, North Carolina, South Carolina, Tennessee, Texas, or Virginia, and zero otherwise.

During the empirical analysis, I tested alternative specifications. Specifically, I explored models with:

- A continuous coding of income (including a quadratic term), education, partisanship, and ideology.
- A dummy for sixty-five-plus citizens in replacement of age (linear and quadratic terms).
- Alternative coding schemes for partisanship and ideology.

The items on tax knowledge are coded with a one if the respondent reports the correct answer, zero if the answer is incorrect, and missing value (NA) if they do not answer.

The majority of the models reported in the text were estimated with ordinary least squares, with the exception of the binary logistic models using NPR 2003 as a data source. The models include standard errors and are robust to heteroscedasticity. In the case of the survey experiments, the average treatment effect (or conditional average treatment effect) are estimated with HC3 robust standard errors.

As additional robustness checks, I reestimate the models under different modeling assumptions. Specifically, I run binary logistic (one = unfair, and zero = fair) and ordinal logistic models for the following outcomes: tax fairness, tax change preferences, desire to eliminate tax expenditures, and decrease federal spending. For the binary models, I used the maximum likelihood estimation and penalized maximum likelihood estimation to deal with potential problems associated with small sample sizes. Finally, for the tax knowledge models, I estimate different count models (Poisson, quasi-Poisson, negative binomial, and zero inflated). For these robustness checks, the quantity of interest is the average marginal effect and discrete change for binary covariates. In general, these complementary models lead to the same substantive conclusions about the effects of covariates (statistical significance and sign of effect) as linear models. Given the above, I have chosen to report the linear models since they are easy to interpret.

Survey Items

Fairness of tax share, 2012 CCES: "Please click a number on the scale to rate how fair your share of each tax is." Response: five-point scale ranging from "the share I pay is unfair" to "the share I pay is fair," with a "don't know enough to rate" option. Five taxes included: federal income, state income, sales, Social Security, and property. Figure 7.2a shows the percentage of respondents selecting one (unfair) on the scale for each tax, among those giving a response. Figure 3.1a shows the mean scores on the five-point scale for "the share I pay" as well as the mean scores from the same scale asked of "the share low-income people pay" and "the share high-income people pay."

Fairness of amount one pays, 2016, 2019 CCES: "How fair do you regard the amount you have to pay for each tax?" Response: four-point scale ranging from "very fair" to "very unfair," with "I do not have to pay this tax" and "I have no opinion" options. Eight taxes included: federal income, state income, estate, investment, state sales, gasoline, payroll, and property. Figures 3.2a, 4.2a, 5.2a, 7.2b, and 7.6 show the percentage of respondents selecting somewhat or very unfair among those giving a response. Figures 1.1, 4.3, 4.8a, 4.8b, 5.3, 5.5a, 5.5b, 6.3, 7.3, 7.7, and 7.8 show results from multivariate analyses, plotting the average partial effect of select attributes for respondents saying the amount they pay for each tax is unfair or very unfair.

Fairness of federal and state income tax share, 2019 CCES: "Please click a number on the scale to rate the fairness of the share each income group pays in federal income tax." Response: five-point scale ranging from "the share low-income people pay is too low" to "the share low-income people pay is too high." The item was asked three times, for low-, middle-, and high-income individuals. The same items were repeated for "state income taxes." Figure 3.1b shows the mean scores on the five-point scale for the share paid by each of the three income groups for federal and state income taxes.

Fairness of tax, 2019 CCES: "How fair do you think each of these taxes is?" Response: four-point scale ranging from "very fair" to "very unfair," with an "I have no opinion" option. Eight taxes included: federal income, state income, estate, investment, state sales, gasoline, payroll, and property. Figure 3.6 shows the share of respondents deeming each tax fair among those saying a progressive federal income tax system is the most fair versus those saying a proportional or regressive system is most fair.

Most fair and least fair tax, 2016 CCES: After asking respondents how fair they regard the amount they have to pay for each tax, two open-ended items asked respondents, "Which taxes do you consider the most fair, and why?" and "Which taxes do you consider the most unfair, and why?" Figure 3.2b shows the share of respondents mentioning each tax as the most fair and most unfair.

Bothers most, 2016 CCES: "Thinking about paying federal income taxes, which of the following bothers you the most?" Response: "the amount you pay," "the complexity of the tax system," "the way the government spends taxes," "the feeling that some wealthy people don't pay their fair share," or "the feeling that some poor people don't pay their fair share," with an "I have no opinion" option. Figure 6.2 shows the distribution of responses for white racial conservatives and white racial liberals (top and bottom terciles, respectively, of the racial resentment index among whites).

Decrease tax, 2016 CCES: "Should each of the following taxes be increased, decreased, or kept the same?" Response: "increased," "decreased," or "kept the same," with an "I have no opinion" option. Eight taxes included: federal income, state income, estate, investment, state sales, gasoline, payroll, and property. Figures 4.2b, 5.2b, and 7.2c show the percentage of respondents saying decrease among those giving a response. Figure 3.3 shows the ratio of the percentage of respondents wanting to decrease each tax to the percentage wanting to increase each tax. Figures 1.2, 4.4, 4.9a, 4.9b, 5.4, 5.6a, 5.6b, 6.4, 7.4, and 7.9

show results from multivariate analyses, plotting the average partial effect of select attributes for respondents selecting the decrease tax response.

Worst tax, ACIR 1983–94: "Which is the worst tax—that's the least fair?" Asked in 1983–89, 1991, and 1993 for four taxes: federal income, state income, state sales, and local property, with an "I don't know" option. Asked in 1988–90, 1992, and 1994 adding a fifth tax, Social Security. Figure 3.2a shows the distribution of responses across all respondents for the five-tax measure. Figure 5.1 shows responses by party affiliation for the four-tax measure. The ACIR surveys were conducted by telephone.

Dislike most, 2019 CCES: "Below is a list of different taxes. Please rank them from the tax you dislike the most (number one) to the tax you dislike the least (number five) by dragging your choices to the numbered boxes on the right." Asked of five taxes: federal income, state income, Social Security, state sales, and property. Figure 3.2a shows the share of respondents ranking each tax as the most disliked (the share selecting number one). Figure 5.1 shows responses by party affiliation.

Taxes now versus 1980, 2012 CCES: "Compared to 1980, do the following groups of people now pay more of their income in federal income taxes, less of their income in federal income taxes, or pay about the same amount?" Response: "pay much more now," "pay more now," "pay about the same amount now," "pay less now," or "pay much less now," with an "I don't know" option. Asked of four groups: "middle-income people," "low-income people," "high-income people," and "people like you." Figure 3.11 shows the proportion of respondents saying how much of their income each income group (low, middle, high, and people like you) pays in federal income tax now compared to 1980.

Tax incidence knowledge, 2016 CCES: "Is each of these taxes progressive (high-income people pay a greater share of their income in tax than lower-income people), regressive (high-income people pay a smaller share of their income in tax than lower-income people), or proportional (people of all income levels pay the same share of their income in tax)," with an "I don't know enough to say" option. Asked of eight taxes: federal income, state income, payroll, estate, state sales, local property, gasoline, and investment (capital gains and dividend taxes). The index of knowledge about progressive taxes is based on the number of correct responses for the four progressive taxes (estate, investment, federal income, and state income). The index of knowledge about regressive taxes is based on the number of correct responses for the four regressive taxes (local property, gasoline, payroll, and state sales). Figure 3.8 shows the distribution of answers for all respondents. Figures 4.6b–4.6c show the level of knowledge of progressive and regressive taxes, respectively, among demographic and political groups. Figure 4.7 shows results from multivariate analyses, plotting the marginal effect of select attributes on respondents' level of knowledge about progressive and regressive taxes.

General tax knowledge, 2016 CCES: Two items tapped general tax knowledge. First, "Do you think the amount deducted from one's paycheck for Social Security and Medicare is part of the federal income tax, or not?" Response: "it is part of the federal income tax" or "it is not part of the federal income tax" (the correct response), with an "I don't know enough to say" option. Second, "Compared with citizens of Western European countries, do you think Americans pay a higher or smaller percentage of their income in taxes?" Response: "Americans pay a higher percentage" or "Americans pay a lower percentage" (the correct answer), with an "I don't know enough to say" option. Figure 4.6a adds these two items together and shows the mean number of correct responses on a zero-to-two scale among demographic and political groups. Figure 4.7 shows results from multivariate analyses, plotting the marginal effect of select attributes on respondents' level of general tax knowledge.

Interest in taxes, CCES 2016: "How closely do you follow news of the following . . ." asked of "taxes." Response: "very closely," "somewhat closely," and "not at all closely," with an "I don't know" option. Figure 8.1a shows the mean score on a zero-to-two scale among demographic and political groups in which "very closely" is scored as 2, "somewhat closely" as 1, and "not at all closely" as 0.

Participation around taxes, CCES 2016:

Tax voting: "In the past five years, have you taken into account the position of a candidate in relation to taxes in deciding how to vote?" Response: "yes," "no," or "don't know." "No" and "don't know" responses are combined for our analyses.

Tax contacting: "In the past five years, have you contacted a government official to complain about taxes?" Response: "yes," "no," or "don't know." "No" and "don't know" responses are combined for our analyses.

Tax contributing: "In the past five years, have you given a campaign contribution based, at least in part, on your concern about taxes?" Response: "yes," "no," or "don't know." "No" and "don't know" responses are combined for our analyses.

Index of tax participation: the three tax participation items were summed to create a zero-to-three scale, with high values indicating high levels of participation around taxes. Figure 8.1b shows the mean number on the zero-to-three scale among demographic and political groups.

Uncued and cued items, 2003 NPR Taxes Study: the following items do not include an explicit "I don't know" option. Figure 5.7 shows the results from a multivariate analysis where the outcome is dichotomous (federal income tax too high, as opposed to about right or too low, and so on). Figure 5.1 shows responses to the "most disliked tax" item by party affiliation.

The four uncued general tax system items include:

"Do you consider the amount of federal income tax you have to pay as too high, about right, or too low?" Response: "too high," "about right," "too low," or "don't know" (volunteered). Outcome is dichotomous (too high versus other responses).

"How fair do you think our present federal tax system is? Overall, would you say that our tax system is . . . very fair, moderately fair, not too fair, or not fair at all?" Response: "very fair," "moderately fair," "not too fair," "not fair at all," or "don't know" (volunteered). Outcome is dichotomous (very or moderately fair versus other responses).

"How complex do you think the current federal income tax system is? Do you think it is very complex, somewhat complex, not too complex, or not complex at all?" Response: "very complex," "somewhat complex," "not too complex," "not complex at all," or "don't know" (volunteered). Outcome is dichotomous (very or somewhat complex versus other responses).

"Some of the biggest taxes that individuals have to pay are (*rotate order*: income taxes, Social Security taxes, sales taxes, and property taxes). No one likes to pay taxes, but thinking about these four kinds of taxes, I'd like you to rank them, starting with the one you dislike the most." Outcome: ranking of "income tax," "Social Security tax," "sales tax," and "property tax" as most disliked, or "don't know" (volunteered).

The four politically cued items include:

"As you may know, in 2001 Congress passed President Bush's proposals for tax cuts that are to be phased in over the next few years. Do you favor or oppose speeding up those tax cuts so they go into effect sooner or don't you know enough to say?" Response: "favor," "oppose," or "don't know enough to say." Outcome is dichotomous (favor versus other responses).

"As you may know, the 2001 tax cuts are set to expire in 2011. Do you support or oppose making those tax cuts permanent, or don't you know enough to say?" Response: "support," "oppose," or "don't know enough to say." Outcome is dichotomous (support versus other responses).

"There is a federal estate tax—that is, a tax on the money people leave when they die. Do you favor or oppose eliminating this tax, or don't you know enough to say?" Half of the sample was asked this "estate tax" wording, and the other half was told, "There is a federal estate tax that some people call the death tax." Response: "favor," "oppose," or "don't know enough to say." Outcome is dichotomous (favor versus other responses). Figure 5.7 combines responses for these two versions of the question.

"Do you favor or oppose eliminating the tax on dividends, or haven't you heard enough about it to have an opinion?" Response: "favor, "oppose," or "have not heard enough about it to have an opinion." Outcome is dichotomous (favor versus other responses). This item was asked of the respondents who in a previous question said that they had "heard about" a "proposal in Washington . . . to do away with personal income taxes on corporate dividends. Dividends are what many companies pay to owners of their stock." Because only a subset of respondents had heard about dividend elimination and therefore were asked their opinion, the coefficients shown in figure 5.7 have larger confidence intervals than is the case for the other outcomes displayed in the figure.

Trump tax cut cued and uncued items, 2019 CCES: "In December 2017, a new tax bill was passed [by Congress and signed by President Trump], the TCJA, which affected taxes beginning in 2018. Do you approve or disapprove of the TCJA, or don't you know enough to say?" Figure 5.8 shows the results from a multivariate analysis where the outcome is approval for the TCJA, and half of the sample was given the cued version that included the words in brackets.

Federal income tax too high, 1947–73 Gallup, 1976–2018 GSS: "Do you consider the amount of federal income tax you have to pay as too high, about right, or too low?" Figures 5.9, 6.6, 7.5, and A.7 show the results from multivariate analyses, plotting the average partial effect of select attributes for respondents saying the amount they pay is too high. Appendix figures A.4, A.5, A.6, A.8, and A.9 show the corresponding descriptive data.

Federal income tax attitudes, 2004 ANES:

Amount respondent pays: "Next are a few questions about federal income taxes. Do you feel you are asked to pay *more than you should* in federal income taxes, about the *right amount*, or *less than you should*?"

Amount the rich pays: "What about rich people? Do you feel rich people are asked to pay *more than they should* in federal income taxes, about the *right amount*, or *less than they should*?"

Amount the poor pays: "What about poor people? Do you feel poor people are asked to pay *more than they should* in federal income taxes, about the *right amount*, or *less than they should*?"

Response: "more than should pay," "about right," "less than should pay," and "don't pay at all," with a "don't know" option. Paying more than one should is coded high. These items are discussed in chapter 6; online appendix tables OA.37–OA.39 show results for multivariate analyses.

Progressive tax attitudes, 1981 Harris: "For the past sixty-eight years, the federal income tax has been based on the principle that higher-income people not only have to pay more in taxes but also must pay a greater percentage of their income in taxes. Do you feel that principle is fair and equitable, or not?" Response: "fair principle" or "not fair principle." Table 3.2 shows the distribution of responses for this item.

Progressive tax attitudes, 1987, 2000, 2008 NORC: "Do you think that people with high incomes should pay a larger share of their income in taxes than those with low incomes, the same share, or a smaller share?" Response: "much larger," "larger," "same," "smaller share," or "much lower." Table 3.2 shows the range of the distribution of responses for this item.

Progressive tax attitudes, 2008 American Patriot Survey: "Now I am going to read you some proposals that a candidate for president might make because he says they embody America's best, most patriotic ideals. After each one, please tell me whether it is a good way or bad way to express America's patriotism.... Make federal taxes more progressive, so the rich pay a significantly higher share of their income than the middle class or poor." Response: "very good," "somewhat good," "somewhat bad," or "very bad," with a "don't know / refused" option. Table 3.2 shows the share of respondents who answer "very good" or "somewhat good."

Progressive tax reform, 2009 CBS/*New York Times*: "Do you think the new tax code should be changed so that middle- and lower-income people pay less than they do now, and upper-income people pay more in taxes than they do now, or don't you think the tax code should be changed?" Response: "should be changed so upper-income people pay more" or "should not." Table 3.2 shows the distribution of responses for this item.

Amount high-income people pay, 1977–92 Roper: "For each one, would you tell me whether you think they have to pay too much in taxes, too little in taxes, or about the right amount. . . . High-income families?" Response: "too much in taxes," "about right," or "too little in taxes." This question was asked in 1977, and twice in 1978, 1979 1985, 1986, and 1992. Table 3.2 shows the range of the share of respondents who believe high-income families pay too little in taxes.

Amount high-income people pay, 1992–2016 Gallup: "As I read off some different groups, please tell me if you think they are paying their fair share in federal taxes, paying too much, or paying too little. . . . Upper-income people?" This question was asked in 1992, 1993, 1994, 1996, and 1999, and every year from 2003 to 2016. Table 3.2 shows the range of the share of respondents who believe upper-income people pay too little in federal taxes.

Amount corporations pay, 2004–16 Gallup: "As I read off some different groups, please tell me if you think they are paying their fair share in federal taxes, paying too much, or paying too little. . . . Corporations?" This question was asked every year from 2004 to 2016. Table 3.2 shows the range of the share of respondents who believe that corporations pay too little in federal taxes.

Progressive tax attitudes, 1972 ANES: "As you know, in our tax system people who earn a lot of money already have to pay higher rates of income tax than those who earn less. Some people think that those with high incomes should pay even more of their income into taxes than they do now. Others think that the rates shouldn't be different at all—that everyone should pay the same portion of their income, no matter how much they make. Where would you place yourself on this scale or haven't you thought much about this?" Outcome: seven-point scale from "increase the tax rate for high incomes" to "have the same tax rate for everyone." Preference for a flat tax is coded high. Results are described in chapter 6; online appendix table OA.36 shows results for multivariate analyses.

Progressive tax attitudes, 2008 ANES: "Which one of the following opinions best agrees with your view?" Response: "people who make more money should pay a *larger percent* of their income in taxes to the government than people who make less money," "people who make more money should pay a *smaller percent* of their income in taxes to the government than people who make less money," or "the amount of money people make *should not determine* what percent of their income they pay in taxes." Preference for a flat tax is coded high. Results are described in chapter 6; online appendix table OA.40 shows results from multivariate analyses.

Progressive tax attitudes, 2012 CCES: Progressive system item: "A progressive tax system is one in which the tax rate a person pays *increases* as the amount of income that person makes increases. A flat tax system is one in which the tax rate is the *same* for all income levels. A regressive tax system is one in which the tax rate a person pays *decreases* as the amount of income that person makes increases. Please indicate how fair you think each tax system is (progressive, flat, and regressive)." Response: four-point scale from "very fair" to "very unfair."

Estate tax item: "An estate tax is a tax on the property left behind by a deceased person. Different people have different views about what types of estates should be taxed or if there should be an estate tax at all. What's your view?" Response: "all estates should be taxed regardless of the value of the deceased person's property," "only the estates of very wealthy deceased persons should be taxed," or "no estates should be taxed."

Capital gains tax item: "A capital gains tax is a tax on money earned from the sale of stocks or assets. Different people have different views about how such income should be taxed. What's your view?" Response: "money earned from the sales of stocks or assets should be taxed at a *higher/same/lower* rate than income earned as wages and salaries."

Bush tax cuts item (from CCES 2012 Common Content): "Congress considered many important bills over the past two years. For each of the following, tell us whether you support or oppose the legislation in principle. . . . The Tax Hike Prevent Act. Would extend Bush era tax cuts for all individuals regardless of income. Would increase the budget deficit by an estimated $405 billion." Response: "support" or "oppose."

Federal income tax on high earners item: "Do you think that the federal income tax rates for families making more than $250,000 per year should be increased, decreased, or kept at the current level?" Response: "increased," "decreased," or "kept at the current level," with an "I have no opinion" option.

Figures 3.7 shows the relationship between responses to the progressive system item and attitudes toward each individual tax policies. Figure 6.5 shows results from multivariate analyses for each of the above items.

Abstract tax system preferences, 2019 CCES: "Thinking about the federal income tax, which is most fair: a progressive system (high-income people pay a greater share of their income in tax than lower-income people), a regressive system (high-income people pay a smaller share of their income in tax than lower-income people), or a proportional system (people of all income levels pay the same share of their income in tax)?" Response: "progressive," "regressive," or "proportional," with an "I don't know enough to say" option. Figures 4a–b show results from multivariate analyses for the subset of respondents selecting each tax system as the most fair.

Perceived distribution of tax expenditures, 2003 NPR, 2016 CCES: "The federal income tax system has a number of credits, deductions, and exclusions that can reduce the taxes paid by qualified taxpayers. For each of these tax breaks, what kind of people get the biggest tax reduction on average?" Asked of: CTC, deduction for high medical expenses, deduction for charitable contributions, home mortgage interest deduction, lower tax rate on capital gains, tax break for employer-provided health insurance, tax break for employer-provided retirement plan, and EITC. Response: "low-income people," "middle-income people," or "high-income people," with an "I don't know enough to say" option. Figure 3.9 shows the percentage of respondents saying that low-, middle-, or high-income people get the biggest tax reduction on average.

Tax expenditure fairness, 2016 CCES: "When two families have the same income, do you think it is fair or unfair that one family pays less tax because they . . . ?" Asked of: dependent children, medical expenses, charity, mortgage, investments, health insurance, and retirement plan. Response: "fair," "unfair," or "I have no opinion." This item is mentioned in chapter 3.

Tax expenditure elimination, 2016 CCES: "Would you like to eliminate any of these tax breaks, reduce their value, or keep them as is?" Asked of: CTC, deduction for high medical expenses, deduction for charitable contributions, home mortgage interest deduction, lower tax rate on capital gains, tax break for employer-provided health insurance, tax break for employer-provided retirement plan, and EITC. Figure 3.5 shows the share of respondents who want to eliminate, reduce, or keep each tax expenditure, among those giving a response. Figure 6.7 shows results from multivariate analyses where a desire to eliminate the tax expenditure is coded high.

Federal spending preferences, 2016 CCES: "Should federal spending on each of the following be increased, decreased, or kept the same?" Asked of (in a randomized order): Social Security, Medicare (public health insurance for older people), Medicaid (public health insurance for low-income people), food stamps, public schools, infrastructure (such as bridges and roads), financial aid for college, national defense, housing rental vouchers, cash welfare, and childcare. Response: "increased," "decreased," or "kept the same," with an "I have no opinion" option. Figure 6.1 shows results from multivariate analyses where a preference for decreased spending is coded high. Figure 7.1b shows the share of white and Black respondents wanting federal spending on each program increased.

Millionaire taxes, 2012, 2016, and 2020 ANES: "Do you favor, oppose, or neither favor nor oppose increasing income taxes on people making over $1 million per year?" Response: "favor," "oppose," or "neither favor nor oppose," with a "don't know" option. Opposition to the millionaire tax is coded high. Results are described in chapter 6; online appendix tables OA.41–OA.43 show results for multivariate analyses.

Racial attitudes, CCES: For the 2012 CCES, the racial resentment index is composed of two items from the survey's Common Content: "The Irish, Italians, Jews and many other minorities overcame prejudice and worked their way up. Blacks should do the same without any special favors." And "generations of slavery and discrimination have created conditions that make it difficult for Blacks to work their way out of the lower class." Response: five-point scale ranging from "strongly agree" to "strongly disagree." The two items were reverse coded and summed, with higher values indicating higher levels of racial resentment.

For the 2016 and 2019 CCES, the racial resentment index is composed of responses to four questions: "Over the past few years, Blacks have gotten less than they deserve"; "Irish, Italian, Jewish, and many other minorities overcame prejudice and worked their way up. Blacks should do the same"; "Generations of slavery and discrimination have created conditions that make it difficult for Blacks to work their way out of the lower class"; and "It's really a matter of some people not trying hard enough; if Blacks would only try harder, they could be just as well-off as whites." Response for each question: four-point scale from "strongly agree" to "strongly disagree." The appropriate items were reverse coded and summed, with higher values indicating higher levels of racial resentment.

Racial attitudes, GSS: For the GSS, the racial resentment index is composed of RACDIF1 and RACDIF4 for a longer time span, and those two items plus WRKWAYUP for a shorter time span, as shown in figure 6.6. For RACDIF1 and RACDIF4, the respondent is prompted with the sentence, "On the average, African Americans have worse jobs, income, and housing than white people." RACDIF1 asks, "Do you think these differences are mainly due to discrimination?" RACDIF4 asks, "Do you think these differences are because most African Americans just don't have the motivation or willpower to pull themselves up out of poverty?" Response: "yes" or "no," with a "don't know" option. WRKWAYUP asks, "Irish, Italians, Jewish, and many other minorities overcame prejudice and worked their way up. Blacks should do the same without special favors." Response: "agree strongly," "agree somewhat," "neither agree nor disagree," "disagree somewhat," or "disagree strongly," with a "don't know" option. The appropriate items were reverse coded and summed, with higher values indicating higher levels of racial resentment.

We also explore six alternative racial attitude measures from the GSS:

"B less intelligent" uses INTLBLKS: "Do people in these groups tend to be unintelligent or tend to be intelligent" (for Blacks). Response: seven-point scale from unintelligent to intelligent. The item is coded such that a belief that Black people are unintelligent is high. This question was asked intermittently between 1990 and 2018.

"Oppose relative marry B" uses MARBLK: "How about having a close relative or family member marry a Black person? Would you be very in favor of it happening, somewhat in favor, neither in favor nor opposed to it happening, somewhat opposed, or very opposed to it happening?" Response: "strongly favor, "favor," "neither favor nor oppose," "oppose," or "strongly oppose," with a "don't know" option. The item is coded such that "oppose" or "strongly oppose" are high. This question was asked intermittently between 1990 and 2018.

"B less ability" uses RACDIF2: "On average, (Negroes/Blacks / African Americans) have worse jobs, income, and housing than white people. Do you think these differences are . . . because most (Negroes/Blacks / African Americans) have less inborn ability to learn?" Response: "yes," "no," or "don't know." The item is coded such that a belief that Black people have less inborn ability to learn is high. This question was asked intermittently between 1977 and 2018.

"Ban B-W marriage" used RACMAR: "Do you think there should be laws against marriages between (Negroes/Blacks / African Americans) and whites?" Response: "yes," "no," or "don't know." The item is coded such that favoring a law against interracial marriage is high. This question was asked intermittently between 1972 and 2002.

"Not vote for B pres" uses RACPRES: "If your party nominated a (Negro/Black / African American) for president, would you vote for him if he were qualified for the job?" Response: "yes," "no," or "don't know." The item is coded such that not voting for a Black candidate is high. This question was asked intermittently between 1972 and 2010.

"Favor seg neighborhood" uses RACSEG: "White people have a right to keep (Negroes/Blacks / African Americans) out of their neighborhoods if they want to and (Negroes/Blacks / African Americans) should respect that right." Response: "agree strongly," "agree slightly," "disagree slightly," or "disagree strongly," with a "don't know" option. The item is coded such that agreement with this statement is high. This question was asked intermittently between 1972 and 1996. Appendix figure A.7 shows results for multivariate analyses of these items.

Racial attitudes, ANES: For the ANES, various measures of racial sentiment and ethnocentrism are constructed based on question availability.

For 1972, the first old-fashioned racism measure uses the question, "Are you in favor of desegregation, strict segregation, or something in between?" with a "don't know" option. Responses were coded such that higher values indicate a preference for segregation. The 1972 alternative old-fashioned racism measure is composed of responses to two questions: "In *American life and politics*, do Blacks have too much, about the right amount of, or too little influence?" and "In *American politics*, do Blacks have too much, about the right amount, or too little influence?" Response: "too much influence," "just about the right amount of influence," or "too little influence," with a "don't know" option. These two items were reverse coded and summed, with higher values indicating higher levels of racial resentment.

For 2004, 2008, 2012, 2016, and 2020, the symbolic racism measure is composed of responses to four questions. The first question reads, "In past studies, we have asked people why they think white people seem to get more of the good things in life in America—such as better jobs and more money—than Black people do. These are some of the reasons given by both Blacks and whites. Please tell me whether you agree or disagree with each reason as to why white people seem to get more of the good things in life: generations of slavery and discrimination have created conditions that make it difficult for Blacks to work their way out of the lower class." The next three questions ask respondents to indicate their level of agreement with the following statements: "Irish, Italians, Jewish, and many other minorities overcame prejudice and worked their way up. Blacks should do the same without any special favors"; "It's really a matter of some people not trying hard enough; if Blacks would only try harder, they could be just as well-off as whites"; "Over the past years, Blacks have gotten less than they deserve." Response: "agree strongly," "agree somewhat," "neither agree nor disagree," "disagree somewhat," or "disagree strongly," with a "don't know" option. All four responses were coded such that high values indicate high levels of racial resentment, then summed to create the symbolic racism index.

For 1972, 2004, 2008, 2012, 2016, and 2020, the first racial attitude measure is composed of responses to two feeling thermometer questions: "Using the thermometer, how would you rate the following groups" (for Blacks and whites)? Response: zero-to-one-hundred scale with a "don't know" option. The Black feeling thermometer score is subtracted from the white feeling thermometer to create a score where high values indicate high levels of racial resentment.

For 2004, 2008, 2012, 2016, and 2020, a second racial attitude measure is composed of responses to four questions about the traits possessed by different racial/ethnic groups. The 2004, 2008, and 2012 measures utilize a hardworking-lazy scale placement for whites and Blacks, and an intelligent-unintelligent scale placement for whites and Blacks. The hardworking-lazy scale placement reads as follows: "I'm going to show you a seven-point scale on which the characteristics of the people in a group can be rated. In the first statement, a score of one means that you think almost all the people in that group tend to be 'hardworking.' A score of seven means that almost all the people in the group are 'lazy.' A score of four means that you think that most people in the group are not closer to one end or the other, and of course you may choose any number in between. Where would you rate [whites/Blacks] in general on this scale?" All outcomes are measured on a one-to-seven scale with a "don't know" option. Responses are reverse coded, then the Black score is subtracted from the white score for each trait. The difference between white and Black scores is averaged over the two trait questions to create a racial attitude measure. In 2016 and 2020, the ANES survey drops the intelligent-unintelligent scale and adds a peaceful-violent scale. The racial attitude measures for 2016 and 2020 utilize the average difference in scores across the hardworking-lazy and peaceful-violent scales for white and Black respondents.

For 2004, 2008, and 2012, the first ethnocentrism measure utilizes the hardworking-lazy and intelligent-unintelligent scales, this time including attitudes toward Asians and Hispanics in addition to Blacks and whites. For 2016 and 2020, the same ethnocentrism measure utilizes the hardworking-lazy and peaceful-violent scales for each racial/ethnic group. For each trait, the Black, Asian, and Hispanic scores are averaged and subtracted from the white score. This score is then averaged over the two available trait questions to create an index of ethnocentrism with high levels of ethnocentrism coded high.

For 2004, 2008, 2012, 2016, and 2020, the second ethnocentrism measure utilizes the feeling thermometer questions, this time including feelings toward Asians and Hispanics in addition to Blacks and whites. The Black, Asian, and Hispanic thermometer scores are averaged and subtracted from the white thermometer score. The outcome is an index of ethnocentrism with high levels of ethnocentrism coded high.

Government trust, 2012, 2016 CCES; GSS; ANES: "How much of the time do you trust the federal government to do what is right?" Response: "just about always," "most of the time," "only some of the time," or "none of the time." Outcome is dichotomous ("just about always" or "most of the time" versus other responses).

Supplementary Figures

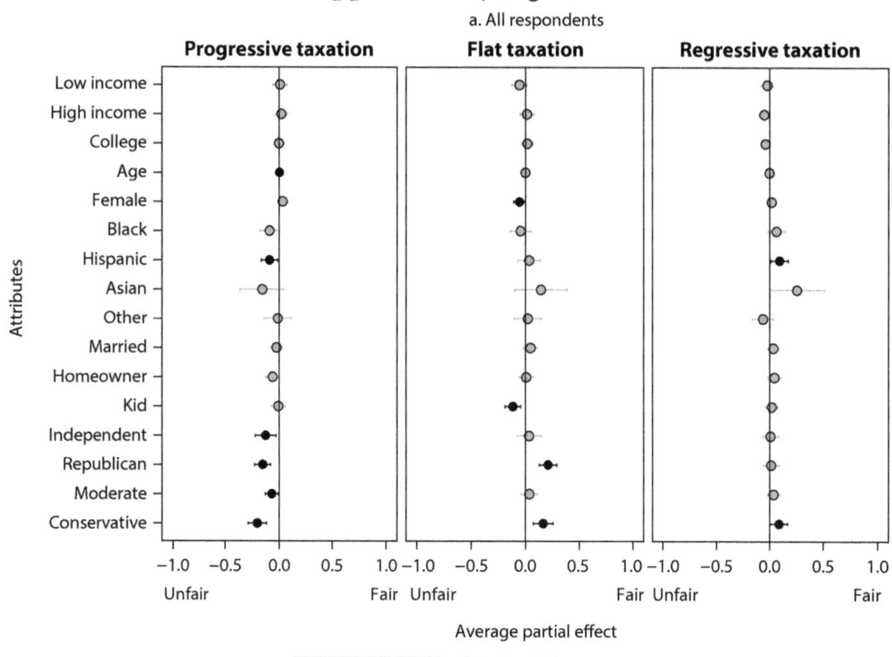

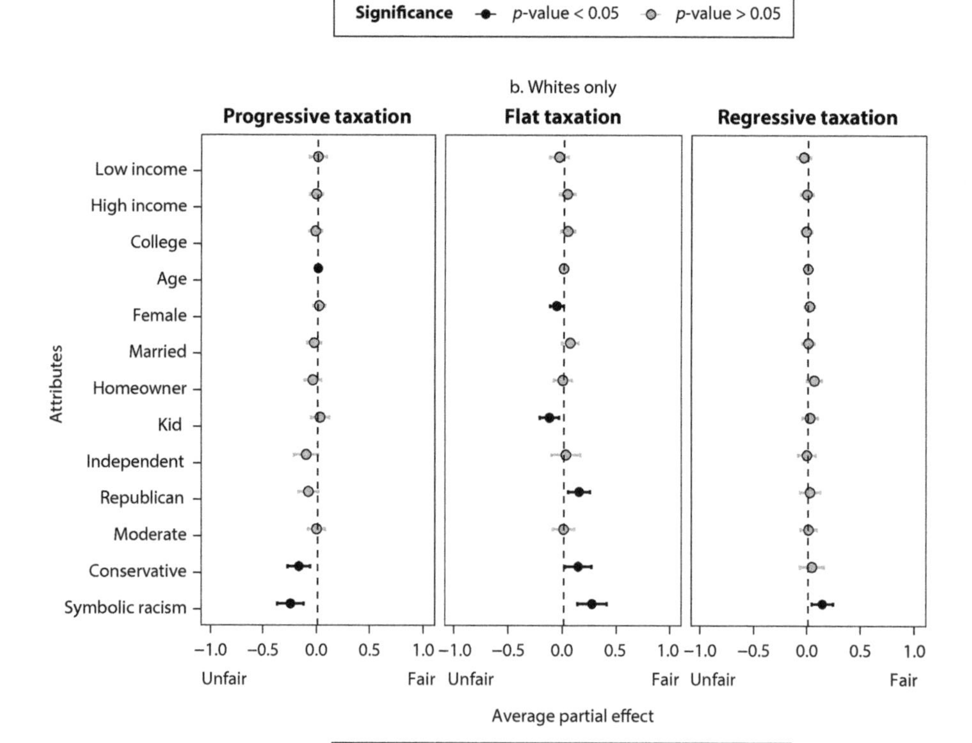

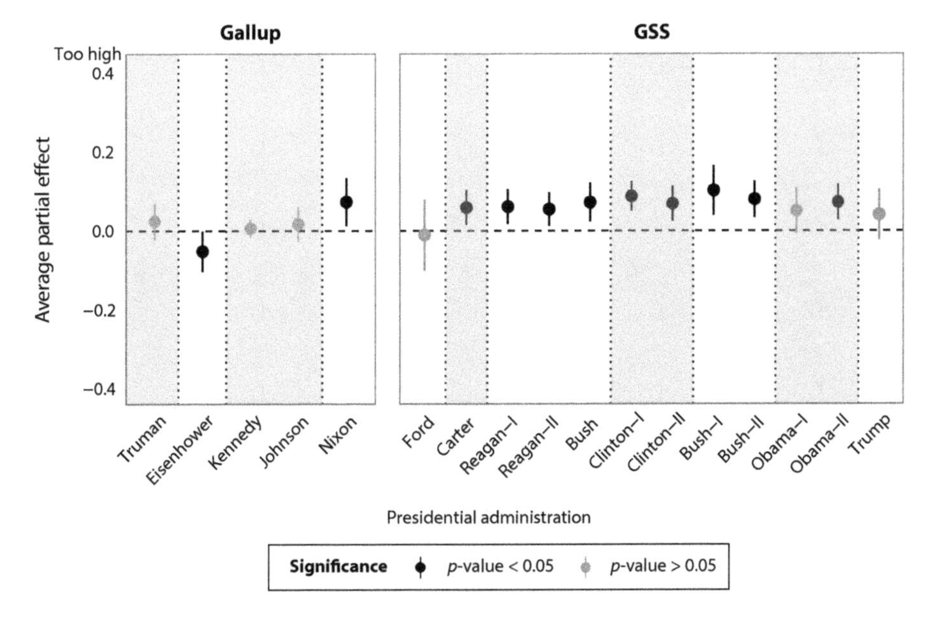

FIGURE A.2 Federal Income Taxes Too High for Top Income Quintile across Presidential Administrations

Note: "Federal income tax too high" is coded high. Full sample. Ordinary least squares model. Figure shows the average partial effect for the top income quintile (approximately) compared to the bottom 80 percent. Democratic presidential administrations shaded. Gallup results on the left control for income, education, gender, age, race/ethnicity, and homeowner; GSS results on the right additionally control for marital status, children, "other" race group, partisanship, and ideology. Model includes year fixed effects. The results are largely the same when GSS covariates are limited to those available in Gallup. Government trust not included in these analyses.

Source: Gallup 1947–73; GSS 1976–2018.

FIGURE A.1 Correlates of Abstract Tax Principles, 2012

Note: Each type of tax system is evaluated separately, and "very fair" is coded high. Ordinary least squares model. (a) is for the full sample; (b) is for whites only, adding symbolic racism as a correlate. Low and high incomes are approximately the bottom and top 20 percent of income, respectively; reference category is the middle 60 percent. Reference category for party is Democrat; for ideology, it is liberal.

Source: 2012 CCES.

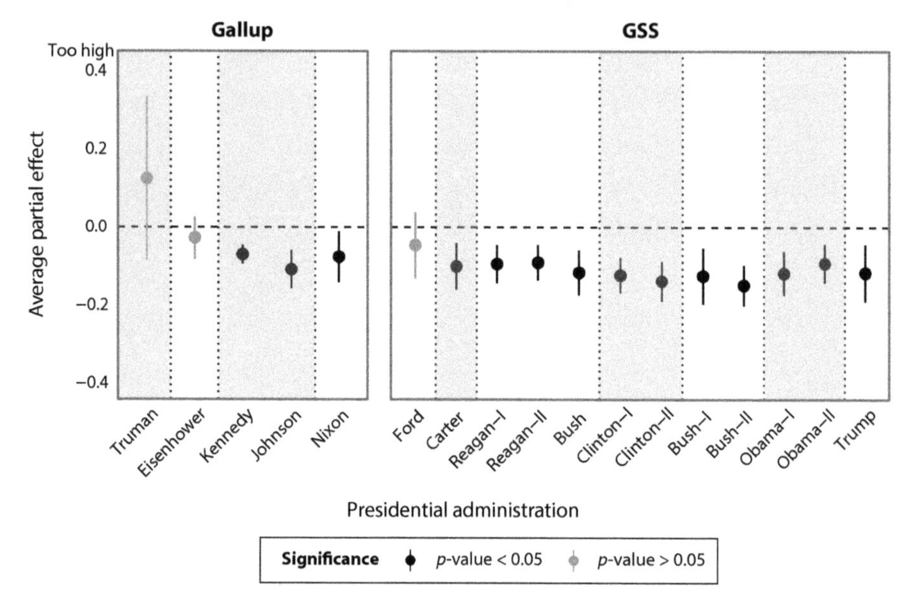

FIGURE A.3 Federal Income Tax Too High for Bottom Income Quintile across Presidential Administrations

Note: "Federal income tax too high" is coded high. Full sample. Ordinary least squares model. Figure shows the average partial effect for the bottom income quintile (approximately) compared to the top 80 percent. Democratic presidential administrations shaded. Gallup results on the left control for income, education, gender, age, race/ethnicity, and homeowner; GSS results on the right additionally control for marital status, children, "other" race group, partisanship, and ideology. Model includes year fixed effects. The results are largely the same when GSS covariates are limited to those available in Gallup. Government trust not included in these analyses.

Source: Gallup 1947–73; GSS 1976–2018.

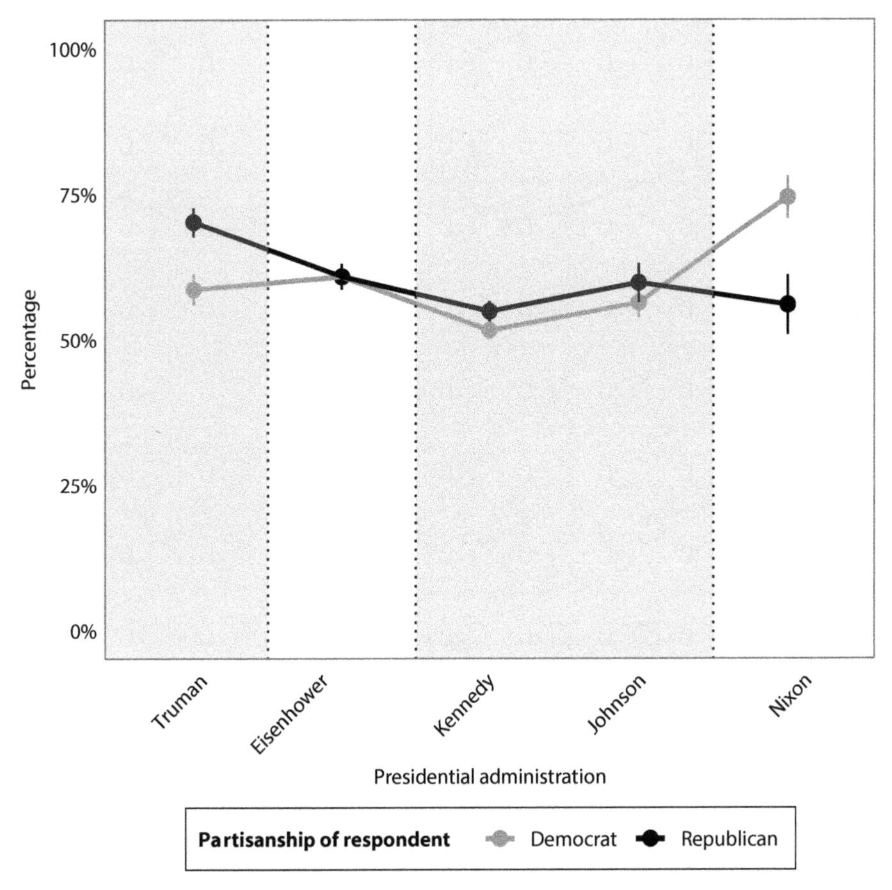

FIGURE A.4 Federal Income Taxes Too High by Party, 1947–73
Note: Descriptive version of Gallup data from figure 5.9. "Federal income tax too high" is coded high. Figure shows the percentage of respondents in each party saying that federal income taxes are too high. Democratic presidential administrations shaded.
Source: Gallup 1947–73.

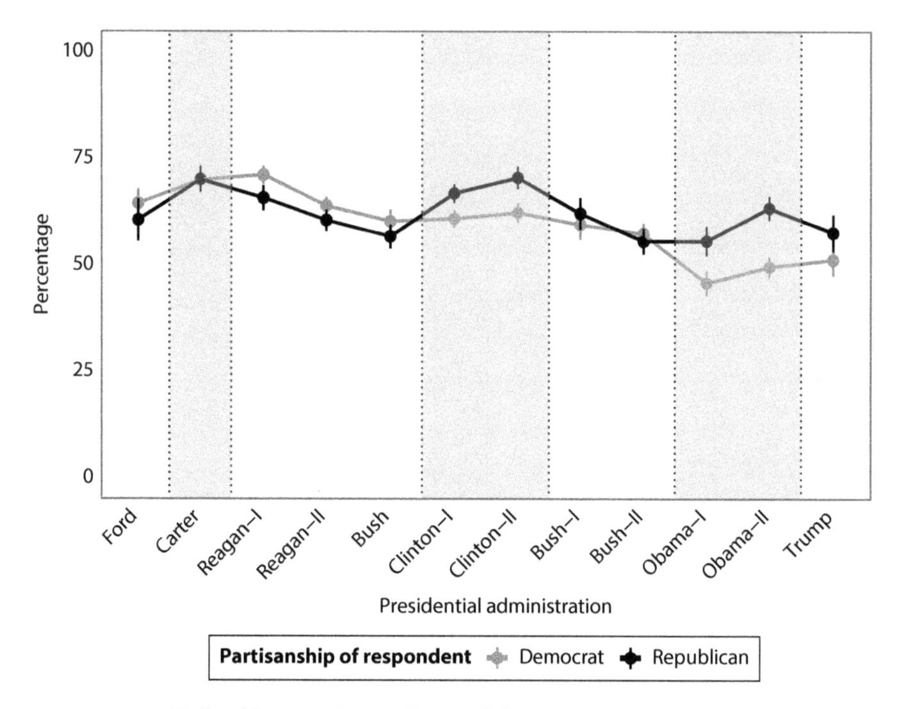

FIGURE A.5 Federal Income Taxes Too High by Party, 1976–2018
Note: Descriptive version of GSS data from figure 5.9. "Federal income tax too high" is coded high. Figure shows the percentage of respondents in each party saying that federal income taxes are too high. Democratic presidential administrations shaded.
Source: GSS 1976–2018.

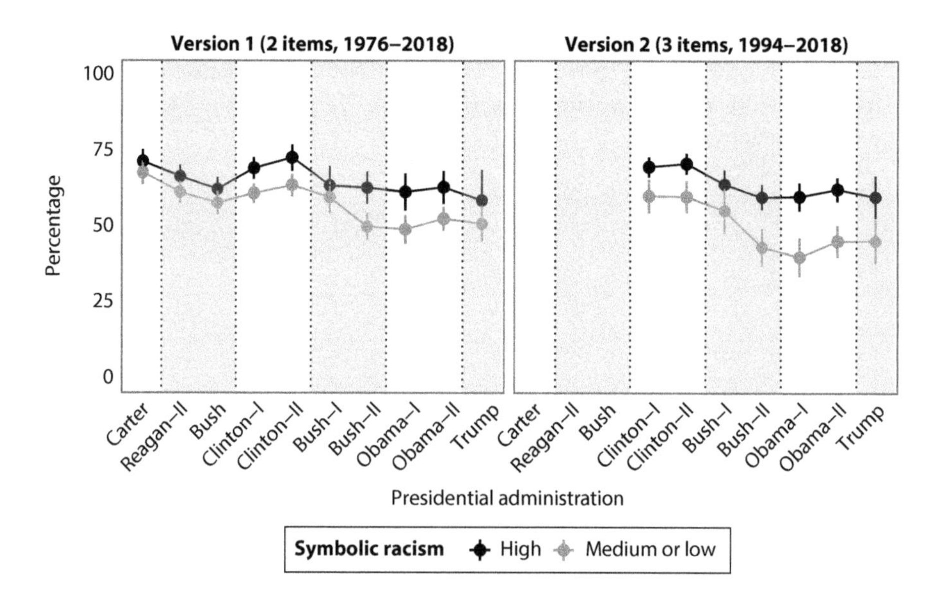

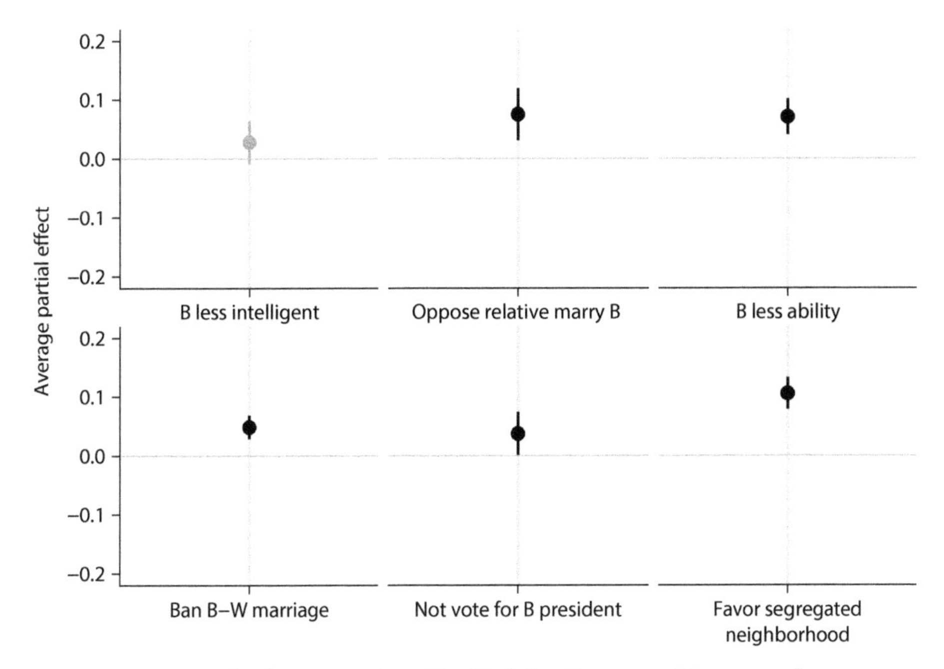

FIGURE A.7 Federal Income Taxes Too High by Alternative Measures of Racism

Note: Results from chapter 6 discussion of alternative measures of racism. A belief that "federal income taxes are too high" is coded high. White sample. Average partial effects are calculated from logit models. Includes a year fixed effect, and controls for income, education, gender, age, marital status, homeowner, children, ideology, and partisanship. For a description of each alternative racism survey item, see appendix.

Source: GSS 1972–2018.

FIGURE A.6 Federal Income Taxes Too High by Racial Resentment across Presidential Administrations

Note: Descriptive version of figure 6.6. Figure shows the percentage of white respondents saying the federal income taxes they have to pay this year are too high, divided into terciles of racial resentment.

Source: GSS 1976–2018.

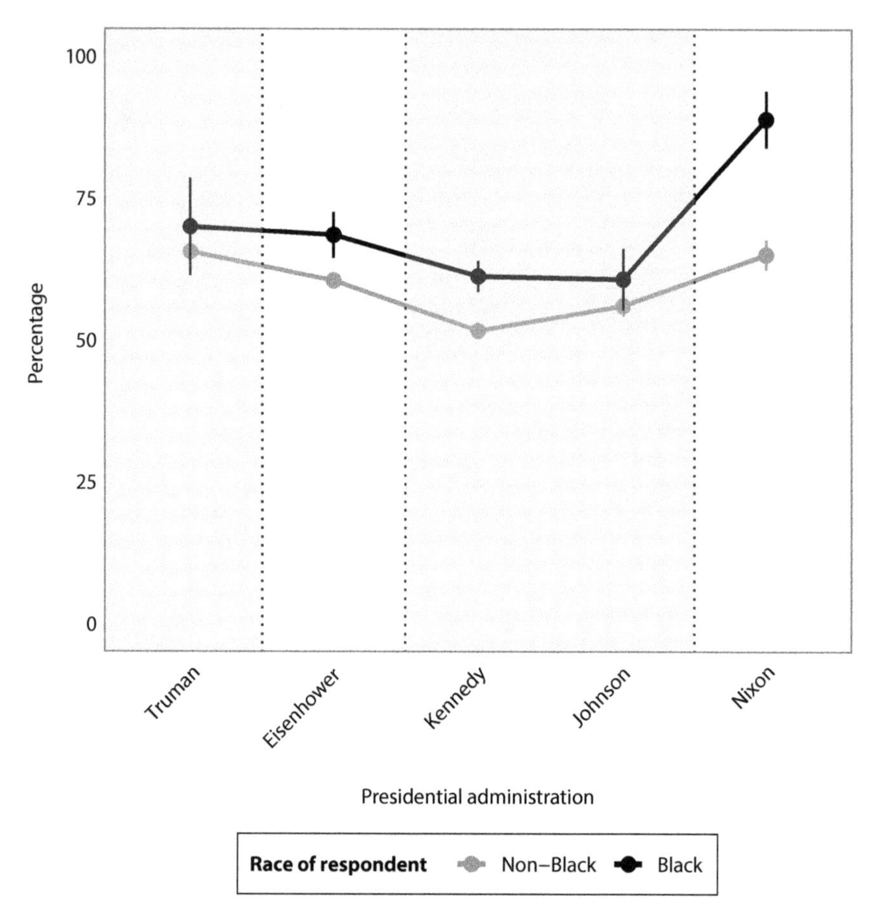

FIGURE A.8 Federal Income Taxes Too High by Race, 1947–73
Note: Descriptive version of Gallup data from figure 7.5. Figure shows the percentage of Black and non-Black respondents indicating that federal income taxes are too high. Full sample. Democratic presidential administrations shaded.
Source: Gallup 1947–73.

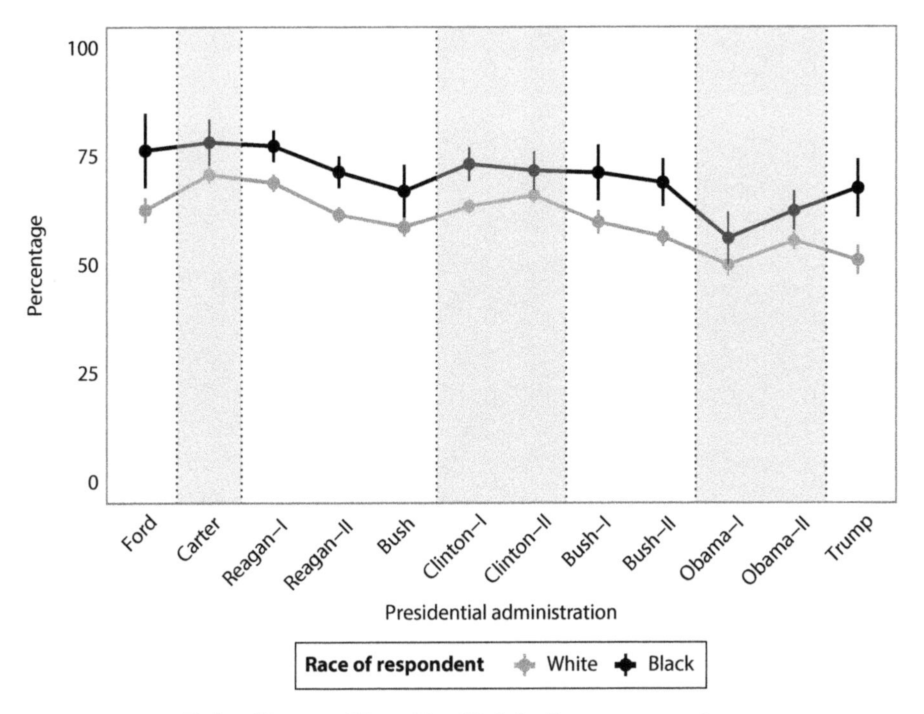

FIGURE A.9 Federal Income Taxes Too High by Race, 1976–2018
Note: Descriptive version of GSS data from figure 7.5. Figure shows the percentage of Black and white respondents indicating that federal income taxes are too high. Democratic presidential administrations shaded.
Source: GSS 1976–2018.

NOTES

1 Introduction

1. When I say "the rich," I usually mean high-income individuals and households, although sometimes, as when discussing taxes on wealth such as the estate tax or capital gains tax, I mean high-wealth individuals. There is a difference between income and wealth, which my language somewhat elides, but as economist Edward Wolff (2017) has shown, wealth rises monotonically with income. Synonyms include "the privileged," "those at the top of the income (sometimes wealth) spectrum," "the well-heeled," and so on.

2. "Latino" might be the preferred term, and the term often used in the critical tax theory literature, but the survey data I employ use the term "Hispanic."

3. Brown 2021; Infanti and Crawford 2009; Moran and Whitford 1996.

4. Berry 2021; Avenancio-Leon and Howard 2020; Kahrl 2024.

5. Brown 2021; Martinez and Martinez 2011.

6. Lowery and Sigelman 1981; Sears and Citrin 1985; Sigelman, Lowery, and Smith 1983; Bartels 2016; Graetz and Shapiro 2005; Hacker and Pierson 2010.

7. Taxes do figure more prominently in political economy and comparative politics. See, among many others, Barnes 2015, 2022; Kato 2003; Levi 1988; Martin and Gabay 2018; Morgan and Prasad 2009; Prasad 2006; Steinmo 1993; Tilly 1990; Wilensky 2002, 2012. There is also a newer experimental literature. See, for example, Ashok and Huber 2020; Haselswerdt and Bartels 2015; McCaffery and Baron 2004.

8. Cameron Ballard-Rosa, Lucy Martin, and Kenneth Scheve (2017) find in a conjoint experiment that respondents prefer lower income tax rates on their own income group than other respondents prefer on average.

9. In their *Winner-Take-All* book, Jacob Hacker and Paul Pierson (2010) do not mention race at all; Larry Bartels (2016) excludes nonwhites from many of his *Unequal Democracy* analyses. See Soss and Weaver 2016.

10. For overviews of the policy feedback literature, see Beland, Campbell, and Weaver 2022; Campbell 2012b; Larsen 2019; Mettler and SoRelle 2018.

11. Erikson, Wright, and McIver 1993; Erikson, MacKuen, and Stimson 2001; Page and Shapiro 1983; Stimson 2004. Elections are a chief mechanism of influence, with politicians considering (Downs 1957; Mayhew 1974) or anticipating (Arnold 1990) their constituents' opinions. Paul Burstein (2014) argues that these works overstate responsiveness—the effect of opinion on policy—because they tend to examine highly salient policies, and his more random sample of policies shows less responsiveness. For a more recent analysis demonstrating policy responsiveness at the state level, see Caughey and Warshaw 2022.

12. Bartels 2016; Gilens 2012; Witko et al. 2021. The mechanisms through which economic elites influence policy include campaign donations, interest group pressure (Hacker and Pierson 2010), and shared social backgrounds and networks (Carnes 2013).

13. See, for example, Barnes et al. 2018; Ellis and Faricy 2021; Haselswerdt and Bartels 2015; Ashok and Huber 2020; Mettler 2011.

14. Mayer 1993; Page and Shapiro 1992; Stimson 2004.

15. Edsall and Edsall 1991; Michelmore 2012.

16. The United States is one of the few countries in the world that does not have a VAT. VAT is collected by each seller in the chain of production and remitted to the tax authorities. In most countries, prices include the tax. In contrast, state sales taxes, which are the main form of consumption tax in the United States, are collected by the retailer at the point of final sale and sent to the tax authorities. The sales tax is typically separately listed and added to the retail price of a good or service.

17. In a multivariate analysis of the 2016 CCES, controlling for the usual demographic, partisan, and ideological covariates, whites who trust government more are more likely to say each of the eight taxes in the survey is fair. The trusting are less likely to want taxes decreased (that's true for five of the eight taxes, with the trust coefficients for the other three—estate, investment, and payroll taxes—just missing statistical significance). Thus high-trust whites are less likely to say taxes are unfair or should be decreased. Aaron Rosenthal (2021), in his analysis of in-depth interviews with a variety of Americans about how they view government, might predict a different relationship for Black Americans. He asserts that "people link their distrust to the most visible parts of government in their lives" (1099). When whites think of government, they think of welfare, he finds, while Black interviewees think about the police and carceral state. As a result, "white distrust is connected to welfare attitudes, while distrust among people of color is associated with feelings about the police" (1099). I find in survey data, however, that among Black Americans, the trust-tax relationship is the same as for whites: Black respondents who are most trusting of government are less likely to say taxes are unfair or should be decreased (although because of a smaller sample size, the coefficients do not always reach statistical significance).

18. Hetherington 2005; Hetherington and Rudolph 2015; Jacoby 2000; McCloskey and Zaller 1984; Rosenthal 2021.

19. On the decline of government trust, see Pew 2022.

2 History and Nature of the American Tax System

1. For overviews of the structure of the American tax system, see Burman and Slemrod 2020; Slemrod and Bakija 2017; Thom 2017; Berger and Toder 2019; Tax Policy Center 2020a. Excellent histories include Bank, Stark, and Thorndike 2008; Brownlee 2016; Graetz 1997; Hansen 1983; Leff 1983; Mehrotra 2013; Michelmore 2012; Prasad 2018; Ratner (1942) 1967; Sparrow 2011; Stein 1996; Thorndike 2013; Witte 1985; Zelizer 1998.

2. Article I, Section 9 of the Constitution states that "no Capitation, or other direct, Tax shall be laid, unless in Proportion to the Census or Enumeration herein before directed to be taken."

3. Bank, Stark, and Thorndike 2008, quoted in Brownlee 2016, 67.

4. Brownlee 2016; Sparrow 2011; Scheve and Stasavage 2016.

5. Hill 1894; US Bureau of the Census, n.d., 41, 240.

6. Most Americans earned their incomes from small businesses or farms, and the commissioner did not have the administrative capacity to collect from these sources (Brownlee 2016). Withholding at the source, however, was introduced in 1862 for government and some railroad, bank, and insurance company employees (Ratner [1942] 1967, 75).

7. Ratner (1942) 1967, 276–77; Stanley 1993.

8. Ratner (1942) 1967, chap. 8; Seligman 1911, chap. 4.

9. Slemrod and Bakija 2017. On the history of corporate taxation, see Bank 2010.

10. On the explicitly redistributive motivation behind the 1913 income tax, see Morgan and Prasad 2009.

11. As Boris I. Bittker, Elias Clark, and Grayson M. P. McCouch (2011, 5) write in their seminal legal account of the estate and gift tax, some writers justified the inheritance tax as a fee for administering the transfer of property at death or "belated fee" to the state for protecting private property during life, but modern writers plainly view the estate tax as an important mechanism of progressivity.

12. Brownlee 2016; Sparrow 2011; Scheve and Stasavage 2016.

13. Note that there is controversy around the reasons for the initial exclusion of agricultural and domestic workers from Social Security pension coverage. The conventional wisdom, as argued by Linda Gordon (1994) and Robert C. Lieberman (1998), is that southern white lawmakers opposed federal aid as a threat to the political economy of the South, which was still centered around Black labor. But Larry DeWitt (2010) argues that this concern revolved around Title I of the Social Security Act, about cash welfare, not Title II, the retirement pension, where work was in fact a prerequisite for participation in the pension scheme. It was Roosevelt administration bureaucrats who sought to avoid "an onerous task for the Treasury" by limiting initial participation to those occupations from which payroll taxes could easily be collected (DeWitt 2010, 63).

14. In order of adoption, individual income tax adopters between 1911 and 1920 were Wisconsin, Mississippi, Oklahoma, Massachusetts, Virginia, Delaware, Missouri, New York, and North Dakota, and between 1921 and 1931 were North Carolina, South Carolina, New Hampshire, Arkansas, Georgia, Oregon, Idaho, Tennessee, Utah, and Vermont. Those adopting during the Depression, between 1933 and 1937, were Alabama, Arizona, Kansas, Minnesota, Montana, New Mexico, Iowa, Louisiana, California, Kentucky, Colorado, and Maryland.

15. Wisconsin, the first state to pass an income tax in 1911, became a cautionary tale about state action: Wisconsin industry suffered because its capital costs were now higher than were its competitors' in other states. Other states avoided implementing income taxes until the Depression forced their hands (Brownlee 2016, chap. 3).

16. Author's calculation from "State Government Revenue by Source: 1902–1996," US Census Bureau, n.d., table Ea348-384. Currently, forty-five states collect sales taxes and forty-two have a personal income tax.

17. IRS 2024a; Joint Committee on Taxation 2003.

18. On the public relations campaigns intended to foster a strong sense of "fiscal citizenship," see Sparrow 2011.

19. The United States entered the Korean War on June 27, 1950, two days after the Northern Korean People's Army invaded South Korea.

20. Between 1955 and 1973, employment increased 120 percent at the state and local levels, compared to 17 percent for the federal government and 36 percent in the private sector (ACIR 1975, 2–3).

21. After the Yom Kippur War between Israeli and Arab forces in October 1973, Arab countries imposed an embargo of oil shipments to the United States, which lasted five months, followed by a nearly 400 percent increase in the price of oil by the Organization of Petroleum Exporting Countries (Patterson 1996, 784). A second oil crisis came in the wake of the Iranian Revolution, during which the US-backed shah fled and Ayatollah Khomeini established an Islamic republic. These events set off a period of economic crisis that lasted until 1983 (Levy 1987).

22. For historical tax bracket information, see www.taxpolicycenter.org/TaxFacts/Tfdb/Content/PDF/individual_rates.pdf.

23. On the connection between trust and taxes, see Hetherington 2005.

24. Gilens 1999; Mueller 1973, 56.

25. "Property Tax on Elderly Is Assailed" 1972.

26. These included a 1978 attempt by the IRS to revoke the tax-exempt status of Christian schools (Stonecash 2000).

27. See, among others, Brownlee 2016; Edsall and Edsall 1991; Hacker and Pierson 2010; Prasad 2006, 2018.

28. To address the budget deficits that arose after the 1981 tax cuts, tax increases were passed in 1982 and 1984, but they garner less attention as they were implemented quietly by reducing some tax breaks. See Brownlee 2016, 188–90.

29. Baumgartner et al. 2009; Graetz and Shapiro 2005.

30. David Karol (2009) dates the Republican focus on tax cuts over budget balancing to the 1970s, but this transition was completed under the Bush administration, which did not offset its deficits after tax cuts with tax increases as Reagan had in 1982 and 1984.

31. High earners now pay an extra 0.9 percent Medicare tax, and an extra 3.8 percent capital gains and dividend tax.

32. Institutional rules thwarted Republicans' goal of permanently repealing the estate tax; budgetary rules dictated that after 2010, all the Bush tax cuts would expire, and the estate tax would automatically return to its pre-2001 level. Democrats, who gained control of the White House and Congress, ran on an anti-inequality platform, but their ability to bargain with Republicans was undermined when they lost control of the House in the 2010 midterm elections. The December 2010 Tax Relief Act during the Great Recession restored the estate tax, but only for two years. The American Taxpayer Relief Act of 2012, passed on January 1, 2013, restored the estate tax (in part because although the Great Recession focused public concern on inequality, Democratic senators from high-income states such as New York, New Jersey, California, and Massachusetts were loath to impose significant new income taxes on their top earners; senators with ties to Wall Street had little interest in increasing taxes on carried interest either, leaving the estate tax as a "relatively easy sell" due to its tight focus on the very wealthiest).

33. The increased estate tax exemption expires after 2025 and will revert to its pre-2018 level of $5 million, adjusted for intervening inflation, unless Congress takes action.

34. IRS 2022; Centers for Disease Control and Prevention 2022; OMB, n.d., tables 2.1, 2.5.

35. On the tax planning and avoidance industry, see Kiel 2022; Rostain and Regan 2014.

36. Pass-through business owners with taxable incomes below $315,000 for married couples and $157,500 for other filers are allowed to deduct 20 percent of business income from their taxable income.

37. In October 2021, 136 nations agreed to a global minimum tax intended to reduce global tax competition and corporate exploitation of tax havens (low-tax countries). It is unclear what the agreement means for US federal revenues; one analysis projects that the combination of low domestic rates, thanks to the TCJA, combined with minimum tax rates on foreign income may increase revenues. See Arnon 2021.

38. About one-third of state revenues comes from federal funding, and the remaining one-fifth from charges and miscellaneous sources. Among the tax sources, sales taxes are the most important, generating 23 percent of general revenues, while 18 percent comes from individual income taxes, 2 percent from corporate income taxes, and 5 percent from other taxes (such as license fees and estate taxes). As a percentage of GDP, corporate income taxes have fallen as a source of state revenues since 1977, just as they have at the federal level. Sales tax revenues are flat as a percentage of GDP, while individual income taxes have increased slightly, intergovernmental transfers more substantially, and charges significantly—the latter mostly because state university tuitions have climbed to offset dramatic decreases in state support for higher education. Tax Policy Center 2020a.

39. Auten and Splinter 2023; Splinter 2019.

40. Calculating total taxes paid as a percentage of wealth rather than income—an alternative way of thinking about the ability to pay—reveals a regressive system. In 2019, total taxes were

7.2 percent of net worth for the bottom 99 percent of households and just 3.2 percent of net worth for the wealthiest 0.1 percent (Saez and Zucman 2019a). For an alternative calculation that also shows the average effective tax rates falling with wealth, see Bricker et al. 2020.

41. Thorndike 2013; Zelenak 2010.

42. Sven Steinmo (1993) notes that many may assume that countries such as Sweden rely heavily on progressive taxation to fund their sizable welfare states, whereas in fact the US system has been the more progressive one, and many European nations use robust regressive sources such as VATs in addition to progressive income taxes to fund government spending.

43. For example, because of the standard deduction, married couples filing jointly did not pay federal income tax on the first $29,900 of earnings in 2024. The figure for single filers was $14,600.

44. Qualified dividends are taxed at the preferential capital gains rates, which were 0, 15, and 20 percent in 2024 (as opposed to the 10 to 37 percent rates on earned income). Most dividends paid by US corporations are deemed "qualified" by the IRS. High-income taxpayers pay an additional 3.8 percent in capital gains taxes, implemented in 2013 to help fund the Affordable Care Act health reform.

45. Faricy 2015; Howard 1997.

46. Tax expenditures can be made "refundable," meaning people get money back from the government if the tax break exceeds their tax liability. On sentiments toward workers and nonworkers, see Ashok and Huber 2020; Cook and Barrett 1992; Gilens 1999; Haselswerdt and Bartels 2015.

47. Jake Haselswerdt (2014) argues contrarily that tax breaks have a shorter lifespan than direct spending programs.

48. Surrey and McDaniel 1985; Witte 1985.

49. For the distribution of key tax expenditures by income, see Joint Committee on Taxation 2022.

50. See also Kinsey, Grasmick, and Smith 1991, which finds that those who use tax breaks feel entitled to them, while those unable to claim tax breaks—often lower-income people—feel they are missing out on benefits that only higher-income people can access, with these perceptions leading them to view the tax system as unfair.

51. Much of such billionaires' wealth lies in assets that do not prompt income taxation unless sold (that is, unrealized capital gains).

52. Alesina, Baqir, and Easterly 1999; Alesina and Glaeser 2004.

53. Brown 2021; Einhorn 2006; Martin and Beck 2017; Walsh 2018.

3 Self-Interest I: Attitudes across Taxes

1. Page, Bartels, and Seawright 2013; Page, Seawright, and Lacombe 2019.

2. Campbell et al. 1960, 208.

3. Shapiro and Mahajan 1986; Mansbridge 1985; Day 1990; Lau and Sears 1981; Schlozman and Verba 1979; Tedin et al. 1977; Sears et al. 1980. For reviews, see Citrin and Green 1990; Green and Gerken 1989.

4. Tedin, Matland, and Weiher 2001, among many other studies.

5. Attiyeh and Engle 1979; Bowler and Donovan 1995; Lowery and Sigelman 1981.

6. MacManus 1995; Mayer 1993.

7. Citrin and Green 1990, 18; Chong, Citrin, and Conley 2001.

8. Outside of tax, a few more examples of opinions congruent with self-interest have emerged. Robin Wolpert and James Gimpel (1998) find that gun owners are less supportive of proposals to ban handguns or impose a waiting period before gun purchase. William Marble and Clayton Nall (2021) show that established homeowners are less supportive of new housing development, which they fear might dilute their property values. This includes liberals who

normally support redistributive policy, including on housing—just not right where they live (see also Einstein, Palmer, and Glick 2019). Michael Hankinson (2018) finds renters too oppose nearby development for self-interested reasons (fear of gentrification and rising rents), even if they are liberals and support more housing in general.

9. People may also be more likely to give researchers their honest opinions about taxes as opposed to more culturally fraught issues where they may self-censor to avoid seeming racist, sexist, or so on. In that case, the measurement of tax issues would be less subject to social desirability bias than other attitude objects, and the complications associated with tax attitudes and their measurement would arise not from self-censorship but rather respondents' actual complicated and perhaps misguided preferences. Many thanks to Morgan Gillespie for this point. Whether tax attitudes are less subject to social desirability bias could be an avenue for future research.

10. On group interests as distinct from self-interest, see Haidt 2012; Haselswerdt 2020; Huddy 2013; Kinder 1998. On long-term interests transforming into group interests, social status, or symbolic attachments, see Kinder 1998; Lau and Redlawsk 2006; Sears and Funk 1990; Sears et al. 1980.

11. See also Lau and Redlawsk 2006; Sears and Funk 1990.

12. Pacheco underscores the ways in which the effect of self-interest may be heterogeneous among partisans (sometimes people are cross pressured, such as Republicans in need of health insurance who are more positive toward the Affordable Care Act than their copartisans). Such cross pressures can mute the apparent effect of self-interest.

13. Page, Bartels, and Seawright 2013; Suhay, Klašnja, and Rivero 2021.

14. Freeland 2012; Page, Bartels, and Seawright 2013; West 2014.

15. There is a debate in the literature about the progressivity of the property tax. An older view saw it as a regressive tax with respect to income; a new view sees it as a progressive tax. In these data, the tax is mildly regressive, and I will treat it as a regressive tax in the analyses ahead.

16. Findings from American Patriot Survey reported in Thorndike 2013, 3.

17. Harris and NORC surveys reported in Bowman, Sims, and O'Neil 2017, 47; see the "Progressivity" section, 44–50. Although large shares want the well-off to pay more, there is not support for confiscatory taxation. Historical surveys show that preferred tax levels, even for the affluent, top out at fairly low levels (like 25 percent).

18. Question wording in the 2016 and 2019 CCES for the fairness of the amount that a respondent pays was as follows: "How fair do you regard the amount you have to pay for each tax?" The question was asked in relation to federal income tax, state income tax, payroll tax for Social Security and Medicare, estate tax, state sales tax, local property tax, gasoline tax, and taxes on investments (capital gains and dividend taxes). The respondent could answer as follows: very fair, somewhat fair, somewhat unfair, very unfair, I do not pay this tax, or I have no opinion.

19. Figure 3.2a shows the result for ACIR data from 1988 to 1994, but the ACIR asked another version of the question excluding Social Security taxes beginning in 1972, which political scientists Richard Cole and John Kincaid (2006) later replicated through 2006. In each year, the federal income and property taxes were always the two "worst" taxes, while state income, sales, and Social Security taxes ranked far behind. Whether federal income or property taxes were deemed the worst in any given year depended on particular events. Property taxes were in the news in 1972 thanks to an ACIR report showing significant disparities in tax burdens across regions and demographic groups, prompting the Nixon administration to briefly propose a VAT to ease the toll (shot down by the National Governors' Conference, which disapproved of competition with state sales taxes ["Property Tax on Elderly Is Assailed" 1972; "Value-Added Tax Opposed in a Poll" 1972; Weaver 1972]). Ire toward the income tax grew during the late 1970s, as the tax revolt gained stream and public opinion shifted in a conservative direction, culminat-

ing in Reagan's presidential victory in 1980. The proportion saying the income tax is the worst one fell after the Reagan tax reductions, but then climbed again after Clinton's 1993 tax increase. Toward the end of the series, the proportion saying the federal income tax is the worst falls again, presumably because of the 2001 and 2003 Bush tax cuts.

20. I included the "most fair" question because, as Vanessa Williamson (2017) points out, most assessments of American attitudes toward taxes are framed negatively.

21. Another 2016 CCES item asked, "When two families have the same income, do you think it is fair or unfair that one family pays less tax because they" are in a particular circumstance? Majorities giving an answer said the following breaks were fair: have more medical expenses than the other family (70 percent), have more dependent children than the other family (68 percent), give more to charity than the other family (61 percent), have a retirement plan through an employer (59 percent), have a home mortgage while the other family does not (56 percent), and have health insurance through an employer (51 percent). The only tax break for which there was only minority support was the preferential capital gains rate: just 38 percent said it was fair if one family "receive(s) more of their income from investments than the other family."

22. Michael Roberts, Peggy Hite, and Cassie Bradley (1994, 165) find a majority of subjects supporting progressive taxation as a concept, but also favoring flat rather than progressive taxes "in response to concrete questions."

23. The definitions were provided both in the question itself and again in the response set.

24. Also, renters, who tend to be lower income than homeowners, pay part of the property tax in higher rent, contributing to property tax regressivity.

25. The proportion of respondents saying "don't know" to the tax expenditure incidence questions are: retirement plan (36 percent), health insurance (35 percent), medical (31 percent), investment (24 percent), mortgage interest (23 percent), EITC (23 percent), CTC (20 percent), and charity (19 percent).

26. Bartels 2016; Graetz and Shapiro 2005.

27. In other policy arenas, whether individuals have personal control and agency over their fate, or are subject to government control and coercion, dramatically affects attitudes toward policy and government, including how much they trust government and how fair they feel government is, as examples from social and criminal justice policies show. Under No Child Left Behind and other "standards-based" reforms, parents of schoolchildren exposed to high-stakes testing regimes and government takeover of poorly performing schools had lower trust in government and lower levels of political efficacy than other parents (Rhodes 2015). Individuals in means-tested social assistance programs subject to work requirements and government monitoring have less political interest and political efficacy (Watson 2015). Contact with the criminal justice system undermines feelings toward government and political participation (Soss and Weaver 2016; Weaver and Lerman 2010; White 2019).

28. It has long been true that majorities believe they pay more in federal income tax than in payroll tax. The share of people saying so in the 2003 NPR Taxes Study was almost identical to that in the more contemporary CCES surveys.

29. On sales taxes, see Brunori 2001.

30. The same item on the 2012 CCES found that respondents were three times as likely to agree as disagree that they didn't mind paying as long as they did not have to pay more when they filed (60 to 19 percent, with 20 percent having no opinion).

31. On administrative burden, see Herd and Moynihan 2018.

32. Forty-three percent of self-preparers say the state income tax should be decreased, compared to 34 percent of those using a tax preparer or software, and 31 percent of those using a friend or family member.

33. See, among others, Hacker and Pierson 2010; Soss 1999.

34. Brunori 2001; Kuttner 1980.

35. Complete question wording: "The United States has a graduated federal income tax system. That is, people with higher incomes are taxed at a higher percentage than people with lower incomes. Some people would like to change the current tax system so that everyone would pay the same income tax rate (for example, 10 or 20 percent). Would you favor such a flat rate system, prefer keeping the system we have now, or don't know enough to say?"

36. On the politics of Social Security and the solvency crisis predicted for 2034, when incoming payroll tax revenues will only cover about 80 percent of the promised benefits unless Congress takes action, see Arnold 2022.

37. Experiments show that tax compliance increases when people are reminded of the government services and public goods that taxes provide (Bott et al. 2020; Hallsworth et al. 2017).

38. Question wording: "Compared to 1980, do the following groups of people now pay more of their income in federal income taxes, less of their income in federal taxes, or about the same amount? Middle-income people, low-income people, high-income people, and people like you."

4 Self-Interest II: Attitudes across Individuals

1. Figures 4.2a–b show the results among respondents who offered an opinion. The figures exclude those who say they don't know; figure 4.2a also excludes those who say "they do not pay the tax." Many respondents provided an answer to that item even when it seems likely they do not pay the tax (such as the estate tax). The 2019 CCES contained an alternative question wording on the fairness of the tax in general, and the pattern of responses by income was similar.

2. Marriage bonuses are more likely when the difference in spouses' incomes is greater (meaning that the married couple filing jointly pays less in tax than a single filer at the same income), and marriage penalties are more likely when the spousal income difference is smaller (McNair 2023).

3. The 2017 TCJA eliminated personal exemptions and increased the size of the standard deduction instead.

4. Figure 4.3 shows the results for the entire sample. Among whites only (not shown), the results are similar in that married whites are more likely to say the payroll tax is fair. Whites differ from the full sample in a couple of regards: affluent whites are more likely than the bottom four quintiles to say the property tax is fair (while in the full sample, the affluent were more likely to say the property tax is unfair, perhaps reflecting the negative experience of Black and Hispanic people when it comes to property taxation; see chapter 7). Whites also differed from the full sample in that those with children saw the estate and property taxes as more fair than those without. Among Black and Hispanic respondents, none of the self-interest indicators are statistically significant (in part because sample sizes among the nonwhite groups in the survey are small).

5. Among whites only (not shown), homeowners similarly want the property tax decreased, and the top income quintile is more likely to want the capital gains tax decreased. Otherwise, preferences on tax rates do not differ by income, marital status, parental status, or age, even though actual taxes paid do vary across those demographic subgroups. Among Black and Hispanic respondents, none of the self-interest indicators are statistically significant.

6. Dan Hopkins (2010) finds that opinion about immigration in areas where their numbers have grown only turns negative when immigration becomes a nationally salient issue reported widely in the media.

7. The gap was slightly smaller by 2019, with seniors overall 10 percent less likely to say their federal income taxes are too high compared to those under sixty-five.

8. Sexual preference is another individual-level characteristic relevant for tax attitudes. Prior to the Supreme Court's 2015 *Obergefell* ruling allowing same-sex marriage nationwide, many same-sex couples were overtaxed at the federal level, unable to file jointly. The heterosexual privilege of the Internal Revenue Code may have become more visible during the period when same-sex couples were able to marry and file jointly in some states, but not at the federal level. On gay couples' tax disadvantages, see Cain 2000.

9. The 2016 CCES only asked about the fairness of what individuals pay for each tax, not the fairness of the tax in general. In theory, nonworkers did not answer the former item, but some did anyway. There is no difference between working and nonworking married women in their attitudes.

10. The model includes regressivity and income, and also controls for education, gender, age, race, marital status, homeownership, children under eighteen, party identification, and ideology. Standard errors are clustered at the state level.

11. The ACIR results are from Shaun Bowler and Todd Donovan (1995). They also find that respondents were likely to choose the state income or sales tax as the most disliked in states that do not have those taxes.

12. These data come from a survey conducted by the Roper Organization for H&R Block in May 1978. The question asked respondents to read down a list of "deductions, exemptions and credits that are now allowed for federal income tax purposes and some types of income that are not subject to federal income tax," and say whether they believe each "is perfectly reasonable for it to be deductible or non-taxable, or whether you think it is really a tax loophole." "Half the profit (capital gains) from the sale of stock or property held more than 9 months." The responses: 43 percent said this was a reasonable deduction, 41 percent said tax loophole, and 16 percent said don't know.

13. Specifically, in a multivariate analysis of respondents aged sixty-five and over in the pooled GSS data, the coefficient on a dummy variable for 1984 and thereafter is negative and statistically significant, indicating that seniors became less likely to say their federal income taxes are too high. The coefficient for income is positive, indicating that higher-income seniors are more likely to say their federal income taxes are too high, and the interaction term between income and the post-1984 indicator is also significant, indicating that high-income seniors became even more likely to say their taxes are too high after 1984, when taxation of Social Security benefits for high-income seniors began. But both of these coefficients are substantively small, and neither is statistically significant.

14. Other model specifications reveal the same results.

15. Pacheco 2014, 4, drawing on Kam 2005.

16. Figures 4.6b–c and 4.7 show the results for 2016. The 2019 results are similar except that Republicans and conservatives were more likely to correctly identify progressive taxes in 2019 than in 2016 (possibly the effect of the Trump tax cut).

17. Michael Alvarez and Edward McCaffery (2003) also find that women are more likely to decline to answer survey questions about taxes.

18. But see Barnes et al. 2018. Lucy Barnes and coauthors provided "taxpayer receipts" to British taxpayers in cooperation with the tax authorities, listing personalized accounts of government spending. The coauthors found that recipients became more knowledgeable about government spending, but did not change their attitudes toward government (waste or trust) or redistribution (taxes on the poor, rich, or themselves).

19. For example, Adam Thal (2020) finds in social media experiments that competition for social status drives affluent Americans toward conservative economic policies, with the effect more pronounced among men.

20. In their seminal works on representation by income, Gilens (2012) uses the top 20 percent of survey respondents and Bartels (2016, chap. 8) the top third. Delli Carpini and

Keeter (1996) compare general political knowledge among the top 15 percent compared to the bottom one-third.

21. Cameron Ballard-Rosa, Lucy Martin, and Kenneth Scheve (2017) find in a conjoint experiment on preferred income tax rates that respondents have progressive preferences, preferring higher rates for high-income groups, but that they are indifferent across rates for those making more than $375,000.

5 Partisan Identification and Ideology

1. Brownlee 2016; Zelizer 1998.

2. Saulnier 1991; Sloan 1991; Stein 1996.

3. Blessing 2014; Prasad 2018; Stimson 2004, 71.

4. John Petrocik (1996, 832) is the issue ownership pioneer, using a small number of polls from 1988 to 1991, while Jeremy Pope and Jonathan Woon (2009, 656) aggregate scores of polls from 1978 to 2004, and Patrick Egan (2013, 2) reports results of surveys from 1981 to 2012. All show that despite some occasional shifts, Republicans clearly own the tax issue and have an enduring reputational advantage with the public on "handling" taxes. Using open-ended ANES questions from 1952 to 1988, John Geer (1992) similarly finds Republicans favored on economic issues, including tax policy. Egan (2013, 8) shows that a party "owns" an issue not because it delivers "popular policies" or "superior performance on [its] owned issue" but rather because it prioritizes its owned issues when it holds power in Washington. People pay too little attention to assess parties' performance, Egan argues. Issue ownership "weakens the relationship between citizens' preferences and public policies" because party activists especially are "rigid on their owned issues," forcing lawmakers to be "ideologically pure" on these issues even when public preferences have changed (Egan 2013, 12).

5. Sears et al. 1980; Lodge and Taber 2013.

6. Bartels 2002; Evans and Andersen 2006; Gerber and Huber 2009; Wlezien, Franklin, and Twiggs 1997.

7. Another form of wishing something to be true: Republicans who have received a government program are less likely than Democrats to admit to it, apparently because they associate such programs, especially social policies, as being for low-income and nonwhite individuals (SoRelle and Shanks 2024). Partisanship also has behavioral consequences: people engage in more consumer spending when their copartisan has recently won the presidential election (Gerber and Huber 2009).

8. In this chapter, I show results for all respondents, just as in chapters 3 and 4. Chapter 7 shows that Black and Hispanic respondents have more negative tax attitudes than whites. Because these respondents are more likely than whites to be Democrats, including them in the analyses of partisanship in this chapter reduces the size of the Republican-Democrat gaps in tax opinion. Analyses conducted with whites only, however, reveals the same patterns: few differences in opinions across partisan groups for regressive taxes, and stronger differences for the progressive federal income, estate, and investment taxes, where white Republicans are more likely than white Democrats to say they are unfair and want them decreased, all things being equal.

9. Note that in the released ACIR data, independent leaners are included with independents, whereas in the NPR, CCES, and other datasets in this book, I code independent leaners with partisans. Also note that the ACIR item in figure 5.1 was asked annually between 1983 and 1989 as well as in 1991 and 1993.

10. A large literature argues that independents who lean toward one party or the other exhibit attitudinal as well as behavioral patterns similar to those of partisans (Keith et al 1992; Magleby, Nelson, and Westlye 2011; Petrocik 2009). "Pure" independents are also called "true" or "no lean" independents in the literature.

11. See also Magleby and Nelson 2012. Magleby, Nelson, and Westlye (2011) as well as Keith and coauthors (1992) find pure independents are less educated, less interested in politics, and less politically knowledgeable than partisans or leaners. Helmut Norpoth and Yamil Velez (2012) find they pay less attention to politics. I find, however, that pure independents are not less knowledgeable about taxes, although I include a "don't know" option so that I measure knowledge levels only among those who answered tax knowledge questions.

12. Anthony Fowler and coauthors' (2023) examination of political moderates may provide a model for inquiry.

13. Similarly, Cameron Ballard-Rosa, Lucy Martin, and Kenneth Scheve (2017) find in their conjoint experiment on income tax rates that both Republican and Democratic identifiers prefer progressive rates.

14. The cued version included these words in brackets: "In December 2017, a new tax bill was passed [by Congress and signed by President Trump], the Tax Cuts and Jobs Act (TCJA), which affected taxes beginning in 2018. Do you approve or disapprove of the TCJA, or don't you know enough to say?"

15. The results are the same when missing respondents are included and with alternative specifications such as logistic regression.

16. Sixteen percent of respondents said the TCJA had caused their federal income taxes to go up, 20 percent said go down, 25 percent said stay the same, and 39 percent said they didn't know.

17. For a compilation of Warshaw's poll, see Sides 2017.

18. Recall that the tax increases imposed under Reagan in 1982 and 1984 went through with barely a peep. George H. W. Bush lost his reelection bid in 1992 after raising taxes, in violation of his "read my lips, no new taxes" pledge. Some observers attribute his loss to the tax increase, but the country was also in a recession, and Republicans had held the presidency for three terms at that point, so party fatigue may have been a factor as well. That said, because tax cuts are now party orthodoxy, it is difficult to imagine a Republican president advocating increases.

19. On regressive taxation in support of welfare state spending, see Kato 2003.

6 Racial Resentment and Tax Attitudes among White Americans

1. In their examination of eight possible explanations for the late 1970s' tax revolt, David Lowery and Lee Sigelman (1981) look at the individual correlates of an ANES question asking respondents whether they would support a property tax initiative similar to Prop 13 in their own state. Much as is the case here, they don't find support for any of the eight, including various measures of self-interest, tax level, party identification, ideology, concerns about government waste, or worries about the distribution of the tax burden. They say instead that tax sentiment is "symbolic" in nature, but they do not test symbolic racism, which here turns out to be the most powerful factor in whites' attitudes.

2. Gilens 1999; Kellstedt 2003; Quadagno 1994; Kinder and Sanders 1996; Winter 2006.

3. Sherif 1988; Tajfel 1982; Tajfel and Turner 1979.

4. Works invoking group-based theories include, among others, Winter 2008; Achen and Bartels 2016; Mason 2018. Predating Tajfel and Turner's work, Campbell et al. 1960 and Converse 1964 noted the importance of groups to political thinking.

5. Kinder 2003; Davis and Wilson 2022.

6. See also Krimmel and Rader 2017, 748.

7. Cook and Barrett 1992; Gilens 1999; Grogan and Park 2017; Michener 2020, 2021; Kinder and Sanders 1996; Quadagno 1994; DeSante 2013; Tesler 2016. Racial resentment is linked to

low support for redistributive policies beyond social policy as well. See, among others, Bobo and Kluegel 1993; Tesler 2012.

8. Jacoby 1994; Krimmel and Rader 2017; Huber and Paris 2013. See also Goren 2008. When survey recipients think "welfare," they think cash welfare, public housing, and food stamps, while when they think about "programs for the poor," they think of those programs as well as a suite of more popular ones such as Medicaid, homeless shelters / soup kitchens / food banks, day care / Head Start, EITC, Social Security / Medicare, and disability insurance / unemployment insurance. Gregory Huber and Celia Paris posit that the different collections of programs considered "welfare" versus "assistance to the poor" help explain why spending on the latter is more popular than spending on the former.

9. See, for example, Alesina, Baqir, and Easterly 1999. On the challenges facing diverse democracies, see Mounk 2022.

10. See, for example, Sniderman and Tetlock 1986; Kinder and Sears 1981.

11. See also Tarman and Sears 2005; Kinder and Sears 1981.

12. Specifically, Winter (2008) runs experiments in which subjects read an article emphasizing that Social Security is a program for "hardworking" Americans. Those in the treatment group also read an argument that Social Security privatization will free up money for "other programs." He finds that compared to the control group, racial conservatives in the treatment group are more opposed to privatization, which would take money away from hardworking (white) Americans and spend it on other programs (for Black Americans). Concomitantly, racial liberals become more supportive of privatization after reading it will free up money for other programs. This experiment "works"—the experimental subjects are able to connect their racial schemata to the group implications of the privatization question—because elite rhetoric has long linked them. Evidence that these linkages are prevalent comes from survey data over time, which show that racially conservative whites are less supportive of welfare spending and more supportive of Social Security spending than racially liberal whites. Other researchers such as Fay Lomax Cook and Edith Barrett (1992) have also found that welfare and Social Security are coded in racialized ways, with survey respondents much more likely to say that Social Security recipients really need the benefits and will use them wisely compared to welfare recipients. See also Kellstedt 2003.

13. See also Gilens 1999; Hutchings and Valentino 2004.

14. On the historical origins of the "white racial frame," see Feagin 2013.

15. The quoted phrase comes from Jeff Shesol (2022), in a review of Jefferson Cowie's (2022) *Freedom's Dominion*, which examines resistance to federal power among white Alabamians during four periods, ranging from the nineteenth-century rush to settle land seized from the Creek Nation to the twentieth-century civil rights era. As Shesol notes, "White Southerners portrayed the oppression of Black people and Native Americans not as a repudiation of freedom but its precondition, its very foundation."

16. Campbell 2014; Lieberman 1998; Quadagno 1994; Soss, Fording, and Schram 2011.

17. Gallup 2024a; Newport 2019. See also Cook, Jacobs, and Kim 2010.

18. Kellstedt's (2003) work on media cues and welfare state attitudes shows how the media shifted from giving "egalitarian cues" during the 1950s and early 1960s to providing more "individualism cues" beginning in the 1970s, which fed an increasing correlation between race and welfare state attitudes over the same period.

19. The first private pensions began earlier. The American Express Company started offering a private pension in 1875, and large employers in manufacturing, banking, and utilities soon followed. Pension Benefit Guaranty Corporation 2022.

20. On the social construction of the white working class during the nineteenth century, see Roediger 2007. David Roediger (2007, 13–14) details a "construction of identity through otherness" that elevated white workers, who feared "dependency on wage labor and . . . the necessities

of capitalist work discipline," over Black workers by constructing "an image of the Black population as 'other'—as embodying the preindustrial, erotic, careless style of life the white worker hated and longed for." Following on W. E. B. Du Bois, Roediger (2007, 12) argues that "white labor does not just receive and resist racist ideas but embraces, adopts and, at times, murderously acts upon those ideas. The problem is not just that the white working class is at critical junctures manipulated into racism, but that it comes to think of itself and its interests as white."

21. Morgan 2007; Martin 2008, 7–9.

22. On party platform and political advertising data, see Smith 2007, 139–41. On the tax mentions in the ANES, see Campbell 2009.

23. See also Sears and Citrin 1985.

24. DeLong (2022) makes a similar argument about the failure of the postwar social welfare state creating an opening for neoliberalism beginning in the 1970s.

25. On the power of national-level rhetoric to tap latent public opinion, see Hopkins 2010.

26. Whites constitute 96 percent of all farmers in the United States and own 98 percent of all farmland (Congressional Research Service 2021).

27. See also Stimson 2004, 18. Marisa Abrajano and Zoltan Hajnal (2015) posit that immigration affects white Americans' political attitudes and behaviors through a threat mechanism as well. Political elites fan an "immigrant threat narrative" (13) that links education, health, social policy, criminal justice, and taxation. Immigrants—especially Latinos—are framed as creating a substantial fiscal drain on the nation because of their use of education and health services while not paying commensurate amounts of tax.

28. In *Dying of Whiteness*, physician Jonathan Metzl (2019, 211) interviews white Americans who decline to sign up for social programs such as the Affordable Care Act health insurance to maintain their place in the racial hierarchy. He ascribes poor whites' support of social spending cuts to a feeling that "government is wasting money on 'people who do not deserve it,' alongside guilt that they themselves need help."

29. Howard 1997; Mettler 2011; SoRelle and Shanks 2024. Christopher Ellis and Christopher Faricy (2021) show that racial resentment is related to EITC attitudes. The data here confirm that finding and reveal the same effect for the CTC.

30. Compared to racial liberals, racial conservatives are less educated, older, more likely to have children under eighteen, more likely to be homeowners, and more likely to be Republican and conservative, all things being equal (there is no difference by income). Descriptively, they are more likely to be married and less likely to be single, although the effect of marital status goes away in a multivariate analysis.

31. The same bivariate and multivariate results obtain in the 2019 CCES data as well.

32. Question wording on estate tax item: "An estate tax is a tax on the property left behind by a deceased person. Different people have different views about what types of estates should be taxed, or if there should be an estate tax at all. What's your view?" Responses: "All estates should be taxed regardless of the value of the deceased person's property"; "Only the estates of very wealthy deceased persons should be taxed"; or "No estates should be taxed." Question wording on capital gains tax item: "A capital gains tax is a tax on money earned from the sale of stocks or assets. Different people have different views about how such income should be taxed. What's your view?" Responses: "Money earned from the sales of stocks or assets should be taxed at a higher/same/lower rate than income earned as wages and salaries." Question wording on income taxation of high earners: "Do you think that the federal income tax rates for families making more than $250,000 per year should be increased, decreased, or kept at the current level?" Response: "increased," "decreased," or "kept at the current level," with an "I have no opinion" option.

33. Another finding along these lines is that in a 2016 CCES item asking about support for flat tax reform of the income tax, support is higher among the more racially resentful. The item asked

about support for changing from a "graduated federal income tax system" in which "people with higher incomes are taxed at a higher percentage than people with lower incomes" to a system in which "everyone would pay the same income tax rate." Among those scoring in the bottom tercile of racial resentment, support was 25 percent, rising to 55 percent in the top tercile.

34. Racial resentment items were not included in the 2002 ANES dataset Bartels used.

35. The GSS welfare and Social Security spending items are NATFARE ("welfare") and NATSOC ("Social Security"): "We are faced with many problems in this country, none of which can be solved easily or inexpensively. I'm going to name some of these problems, and for each one I'd like you to tell me whether you think we're spending too much money on it, too little money, or about the right amount."

36. Monica Prasad's (2018, table 4.1) analysis of the 1980 ANES confirms this finding: during the Reagan era, racially intolerant whites were more favorable toward a tax cut.

37. Christopher Tarman and Sears (2005) identify RACDIF1, RACDIF4, WRKWAYUP, and BLKGOVT as symbolic racism measures in the GSS; the first two are available for the longest time span and appear in the left panel of figure 6.6. The third item is available for the shorter period and is included with the first two in the right panel. Question wording: "On the average, African Americans have worse jobs, income, and housing than white people." RACDIF1: "Do you think these differences are mainly due to discrimination?" RACDIF4: "Because most African Americans just don't have the motivation or willpower to pull themselves up out of poverty?" WRKWAYUP: "Irish, Italians, Jewish, and many other minorities overcame prejudice and worked their way up. Blacks should do the same without special favors."

38. The analysis in figure 6.6 is from a generalized linear mixed model allowing baseline tax attitudes along with the association between symbolic racism and tax attitudes to vary by presidential administration (a random effects model). A fixed effects model finds similar effects—those scoring high on racial resentment are always more likely than others to say their federal income taxes are too high—except that the coefficients for the Jimmy Carter, Reagan, and Bush administrations do not quite reach traditional levels of statistical significance.

39. We cannot measure the role of racial liberalism/conservatism in prior decades, but political liberalism/conservatism is related to civil rights attitudes in earlier periods. Using Gallup data from the 1930s and 1940s, Eric Schickler (2016, chap. 5) finds that more economically liberal whites (those giving liberal answers to survey items about the government's role in the economy) were more supportive of civil rights as well.

40. A similar analysis of 2019 CCES data shows that the racially resentful are more likely to say their federal income taxes are too high that year as well.

41. Winter (2006, 2008) and Christopher DeSante (2013) also find a strong relationship between racial resentment and opposition to means-tested program spending.

42. I also find in a multivariate analysis of the 2012 ANES data, which contains Jardina's measures of white identity, that there is no relationship between white identity and saying that the government wastes a lot of the money that it collects in taxes. But the racially resentful are more likely to say so, demographic and political variables held constant. This squares with the CCES findings that what bothers the racially resentful the most about taxes is "how the money is spent."

43. Among whites in the 2002 ANES, there is a modest bivariate relationship between the white feeling thermometer and favorability toward estate/death tax elimination. Whites favoring estate tax elimination score 69.3 on the white feeling thermometer compared to 65 among those opposing elimination ($p < 0.01$).

44. Another factor that could be tested in the future is "inequity aversion." Krimmel and Rader (2021) show that attitudes toward government spending—perceptions of how fair it is—are influenced not just by partisanship, ideology, and racial resentment but also by inequity aversion: those who believe their racial group gets less than it deserves are less supportive of government spending. The effect obtains for white, Black, and Hispanic respondents.

45. Spencer Piston (2018, chaps. 3–4) argues that nonrich Americans resent the rich and want them to pay more in taxes. Others such as Leslie McCall (2013) say that inequality attitudes turn more on attitudes toward the rich than toward the poor, but that people want to address inequality through better jobs and pay, not through progressive taxation, whose link to solving inequality is harder for many to see.

46. These differences are statistically significant at $p < 0.001$.

47. These analyses are for whites only. Dependent variables concern the estate tax (which estates should be taxed: all estates, only those of the wealthy, or no estates), capital gains tax (money earned from the sale of stocks or assets should be taxed at a higher, same, or lower rate than income earned as wages and salaries), and federal income tax (rates for families making more than $250,000 per year should be increased, kept at the current level, or decreased). The equations also control for measures of self-interest (income, investor, belief one would be rich someday, and that taxing the rich more today means taxing oneself more in the future), political ideology, a two-item index of inequality attitudes, an item asking whether trying to tax the rich is futile, and demographics (education, age, and gender). Government trust is not available in this dataset. Ordinary least squares and multinomial logistic regression produce largely the same results.

48. As mentioned in chapter 2, taxpayers have to itemize their deductions to take the home mortgage interest deduction. Only 30 percent did so before the TCJA of 2017, and only 10 percent did so afterward. The affluent overwhelmingly benefit from this tax break.

49. On negative stereotypes around Black Americans and means-tested programs, see Gilens 1999; Kellstedt 2003; Kluegel and Smith 1986; McCabe 2018. In his analysis of social policy for children in the United States, Canada, and the United Kingdom, Joshua McCabe (2018, 7–8) notes that both taxpayers and children in the United States are seen as "worthy of benefits," but that deservingness is not enough to secure benefits; there has to be a match with the type of benefit. In the United States, direct spending was eschewed for tax credits. The "cultural legacy of institutions" gave a "discursive springboard to taxpayers," asserts McCabe—something families with children never gained.

50. In December 2021, 61.2 million children in 36 million households received the credit.

51. The relative unpopularity of the new universally expanded CTC also reveals what makes Social Security popular: less that it is universal and more that it is earned through payroll tax contributions. In its attitudinal structure, the CTC more closely resembles welfare than Social Security. From a political strategy perspective, Eric Patashnik (2023, 188) argues that CTC proponents should have accepted the requirement of Senator Joe Manchin (D-WV), the pivotal vote on President Biden's American Rescue Plan, that a work attachment be included in the expanded CTC. Then after the expanded program became "deeply embedded in the social fabric," proponents could find ways to extend coverage to the nonworking poor.

52. First, the results for tax unfairness. Tax knowledge: the association between racial resentment and tax unfairness is greater at higher knowledge levels for every tax except sales and property taxes, where there is no correlation with racial resentment at any level of tax knowledge. Education: the relationship between racial resentment and tax unfairness is greater among high-education whites for the investment and property taxes. For all other taxes, the relationship is the same for both high- and low-education whites: either racial resentment is not correlated with unfairness at either education level (sales tax), or it is correlated at both high- and low-education levels (federal income, state income, estate, payroll, and gas taxes). Income: the pattern is very much like that for education. The relationship between racial resentment and tax unfairness is greater among high-income whites for the property tax. Racial resentment is not correlated with unfairness at either income level for the sales tax, and it is correlated at both high- and low-income levels for all other taxes. Thus there is no evidence that racial resentment is substituting for knowledge or sophistication—either the sophisticated have better alignment between their racial resentment and tax attitudes (when sophistication is measured by tax

knowledge, which loses a lot of cases) or the alignment is mostly the same (when sophistication is measured by education or income).

Second, the results for decrease taxes. Tax knowledge: the association between racial resentment and the desire to decrease taxes is greater at high-knowledge levels for all four progressive taxes plus the gas tax. Racial resentment not related to sales or property decreases at any level of knowledge, and it is related to a desire to decrease the payroll tax at all levels of knowledge. Education: the association between racial resentment and decrease tax is the same or greater at higher-education levels, and never greater at low-education levels. Income: the results are similar to those for education. The association of racial resentment and decrease tax is the same or stronger at higher-income levels, and never greater at low-income levels.

Also, the same patterns exist for attitudes on federal spending on means-tested programs as for taxes and tax expenditures. Either the correlation between racial resentment and federal spending opinion is greater at high-sophistication levels (when sophistication is measured by general tax knowledge), or the correlation is the same across sophistication levels (when sophistication is measured by education or income). The one exception is Social Security: attitudes toward that program are not correlated with racial resentment among either high- or low-sophistication respondents, regardless of the way sophistication is measured. These results provide further evidence that the structure of tax attitudes is similar to that of spending attitudes in the United States.

53. My conclusions on tax attitudes echo those of Zoltan Hajnal (2020) for other policy areas. He finds that race is an enormously important factor in Americans' vote choices and public policy preferences, exceeding the influence of partisanship or income, and among whites, racial resentment plays a larger role in tax attitudes than does partisanship, ideology or income, or other personal characteristics.

54. Also, the EITC and CTC have been "refundable" to varying degrees, meaning that one can receive a cash payment from the IRS if the credit exceeds one's tax liability. To the degree to which racially resentful survey respondents know that some EITC and CTC recipients get money back from the government, they may disfavor the credit even more.

55. Gilens 1999; Winter 2008.

56. On the effect of racial resentment on attitudes toward seemingly race-neutral policies, see Gilens 1998. For an overview of racial resentment and white attitudes, see Hutchings and Valentino 2004. On white animus toward Latinos, see Ramirez and Peterson 2020.

57. Joe Soss and Sanford Schram (2007) show that after the 1996 welfare reform, which ended welfare entitlement as well as introduced lifetime limits and work requirements, attitudes toward the program, its recipients, and the party that adopted the reforms (Democrats under Clinton) remain unchanged.

58. Brown 2021; Ott 2019; Williams 2021.

7 State Coercion and Tax Attitudes among Black and Hispanic Americans

1. Dawson 1994, 183; Hajnal 2020; Kinder and Sanders 1996, 30.

2. See also Soss and Weaver 2017. Jacob Hacker and Paul Pierson (2010) contend that political scientists devote too much attention to electoral politics, and who gets what is really determined by the "combat" among interest groups. Soss and Weaver say both of these schools—the electoral politics and organized combat perspectives—miss the second face of government power: coercion and repression.

3. Brown 1997, 2021; Henricks and Seamster 2017; Martinez and Martinez 2011; Moran and Whitford 1996.

4. On race and property taxes, see, among others, Berry 2021; Kahrl 2018, 2019, 2024; Martin and Beck 2017. On race and EITC audits, see Elzayn et al. 2023.

5. Dawson 1994, 183; Hajnal 2020; Kinder and Sanders 1996, 30.

6. Researchers have long distinguished between abstract and operational aspects of Americans' attitudes toward government. See Cantril 1951; Ellis and Stimson 2012; Page and Jacobs 2009; Stimson 2004.

7. Similarly, over time, the share of GSS respondents saying their federal income taxes are about right or too low (rather than too high) rises and falls with aggregated opinion on the federal spending items. On the "public mood," see Stimson 2004. The spending and tax components tend to move together.

8. See King and Smith 2005; Lieberman 1995, 1998, 2005.

9. On the negative citizenship messages conveyed by interactions with social assistance programs, see, among others, Soss 1999; Michener 2018.

10. Soss and Weaver 2016, 74. See also Soss, Fording, and Schram 2011. On politics as combat among organized interests, see Hacker and Pierson 2010.

11. Sentencing Project 2018; Weaver 2007; Western 2006.

12. Michener 2016; Pager 2007; Western 2006.

13. Soss, Fording, and Schram 2011; Michener 2019.

14. Note that I am aware of Claire Jean Kim's critique of the two directions in which discussing race beyond a Black-white binary has unfolded. One approach has been to talk about each group separately (much as I do here in mentioning Native American dispossession and Asian exclusion). The other approach has been to impose a racial hierarchy with "whites on the top, Blacks on the bottom, and all other groups somewhere in between," as Kim (1999, 106) puts it. She argues instead that racialization processes are "mutually constitutive of one another": groups are racialized in relation to each other. I agree with her critique, but her point is somewhat beyond the scope of this book, which simply seeks to take a first look at how different groups' tax attitudes may vary with their treatment in tax policy.

15. As mentioned in chapter 2, there is a debate about intentionality here. Robert C. Lieberman contends that Black-dominated occupations were intentionally excluded from Social Security at the behest of southern white congresspeople. Larry DeWitt (2010) argues convincingly that such occupations were left out at the behest of the Roosevelt administration framers of the law, who felt it was too difficult to collect payroll taxes on workers outside commerce and industry. This debate aside, the policy effect was that Black Americans did not participate in Social Security in great numbers until the expansionary amendments of the 1950s.

16. Katznelson 2005; Williams 2021.

17. Craigie, Grawert, and Kimble 2020; Pager 2007. On the relationship between punitiveness in public opinion, which includes a strong racial attitude element, and the rise of mass incarceration in the United States, see Enns 2016.

18. Derenoncourt et al. 2022; Katznelson 2005.

19. Trounstine 2018; Williams 2021; Rothstein 2017; Thurston 2018; Conley 1999; Oliver and Shapiro 2006.

20. Massey and Denton 1993; Freund 2007; Jackson 1985; Kahrl 2018; Oliver and Shapiro 2006; Perry, Rothwell, and Harshbarger 2018. On the narratives whites produced to justify segregation during the Great Migration of southern Blacks to northern cities, see Hayward 2013.

21. Kahrl (2019) terms this getting the "short end of both sticks." Precisely because of these practices, and because returns on homeownership exceed those of equities only in certain times and places, some observers argue that homebuying should be viewed as consumption, not investment, and that the American focus on homeownership is misplaced and generates a host of other problems (sprawl, congestion, and environmental degradation), not to mention racial inequalities. See Demsas 2022.

22. Kahrl 2018; Berry 2021. Black Americans were also targeted by subprime lending in the 1990s and 2000s, leading to the financial crisis of 2008 and increasing their vulnerability to tax delinquency. See Kahrl 2017, 2024.

23. Thomas Pettigrew (1979, 114) calls racial segregation through housing policy and practices the "structural linchpin of modern race relations."

24. See, among others, Brown 2021; Ott 2019; Moran and Whitford 1996. For a compendium of critical legal studies examinations of tax policy, see Infanti and Crawford 2009.

25. Livingston 2001–2, as reprinted in Infanti and Crawford 2009, 271. See also Brown 2021; Moran and Whitford 1996; Strand and Mirkay 2020.

26. Moran and Whitfield 1996; Brown 2021. In 2016, 60 percent of white families but only 34 percent of Black families had retirement accounts, and white families have higher assets, with the white-to-Black ratio in average value of retirement accounts growing from two times in 1989 to three times in 2016, according to the Survey of Consumer Finances (Tax Policy Center 2020b).

27. Lawrence Zelenak (1998) argues that the critical tax policy critiques are too selective in choosing tax code provisions that are discriminatory and there may be other provisions, such as the EITC, that advantage such groups. But Leo Martinez and Jennifer Martinez (2011) contend that while that may be true, the value of the EITC and any other such provisions is greatly overshadowed by all the other discriminatory parts of the code.

28. For an additional list of tax provisions with differential effects across race, see Tax Policy Center 2020b.

29. On the imputed income bonus for one-earner couples, see McCaffery 1997.

30. For additional accounts of the political and economic factors affecting state tax burdens, see Berch 1995; Chernick 2005; Dennis, Moore, and Somerville 2007; Hansen 1983; Hayes and Vidal 2015; Lowery 1987; Morgan 1994. Even contemporarily, the gap between Black and white evaluations of local public services are greater in the South than non-South. In the 2016 CCES, respondents were asked to grade local services on a five-point scale. Black respondents gave lower grades on public schools than white respondents, but the Black-white difference was nearly three times greater in the South. On low levels of investment in education in the South, see Goldin and Katz 1998.

31. See also Martin 2008.

32. On lags in updated assessments in high-priced neighborhoods, see Sances 2016.

33. Specifically, the assessed value on which property tax is based is often a higher share of the sales price of lower-value homes than higher-value ones. Berry finds this regressivity throughout the nation, and on average in a given jurisdiction, a property with a sales price in the lowest decile pays an effective property tax rate that is double that of a property with a sales price in the highest decile.

34. On the underrepresentation of the working class in Congress and its effect on policymaking, see Carnes 2013.

35. Edward Wolff (2017) notes that the racial wealth gap is far larger than the racial income gap.

36. Kent and Ricketts 2021; Brown 2021.

37. Additional sources of personal experience could include the "counterpublic" of barbershops, Black Entertainment Television, and the Black church, which constitute a source of Black political thought in Melissa Victoria Harris-Lacewell's (2004) telling, along with the realizations that arise from the experience of living in urban and suburban spaces that are racialized due to stories about "the Black and white races" being differentially qualified for and deserving of homeownership. "A city dweller walks the streets and learns his place," Hayward (2013, 198) writes, making for "corporeal learning" that reinforces "identitarian lessons."

38. Question wording in the 2012 CCES: "Please click a number on the scale to rate how fair your share of each tax is" (five-point scale ranging from "the share I pay is unfair" to "the share I pay is fair," with a "don't know enough to rate" option). Figure 7.2a shows the percentage of respondents selecting one on the scale. Question wording in the 2016 CCES: "How fair do you

regard the amount you have to pay for each tax?" (four-point scale ranging from very fair to very unfair, with "I do not have to pay this tax" and "I have no opinion" options). Figure 7.2b shows the percentage of respondents selecting three or four on the scale (somewhat or very unfair).

39. When asked in 2019 about the fairness of taxes in general, not the amount one pays, Black respondents were most likely to cite the property, federal income, gas, and estate taxes as unfair, and more likely to cite these taxes plus the sales tax as unfair relative to whites.

40. Moran and Whitford's (1996) finding that Black households pay more in federal income tax than white ones at every income level is reflected in opinion as well: at every income level, Black respondents in pooled GSS data are more likely to say their federal income taxes are too high, by 10 to 16 percentage points depending on the income quintile (the share of white and Black respondents who say their federal income taxes are too high is 51 and 62 percent, respectively, for the lowest-income quintile, 55 and 69 percent for the second quintile, 61 and 71 percent for the middle quintile, 65 and 78 for the fourth quintile, and 65 and 81 percent for the highest quintile. All of these differences are statistically significant). And Brown's (2021) argument that Black married couples pay more federal income tax than white married couples on average because they are more likely to be two-earner couples and have similar incomes is reflected in opinion too: Black married respondents are more likely to say their federal income taxes are too high than white couples in the pooled GSS, 74 to 63 percent.

41. ITEP 2018; Tax Foundation 2020a, 2020b, 2021, 2022.

42. Corroborating these findings in which Black southerners have distinctive attitudes on burdensome state taxes are other findings from the 2019 CCES. That survey asked respondents from which level of government they feel they get the most and the least for their money. The modal answer for "most value" for southern Black respondents was the federal government, while for non-South Black respondents it was state government, and for both southern and nonsouthern whites it was local government. The modal answer for "least value" for southern Black respondents was local government, while it was the federal government for nonsouthern Black respondents and both white groups. Compared to other Black and white respondents, Black southerners stand out for their positive regard toward the federal government and negative regard toward local government (in many southern states, local governments impose sales taxes on top of state sales taxes).

43. Gennetian, Hill, and Ross-Cabrera 2020; Bitler et al. 2021.

44. I will mostly use the term "Hispanic Americans" because the datasets I employ ask whether respondents are Hispanic, not Latino. Whenever I refer to whites, I mean non-Hispanic whites. In the analyses here, I include all Hispanic respondents, citizens and noncitizens, as the number of noncitizens is small and noncitizens pay many taxes.

45. Martinez 2017; Martinez and Martinez 2011. On the Hispanic experience of segregation and discrimination, see Garcia Bedolla 2014. On Hispanic political experiences arising from anti-immigrant legislation, see Merolla et al. 2012; Pantoja, Ramirez, and Segura 2001.

46. See also Lipman 2006.

47. KFF 2019b.

48. Martinez 2017; Larrea 2013. Martinez maintains that undocumented persons paying Social Security taxes for benefits they can never claim turns the benefits theory of taxation "on its head."

49. On Latino political information, see Abrajano 2015. On information networks among Latina women, see Hardy-Fanta 1993.

50. Gabriel Sanchez and Natalie Masuoka (2010) find a Dawson-style sense of linked fate among Latino survey respondents, although it is stronger among lower-income, Spanish-dominant, and immigrant (versus second-generation and beyond) respondents.

51. We might additionally hypothesize that Asian Americans experience the tax system as yet another coercive arm of the state. Historically, Asians have been discriminated against in

immigration policy, the Japanese internment during World War II, and so on. Asian Americans are also disadvantaged in the tax code, even though they have higher average household incomes than white Americans (US Bureau of the Census 2018) and therefore may appear to have better access to tax-saving provisions than other minority groups. Asian homeownership rates are higher than those of Blacks and Latinos, but below whites' rates, reducing access to the home mortgage interest deduction and other tax breaks associated with homeownership. Asian American couples are more likely than white ones to have two earners and so are less likely to enjoy the untaxed imputed income of a nonworking spouse. For these and additional reasons, Asian Americans may experience "less favorable tax treatment" than whites (Uy 2004).

Unfortunately, there are even fewer Asian respondents in the CCES than Black or Hispanic ones, limiting my ability to examine their tax attitudes. The findings suggest, however, that like Black and Hispanic Americans, Asian Americans are generally more progovernment than whites, but not concomitantly more protax. On average, the Asian CCES respondents are more liberal than whites and score higher on the government services scale. Combining 2016 and 2019 data, and performing a multivariate analysis similar to figures 7.3 and 7.8 for Black and Hispanic respondents, I find that Asian respondents' views on the fairness of what they pay for various taxes do not differ statistically from those of whites. The point estimates indicate that Asians are more likely to say many taxes are unfair, but given the small number of Asian respondents in the datasets, the coefficients cannot be distinguished from zero. Similarly, Asian respondents do not differ from whites in their desire to see taxes decreased.

The Asian American population is quite diverse, with pronounced differences by country of origin, generation in the United States, income level, and so on. The CCES data are not fine-grained enough to allow exploration of attitudes within this group. Analysis of Asian Americans' tax attitudes is a ripe area for future research.

52. See also Harris-Lacewell 2004.

53. Garcia and Sanchez 2008; Garcia Bedolla 2014.

54. On the effect of state and local tax policy on racial equity, see Davis and Wiehe 2021.

55. On race and public policy, see, among others, Einhorn 2006; Lieberman 1998; Quadagno 1994; Michener 2019.

56. With data spanning from 1860 to 2020, Ellora Derenoncourt and coauthors (2022) trace how the white-Black wealth gap shrank for five decades after Emancipation, and continued to shrink at a slower rate until 1950. From the 1960s to the 1980s, the rate of convergence sped up, which they attribute in part to government actions such as extensions of civil rights, social program expansion, and improved labor standards. Since the 1980s, the gap has grown again, apparently because whites are more likely to own stocks than Black households, which hold most of their wealth in housing. Stocks have appreciated in value much more than housing over this period.

57. Soss and Weaver 2016, 74; Michener 2019.

58. Henricks and Seamster 2017, 169; Strand and Mirkay 2020. On the rise of market model programs in the neoliberal era and their racially disparate effects, see Dawson and Francis 2015.

59. Graetz and Shapiro 2005; Sahadi 2017; Tax Policy Center 2020a.

60. Bittman 2021; Rappeport 2022.

61. On the administrative burden in public policy, see Herd and Moynihan 2018.

62. See also Griffin and Newman 2007, 2008.

8 Conclusion

1. In 2013, 93.9 percent of the top 1 percent of wealth holders were white, 1.7 percent were Black, 1.0 percent were Hispanic, and 3.4 percent were Asian or other. Three decades earlier, in 1983, wealth was a bit more concentrated among whites: 97.9 percent in the top 1 percent of

wealth holders were white, 0.5 percent were Black, virtually none were Hispanic, and 1.6 percent were Asian or other.

2. Historians argue that taxes and race have always been connected in the United States. See Einhorn 2006; Michelmore 2012; Walsh 2018.

3. Or as Cameron Ballard-Rosa, Lucy Martin, and Kenneth Scheve (2017, 2) put it, having found that their conjoint experiment subjects are indifferent over income tax rates on those earning more than $375,000, “relatively flat citizen preferences” over taxation at the top of the income spectrum gives politicians “leeway” to enact their own preferences or those of “highly organized wealthy interests.”

4. Adam Seth Levine (2015) examines a related asymmetry: reminding people of inequality and their own financial insecurity demobilizes them.

5. See also McGhee 2021.

6. Rodden 2019; McGhee 2014.

7. Gilens 1996; Miler 2018; Witko et al. 2021.

8. Wilensky 2012; Martin and Gabay 2018.

9. Liberal welfare regimes like the United States, United Kingdom, and Canada make wider use of tax expenditures than Germany and the Netherlands. But the United States stands apart even from the United Kingdom and Canada in using deductions, exemptions, and exclusions more than credits, with the former set of instruments aiding higher-income households more than lower-income ones

10. Elliott and Kiel 2019; Matthews 2019.

11. The United States has lower tax compliance than Sweden and the United Kingdom, but higher than Italy. For a cross-national comparison of the effect of institutions and attitudes on tax compliance, see Pampel, Andrighetto, and Steinmo 2019.

12. For discussions of wealth taxation, see Saez and Zucman 2019b; Wolff 2017, chap. 14.

13. Congressional Budget Office 2023; IRS 2024b.

14. The question wording in the 2016 CCES: “In the past five years, have you taken into account the position of a candidate in relation to taxes in deciding how to vote? In the past five years, have you contacted a government official to complain about taxes? In the past five years, have you given a campaign contribution based, at least in part, on your concern about taxes?”

15. Including the seminal work of, among others, Kato 2003; Levi 1988; Prasad 2006; Tilly 1990; Wilensky 2002, 2012.

16. Nonetheless, comparative politics analyses on tax attitudes include, among others, Ansell, Cansunar, and Elkjaer 2022; Barnes 2015, 2022; Martin and Gabay 2018.

17. On tax attitudes and context, see Ansell, Cansunar, and Elkjaer 2022.

18. Dawson 1994; Soss and Weaver 2016. See also White and Laird 2020.

19. Racial and ethnic minorities display different levels of traditional political knowledge even when given more time to complete questions as well as offered a monetary incentive for correct answers. See Prior and Lupia 2008.

REFERENCES

Abrajano, Marisa. 2015. "Reexamining the 'Racial Gap' in Political Knowledge." *Journal of Politics* 77 (1): 44–54.

Abrajano, Marisa, and Zoltan L. Hajnal. 2015. *White Backlash: Immigration, Race, and American Politics*. Princeton, NJ: Princeton University Press.

Abreu, Alice G. 2009. "Tax Counts: Bringing Money-Law to LatCrit." In *Critical Tax Theory: An Introduction*, edited by Anthony C. Infanti and Bridget J. Crawford, 109–15. New York: Cambridge University Press.

Abreu, Alice G., and Richard K. Greenstein. 2018. "Rebranding Tax / Increasing Diversity." *Denver Law Review* 96 (1): 1–50.

Achen, Christopher H., and Larry M. Bartels. 2016. *Democracy for Realists: Why Elections Do Not Produce Responsive Government*. Princeton, NJ: Princeton University Press.

Advisory Commission on Intergovernmental Relations (ACIR). 1975. "Trends in Fiscal Federalism, 1954–1974." Report M-86, February. Washington, DC: ACIR.

———. 1980. "Significant Features of Fiscal Federalism, 1979–80." Report M-183, October. Washington, DC: ACIR.

Advisory Commission on Intergovernmental Relations in UNT Digital Library. n.d. University of North Texas Libraries. https://digital.library.unt.edu/explore/collections/ACIR/.

Alesina, Alberto, Reza Baqir, and William Easterly. 1999. "Public Goods and Ethnic Divisions." *Quarterly Journal of Economics* 114 (4): 1243–84.

Alesina, Alberto, and Edward Glaeser. 2004. *Fighting Poverty in the US and Europe: A World of Difference*. New York: Oxford University Press.

"All Stick No Carrot: Racism, Property Tax Assessments, and Neoliberalism Post 1945 Chicago." 2019. *Metropole* (blog), Urban History Association. https://themetropole.blog/2019/05/09/all-stick-no-carrot-racism-property-tax-assessments-and-neoliberalism-post-1945-chicago/.

Altig, David, Alan Auerbach, Patrick Higgins, Darryl Koehler, Laurence Kotlikoff, Ellyn Terry, and Victor Ye. 2020. "Did the 2017 Tax Reform Discriminate against Blue State Voters?" *National Tax Journal* 74 (4): 1087–108.

Alvarez, R. Michael, and Edward J. McCaffery. 2003. "Are There Sex Differences in Fiscal Political Preferences?" *Political Research Quarterly* 56 (1): 5–17.

Ansell, Ben, Asli Cansunar, and Mads Andreas Elkjaer. 2022. "Tax Exposure and Political Preferences." Working paper, Oxford University, September 23.

Arnold, R. Douglas. 1990. *The Logic of Congressional Action*. New Haven, CT: Yale University Press.

———. 2022. *Fixing Social Security: The Politics of Reform in a Polarized Age*. Princeton, NJ: Princeton University Press.

Arnon, Alex. 2021. "Revenue and Profit Shifting for the U.S. in a Global Minimum Tax Agreement." University of Pennsylvania Wharton School, October 13. https://budgetmodel.wharton.upenn.edu/issues/2021/10/13/oecd-global-minimum-tax-risks.

Ashok, Vivekinan L., and Gregory A. Huber. 2020. "Do Means of Program Delivery and Distributional Consequences Affect Policy Support? Experimental Evidence about the Sources of Citizens' Policy Opinions." *Political Behavior* 42:1097–118.

Attiyeh, Richard, and Robert F. Engle. 1979. "Testing Some Propositions about Proposition 13." *National Tax Journal* 32:131–46.

Auten, Gerald, and David Splinter. 2023. "Income Inequality in the United States: Using Tax Data to Measure Long-Term Trends." September 29. https://davidsplinter.com/AutenSplinter-Tax_Data_and_Inequality.pdf.

Avenancio-Leon, Carlos, and Troup Howard. 2020. "The Assessment Gap: Racial Inequalities in Property Taxation." Working paper. Haas School of Business, University of California at Berkeley, June.

Ballard-Rosa, Cameron, Lucy Martin, and Kenneth Scheve. 2017. "The Structure of American Income Tax Policy." *Journal of Politics* 79 (1): 1–16.

Bank, Steven A. 2010. *From Sword to Shield: The Transformation of the Corporate Income Tax, 1861 to Present*. New York: Oxford University Press.

Bank, Steven A., Kirk J. Stark, and Joseph J. Thorndike. 2008. *War and Taxes*. Washington, DC: Urban Institute Press.

Barber, James David. 1973. *Citizen Politics*. 2nd ed. Chicago: Markham Publishing.

Barnes, Lucy. 2015. "The Size and Shape of Government: Preferences over Redistributive Tax Policy." *Socio-Economic Review* 13 (1): 55–78.

———. 2022. "Taxing the Rich: Public Preferences and Public Understanding." *Journal of European Public Policy* 29 (5): 787–804.

Barnes, Lucy, Avi Feller, Jake Haselswerdt, and Ethan Porter. 2018. "Information, Knowledge, and Attitudes: An Evaluation of the Taxpayer Receipt." *Journal of Politics* 80 (2): 701–6.

Bartels, Larry M. 2002. "Beyond the Running Tally: Partisan Bias in Political Perceptions." *Political Behavior* 24 (2): 117–50.

———. 2016. *Unequal Democracy: The Political Economy of the New Gilded Age*. 2nd ed. Princeton, NJ: Princeton University Press.

Baumgartner, Frank R., Jeffrey M. Berry, Marie Hojnacki, David C. Kimball, and Beth L. Leech. 2009. *Lobbying and Policy Change: Who Wins, Who Loses, and Why*. Chicago: University of Chicago Press.

Béland, Daniel, Andrea Louise Campbell, and R. Kent Weaver. 2022. *Policy Feedback: How Policies Shape Politics*. Cambridge: Cambridge University Press.

Bentham, Jeremy. 1843. *Principles of the Civil Code*. PCC part 2, chapter 3. https://www.laits.utexas.edu/poltheory/bentham/pcc/pcc.pa02.c03.html.

Berch, Neil. 1995. "Explaining Changes in the Tax Incidence in the States." *Political Research Quarterly* 48:629–41.

Berger, Daniel, and Eric Toder. 2019. "Distributional Effects of Individual Income Tax Expenditures after the 2017 Tax Cuts and Jobs Act." Urban-Brookings Tax Policy Center, June 4. www.taxpolicycenter.org/publications/distributional-effects-individual-income-tax-expenditures-after-2017-tax-cuts-and-jobs/full.

Berry, Christopher. 2021. "Reassessing the Property Tax." Unpublished manuscript, March 1.

Bitler, Marianne, Lisa A. Gennetian, Christina Gibson-Davis, and Marcos A. Rangel. 2021. "Means-Tested Safety Net Programs and Hispanic Families: Evidence from Medicaid, SNAP, and WIC." *Annals of the American Academy for Political and Social Science* 696 (1): 274–305.

Bittker, Boris I., Elias Clark, and Grayson M. P. McCouch. 2011. *Federal Estate and Gift Taxation*. 10th ed. Saint Paul, MN: West.

Bittman, Mark. 2021. "Black Farmers May Finally Get the Help They Deserve." *New York Times*, March 4. www.nytimes.com/2021/03/04/opinion/black-farmers-covid-relief.html.

Blessing, Laura. 2014. "The New Politics of Taxation: The Republican Party and Anti-Tax Positions." PhD diss., University of Virginia.
Bobo, Lawrence, and James R. Kluegel. 1993. "Opposition to Race-Targeting: Self-Interest, Stratification Ideology, or Racial Attitudes?" *American Sociological Review* 58 (4): 443–64.
Bonica, Adam, Nolan McCarty, Keith T. Poole, and Howard Rosenthal. 2013. "Why Hasn't Democracy Slowed Rising Inequality?" *Journal of Economic Perspectives* 27 (3): 103–24.
Bott, Kristina M., Alexander W. Cappelen, Erik Ø. Sørensen, and Bertil Tungodden. 2020. "You've Got Mail: A Randomized Field Experiment on Tax Evasion." *Management Science* 66 (7): 2801–19.
Bowler, Shaun, and Todd Donovan. 1995. "Popular Responsiveness to Taxation." *Political Research Quarterly* 48:79–99.
Bowman, Karlyn. 2019. "Tax Attitudes: What Has Changed, What Has Not." American Enterprise Institute, April 12.
Bowman, Karlyn, Heather Sims, and Eleanor O'Neil. 2017. "Public Opinion on Taxes: 1937 to Today." AEI Public Opinion Studies. American Enterprise Institute, April.
Bricker, Jesse, Kevin B. Moore, Sarah J. Reber, and Alice Henriques Volz. 2020. "Effective Tax Rates by Income and Wealth Class." *National Tax Journal* 73 (4): 987–1004.
Broockman, David E., and Christopher Skovron,. 2018. "Bias Perceptions of Public Opinion among Political Elites." *American Political Science Review* 112 (3): 542–63.
Brown, Dorothy A. 1997. "The Marriage Bonus/Penalty in Black and White." *University of Cincinnati Law Review* 65:787–98.
———. 2013. "The 535 Report: A Pathway to Fundamental Tax Reform." *Pepperdine Law Review* 40:1155–72.
———. 2021. *The Whiteness of Wealth: How the Tax System Impoverishes Black Americans—and How We Can Fix It*. New York: Crown.
Brownlee, W. Elliot. 2016. *Federal Taxation in America: A History*. 3rd ed. New York: Cambridge University Press.
Brunori, David. 2001. *State Tax Policy: A Political Perspective*. Washington, DC: Urban Institute.
Burman, Leonard E., and Joel Slemrod. 2020. *Taxes in America: What Everyone Needs to Know*. 2nd ed. New York: Oxford University Press.
Burstein, Paul. 2014. *American Public Opinion, Advocacy, and Policy in Congress: What the Public Wants and What It Gets*. New York: Cambridge University Press.
Bush, George W. 2001. "Remarks at Truman High School in Independence, Missouri." American Presidency Project, August 21. www.presidency.ucsb.edu/documents/remarks-truman-high-school-independence-missouri.
———. 2004. "Remarks in Columbus, Ohio." American Presidency Project, September 1. www.presidency.ucsb.edu/documents/remarks-columbus-ohio-1.
Cabral, Marika, and Caroline Hoxby. 2012. "The Hated Property Tax: Salience, Tax Rates, and Tax Revolts." Working paper 18514. Cambridge, MA: National Bureau of Economic Research.
Cain, Patricia A. 2000. "Heterosexual Privilege and the Internal Revenue Code." *University of San Francisco Law Review* 34 (3): article 4.
Campbell, Andrea Louise. 2003. *How Policies Make Citizens: Senior Political Activism and the American Welfare State*. Princeton, NJ: Princeton University Press.
———. 2009. "What Americans Think of Taxes." In *The New Fiscal Sociology*, edited by Monica Prasad, Isaac Martin, and Ajay Mehrotra, 48–67. New York: Cambridge University Press.
———. 2012a. "America the Undertaxed." *Foreign Affairs* 91 (September–October): 99–112.
———. 2012b. "Policy Makes Mass Politics." *Annual Review of Political Science* 15:333–51.
———. 2014. *Trapped in America's Safety Net: One Family's Struggle*. Chicago: University of Chicago Press.

———. 2017. "Americans' Conflicted Attitudes about Taxing the Wealthy." Paper presented at the Annual Meeting of the American Political Science Association, San Francisco.
———. 2018. "Tax Designs and Tax Attitudes." *Forum* 16 (3): 369–98.
Campbell, Angus, Philip E. Converse, Warren E. Miller, and Donald E. Stokes. 1960. *The American Voter*. New York: John Wiley and Sons.
Cantril, Hadley. 1951. *Public Opinion, 1935–1946*. Princeton, NJ: Princeton University Press.
Carnegie, Andrew. 2006. *The "Gospel of Wealth": Essays and Other Writings*. New York: Penguin.
Carnes, Nicholas. 2013. *White-Collar Government: The Hidden Role of Class in Economic Policy Making*. Chicago: University of Chicago Press.
Caughey, Devin, and Christopher Warshaw. 2022. *Dynamic Democracy: Public Opinion, Elections, and Policymaking in the American States*. Chicago: University of Chicago Press.
Cavaille, Charlotte. 2023. *Fair Enough? Support for Redistribution in the Age of Inequality*. New York: Cambridge University Press.
Centers for Disease Control and Prevention. 2022. "Mortality in the United States, 2021." www.cdc.gov/nchs/products/databriefs/db456.htm#:~:text=Statistics%20System%2C%20Mortality.-,Summary,2020%20to%20416%2C893%20in%202021.
Chernick, Howard. 2005. "On the Distribution of Subnational Tax Progressivity in the U.S." *National Tax Journal* 58:93–112.
Chong, Dennis, Jack Citrin, and Patricia Conley. 2001. "When Self-Interest Matters." *Political Psychology* 22 (3): 541–70.
Citibank. 2020. *Closing the Racial Inequality Gaps: The Economic Cost of Black Inequality in the U.S.* https://icg.citi.com/icghome/what-we-think/citigps/insights/closing-the-racial-inequality-gaps-20200922.
Citrin, Jack, and Donald P. Green. 1990. "The Self-Interest Motive in American Public Opinion." In *Research in Micropolitics*, edited by Samuel Long. Greenwich, CT: JIA Press.
Clark, Christopher J. 2019. *Gaining Voice: The Causes and Consequences of Black Representation in the American States*. New York: Oxford University Press.
Cohen, Cathy J., and Matthew D. Luttig. 2020. "Reconceptualizing Political Knowledge: Race, Ethnicity, and Carceral Violence." *Perspectives on Politics* 18 (3): 805–18.
Cole, Richard L., and John Kincaid. 2006. "Public Opinion on U.S. Federal and Intergovernmental Issues in 2006: Continuity and Change." *Publius* 36:443–59.
Condon, Meghan, and Amber Wichowsky. 2020. *The Economic Other: Inequality in the American Political Imagination*. Chicago: University of Chicago Press.
Congressional Budget Office. 2018. "Options for Reducing the Deficit: 2019 to 2028." December 13. www.cbo.gov/publication/54667.
———. 2022. "Distribution of Household Income, 2019." November 15. www.cbo.gov/publication/58353#data.
———. 2023. "The Budget and Economic Outlook: 2023 to 2033." February. www.cbo.gov/publication/58848.
———. 2024. "The Long-Term Budget Outlook: 2024 to 2054." March 20. www.cbo.gov/publication/59711.
Congressional Research Service. 2021. "Racial Equity in U.S. Farming: Background in Brief." November 19. https://crsreports.congress.gov/product/pdf/R/R46969.
Conley, Dalton. 1999. *Being Black, Living in the Red: Race, Wealth, and Social Policy in America*. Berkeley: University of California Press.
Converse, Philip E. 1964. "The Nature of Belief Systems in Mass Publics." In *Ideology and Discontent*, edited by David Apter, 206–61. New York: Free Press.
Cook, Fay Lomax, and Edith J. Barrett. 1992. *Support for the American Welfare State: The Views of Congress and the Public*. New York: Columbia University Press.

Cook, Fay Lomax, Lawrence R. Jacobs, and Dukhong Kim. 2010. "Trusting What You Know: Information, Knowledge, and Confidence in Social Security." *Journal of Politics* 72 (2): 397–412.

Cowie, Jefferson. 2022. *Freedom's Dominion: A Saga of White Resistance to Federal Power*. New York: Basic Books.

Craigie, Terry-Ann, Ames Grawert, and Cameron Kimble. 2020. "Conviction, Imprisonment, and Lost Earnings: How Involvement with the Criminal Justice System Deepens Inequality." Brennan Center for Justice, September 15. www.brennancenter.org/our-work/research-reports/conviction-imprisonment-and-lost-earnings-how-involvement-criminal.

Davis, Carl, Misha Hill, and Meg Wiehe. 2021. "Taxes and Racial Equity: An Overview of State and Local Policy Impacts." Institute on Taxation and Economic Policy, March 31. https://itep.org/taxes-and-racial-equity/.

Davis, Darren W., and David C. Wilson 2022. *Racial Resentment in the Political Mind*. Chicago: University of Chicago Press.

Davis, Julie Hirschfeld, and Kate Kelly. 2017. "Two Bankers Are Selling Trump's Tax Plan. Is Congress Buying?" *New York Times*, August 28. www.nytimes.com/2017/08/28/us/politics/trump-tax-plan-cohn-mnuchin.html.

Dawson, Michael C. 1994. *Behind the Mule: Race and Class in African-American Politics*. Princeton, NJ: Princeton University Press.

Dawson, Michael C., and Megan Ming Francis. 2015. "Black Politics and the Neoliberal Racial Order." *Public Culture* 28 (1): 23–62.

Day, Christine L. 1990. *What Older Americans Think: Interest Groups and Aging Policy*. Princeton, NJ: Princeton University Press.

Delli Carpini, Michael X., and Scott Keeter. 1996. *What Americans Know about Politics and Why It Matters*. New Haven, CT: Yale University Press.

DeLong, J. Bradford. 2022. *Slouching towards Utopia: An Economic History of the Twentieth Century*. New York: Basic Books.

Demsas, Jerusalem. 2022. "The Homeownership Society Was a Mistake." *Atlantic*, December 20. www.theatlantic.com/newsletters/archive/2022/12/homeownership-real-estate-investment-renting/672511/.

Dennis, Christopher, William H. Moore, and Tracey Somerville. 2007. "The Impact of Politics on the Distribution of State and Local Tax Burdens." *Social Science Journal* 44 (2): 339–47.

Derenoncourt, Ellora, Chi Hyun Kim, Moritz Kuhn, and Moritz Schularick. 2022. "Wealth of Two Nations: The U.S. Racial Wealth Gap, 1860–2020." NBER working paper 30101, June. www.nber.org/papers/w30101.

Derthick, Martha. 1979. *Policymaking for Social Security*. Washington, DC: Brookings.

DeSante, Christopher. 2013. "Working Twice as Hard to Get Half as Far: Race, Work Ethic, and America's Deserving Poor." *American Journal of Political Science* 57 (2): 342–56.

DeSilver, Drew. 2013. "Black Incomes Are Up, but Wealth Isn't." Pew Research Center, August 30. www.pewresearch.org/fact-tank/2013/08/30/black-incomes-are-up-but-wealth-isnt/.

DeWitt, Larry. 2010. "The Decision to Exclude Agricultural and Domestic Workers from the 1935 Social Security Act." *Social Security Bulletin* 70 (4): 49–68.

Donovan, Todd, and Shaun Bowler. 2020. "Who Wants to Raise Taxes?" *Political Research Quarterly* 75 (1): 35–46.

Downs, Anthony. 1957. *An Economic Theory of Democracy*. New York: Harper and Row.

Druckman, James N., Erik Peterson, and Rune Slothuus. 2018. "How Elite Partisan Polarization Affects Public Opinion Formation." *American Political Science Review* 107 (1): 57–79.

Edsall, Thomas Byrne, and Mary D. Edsall. 1991. *Chain Reaction: The Impact of Race, Rights, and Taxes on American Politics*. New York: W. W. Norton.

Edwards, Khadijah. 2023. "Black Americans View Capitalism More Negatively than Positively but Express Hope in Black Businesses." Pew Research Center, March 8. www.pewresearch.org/short-reads/2023/03/08/black-americans-view-capitalism-more-negatively-than-positively-but-express-hope-in-black-businesses/.

Egan, Patrick J. 2013. *Partisan Priorities: How Issue Ownership Drives and Distorts American Politics*. New York: Cambridge University Press.

Einhorn, Robin. 2006. *American Taxation, American Slavery*. Chicago: University of Chicago Press.

Einstein, Katherine Levine, Maxwell Palmer, and David M. Glick. 2019. "Who Participates in Local Government? Evidence from Meeting Minutes." *Perspective on Politics* 17 (1): 28–46.

Eisenger, Jesse, Jeff Ernsthausen, and Paul Kiel. 2021. "The Secret IRS File: Trove of Never-Before-Seen Records Reveal How the Wealthiest Avoid Income Tax." ProPublica, June 8. www.propublica.org/article/the-secret-irs-files-trove-of-never-before-seen-records-reveal-how-the-wealthiest-avoid-income-tax.

Elliott, Justin, and Paul Kiel. 2019. "Inside TurboTax's 20-Year Fight to Stop Americans from Filing Their Taxes for Free." ProPublica, October 17. www.propublica.org/article/inside-turbotax-20-year-fight-to-stop-americans-from-filing-their-taxes-for-free.

Ellis, Christopher, and Christopher Faricy. 2021. *The Other Side of the Coin: Public Opinion toward Social Tax Expenditures*. New York: Russell Sage.

Ellis, Christopher, and James A. Stimson. 2012. *Ideology in America*. New York: Cambridge University Press.

Elzayn, Hadi, Evelyn Smith, Thomas Hertz, Arun Ramesh, Robin Fisher, Daniel E. Ho, and Jacob Goldin. 2023. "Measuring the Mitigating Racial Disparities in Tax Audits." Stanford University, Institute for Economic and Policy Research, January 30. https://siepr.stanford.edu/publications/measuring-and-mitigating-racial-disparities-tax-audits.

Enns, Peter K. 2016. *Incarceration Nation: How the United States Became the Most Punitive Democracy in the World*. New York: Cambridge University Press.

Enns, Peter K., Nathan J. Kelly, Jana Morgan, Thomas Volscho, and Christopher Witko. 2014. "Conditional Status Quo Bias and Top Income Shares: How U.S. Political Institutions Have Benefited the Rich." *Journal of Politics* 76 (2): 289–303.

Enten, Harry. 2017. "The GOP Tax Cuts Are Even More Unpopular Than Past Tax Hikes." FiveThirtyEight, November 29. https://fivethirtyeight.com/features/the-gop-tax-cuts-are-even-more-unpopular-than-past-tax-hikes/.

Erikson, Robert S., Michael B. MacKuen, and James A. Stimson. 2002. *The Macro Polity*. New York: Cambridge University Press.

Erikson, Robert S., and Kent L. Tedin. 2019. *American Public Opinion*. 10th ed. New York: Routledge.

Erikson, Robert S., Gerald C. Wright, and John P. McIver. 1993. *Statehouse Democracy*. New York: Cambridge University Press.

Evans, Geoffrey, and Robert Andersen. 2006. "The Political Conditioning of Economic Perceptions." *Journal of Politics* 68 (1): 194–207.

Faricy, Christopher G. 2015. *Welfare for the Wealthy: Parties, Social Spending, and Inequality in the United States*. New York: Cambridge University Press.

Faricy, Christopher G., and Christopher Ellis. 2014. "Public Attitudes toward Social Spending in the United States: The Differences between Direct Spending and Tax Expenditures." *Political Behavior* 36: 53–76.

Feagin, Joe R. 2013. *The White Racial Frame: Centuries of Racial Framing and Counter-Framing*. 2nd ed. New York: Routledge.

Federal Interagency Forum on Aging-Related Statistics. 2020. *Older Americans 2020: Key Indicators of Well-Being*. Washington, DC: US Government Printing Office. https://agingstats.gov/docs/LatestReport/OA20_508_10142020.pdf.

Fisher, Glenn W. 1996. *The Worst Tax? A History of the Property Tax in America*. Lawrence: University Press of Kansas.
Fitzgerald, F. Scott. 2007. *All the Sad Young Men*. Edited by James L. W. West III. New York: Cambridge University Press.
Flynn, D. J., Brendan Nyhan, and Jason Reifler. 2017. "The Nature and Origins of Misperceptions: Understanding False and Unsupported Beliefs about Politics." *Advances in Political Psychology* 38 (supp. 1): 127–50.
Fowler, Anthony, Seth J. Hill, Jeffrey B. Lewis, Chris Tausanovitch, Lynn Vavreck, and Christopher Warshaw. 2023. "Moderates." *American Political Science Review* 117 (2): 643–60.
Freeland, Chrystia. 2012. *Plutocrats: The Rise of the New Global Super-Rich and the Fall of Everyone Else*. New York: Penguin Press.
Friedman, Milton, and Rose D. Friedman. 1998. *Two Lucky People: Memoirs*. Chicago: University of Chicago Press.
Freund, David M. P. 2007. *Colored Property: State Policy and White Racial Politics in Suburban America*. Chicago: University of Chicago Press.
Gallup. 2024a. "Social Security." https://news.gallup.com/poll/1693/social-security.aspx (accessed 2/21/23).
———. 2024b. "Taxes." https://news.gallup.com/poll/1714/taxes.aspx.
Garcia, F. Chris, and Gabriel R. Sanchez. 2008. *Hispanics and the U.S. Political System: Moving into the Mainstream*. Upper Saddle River, NJ: Pearson Prentice Hall.
Garcia Bedolla, Lisa. 2014. *Latino Politics*. 2nd ed. Cambridge, UK: Polity.
Geer, John G. 1992. "New Deal Issues and the American Electorate, 1952–88." *Political Behavior* 14 (1): 45–65.
General Accounting Office (GAO). n.d. "Tax Expenditures: Issue Summary." www.gao.gov/tax-expenditures.
Gennetian, Lisa A., Zoelene Hill, and Dakota Ross-Cabrera. 2020. "State-Level TANF Policies and Practice May Shape Access and Utilization among Hispanic Families." National Research Center on Hispanic Children and Families. October 15. www.hispanicresearchcenter.org/research-resources/state-level-tanf-policies-and-practice-may-shape-access-and-utilization-among-hispanic-families/.
Gerber, Alan S., and Gregory A. Huber. 2009. "Partisanship and Economic Behavior: Do Partisan Differences in Economic Forecasts Predict Real Economic Behavior?" *American Political Science Review* 103 (3): 407–26.
Gilens, Martin. 1996. "'Racial Coding' and White Opposition to Welfare." *American Political Science Review* 90 (3): 593–604.
———. 1998. "Racial Attitudes and Race-Neutral Social Policies: White Opposition to Welfare and the Politics of Racial Inequality." In *Perception and Prejudice: Race and Politics in the United States*, edited by Jon Hurwitz and Mark Peffley, 171–201. New Haven, CT: Yale University Press.
———. 1999. *Why Americans Hate Welfare: Race, Media, and the Politics of Antipoverty Policy*. Chicago: University of Chicago Press.
———. 2001. "Political Ignorance and Collective Policy Preferences." *American Political Science Review* 91:379–96.
———. 2012. *Affluence and Influence: Economic Inequality and Political Power in America*. New York: Russell Sage.
Goldin, Claudia, and Lawrence F. Katz. 1998. "Human Capital and Social Capital: The Rise of Secondary Schooling in America, 1910 to 1940." NBER working paper 6439, March.
Good, Chris. 2012. "Norquist's Tax Pledge: What It Is and How It Started." ABC News, November 26. https://abcnews.go.com/blogs/politics/2012/11/norquists-tax-pledge-what-it-is-and-how-it-started.

Gordon, Linda. 1994. *Pitied but Not Entitled: Single Mothers and the History of Welfare, 1890–1935*. New York: Free Press.

Goren, Paul. 2008. "The Two Faces of Government Spending." *Political Research Quarterly* 61 (1): 147–57.Graetz, Michael J. 1997. *The Decline (and Fall?) of the Income Tax*. New York: W. W. Norton.

———. 2024. *The Power to Destroy: How the Antitax Movement Hijacked America*. Princeton, NJ: Princeton University Press.

Graetz, Michael J., and Ian Shapiro. 2005. *Death by a Thousand Cuts: The Fight over Taxing Inherited Wealth*. Princeton, NJ: Princeton University Press.

Green, Donald Philip, and Ann Elizabeth Gerken. 1989. "Self-Interest and Public Opinion toward Smoking Restrictions and Cigarette Taxes." *Public Opinion Quarterly* 53:1–16.

Green, Donald Philip, Bradley Palmquist, and Eric Schickler. 2002. *Partisan Hearts and Minds: Political Parties and the Social Identities of Voters*. New Haven, CT: Yale University Press.

Griffin, John D., and Brian Newman. 2007. "The Unequal Representation of Latinos and Whites." *Journal of Politics* 69:1032–46.

———. 2008. *Minority Report: Evaluating Political Equality in America*. Chicago: University of Chicago Press.

Grogan, Colleen M., and Sunggeun (Ethan) Park. 2017. "The Racial Divide in State Medicaid Expansions." *Journal of Health Politics, Policy and Law* 42 (3): 539–72.

Hacker, Jacob S., and Paul Pierson. 2010. *Winner-Take-All Politics: How Washington Made the Rich Richer—and Turned Its Back on the Middle Class*. New York: Simon and Schuster.

Haidt, Jonathan. 2012. *The Righteous Mind: Why Good People Are Divided by Politics and Religion*. New York: Pantheon.

Hajnal, Zoltan L. 2020. *Dangerously Divided: How Race and Class Shape Winning and Losing in American Politics*. New York: Cambridge University Press.

Hallsworth, Michael, John A. List, Robert D. Metcalfe, and Ivo Vlaev. 2017. "The Behavioralist as Tax Collector: Using Natural Field Experiments to Enhance Tax Compliance." *Journal of Public Economics* 148:14–31.

Hankinson, Michael. 2018. "When Do Renters Behave Like Homeowners? High Rent, Price Anxiety, and NIMBYism." *American Political Science Review* 112 (3): 473–93.

Hansen, Kristina Jessen. 2023. "Greed, Envy, and Admiration: The Distinct Nature of Public Opinion about Redistribution from the Rich." *American Political Science Review* 117 (1): 217–34.

Hansen, Susan B. 1983. *The Politics of Taxation: Revenue without Representation*. New York: Praeger.

Hardy-Fanta, Carol. 1993. *Latina Politics, Latino Politics: Gender, Culture, and Political Participation in Boston*. Philadelphia: Temple University Press.

Harris-Lacewell, Melissa Victoria. 2004. *Barbershops, Bibles, and BET: Everyday Talk and Black Political Thought*. Princeton, NJ: Princeton University Press.

Harvey, Catherine. 2017. "Access to Workplace Retirement Plans by Race and Ethnicity." AARP Public Policy Institute, February. www.aarp.org/ppi/info-2017/Access-to-Workplace-Retirement-Plans-by-Race-and-Ethnicity.html.

Haselswerdt, Jake. 2014. "The Lifespan of a Tax Break: Comparing the Durability of Tax Expenditures and Spending Programs." *American Politics Research* 42 (5): 731–59.

———. 2020. "Carving Out: Isolating the True Effect of Self-Interest on Policy Attitudes." *American Political Science Review* 114 (4): 1103–16.

Haselswerdt, Jake, and Brandon Bartels. 2015. "Public Opinion, Policy Tools, and the Status Quo: Evidence from a Survey Experiment." *Political Research Quarterly* 68 (3): 607–21.

Hawthorne, Michael R., and John E. Jackson. 1987. "The Individual Political Economy of Federal Tax Policy." *American Political Science Review* 81:757–74.

Hayes, Thomas J., and D. Xavier Medina Vidal. 2015. "Fiscal Policy and Economic Inequality in the U.S. States: Taxing and Spending from 1976 to 2006." *Political Research Quarterly* 68 (2): 392–407.

Hayward, Clarissa. 2013. *How Americans Make Race: Stories, Institutions, Spaces*. New York: Cambridge University Press.

Henricks, Kasey, and Louise Seamster. 2017. "Mechanisms of the Racial Tax State." *Critical Sociology* 43 (2): 169–79.

Herd, Pamela, and Donald P. Moynihan. 2018. *Administrative Burden: Policymaking by Other Means*. New York: Russell Sage.

Hertel-Fernandez, Alexander, and Theda Skocpol. 2015. "Asymmetric Interest Group Mobilization and Party Coalitions in U.S. Tax Politics." *Studies in American Political Development* 29 (October): 235–49.

Herzig, David J. 2018. "The Income Equality Case for Eliminating the Estate Tax." *Southern California Law Review* 90:1143–98.

Hetherington, Marc J. 2005. *Why Trust Matters: Declining Political Trust and the Demise of American Liberalism*. Princeton, NJ: Princeton University Press.

Hetherington, Marc J., and Thomas J. Rudolph. 2015. *Why Washington Won't Work: Polarization, Political Trust, and the Governing Crisis*. Chicago: University of Chicago Press.

Hill, Joseph A. 1894. "The Civil War Income Tax." *Quarterly Journal of Economics* 8.

"Homeownership Rate by Race." 2023. USAFacts, October 3. https://usafacts.org/articles/homeownership-rates-by-race/.

Hopkins, Daniel J. 2010. "Politicized Places: Explaining Where and When Immigrants Provoke Local Opposition." *American Political Science Review* 104 (1): 40–60.

———. 2023. *Stable Condition: Elites' Limited Influence on Health Care Attitudes*. New York: Russell Sage.

Howard, Christopher. 1997. *The Hidden Welfare State: Tax Expenditures and Social Policy in the United States*. Princeton, NJ: Princeton University Press.

Huber, Gregory A., and Celia Paris. 2013. "Assessing the Programmatic Equivalence Assumption in Question Wording Experiments: Understanding Why Americans Like Assistance to the Poor More Than Welfare." *Public Opinion Quarterly* 77 (1): 385–97.

Can Politics." *Annual Review of Political Science* 7:383–408.

Infanti, Anthony C., and Bridge J. Crawford, eds. 2009. *Critical Tax Theory: An Introduction*. New York: Cambridge University Press.

Institute on Taxation and Economic Policy (ITEP). 2015. "Who Pays? A Distributional Analysis of the Tax Systems in All 50 States." 5th ed. January.

———. 2018. "Who Pays? A Distributional Analysis of the Tax Systems in All 50 States." 6th ed. October.

———. 2019. "TCJA by the Numbers, 2020." August 28. https://itep.org/tcja-2020/.

———. 2020. "Who Pays Taxes in America in 2020?" July 14. https://itep.org/who-pays-taxes-in-america-in-2020.

———. 2024. "Who Pays Taxes in America in 2024?" April. https://sfo2.digitaloceanspaces.com/itep/ITEP-Who-Pays-Taxes-in-America-in-2024.pdf.

Internal Revenue Service (IRS). 2022. "Estate Tax Filing Year Tables." www.irs.gov/statistics/soi-tax-stats-estate-tax-filing-year-tables.

———. 2023. "Taxpayer Compliance Burden." www.irs.gov/pub/irs-pdf/p5743.pdf.

———. 2024a. "U.S. Corporation Income Tax: Tax Brackets and Rates, 1909–2010." Historical Table 24, June 18. www.irs.gov/statistics/soi-tax-stats-historical-table-24.

———. 2024b. "Tax Gap Projections for Tax Year 2022." October. www.irs.gov/pub/irs-pdf/p5869.pdf.

Jackson, Kenneth. 1985. *Crabgrass Frontier: The Suburbanization of America*. New York: Oxford University Press.

Jacobs, Lawrence R., and Robert Y. Shapiro. 1998. "Myths and Misunderstandings about Public Opinion toward Social Security." In *Framing the Social Security Debate: Values, Politics, and Economics*, edited by R. Douglas Arnold, Michael J. Graetz, and Alicia H. Munnell, 355–88. Washington, DC: National Academy of Social Insurance.

Jacobson, Darien B., Brian G. Raub, and Barry W. Johnson. n.d. "The Estate Tax: Ninety Years and Counting." Internal Revenue Service. https://www.irs.gov/pub/irs-soi/ninetyestate.pdf.

Jacoby, William G. 1994. "Public Attitudes toward Government Spending." *American Journal of Political Science* 38:336–61.

———. 2000. "Issue Framing and Public Opinion on Government Spending." *American Journal of Political Science* 44 (4): 750–67.

Jardina, Ashley. 2019. *White Identity Politics*. New York: Cambridge University Press.

Johnston, Richard. 2006. "Party Identification: Unmoved Mover or Sum of Preferences." *Annual Review of Political Science* 9:329–51.

Joint Committee on Taxation 2015. "History, Present Law, and Analysis of the Federal Wealth Transfer Tax System." JCX-52-15, March 16. www.jct.gov/publications.html?func=startdown&id=4744 file.

———. 2022. "Estimates of Federal Tax Expenditures for Fiscal Years 2022–2026." JCX-22-22. December 22.

Kahneman, Daniel. 2011. *Thinking, Fast and Slow*. New York: Farrar, Straus and Giroux.

Kahneman, Daniel, and Amos Tversky. 1979. "Prospect Theory: An Analysis of Decision under Risk." *Econometrica* 47 (2): 263–91.

Kahrl, Andrew W. 2017. "Investing in Distress: Tax Delinquency and Predatory Tax Buying in Urban America." *Critical Sociology* 43 (2): 199–219.

———. 2018. "Capitalizing on the Urban Fiscal Crisis: Predatory Tax Buyers in 1970s Chicago." *Journal of Urban History* 44 (3): 382–401.

———. 2019. "The Short End of Both Sticks: Property Assessments and Black Taxpayer Disadvantage in Urban America." In *Shaped by the State: Toward a New Political History of the Twentieth Century*, edited by Brent Cebul, Lily Geismer, and Mason B. Williams, 189–217. Chicago: University of Chicago Press.

______. 2024. *The Black Tax: 150 Years of Theft, Exploitation, and Dispossession in America*. Chicago: University of Chicago Press.

Kam, Cindy D. 2005. "Who Toes the Party Line? Cues, Values, and Individual Differences." *Political Behavior* 27 (2): 163–82.

Karma, Rogé. 2024. "A Baffling Academic Feud over Income Inequality." *Atlantic*, February 27. www.theatlantic.com/ideas/archive/2024/02/one-percent-income-inequality-academic-feud/677564/.

Karol, David. 2009. *Party Position Change in American Politics: Coalition Management*. New York: Cambridge University Press.

Kato, Junko. 2003. *Regressive Taxation and the Welfare State: Path Dependence and Policy Diffusion*. New York: Cambridge University Press.

Katznelson, Ira. 2005. *When Affirmative Action Was White: An Untold History of Racial Inequality in Twentieth-Century America*. New York: W. W. Norton.

Keith, Bruce E., David B. Magleby, Candice J. Nelson, Elizabeth A. Orr, Mark C. Westlye, and Raymond E. Wolfinger. 1992. *The Myth of the Independent Voter*. Berkeley: University of California Press.

Kellstedt, Paul M. 2003. *The Mass Media and the Dynamics of American Racial Attitudes*. New York: Cambridge University Press.

Kent, Ana Hernandez, and Lowell R. Ricketts. 2021. "Wealth Gaps between White, Black and Hispanic Families in 2019." Federal Reserve Bank of Saint Louis, January 5. www.stlouisfed.org/on-the-economy/2021/january/wealth-gaps-white-black-hispanic-families-2019.

KFF 2019. "Employer-Sponsored Coverage Rates for the Nonelderly by Race/Ethnicity." www.kff.org/other/state-indicator/nonelderly-employer-coverage-rate-by-raceethnicity/?currentTimeframe=0&sortModel=%7B%22colId%22:%22Location%22,%22sort%22:%22asc%22%7D.

Kiel, Paul. 2022. "Ten Ways Billionaires Avoid Taxes on an Epic Scale." ProPublica, June 24. www.propublica.org/article/billionaires-tax-avoidance-techniques-irs-files.

Kim, Claire Jean. 1999. "The Racial Triangulation of Asian Americans." *Politics and Society* 271:105–38.

Kinder, Donald R. 1998. "Opinion and Action in the Realm of Politics." In *The Handbook of Social Psychology*, edited by Daniel T. Gilbert, Susan T. Fiske, and Gardner Lindzey, 778–867. Oxford: Oxford University Press.

———. 2003. "Belief Systems after Converse." In *Electoral Democracy*, edited by Michael MacKuen and George Rabinowitz, 13–47. Ann Arbor: University of Michigan Press.

Kinder, Donald R., and Cindy D. Kam. 2010. *Us against Them: Ethnocentric Foundations of American Opinion*. Chicago: University of Chicago Press.

Kinder, Donald R., and Lynn M. Sanders. 1996. *Divided by Color: Racial Politics and Democratic Ideals*. Chicago: University of Chicago Press.

Kinder, Donald R., and David O. Sears. 1981. "Prejudice and Politics: Symbolic Racism versus Racial Threats to the Good Life." *Journal of Personality and Social Psychology* 40:414–31.

Kinsey, Karyl A., Harold G. Grasmick, and Kent W. Smith. 1991. "Framing Justice: Taxpayer Evaluations of Personal Tax Burdens." *Law and Society Review* 25 (4): 845–74.

Kluegel, James R., and Eliot R. Smith. 1986. *Beliefs about Inequality: Americans' Views of What Is and What Ought to Be*. New York: de Gruyter.

Kornhauser, Marjorie E. 1998. "Through the Looking Glass with Alice and Larry: The Nature of Scholarship." *North Carolina Law Review* 76 (5): 1609–28.

Krimmel, Katherine, and Kelly Rader. 2017. "The Federal Spending Paradox: Economic Self-Interest and Symbolic Racism in Contemporary Fiscal Politics." *American Politics Research* 45 (5): 727–54.

———. 2021. "Racial Unfairness and Fiscal Politics." *American Politics Research* 49 (2): 143–56.

Kuttner, Robert. 1980. *Revolt of the Haves: Tax Rebellions and Hard Times*. New York: Simon and Schuster.

Larrea, Luis. 2013. "Taxation Inequality and Undocumented Immigrants." *Law Raza* 5 (1): 1–37.

Larsen, Erik Gahner. 2019. "Policy Feedback Effects on Mass Publics: A Quantitative Review." *Policy Studies Journal* 47 (2), 372–94.

Lau, Richard R., and David P. Redlawsk. 2006. *How Voters Decide: Information Processing during Election Campaigns*. New York: Cambridge University Press.

Lau, Richard R., and David O. Sears. 1981. "Cognitive Links between Economic Grievances and Political Responses." *Political Behavior* 3:279–302.

Lav, Iris J., and Michael Leachman. 2018. "State Limits on Property Taxes Hamstring Local Services and Should Be Relaxed or Repealed." Center on Budget and Policy Priorities, July 18.

League of United Latin American Citizens. 2024. "Criminal Justice Reform." https://lulac.org/advocacy/issues/criminal_justice_reform/.

Leff, Mark H. 1983. "Taxing the 'Forgotten Man': The Politics of Social Security Finance in the New Deal." *Journal of American History* 70:359–81.

———. 1984. *The Limits of Symbolic Reform: The New Deal and Taxation*. New York: Cambridge University Press.

Lenz, Gabriel S. 2012. *Follow the Leader: How Voters Respond to Politicians' Policies and Performance*. Chicago: University of Chicago Press.
Lerman, Amy E., and Vesla M. Weaver. 2014. *Arresting Citizenship: The Democratic Consequences of American Crime Control*. Chicago: University of Chicago Press.
Levi, Margaret. 1988. *Of Rule and Revenue*. Berkeley: University of California Press.
Levine, Adam Seth. 2015. *American Insecurity: Why Our Economic Fears Lead to Political Inaction*. Princeton, NJ: Princeton University Press.
Levy, Frank. 1987. *Dollars and Dreams: The Changing American Income Distribution*. New York: Russell Sage.
Lieberman, Robert C. 1998. *Shifting the Color Line: Race and the American Welfare State*. Cambridge, MA: Harvard University Press.
Lipman, Francine J. 2006. "The Taxation of Undocumented Immigrants: Separate, Unequal, and without Representation." *Harvard Latino Law Review* 9:1–58.
Livingston, Michael A. 2001–2. "Women, Poverty, and the Tax Code: A Tale of Theory and Practice." *Journal of Gender, Race, and Justice* 5:328.
Lodge, Milton, and Charles S. Taber. 2013. *The Rationalizing Voter*. New York: Cambridge University Press.
Lowery, David. 1987. "The Distribution of Tax Burdens in the American States." *Western Political Quarterly* 40:137–58.
Lowery, David, and Lee Sigelman. 1981. "Understanding the Tax Revolt: Eight Explanations." *American Political Science Review* 75 (4): 963–74.
MacManus, Susan A. 1995. "Taxing and Spending Politics: A Generational Perspective." *Journal of Politics* 57:607–29.
Magleby, David B., and Candice Nelson. 2012. "Independent Leaners as Policy Partisans: An Examination of Party Identification and Policy Views." *Forum* 10 (3): article 6.
Magleby, David B., Candice J. Nelson, and Mark C. Westlye. 2011. "The Myth of the Independent Voter Revisited." In *Facing the Challenge of Democracy: Explorations in the Analysis of Public Opinion and Political Participation*, edited by Paul M. Sniderman and Benjamin Highton, 238–64. Princeton, NJ: Princeton University Press.
Mansbridge, Jane J. 1985. "Myth and Reality: The ERA and the Gender Gap in the 1980 Election." *Public Opinion Quarterly* 49:164–78.
Marble, William, and Clayton Nall. 2021. "Where Self-Interest Trumps Ideology: Liberal Homeowners and Local Opposition to Housing Development." *Journal of Politics* 83 (4): 1747–63.
Martin, Isaac William. 2008. *The Permanent Tax Revolt: How the Property Tax Transformed American Politics*. Stanford, CA: Stanford University Press.
Martin, Isaac William, and Kevin Beck. 2017. "Property Tax Limitation and Racial Inequality in Effective Tax Rates." *Critical Sociology* 43, no. 2 (March): 221–36.
Martin, Isaac William, and Nadav Gabay. 2018. "Tax Policy and Tax Protest in 20 Rich Democracies, 1980–2010." *British Journal of Sociology* 69 (3): 647–69.
Martinez, Leo. P. 2017. "Latinos and the Internal Revenue Code: A Tax Policy Primer for the New Administration." *Harvard Latinx Law Review* 20:101–20.
Martinez, Leo P., and Jennifer M. Martinez. 2011. "The Internal Revenue Code and Latino Realities: A Critical Perspective." *University of Florida Journal of Law and Public Policy* 22:377–406.
Mason, Lilliana. 2018. *Uncivil Agreement: How Politics Became Our Identity*. Chicago: University of Chicago Press.
Massey, Douglas S., and Nancy A. Denton. 1993. *American Apartheid: Segregation and the Making of the Underclass*. Cambridge, MA: Harvard University Press.
Matthews, Dylan. 2019. "A Bipartisan Group in Congress Wants to Make It Harder for You to Do Taxes." *Vox*, April 19. www.vox.com/2019/4/9/18301943/last-minute-tax-preparation-h-r-block-turbotax.

Mayer, William G. 1993. *The Changing American Mind: How and Why American Public Opinion Changed between 1960 and 1988*. Ann Arbor: University of Michigan Press.

Mayhew, David. 1974. *Congress: The Electoral Connection*. New Haven, CT: Yale University Press.

McCabe, Joshua T. 2018. *The Fiscalization of Social Policy: How Taxpayers Trumped Children in the Fight against Child Poverty*. New York: Oxford University Press.

McCaffery, Edward J. 1997. *Taxing Women*. Chicago: University of Chicago Press.

———. 1999. "The Burden of Benefits." *Villanova Law Review* 44 (3): 445–94.

———. 2008. "Where's the Sex in Fiscal Sociology? Taxation and Gender in Comparative Perspective." USC CLEO Research Paper No. C07–12.

McCaffery, Edward J., and Jonathan Baron. 2004. "Thinking about Tax." USC CLEO Research Paper No. C04–10. July 16. https://ssrn.com/abstract=567767.

McCall, Leslie. 2013. *The Undeserving Rich: American Beliefs about Inequality, Opportunity, and Redistribution*. New York: Cambridge University Press.

McCloskey, Herbert, and John Zaller. 1984. *The American Ethos: Public Attitudes toward Democracy and Capitalism*. Cambridge, MA: Harvard University Press.

McGhee, Eric. 2014. "Measuring Partisan Bias in Single-Member District Electoral Systems." *Legislative Studies Quarterly* 39 (1): 55–85.

McGhee, Heather. 2021. *The Sum of Us: What Racism Costs Everyone and How We Can Prosper Together*. New York: One World.

McNair, Kamaron. 2023. "How to Tell If You'll Receive a Marriage Penalty—or Bonus—on Your Taxes." CNBC. April 17. www.cnbc.com/2023/04/17/taxes-how-to-tell-if-youll-receive-a-marriage-penalty-or-bonus.html.

Mehrotra, Ajay K. 2013. *Making the Modern American Fiscal State: Law, Politics, and the Rise of Progressive Taxation, 1877–1929*. New York: Cambridge University Press.

Meltzer, Allan H., and Scott F. Richard. 1981. "A Rational Theory of the Size of Government." *Journal of Political Economy* 89 (5): 914–27.

Merolla, Jennifer, Adrian Pantoja, Ivy Cargile, and Juana Mora. 2012. "From Coverage to Action: The Immigration Debate and Its Effect on Participation." *Political Research Quarterly* 66 (2): 322–35.

Mettler, Suzanne. 2011. *The Submerged State: How Invisible Government Policies Undermine American Democracy*. Chicago: University of Chicago Press.

Mettler, Suzanne, and Mallory SoRelle. 2018. "Policy Feedback Theory. In *Theories of the Policy Process*, edited by Christopher M. Weible and Paul A. Sabatier, 103–34. 4th ed. New York: Routledge.

Metzl, Jonathan. 2019. *Dying of Whiteness: How the Politics of Racial Resentment Is Killing America's Heartland*. New York: Basic Books.

Michelmore, Molly C. 2012. *Tax and Spend: The Welfare State, Tax Politics, and the Limits of American Liberalism*. Philadelphia: University of Pennsylvania Press.

Michener, Jamila. 2018. *Fragmented Democracy: Medicaid, Federalism, and Unequal Politics*. New York: Cambridge University Press.

———. 2019. "Policy Feedback in a Racialized Polity." *Policy Studies Journal* 47 (2): 423–50.

———. 2020. "Race, Politics and the Affordable Care Act." *Journal of Health Politics, Policy and Law* 45 (4): 547–66.

———. 2021. "Politics, Pandemic, and Racial Justice through the Lens of Medicaid." *American Journal of Public Health* 112 (4): 643–46.

Miler, Kristina C. 2018. *Poor Representation: Congress and the Politics of Poverty in the United States*. New York: Cambridge University Press.

Mill, John Stuart. 1848. *Principles of Political Economy*. Boston: C. C. Little and J. Brown.

Moran, Beverly I., and William Whitford. 1996. "A Black Critique of the Internal Revenue Code." *Wisconsin Law Review* 4:751–820.

Morgan, David R. 1994. "Tax Equity in the American States: A Multivariate Analysis." *Social Science Quarterly* 75:510–23.

Morgan, Kimberly J. 2007. "Constricting the Welfare State: Tax Policy and the Political Movement against Government." In *Remaking America: Democracy and Public Policy in an Age of Inequality*, edited by Joe Soss, Jacob S. Hacker, and Suzanne Mettler, 27–50. New York: Russell Sage.

Morgan, Kimberly J., and Monica Prasad. 2009. "The Origins of Tax Systems: A French-American Comparison." *American Journal of Sociology* 114 (5): 1350–94.

Mounk, Yascha. 2022. *The Great Experiment: Why Diverse Democracies Fall Apart and How They Can Endure*. New York: Penguin.

Mueller, John E. 1973. *War, Presidents and Public Opinion*. New York: John Wiley and Sons.

Nantell, Sharon D. 1999. "A Cultural Perspective on American Tax Policy." *Chapman Law Review* 2 (1): 33–93.

National Archives. n.d. "Congress and the New Deal: Social Security." www.archives.gov/exhibits/treasures_of_congress/text/page19_text.html.

Newman, Katherine S., and Rourke L. O'Brien. 2011. *Taxing the Poor: Doing Damage to the Truly Disadvantaged*. Berkeley: University of California Press.

Newport, Frank. 2019. "Social Security and American Public Opinion." Gallup Polling Matters, June 18. https://news.gallup.com/opinion/polling-matters/258335/social-security-american-public-opinion.aspx.

"The Non-Taxpaying Class." 2002. *Wall Street Journal*, November 20, A20.

Norpoth, Helmut, and Yamil Velez. 2012. "Independent Leaners: Ideals, Myths, and Reality." *Forum* 10 (3): article 7.

Office of Management and Budget (OMB). n.d. "Historical Tables." www.whitehouse.gov/omb/historical-tables.

Oliver, Melvin L., and Thomas M. Shapiro. 2006. *Black Wealth / White Wealth: A New Perspective on Racial Inequality*. 2nd ed. New York: Routledge.

"O'Neill Says Cheney Told Him, 'Deficits Don't Matter.'" 2004. *Chicago Tribune*, January 12. www.chicagotribune.com/news/ct-xpm-2004-01-12-0401120168-story.html.

Organisation for Economic Co-operation and Development (OECD). 2010. Tax Expenditures in OECD Countries.

———. 2023. Revenue Statistics. www.oecd.org/tax/tax-policy/revenue-statistics-2522770x.htm.

Ott, Julia. 2019. "Tax Preference as White Privilege in the United States, 1921–1965." *Capitalism: A Journal of History and Economics* 1 (1): 92–165.

Pacheco, Julianna. 2014. "A Conditional Theory of Self-Interest and Symbolic Politics." Unpublished manuscript, October 6.

Page, Benjamin I., Larry M. Bartels, and Jason Seawright. 2013. "Democracy and the Policy Preferences of Wealthy Americans." *Perspectives on Politics* 11 (1): 51–73.

Page, Benjamin I., and Lawrence R. Jacobs. 2009. *Class War? What Americans Really Think about Economic Inequality*. Chicago: University of Chicago Press.

Page, Benjamin I., Jason Seawright, and Matthew J. Lacombe. 2019. *Billionaires and Stealth Politics*. Chicago: University of Chicago Press.

Page, Benjamin I., and Robert Y. Shapiro. 1983. "Effects of Public Opinion on Policy." *American Political Science Review* 77:175–90.

———. 1992. *The Rational Public: Fifty Years of Trends in Americans' Policy Preferences*. Chicago: University of Chicago Press.

Pager, Devah. 2007. *Marked: Race, Crime, and Finding Work in an Era of Mass Incarceration*. Chicago: University of Chicago Press.

Pampel, Fred, Guilia Andrighetto, and Sven Steinmo. 2019. "How Institutions and Attitudes Shape Tax Compliance: A Cross-National Experiment and Survey." *Social Forces* 97 (3): 1337–64.

Pantoja, Adrian D., Ricardo Ramirez, and Gary M. Segura. 2001. "Citizens by Choice, Voters by Necessity: Patterns in Political Mobilization by Naturalized Latinos." *Political Research Quarterly* 54 (4): 729–50.

Patashnik, Eric M. 2023. *Countermobilization: Policy Feedback and Backlash in a Polarized Age.* Chicago: University of Chicago Press.

Patterson, James T. 1969. *The New Deal and the States: Federalism in Transition.* Princeton, NJ: Princeton University Press.

———. 1996. *Grand Expectations: The United States, 1945–1974.* New York: Oxford University Press.

Penner, Rudolph G. 1998. "A Brief History of State and Local Fiscal Policy." Urban Institute. Series A, no. A-27, October. https://webarchive.urban.org/UploadedPDF/anf27.pdf.

Pension Benefit Guaranty Corporation. 2022. "History of PBGC." November 23. tinyurl.com/3vnpytfd.

Perry, Andre M., Jonathan Rothwell, and David Harshbarger. 2018. "The Devaluation of Assets in Black Neighborhoods: The Case of Residential Property." Brookings, November. www.brookings.edu/wp-content/uploads/2018/11/2018.11_Brookings-Metro_Devaluation-Assets-Black-Neighborhoods_final.pdf.

Petrocik, John R. 1996. "Issue Ownership in Presidential Elections, with a 1980 Case Study." *American Journal of Political Science* 40 (3): 825–50.

———. 2009. "Measuring Party Support: Leaners Are Not Independents." *Electoral Studies* 28:562–72.

Pettigrew, Thomas F. 1979. "Racial Change and Social Policy." *Annals of the American Academy of Political and Social Science* 441:114–31.

Pew Research Center. 2019. "Political Independent: Who They Are, What They Think." March. www.pewresearch.org/politics/2019/03/14/political-independents-who-they-are-what-they-think/.

———. 2022. "Public Trust in Government: 1958–2022." June 6. www.pewresearch.org/politics/2022/06/06/public-trust-in-government-1958-2022/.

Piston, Spencer. 2018. *Class Attitudes in America: Sympathy for the Poor, Resentment of the Rich, and Political Implications.* New York: Cambridge University Press.

Pope, Jeremy C., and Jonathan Woon. 2009. "Measuring Changes in American Party Reputations, 1939–2004." *Political Research Quarterly* 62 (4): 653–61.

Prasad, Monica. 2006. *The Politics of Free Markets: The Rise of Neoliberal Economic Policies in Britain, France, Germany and the United States.* Chicago: University of Chicago Press.

———. 2018. *Starving the Beast: Ronald Reagan and the Tax Cut Revolution.* New York: Russell Sage.

Prior, Markus, and Arthur Lupia. 2008. "Money, Time and Political Knowledge: Distinguishing Quick Recall and Political Learning Skills." *American Journal of Political Science* 52 (1): 169–83.

"Property Tax on Elderly Is Assailed." 1972. *New York Times,* September 15, 25.

Quadagno, Jill. 1994. *The Color of Welfare: How Racism Undermined the War on Poverty.* New York: Oxford University Press.

Ramirez, Mark D., and David A. M. Peterson. 2020. *Ignored Racism: White Animus toward Latinos.* New York: Cambridge University Press.

Rappeport, Alan. 2022. "Black Farmers Fear Foreclosure as Debt Relief Remains Frozen." *New York Times,* February 21. www.nytimes.com/2022/02/21/us/politics/black-farmers-debt-relief.html.

Rappeport, Alan, Emily Flitter, and Kate Kelly. 2022. "The Carried Interest Loophole Survives Another Political Battle." *New York Times,* August 5.

Ratner, Sidney. (1942) 1967. *Taxation and Democracy in America.* New York: John Wiley and Sons.

Rhodes, Jesse. 2015. "Learning Citizenship? How State Education Reforms Affect Parents' Political Attitudes and Behavior." *Political Behavior* 47:181–220.

Roberts, Michael L., Peggy A. Hite, and Cassie F. Bradley. 1994. "Understanding Attitudes toward Progressive Taxation." *Public Opinion Quarterly* 58 (2): 165–90.

Robillard, Kevin. 2012. "Who Are Romney's '47 percent'?" *Politico*, September 18. www.politico.com/story/2012/09/who-are-romneys-47-percent-081326.

Rodden, Jonathan. 2019. *Why Cities Lose: The Deep Roots of the Urban-Rural Political Divide*. New York: Basic Books.

Roediger, David R. 2007. *The Wages of Whiteness: Race and the Making of the American Working Class*. London: Verso.

Rosenthal, Aaron. 2021. "Submerged for Some? Government Visibility, Race, and American Political Trust." *Perspectives on Politics* 19 (4): 1098–114.

Rostain, Tanina, and Milton C. Regan Jr. 2014. *Confidence Games: Lawyers, Accountants, and the Tax Shelter Industry*. Cambridge, MA: MIT Press.

Rothstein, Richard. 2017. *The Color of Law: A Forgotten History of How Our Government Segregated America*. New York: Liveright.

Rudolph, Thomas J., and Jillian Evans. 2005. "Political Trust, Ideology, and Public Support for Government Spending." *American Journal of Political Science* 49 (3): 660–71.

Saez, Emmanuel, and Gabriel Zucman. 2019a. Letter to Senator Elizabeth Warren. January 18. www.warren.senate.gov/imo/media/doc/saez-zucman-wealthtax.pdf.

———. 2019b. "Progressive Wealth Taxation." Brookings Papers on Economic Activity, September 4. www.brookings.edu/wp-content/uploads/2019/09/Saez-Zucman_conference-draft.pdf.

———. 2020. "The Rise of Income and Wealth Inequality: Evidence from Distributional Macroeconomic Accounts." *Journal of Economic Perspectives* 34 (4): 3–26.

Sahadi, Jeanne. 2017. "No, the Estate Tax Isn't Killing Family Farms." CNN Business, October 10. https://money.cnn.com/2017/10/10/news/economy/farmers-estate-tax/index.html.

Sances, Michael W. 2016. "The Distributional Impact of Greater Responsiveness: Evidence from New York Towns." *Journal of Politics* 78 (1): 105–19.

Sanchez, Gabriel R., and Natalie Masuoka. 2010. "Brown-Utility Heuristic? The Presence and Contributing Factors of Latino Linked Fate." *Hispanic Journal of Behavioral Sciences* 32 (4): 519–31.

Saulnier, Raymond J. 1991. *Constructive Years: The U.S. Economy under Eisenhower*. Lanham, MD: University Press of America.

Scheve, Kenneth, and David Stasavage. 2016. *Taxing the Rich: A History of Fiscal Fairness in the United States and Europe*. Princeton, NJ: Princeton University Press.

Schickler, Eric. 2016. *Racial Realignment: The Transformation of American Liberalism, 1932–1965*. Princeton, NJ: Princeton University Press.

Schlozman, Kay Lehman, Henry E. Brady, and Sidney Verba. 2018. *Unequal and Unrepresented: Political Inequality and the People's Voice in the New Gilded Age*. Princeton, NJ: Princeton University Press.

Schlozman, Kay Lehman, and Sidney Verba. 1979. *Insult to Injury: Unemployment, Class, and Political Response*. Cambridge, MA: Harvard University Press.

Sears, David O. 1993. "Symbolic Politics: A Socio-Psychological Theory." In *Explorations in Political Psychology*, edited by Shanto Iyengar and William J. McGuire, 113–49. Durham, NC: Duke University Press.

Sears, David O., and Jack Citrin. 1985. *Tax Revolt: Something for Nothing in California*. Enl. ed. Cambridge, MA: Harvard University Press.

Sears, David O., and Carolyn L. Funk. 1990. "The Limited Effect of Economic Self-Interest on the Political Attitudes of the Mass Public." *Journal of Behavioral Economics* 19:247–71.

Sears, David O., and P. Henry. 2005. "Over Thirty Years Later: A Contemporary Look at Symbolic Racism." *Advances in Experimental Social Psychology* 37:95–150.

Sears, David O., Richard R. Lau, Tom R. Tyler, and Harris M. Allen Jr. 1980. "Self-Interest versus Symbolic Politics in Policy Attitudes and Presidential Voting." *American Political Science Review* 74 (3): 670–84.

Seligman, Edwin R. A. 1911. *The Income Tax: A Study of the History, Theory and Practice of Income Taxation at Home and Abroad.* New York: Macmillan.

Sentencing Project. 2018. "Report to the United States on Racial Disparities in the U.S. Criminal Justice System." April 19. www.sentencingproject.org/reports/report-to-the-united-nations-on-racial-disparities-in-the-u-s-criminal-justice-system/.

Shanks, Trina Williams. 2005. "The Homestead Act: A Major Asset-Building Policy in American History." In *Inclusion in the American Dream: Assets, Poverty, and Public Policy*, edited by Michael Sherraden, 20–41. New York: Oxford University Press.

Shapiro, Robert Y., and Harpreet Mahajan. 1986. "Gender Differences in Policy Preferences: A Summary of Trends from the 1960s to the 1980s." *Public Opinion Quarterly* 50 (1): 42–61.

Sherif, Muzafer. 1988. *The Robbers Cave Experiment: Intergroup Conflict and Cooperation.* Middletown, CT: Wesleyan University Press.

Shesol, Jeff. 2022. "When Freedom Meant the Freedom to Oppress Others." *New York Times*, December 12. www.nytimes.com/2022/12/12/books/review/freedoms-dominion-jefferson-cowie.html.

Sides, John. 2017. "Here's the Incredibly Unpopular GOP Tax Reform Plan—in One Graph." *Washington Post*, November 18. www.washingtonpost.com/news/monkey-cage/wp/2017/11/18/heres-the-incredibly-unpopular-gop-tax-reform-plan-in-one-graph/.

Siev, Joseph J., Daniel R. Rovenpor, and Richard E. Petty. 2024. "Independents, Not Partisans, Are More Likely to Hold and Express Electoral Preferences Based in Negativity." *Journal of Experimental Social Psychology* 110:104538.

Sigelman, Lee, David Lowery, and Roland Smith. 1983. "The Tax Revolt: A Comparative State Analysis." *Western Political Quarterly* 36 (1): 30–51.

Skocpol, Theda. 1991. "Targeting within Universalism: Politically Viable Policies to Combat Poverty in the United States." In *The Urban Underclass*, edited by Christopher Jencks and Paul E. Peterson, 411–36. Washington, DC: Brookings.

———. 1992. *Protecting Soldiers and Mothers: The Political Origins of Social Policy in the United States.* Cambridge, MA: Harvard University Press.

Slemrod, Joel, and Jon Bakija. 2017. *Taxing Ourselves: A Citizen's Guide to the Debate over Taxes.* 5th ed. Cambridge, MA: MIT Press.

Sloan, John W. 1991. *Eisenhower and the Management of Prosperity*. Lawrence: University Press of Kansas.

Smith, Mark A. 2007. "Economic Insecurity, Party Reputations, and the Republican Ascendance." In *The Transformation of American Politics: Activist Government and the Rise of Conservatism*, edited by Paul Pierson and Theda Skocpol, 135–59. Princeton, NJ: Princeton University Press.

Sniderman, Paul, and Philip E. Tetlock. 1986. "Symbolic Racism: Problems of Motive Attribution in Political Debate." *Journal of Social Issues* 42:129–50.

SoRelle, Mallory, and Delphia Shanks. 2024. "The Policy Acknowledgement Gap: Explaining (Mis)perceptions of Government Social Program Use." *Policy Studies Journal* 52 (1): 47–71.

Soss, Joe. 1999. "Lessons of Welfare: Policy Design, Political Learning, and Political Action." *American Political Science Review* 93:363–80.

Soss, Joe, Richard C. Fording, and Sanford F. Schram. 2011. *Disciplining the Poor: Neoliberal Paternalism and the Persistent Power of Race.* Chicago: University of Chicago Press.

Soss, Joe, and Sanford F. Schram. 2007. "A Public Transformed? Welfare Reform as Policy Feedback." *American Political Science Review* 101 (1): 111–27.

Soss, Joe, and Vesla Weaver. 2016. "Learning from Ferguson: Welfare, Criminal Justice, and the Political Science of Race and Class." In *The Double Bind: The Politics of Race and Class Inequalities in the Americas*, edited by Juliet Hooker and Alvin B. Tillery Jr., 73–99. Washington, DC: American Political Science Association.

———. 2017. "Police Are Our Government: Politics, Policy Science, and the Policing of Race-Class Subjugated Communities." *Annual Review of Political Science* 20:565–91.

Sparrow, James T. 2011. *Warfare State: World War II Americans and the Age of Big Government*. New York: Oxford University Press.

Splinter, David. 2019. "U.S. Taxes Are Progressive: Comment on 'Progressive Wealth Taxation.'" October 8. www.davidsplinter.com/Splinter-TaxesAreProgressive.pdf.

Stanley, Robert. 1993. *Dimensions of Law in the Service of Order: Origins of the Federal Income Tax, 1861–1913*. New York: Oxford University Press.

Stein, Herbert. 1996. *The Fiscal Revolution in America: Policy in Pursuit of Reality*. 2nd rev. ed. Washington, DC: AEI Press.

Steinmo, Sven. 1993. *Taxation and Democracy: Swedish, British, and American Approaches to Financing the Modern State*. New Haven, CT: Yale University Press.

Steuerle, C. Eugene. 2004. *Contemporary U.S. Tax Policy*. Washington, DC: Urban Institute Press.

Stewart, Shelly, III, Michael Chui, James Manyika, J. P. Julien, Dame Vivian Hunt, Bob Sternfels, Lola Woetzel, and Haiyang Zhang. 2021. "The Economic State of Black America: What Is and What Could Be." McKinsey Global Institute. www.mckinsey.com/featured-insights/diversity-and-inclusion/the-economic-state-of-black-america-what-is-and-what-could-be#/.

Stimson, James A. 2004. *Tides of Consent: How Public Opinion Shapes American Politics*. New York: Cambridge University Press.

Stonecash, Jeffrey M. 2000. *Class and Party in American Politics*. Boulder, CO: Westview Press.

Strand, Palma Joy, and Nicholas A. Mirkay. 2020. "Racialized Tax Inequity: Wealth, Racism, and the U.S. System of Taxation." *Northwestern Journal of Law and Social Policy* 15:265–304.

Suhay, Elizabeth, Marko Klašnja, and Gonzalo Rivero. 2021. "Ideology of Affluence: Explanations for Inequality and Economic Policy Preferences among Rich Americans." *Journal of Politics* 83 (1): 367–80.

Surrey, Stanley S., and Paul R. McDaniel. 1985. *Tax Expenditures*. Cambridge, MA: Harvard University Press.

Tajfel, Henri. 1982. *Social Identity and Intergroup Relations*. New York: Cambridge University Press.

Tajfel, Henri, and John Turner. 1979. "An Integrative Theory of Intergroup Conflict." In *The Social Psychology of Intergroup Relations*, edited by William G. Austin and Stephen Worchel, 33–47. Monterey, CA: Brooks/Cole.

Tarman, Christopher, and David O. Sears. 2005. "The Conceptualization and Measurement of Symbolic Racism." *Journal of Politics* 67 (3): 731–61.

Tax Foundation. 2020a. "State and Local Sales Tax Rates, Midyear 2020." July 8. https://taxfoundation.org/publications/state-and-local-sales-tax-rates/.

———. 2020b. "State Gasoline Tax Rates as of July 2020." July 29. https://taxfoundation.org/state-gas-tax-rates-2020/.

———. 2022. "Where Do People Pay the Most in Property Taxes?" September 13. https://taxfoundation.org/property-taxes-by-state-county-2022/.

Tax Policy Center. 2013. "T13-0081 Tax Benefit of Preferential Rates on Long-Term Capital Gains and Qualified Dividends." February 3. www.taxpolicycenter.org/model-estimates/individual-income-tax-expenditures/tax-benefit-preferential-rates-long-term-0.

———. 2015. "Average and Marginal Federal Income Tax Rates for Four-Person Families at the Same Relative Position in the Income Distribution, 1955–2014." www.taxpolicycenter.org/statistics/historical-federal-income-tax-rates-family-four.

———. 2020a. *Briefing Book*. https://www.taxpolicycenter.org/sites/default/files/briefing-book/tpc_briefing_book_2020.pdf.

———. 2020b. "Racial Disparities and the Income Tax System." January 30. https://apps.urban.org/features/race-and-taxes/#about-the-data.

Tedin, Kent L., D. W. Brady, M. E. Buxton, B. M. Gorman, and J. L. Thompson. 1977. "Social Background and Political Differences between Pro- and Anti-ERA Activists." *American Politics Quarterly* 5:395–408.

Tedin, Kent L., Richard P. Matland, and Gregory R. Weiher. 2001. "Age, Race, Self-Interest, and Financing Public Schools through Referenda." *Journal of Politics* 63:270–94.

Teles, Steven M. 2013. "Kludgeocracy in America." *National Affairs* (Fall): 97–114.

Tesler, Michael. 2012. "The Spillover of Racialization into Health Care: How President Obama Polarized Public Opinion by Racial Attitudes and Race." *American Journal of Political Science* 56 (3): 690–704.

———. 2016. *Post-Racial or Most-Racial? Race and Politics in the Obama Era*. Chicago: University of Chicago Press.

———. 2020. "Racial Attitudes and American Politics." In *New Directions in Public Opinion*, edited by Adam J. Berinsky, 118–36. 3rd ed. New York: Routledge.

Thal, Adam. 2020. "The Desire for Social Status and Economic Conservatism among Affluent Americans." *American Political Science Review* 114 (2): 426–42.

Thom, Michael. 2017. *Tax Politics and Policy*. New York: Routledge.

Thomson-Deveaux, Amelia. 2023. "Congress's U-Turn Has States Thinking about Giving Parents Cash." FiveThirtyEight, February 9. https://fivethirtyeight.com/features/congresss-u-turn-has-states-thinking-about-giving-parents-cash/.

Thorndike, Joseph J. 2013. *Their Fair Share: Taxing the Rich in the Age of FDR*. Washington, DC: Urban Institute Press.

Thurston, Chloe N. 2018. *At the Boundaries of Homeownership: Credit, Discrimination, and the American State*. New York: Cambridge University Press.

Tilly, Charles. 1990. *Capital, Coercion and European States, AD 990–1990*. Cambridge, UK: Blackwell.

Trounstine, Jessica. 2018. *Segregation by Design: Local Politics and Inequality in American Cities*. New York: Cambridge University Press.

Turner, Cory. 2022. "The Expanded Child Tax Credit Briefly Slashed Child Poverty. Here's What Else It Did." NPR, January 27. www.npr.org/2022/01/27/1075299510/the-expanded-child-tax-credit-briefly-slashed-child-poverty-heres-what-else-it-d.

Tyler, Tom R. 1998. "Trust and Democratic Governance." In *Trust and Governance*, edited by Valerie A. Braithwaite and Margaret Levi, 269–94. New York: Russell Sage.

US Bureau of the Census n.d. *Historical Statistics of the United States: Colonial Times to 1970*.US Department of Housing and Urban Development. 1973. "A Study of Property Taxes and Urban Blight." H-1299. January.

US House Ways and Means Committee. 1998. *1998 Green Book*. Washington, DC: US Government Printing Office.

Uy, Mylinh. 2004. "Tax and Race: The Impact on Asian Americans." *Asian Law Journal* 11:117–43.

"Value-Added Tax Opposed in a Poll." 1972. *New York Times*, August 27, 20.

Walsh, Camille. 2018. *Racial Taxation: Schools, Segregation, and Taxpayer Citizenship, 1869–1973*. Chapel Hill: University of North Carolina Press.

Watson, Sara. 2015. "Does Welfare Conditionality Reduce Democratic Participation." *Comparative Political Studies* 48:645–86.

Weaver, Vesla, and Amy Lerman. 2010. "Political Consequences of the Carceral State." *American Political Science Review* 104:817–33.

Weaver, Warren, Jr. 1972. "Governors Score Value-Added Tax." *New York Times*, June 8, 23.

Wedeen, Jason, and Robert Kurzban. 2017. "Self-Interest Is Often a Major Determinant of Issue Attitudes." *Advances in Political Psychology* 38 (supp. 1): 67–90.

West, Darrell M. 2014. *Billionaires: Reflections on the Upper Crust*. Washington, DC: Brookings.

White, Ariel. 2019. "Misdemeanor Disenfranchisement? The Demobilizing Effects of Brief Jail Spells on Potential Voters." *American Political Science Review* 113 (2): 311–24.

White, Ismail K., and Chryl N. Laird. 2020. *Steadfast Democrats: How Social Forces Shape Black Political Behavior*. Princeton, NJ: Princeton University Press.

Wilensky, Harold L. 2002. *Rich Democracies: Political Economy, Public Policy, and Performance*. Berkeley: University of California Press.

———. 2012. *American Political Economy in Global Perspective*. New York: Cambridge University Press.

Wilkes, Rima. 2015. "We Trust in Government, Just Not in Yours: Race, Partisanship, and Political Trust, 1958–2012." *Social Science Research* 49:356–71.

Williams, Robert B. 2021. "Federal Wealth Policy and the Perpetuation of White Supremacy." *Review of Black Political Economy* 49 (2): 131–51. https://journals.sagepub.com/doi/pdf/10.1177/00346446211000821.

Williamson, Vanessa. 2017. *Read My Lips: Why Americans Are Proud to Pay Taxes*. Princeton, NJ: Princeton University Press.

Winter, Nicholas J. 2006. "Beyond Welfare: Framing and the Racialization of White Opinion on Social Security." *American Journal of Political Science* 96:75–90.

———. 2008. *Dangerous Frames: How Ideas about Race and Gender Shape Public Opinion*. Chicago: University of Chicago Press.

Witko, Christopher, Jana Morgan, Nathan J. Kelly, and Peter K. Enns. 2021. *Hijacking the Agenda: Economic Power and Political Influence*. New York: Russell Sage.

Witte, John F. 1985. *The Politics and Development of the Federal Income Tax*. Madison: University of Wisconsin Press.

Wlezien, Christopher, Mark Franklin, and Daniel Twiggs. 1997. "Economic Perceptions and Vote Choice: Disentangling the Endogeneity." *Political Behavior* 19 (1): 7–17.

Wolff, Edward N. 2017. *A Century of Wealth in America*. Cambridge, MA: Harvard University Press.

Wolpert, Robin M., and James G. Gimpel. 1998. "Self-Interest, Symbolic Politics, and Public Attitudes toward Gun Control." *Political Behavior* 20 (3): 241–62.

Woodward, Bob. 1994. *The Agenda: Inside the Clinton White House*. New York: Simon and Schuster.

Yokley, Eli. 2021. "Voters Are Divided over One-Year Extension of Expanded Child Tax Credit." Morning Consult, December 20. https://morningconsult.com/2021/12/20/child-tax-credit-support-poll-build-back-better/.

Young, Cristobal. 2017. *The Myth of Millionaire Tax Flight: How Place Still Matters for the Rich*. Stanford, CA: Stanford University Press.

Zelenak, Lawrence. 1998. "Taking Critical Tax Theory Seriously." *North Carolina Law Review* 76:1521–80.

———. 2010. "The Federal Retail Sales Tax That Wasn't: An Actual History and an Alternative History." *Law and Contemporary Problems* 73 (1): 149–205.

Zelizer, Julian E. 1998. *Taxing America: Wilbur D. Mills, Congress, and the State, 1945–1975*. New York: Cambridge University Press.

INDEX

Note: Page numbers followed by an italicized *f* or *t* indicate figures or tables on that page. Page numbers followed by an n indicate notes.

PRINCETON STUDIES IN AMERICAN POLITICS

Historical, International, and Comparative Perspectives

Paul Frymer, Suzanne Mettler, and Eric Schickler, Series Editors

Ira Katznelson, Martin Shefter, and Theda Skocpol, Founding Series Editors

Attention, Shoppers!: American Retail Capitalism and the Origins of the Amazon Economy, Kathleen Thelen

Divergent Democracy: How Policy Positions Came to Dominate Party Competition, Katherine Krimmel

The Hollow Parties: The Many Pasts and Disordered Present of American Party Politics, Daniel Schlozman and Sam Rosenfeld

How the Heartland Went Red: Why Local Forces Matter in an Age of Nationalized Politics, Stephanie Ternullo

Laboratories against Democracy: How National Parties Transformed State Politics, Jacob M. Grumbach

Rough Draft of History: A Century of US Social Movements in the News, Edwin Amenta and Neal Caren

Checks in the Balance: Legislative Capacity and the Dynamics of Executive Power, Alexander Bolton and Sharece Thrower

Firepower: How the NRA Turned Gun Owners into a Political Force, Matthew J. Lacombe

American Bonds: How Credit Markets Shaped a Nation, Sarah L. Quinn

The Unsolid South: Mass Politics and National Representation in a One-Party Enclave, Devin Caughey

Southern Nation: Congress and White Supremacy after Reconstruction, David A. Bateman, Ira Katznelson, and John S. Lapinsky

California Greenin': How the Golden State Became an Environmental Leader, David Vogel

Building an American Empire: The Era of Territorial and Political Expansion, Paul Frymer

Racial Realignment: The Transformation of American Liberalism, 1932–1965, Eric Schickler

Paths out of Dixie: The Democratization of Authoritarian Enclaves in America's Deep South, 1944–1972, Robert Mickey

When Movements Anchor Parties: Electoral Alignments in American History, Daniel Schlozman

Electing the Senate: Indirect Democracy before the Seventeenth Amendment, Wendy J. Schiller and Charles Stewart III

Looking for Rights in All the Wrong Places: Why State Constitutions Contain America's Positive Rights, Emily Zackin

The Substance of Representation: Congress, American Political Development, and Lawmaking, John S. Lapinski

Fighting for the Speakership: The House and the Rise of Party Government, Jeffery A. Jenkins and Charles Stewart

Three Worlds of Relief: Race, Immigration, and the American Welfare State from the Progressive Era to the New Deal, Cybelle Fox

Building the Judiciary: Law, Courts, and the Politics of Institutional Development, Justin Crowe

Still a House Divided: Race and Politics in Obama's America, Desmond King and Rogers M. Smith

Reputation and Power: Organizational Image and Pharmaceutical Regulation at the FDA, Daniel Carpenter

The Litigation State: Public Regulation and Private Lawsuits in the U.S., Sean Farhang

Why Is There No Labor Party in the United States?, Robin Archer

Presidential Party Building: Dwight D. Eisenhower to George W. Bush, Daniel J. Galvin

Fighting for Democracy: Black Veterans and the Struggle against White Supremacy in the Postwar South, Christopher S. Parker

The Fifth Freedom: Jobs, Politics, and Civil Rights in the United States, 1941–1972, Anthony S. Chen

A NOTE ON THE TYPE

This book has been composed in Arno, an Old-style serif typeface in the classic Venetian tradition, designed by Robert Slimbach at Adobe.